VEILED DESIRES

MAUREEN SABINE

Veiled Desires

INTIMATE PORTRAYALS
OF NUNS IN POSTWAR
ANGLO-AMERICAN FILM

FORDHAM UNIVERSITY PRESS

New York / 2013

Library of Congress Cataloging-in-Publication Data

Sabine, Maureen.
 Veiled desires : intimate portrayals of nuns in postwar Anglo-American film / Maureen Sabine. — First edition.
     pages cm
 Includes bibliographical references and index.
 ISBN 978-0-8232-5165-0 (cloth : alk. paper) — ISBN 978-0-8232-5166-7 (pbk. : alk. paper)
 1. Nuns in motion pictures. 2. Motion pictures—Great Britain—History. 3. Motion pictures—United States—History. I. Title.
 PN1995.9.N95S23 2013
 791.430941—dc23

                                                                    2012050170

Printed in the United States of America
15 14 13   5 4 3 2 1
First edition

To Martin, for his staunch love,
constancy, and faith, and to Chris, Peter, and Tony,
who make our circle complete.

"Thy firmnes makes my circle
just, And makes me end,
where I begunne."
John Donne, "A Valediction
forbidding mourning"

CONTENTS

ACKNOWLEDGMENTS

I am grateful to the History Department at the University of Hong Kong, which gave me a home away from home where I could work on this book in an intellectual environment of serious engagement with religious history and culture, and in particular, to colleagues Frank Dikotter, Staci Ford, and Bert Becker who supported me so generously with advice and many interesting conversations during the long writing process. The Hong Kong Research Grants Council awarded me the GRF grant, which enabled me to research and devote considerable time to this project. I also wish to thank Daniel Chua, Head of the School of Humanities, for his understanding and encouragement during this period. Behind these individuals are a "company of many," and the memory of their love, friendship, collegiality, and goodness has sustained me over the course of my life. They include my siblings, Rob, Cathy, Tom, and John Fath; my mother-in-law and brother-in-law, Peggy and Roger Sabine; friends made at university, the late Mary Daly and Eileen Warburton; friends made over the course of my academic career, Emma Letley, Maria Yuen, Lena Lau, Rodney Davey, Maryanne Dever, Peter Hutchings, and Greg Lee; friends made in service to Hong Kong education, Kin-Yue Fu, Alice Tai Footman, and Ti Dennig; life-long friends Howard and Christabel Flight, Andrew and Deborah Cullen, John and Bron Walter, Alex and Vicki Harris, and Colin and Peggy Cohen; and the students in English, Comparative Literature, and History who have made teaching so rewarding for me. Thank you all.

VEILED DESIRES

INTRODUCTION

*I*f anyone has suffered from typecasting, it is the cinematic nun. Enveloped in a religious veil and habit that show her only in part and are barriers to imagining her as a whole person, she has been vulnerable to stereotypes that complete the visual process of fragmenting her on-screen.[1] Whether these stereotypes trivialize, sentimentalize, or sanctify her, represent her seriously or sensationally, the result is the same.[2] She has seldom been seen as a totality of mind-body-heart-spirit, rarely been the subject of comprehensive inter-disciplinary analysis, and never been the subject of full-length study. Instead, the screen nun has often become the occasion to talk about something else, something of more interest to the critical viewer than the desires that call her as a woman to the religious life. This book will turn the focus of discussion back on the cinematic nun as a woman and a religious in the twentieth century, one striving for a life that integrates personal and professed, worldly and sacred, traditional and modern, gender and spiritual aspirations. It will sug-

[1] I am indebted to Adrian Stokes's extended essay *Reflections on the Nude* (London: Tavistock, 1967), 3–64, for his psychoanalytic discussion of the wholeness that may be found through contemplation of female figures in the visual arts who embody completeness, fulfillment, and plenitude.

[2] See, for example, Judith Wynn's assertion that "movies about nuns fall into one of two categories: the ridiculous and the sublime" in "The Sappy and Sublime" *Sojourner* 5.6 (1980): 21; Rebecca Sullivan's suggestion at the close of *Visual Habits: Nuns, Feminism, and American Postwar Popular Culture* (University of Toronto Press, 2005), 220, that nice, naughty, and nasty nuns became the prevailing film stereotypes in the late sixties and seventies; and Mary Ann Janosik's classification of women religious in Hollywood film as "the Earth Mother Madonna, the Eccentric Aunt, and the Social Activist Sister" in "Madonnas in our Midst: Representations of Women Religious in Hollywood Film," *U.S. Catholic Historian* 15.3 (1997): 81. Anthony Burke Smith has recently described how "American nuns bore the brunt of stereotyping" in the popular, postwar, photojournalist magazine *Life*. See *The Look of Catholics: Portrayals in Popular Culture from the Great Depression to the Cold War* (Lawrence: University Press of Kansas, 2010), 121–2.

gest the height, breadth, and depth of her desires by looking at a range of postwar mainstream, English-speaking films in which she rose to prominence as an ardent leading character. Desires that reach from earth to heaven and express the longing not only for human but divine love can provoke disquiet at their sheer power, magnitude, and audacity. Stereotypes may manage this unease by belittling or diminishing cinematic nuns in significance and overlooking filmic evidence of their more mature desires as women and religious. The inter-related question I will bear in mind throughout my investigation is whether this stereotyping is the work of filmmakers who saw nuns as a dramatic novelty, reviewers who did not understand or appreciate their religious life, critics who thought the films were only about nuns at face value, or a popular audience who enjoyed seeing them inside a "little nunny world."[3]

The dramatic feature films that I have selected for closer reading and analysis range from pure entertainment to documentary-like realism. However, none portray the religious vocation as a safe and settled life choice for a modern woman, the convent as an escape from a troubling world, or consecrated vows as a release from desire, doubt, dilemma, or darkness. On the contrary, they dramatize the nun protagonist's restless heart as she comes to terms with what is missing in her modern life and questions whether this can be satisfied by a traditional affirmation, more progressive interpretation, or ultimate renunciation of her religious vows. The title of this book, *Veiled Desires*, refers to the paradox driving this study—how the charismatic and photogenic actresses who played chaste nuns draw attention to the desires that their habits were thought to veil and stifle. This paradox is neatly illustrated by the lament of the placid nun heroine who ruefully resumes the holy robe of undesirability at the end of the 1957 film *Sea Wife*: "No one ever looks at the face of a nun." My study investigates this assumption. Indeed, I argue that film viewers most certainly *do* look when the nun in question is played by a young and beautiful starlet such as Joan Collins. However, as the hero (Richard Burton) symbolizes through his fleeting and inattentive glance of non-recognition, where he sees only the stereotype of the asexual religious and not the flesh and blood woman he loves, even B-grade films featuring nuns might be worth a second and closer look.

[3] Theologian and journalist Sister Charles Borromeo Muckenhirn, C.S.C., was quoted by Michael Novak in his article on "The New Nuns" for *The Saturday Evening Post* (July 30, 1966): 22. See Sullivan's discussion in *Visual Habits*, 67, of the gender political issues that nun films raise.

This book also explores how iconic movie stars such as Ingrid Berg-man, Deborah Kerr, Audrey Hepburn, and Diana Rigg brought a per-sonal history of desire to their film roles; how they negotiated their vola-tile status on-screen as desirable women playing religious who both dis-avow the desire for money, sex, and power and forge alternative mean-ings for their vows of poverty, chastity, and obedience; and how their erotic ambivalence can open up new and provocative understandings of the place of the female body, sexuality, and longing in the religious life. My study will further expand the way we see nuns on-screen by con-necting them to the bigger picture that religious and cultural historians have already vividly drawn of Catholic and Anglican sisterhood. At the same time, I focus on films that allow me not only to deconstruct the restrictive stereotypes enclosing cinematic nuns but also to unfold a rich pageantry of intricately coiled and spiraling desires: the desire to escape patriarchal domination in the home and a domestic life without purpose; the desire for female autonomy and independence from men; the de-sire for meaningful work, professional development, and an outlet not only for their talents but their capacity for love; the desire to travel, see the world, and experience adventure; the desire to dedicate their life to Christ, prayer, philanthropy, and evangelism. Taken as a cumulative body, these films suggest how the religious vocation can call women to recognize and live out their deepest desires—desires that take different shape according to each character, movie, historical setting, and period of production—and that cannot always be contained by the veil, the habit, the convent, the chapel, or the cloister.

The subtitle of my book indicates that this is not a comprehensive survey of the postwar cinematic nun but a composition of intimate por-trayals. It alludes to my interest in her screen encounters with intimacy, whether overtures of intimacy constitute a danger or a godsend to her religious life, why intimacy is traditionally avoided, and when it is recog-nized more progressively as "the vocation of every person, single or mar-ried, lay or cleric" (Gustafson 1994: 278). My study encompasses twenty-one feature films in total and examines twelve in depth, predominantly from Hollywood, in which the woman religious appears as a figure of veiled desire. It begins with the end-of-war film *The Bells of St. Mary's* (1945), which immortalized and indelibly typecast the nun as a star who "light(s) up dark lives . . . with luminous Hollywood beauty" (Loudon 1993: 16). It concludes with the twenty-first century film *Doubt* (2008), which depicts the nun as a figure of light and darkness, desire and denial. The six chapters that follow offer close textual, inter-disciplinary, and

historically contextualized readings of films that are presented chronologically and grouped thematically as they represent, in Chapter 1, the
selfless desires of women, their sense of religious mission, and the sacrificial service that can both thwart and give fulfillment; in Chapter 2, their
sexual desires, commitment to a celibate vocation, and the role of sublimation in the religious life; in Chapter 3, the personal and professional
desires that are subject to the vow of obedience and the psychic role of
the family romance in the formation of core subjectivity; in Chapter 4,
the sonorous desires that lift their spirit, lead them out of the convent
but keep them in communion with its religious sounds and spaces; in
Chapter 5, the sacred, strange, and mysterious desires that draw them to
contemplative life; in Chapter 6, the spiritual desires that enable them to
face evil and withstand the power of death with love; and in the Conclusion, darker and more suspect desires that find outlet in the lust for power
and domination, that pervert religious ideals, and that give rise to doubt,
disbelief, and disillusionment.

Audre Lorde's well-known essay on the "Uses of the Erotic: The
Erotic as Power" informs my study of the veiled desires of cinematic
nuns. Lorde initially presented this essay in a setting conducive to scholarship on women religious, namely a 1978 conference on the history of
women at Mount Holyoke College. Mount Holyoke was originally a
female seminary before becoming the first of the Seven Sisters, and the
college founder, Mary Lyon, encouraged her women students to pursue
a path that the cinematic nuns in this study often dramatize: "Go where
no one else will go, do what no one else will do." Lorde defined eros as
the core longings that make us most fully human: for fulfilling work, for
the creation and celebration of beauty, for intellectual and spiritual pursuits, for the enjoyment of friendship, love, connection, and intimacy.
Thus, she potentially provides a framework for seeing nuns on-screen as
whole persons rather than through the lens of partial stereotypes. Lorde
also projected an affirmative vision of eros as a lifeforce that stands in
opposition to dehumanizing pornography and indeed to the "ravaging
eroticism" that twentieth-century Catholic authorities saw threatening
modern love and intimacy.[4] In her passionate insistence that sexuality
and spirituality are interrelated forms of self-expression, she rejected the
mental tendency to separate the soulful self from the sexed and gen-

---

[4]Pope Paul VI's *Evangelica testificatio* is quoted by Sister Mary Dominic Pitts,
O.P., "The Threefold Response of the Vows," in The Council of Major Superiors
of Women Religious, *The Foundations of Religious Life: Revisiting the Vision* (Notre
Dame, Ind.: Ave Maria Press, 2009), 95.

dered body. This split can encourage the perception that nuns cease to be women when they become religious, or worse, lead to the dualistic representation of the good nun as supremely spiritual and the bad or failed nun as incorrigibly female.

Lorde's short, secular but deeply spiritual essay exerted a considerable influence on feminist theologians and religious thinkers who have interrogated Judeo-Christian discourse on love, sexuality, and embodiment, and it inspired them to challenge Anders Nygren's authoritative study of *Agape and Eros*.

Published between 1932 and 1939 as the world went into freefall with the Great Depression and moved inexorably toward another full-scale war, Nygren's sweeping history of Christian ideas of love reflects the pessimism of those grim times. He depicted a fundamental contrast between the selfish and acquisitive cravings of the natural man driven by the baser appetite of eros and the magnanimous and gratuitous gift of divine love to this natural man in agape. In perceiving God as pure Agape and Eros as wholly alien to his being, Nygren not only made egocentric mankind appear unlovable but a theocentric God unlikeable: "Eros finds abundant reason for man to love God, in that God possesses what man lacks and seeks; but no reason for God to love man, since man possesses nothing that God could desire" (1953: xiii). Divine agape for sinful humanity is unveiled at its most exalted in the selfless sacrifice of Christ on the Cross (117, 236). With his death, Christian love is born as a new phenomenon modeled on divine agape and transcending the Hellenistic and pagan religious strivings of eros (160–3). Nygren's definition of Christian agape as a loving and "whole-hearted surrender to God," without reserve, as "obedience to God, without any thought of reward," and as a conversion or change of heart in which "love is awakened in man by God himself," articulates first principles of the religious life that will be reiterated on-screen (1953: viii, 95, 213, 223). Indeed these remain sacred for traditional nuns of the present-day who describe their religious vocation as a divine gift that is "freely given and unmerited," and is expressed by Christ's reminder to his apostles in John 15:16: "You did not choose me, but I chose you." The super-human struggle to imitate Christ by offering in return "the gift and sacrifice of self,"[5] responding to a divine love that is unearned and undeserved, and showing love for those who are dislike-

---

[5] See the essay of Mother Agnes Mary Donovan, S.V., and Sister Mary Elizabeth Wusinich, S.V., on "Religious Consecration—A Particular Form of Consecrated Life" in *The Foundations of Religious Life*, 23–6.

able or hateful, will appear as a subject of serious moral examination in the 1959 feature-length film *The Nun's Story* as well as in the 1975 TV film *In This House of Brede*, and constitute the mysterious heart of the 1995 film *Dead Man Walking*.

Inherent in the comparative contrast Nygren draws between agape as the most pure and altruistic expression of Christian love, and eros as the avaricious love that brands us needy creatures, is the binary he ostensibly repudiates at the outset of his study. Although he insists that his contrast is not between "right and wrong . . . higher and lower," earthly and heavenly, sensual and spiritual love (1953: 39, 50), his discourse repeatedly underlines the superiority of self-giving agape and inferiority of self-seeking eros. Belief in the superiority of agape as divinely inspired love contributed to a hierarchical construct of religious life that would prevail until the Second Vatican Council and that continues to be upheld in modified form by traditional nuns. They insist that "the Church has consistently taught the objective superiority of the state of the evangelical counsels," or three vows of poverty, chastity, and obedience, in living a Christian life. A religious life consecrated to these vows is implicitly the consummate expression of the "state of perfection" and the vocation of love to which all Christians are called.[6] This construct has not only promoted the ideological view that nuns perfect high-souled agape but that eros is a selfish, secular, and sexual manifestation of love wholly renounced in religious life. A major aim of my study is to look at films that deconstruct this view; anticipate changes in religious thinking on love, desire, and intimacy; and suggest how screen nuns negotiate a path between the traditional idealization of agape and the modern valorization of eros.

Theological and spiritual writers who succeeded Lorde have not only contested the dichotomous comparison of eros with agape but have brought to the fore an important chapter in Nygren's religious history.[7] They have recognized the "central and permanent place" eros secured in Catholicism through the influential Church Father Augustine (Nygren 1953: 183, 243, 451, 561). The haunting discourse of Augustine's *Confessions* demonstrates that it is "a constant desiring, a forever reaching out,

---

[6]See the careful argument of Sister M. Maximilia Um, F.S.G.M., on the "Evangelical Mission," *The Foundations of Religious Life*, 170–1.

[7]See the helpful summaries and lists of writers on eros by David M. Carr, *The Erotic Word: Sexuality, Spirituality and the Bible* (New York: Oxford University Press, 2003), 9–11, 181n.24, 182n.31, and by James B. Nelson, *Embodiment: An Approach to Sexuality and Christian Theology* (Minneapolis: Augsburg, 1979), 110–17, 283n.18.

a quest for communion with another, with beauty, with knowledge, with goodness," which give eros its momentum (Nelson 1979: 112). Moreover these religious thinkers have resumed Augustine's attempts at Christian synthesis by arguing that divine and human love exist on a continuum in which agape and eros are not wholly opposed but different manifestations of love in all its majesty and magnitude (Nelson 1979: 109–11; Carr 2003: 182n.31). Their perception of the energy flow between eros and agape makes the mysterious pull of a religious vocation more intelligible. Actual nuns often recount how God's call was felt insistently as "a deep and strong desire to give myself to Him as completely as possible" (Cabrini 2008: 24). They memorably define the religious life as "one long, long yearning" (Kaylin 2000: 166). They speak of religious consecration as not only a "gift and sacrifice of self" but an act of spousal love that "embraces the whole person, soul and body" (Donovan and Wusinich 2009: 23–4; Miller 2009: 49–50, 62). Agapaic and erotic love merge in these statements, suggesting that sexuality is an expression of "the whole person" and passionate feeling has sacred depths, and making nuns' nuptial love for God appear centered rather than unbalanced. In a written account aptly titled "First Love," a Dominican sister recalled the wave of emotions associated with the recognition of a religious vocation, as she felt a love for God suffused with the passion and power of eros and the grateful awareness of agape—that this love was a sublime gift:

> I knew God loved us and that nuns are called "brides of Christ," but I had always taken the latter term as purely poetic. It's astounding to have God look at you like that; both exhilarating and humbling because you know it's totally unmerited. To my surprise, I felt very much like when I had first fallen in love, except it was magnified a hundred times. (Anonymous Dominican Contemplative Nun 2008: 65–6)

These testimonials accord with the view of recent theologians who radically differ from Nygren in the conviction that the God who underwent the Passion on the Cross to save humanity is not an impassive but "an erotic being, longing for us, desiring us, pursuing us, loving us even to distraction with intense emotion and passion" (Blye Howe 1998: 57). As the novelist Rumer Godden would observe after spending several years studying cloistered Benedictines in preparation for *In This House of Brede* (whose film adaptation I discuss in Chapter 5), "nuns are dramatic. Theirs is the greatest love story in the world" (Godden 1989: 279). Film is a particularly apt medium for communicating the erotic dynamism of the religious vocation and projecting the nun on-screen as a desiring and desired person. Indeed, in the course of my research, I was surprised to hear women religious acknowledge the positive role that Hollywood played in their decision to enter the convent.

> It was a vocation I knew little about, except from observing the presence of sisters in our parish and school, and watching with great interest some of the Hollywood classics like *The Bells of St. Mary's*, *The Nun's Story* and *The Sound of Music*. All this touched my heart and stirred my spirit to search for the deeper truths of my faith. (Sister Maria Christine, O.P., 2008: 51)

Of course when Hollywood chose actresses with star power, energy, radiance, and charisma such as Ingrid Bergman, Deborah Kerr, Joan Collins, Audrey Hepburn, Julie Andrews, Diana Rigg, Meg Tilly, and Susan Sarandon to play nuns, it was not thinking of the erotic pull of the religious call but these women's pulling power at the box office. If the cinematic nun has been particularly beautiful, there has been a critical inclination to dismiss her as a romanticized representation or to focus on the mascara, blusher, and lip gloss that emphasize her artificiality. However, the sight of beauty, as Nygren acknowledged in discussing the influence of platonic love on Christianity, can awaken eros in the soul and give intimations of divine beauty (1953: 173, 223). A love of beauty is a persistent feature of monastic history. It is manifest not only in convent architecture, liturgy, music, and devotional objects, but in the nun's graceful rituals, body language, and striking habit, all of which make for visually rich and dramatic spectacle on-screen (Sipe 1994: 196; Burke Smith 2010: 11–12). Both nuns who have left the convent and those who remain concur in the view that the religious life can be compellingly beautiful, a reality that Fred Zinnemann made visible on-screen with the help of his ethereally lovely film star Audrey Hepburn in *The Nun's Story*. Yet James B. Nelson has insisted that cloistered beauty cannot be the product of a sterile celibate culture and that even in religious life "there is an intimate, unbreakable link between sexuality and a sense of beauty" (1979: 92–3). While the least successful films in this study do tend to perpetuate the stereotype that the nun is an incomplete or perfunctory part-self, strange, bland or blank, the most interesting employ her face and gestures to intimate that a whole person with a complex psychic history, inner feelings, and longings is hidden beneath the habit and veil. Occasionally, there is a glimpse of religious life as a living out of the ancient beauty of the Jewish shema where God's first chosen ones were called to love the Lord God with all their heart, soul, mind, and strength.

Scholars now engaged in the study of religion, film, and popular culture recognize the attraction of the religious film may lie in the fact that it is imbued with eros or "a longing for something beyond the world we know" (Grace 2009: 3). In her discussion of devotional objects and sacred relics from the Christian past, Margaret Miles suggested that religious seeing has a numinous quality "in which other human beings, the natural world, and objects appear in their full beauty, transformed" (1985: 2). Both Nygren and the theologians who critiqued him would connect this moment of epiphany to the mysterious alchemy of agape in which divine grace suffuses eros with golden light (Nygren 1953: 223; Nelson 1979: 113). The luminous beauty, the radiance, and the glow that are often remarked upon in the cinematic nun, and disparaged as typecasting, may point to something more powerful: which is the redoubled energy of desire she radiates as a film star and a religious icon in a modern visual era where the cinema has replaced the cathedral (Miles 2002: 25, 189). However, the screen nun is not only or always a vision of beauty and desire. She is also a protagonist in films shaped by the vision of the director and the expectations of a popular audience. With the development of Catholic studies, cultural historians have begun to explore how nun films represent the social desires, hopes, anxieties, and concerns of their historical time. I am also interested in the screen nun's embodiment of religious visions of desire, having to do with the longing to see God, the importance of faith and the power of prayer (Loughlin 2007: 337–40; Ostwalt 1995: 155). While the cinematic nun's entreaties and convictions have often been disregarded as simple elements in her stereotyping, theological and spiritual writers are now cognizant that prayer can express a complex discourse of desire, and that belief is a commitment rooted in the language of the heart (Beattie 2006: 77).[8]

Like theology and spirituality, psychoanalysis also strives to decipher the language of desire. There has been pronounced resistance to the idea that Freud's secular and skeptical theory might in any way illuminate the workings of faith. However, his writing is imbued with a deep knowledge of the Bible and reflects his lifelong fascination with the psychology

---

[8]Diana L. Eck points out that the Latin word "credo" originally meant to give one's heart to the profession of faith, and that "believe" comes from the old English word "belove." Eck, *Encountering God: A Spiritual Journey from Bozeman to Banaras* (Boston: Beacon Press, 1993), 95–6.

that gave rise to collective religion and still inspires individual belief, love, and trust in God. More to the point, Freud anticipated the brief but powerful remarks of Lorde in his view of eros as "the divine spark which is directly or indirectly the driving force—*il primo motore*—behind all human activity" (1910, *SE* 11: 74). Yet eros cannot always be affirmed as a positive lifeforce for cinematic nuns or a means of their female fulfillment and empowerment. For the films in which they achieved prominence were overwhelmingly fashioned by male directors, screenwriters, and producers. These films periodically allude to the patriarchal hierarchy of the institutional Catholic Church and its political struggle with sister nonconformists and reformists. They sometimes depict worship of God as an extension of the obedient daughter's devotion to the father. One major film—*Agnes of God* (1985)—openly debates the competing claims of Freud, the father of psychoanalysis, and God the Father of religion, and dramatizes the clash of the "new science" of psychiatry and the old-fashioned tenets of traditional Catholic faith.

In these instances, Freud's androcentric theories of gender, sexual, and religious psychology help me to understand the oedipal family dynamics that male filmmakers may consciously or otherwise project onto the convent. They also enable me to critique the recurrent filmic motif of the absent, distant, jealous, or abusive mother, a motif that allows the male to be valorized as head of family, church, and state and reflects Freud's mental masculinity. Object-relations theorists such as Donald Winnicott, Melanie Klein, and Ana-Maria Rizzuto supplement my reading of Freud and compensate for his theoretical devaluation of both women and religious believers as immature. Rizzuto and Klein acknowledge the psychological importance of the mother as well as the father in the family romance. Rizzuto argues that both parents can be influential in the early formation of the God representation and the evolution of more mature faith. Winnicott indicates how religion can play creatively as well as destructively with reality. Freudian psychoanalyst Hans Loewald considers the psychic operation of repression and sublimation and suggests how the life energies of eros might be withheld or redirected in the religious life (Miles 1988: 96).

One of the most highly respected films made about the modern nun, *Dead Man Walking* (1995), heralded the revival of serious scholarly interest in women religious. Jo Ann Kay McNamara's magisterial history of *Sisters in Arms: Catholic Nuns Through Two Millennia* appeared only a year later in 1996. Carol K. Coburn and Martha Smith's *Spirited Lives* was published in 1999. It studied the influential role that Catholic nuns played in nineteenth and early twentieth-century American history, and indeed highlighted the pioneering activities of the religious order with which Sister Helen Prejean of *Dead Man Walking* was affiliated, the Sisters of St. Joseph. *Spirited Lives* ended by contrasting the freedom, entrepreneurship, and empowerment that women religious experienced as they expanded the frontiers of American Catholicism with the "great repression" they underwent when this work was done and they were subject in the 1920s to a more restricted life in canonically regulated communities. Fred Zinnemann's 1959 film *The Nun's Story*, which is the subject of Chapter 3, allows me to examine this great repression of veiled desires.

Since then, historians such as Silvia Evangelisti have shown that the desire of Zinnemann's film protagonist Sister Luke to distinguish herself was not so singular after all by recovering the early modern history of female religious energy, purposefulness, and achievement in *Nuns: A History of Convent Life* (Oxford University Press, 2007). Susan Mumm's 1999 work on the emergence of Anglican religious communities in Victorian Britain has provided background reading for my critique of the Powell and Pressburger film *Black Narcissus* (1947), a psychological study of Anglican sisters and the breakdown of their community life during the dying days of the British Indian Empire. It also helped me to appreciate the later social predicament of single Protestant women such as Gladys Aylward who had no congregational base to support their Christian zeal and activism. In dramatizing her life story, *The Inn of the Sixth Happiness* (1958) represents Aylward's solo journey from Britain to become a missionary in China as a search for an alternative *communitas* characterized by lowliness, sacredness, homogeneity, and comradeship (Turner 1969: 96).

Both nuns who stayed in the convent and those who left have also contributed authoritative insider accounts as religious and community historians, sociologists, theologians, feminist activists, and advocates of traditional as well as progressive ideals of religious life. At the same time, professors of English, Comparative Literature, Religion, and Cultural Studies began to analyze Catholic girlhood narratives, the departure accounts of Catholic women who left the convent or Church, and the representation of the nun in fiction with Jeana DelRosso's *Writing Catholic Women* (2005), Debra Campbell's *Graceful Exits* (2003), and Manuela Mourao's *Altered Habits* (2002).

This book is not intended as a work of film studies *per se*, although it certainly considers how key elements of film narration—representation of character, interpretative acting, dialogue, close-ups of the nun's face, the inherent costume drama of the habit and veil, screenplay, color, sound, location, and camera work—all conveyed the complex desires of women religious on-screen (Rosenstone 2006: 25, 47). However, it does regard nun films as a significant genre that has only been partially explored, yet was responsible for bringing the hidden world, desires, and lifestyle of nuns to the attention of a wider general audience. In fact, vocational directors have acknowledged that the dramatic feature films of the postwar era could be the first introduction to traditional nuns and their religious life for young women who had no contact with sisters through parochial school or a church community (Rooney 2001: 12; Reed 2004: 134). Films such as *The Nun's Story* (1959), *In This House of Brede* (1975), and *Agnes of God* (1985) also brought to the screen a category of nuns who were usually invisible, unheard, and anonymous, those in contemplative orders who lived behind cloistered walls, adhered to strict rules of silence and asceticism, and cultivated self-abnegation.[9]

While this book does not claim to contribute new knowledge to the scholarly work that has already been done on the history of nuns, it does consider what aspects of their past might be constructed more vividly, tangibly, and evocatively through the visual medium of film rather than written narrative. Although Rumer Godden would scornfully dismiss Powell and Pressburger's 1947 film adaptation of her novel *Black Narcissus* as having "not an atom of truth" (Godden 1989: 51), their film did examine the meaning of sexuality in the religious life, an issue that was absent from the official histories of nuns and was not openly discussed or positively reevaluated until after the Second Vatican Council (Schneiders 2000: 247; 2001: 160–6). Only two movies in this study approximate history films. Fred Zinnemann's *The Nun's Story* (1959) was based on the fictionalized life story of former nun Marie Louise Habets. The film shows the influence of Robert Flaherty's documentary-like storytelling in its visualization of her congregational induction and training and suggests the director's affinity with the historian in his open-minded and impartial representation of the religious life.[10] Tim Robbins's *Dead Man*

---

[9] Although I use the term "nun" as popularly understand to refer to women religious, I am aware that technically, a nun takes solemn vows and belongs to a contemplative and cloistered religious order, while a *sister* is a member of an active religious order and has traditionally had professional contact with the world through teaching, medical and pastoral care, hospital administration, and social and missionary work. However, Sister Luke in *The Nun's Story* (1959) could be classified as a semi-contemplative who observed rules of enclosure and followed the liturgy of the hours but had restricted work on the outside.

[10] Robert A. Rosenstone cites Robert Flaherty as a pioneer of documentary film narrative in *History on Film / Film on History* (Edinburgh: Pearson Longman,

Walking (1995) could loosely be called a biographical film based on the *testimonio* of Sister Helen Prejean who brought the evils of capital punishment to the attention of a general readership and made it a subject of considerable public debate. However even completely fictional films featuring nuns gave a general audience some awareness of their dramatic past and appreciation of the active role they played on the twentieth-century world stage as participants in the history of working women, wartime, British imperialism, European colonialism, Christian missionary expansion, and American Catholicism.

This book draws on the existing body of written scholarship in order to historically frame the films; ground them chronologically in the evolving twentieth-century experiences of modern women religious; connect them to the religious and conventual culture they dramatize, and to the social period and circumstances in which they were produced; and examine the literary history behind some of the films. My training in English literary interpretation and close reading has also prompted me to look at the texts that inspired key films and that either Pinewood or Hollywood appropriated for its own purposes. Thus I consider how female writers—the British-Indian novelist Rumer Godden, the fictional biographer Kathryn Hulme, and the testimonial writer Sister Helen Prejean—originally conceived their life stories of nuns and how their narratives of religious life were realized or altered by the male filmmakers who brought them to the screen in *Black Narcissus* (1947), *The Nun's Story* (1959), *In This House of Brede* (1975), and *Dead Man Walking* (1995).Throughout my study, I ask questions that are important not only to historians but literary and cultural critics: What were the sources for the nun film; how did filmmakers bring her story to the screen; what were their intentions; does the film make an audience think more meaningfully about her religious life and history; and what might have been changed to make it a more authentic construct of the nun's world and *weltanschauung* (Rosenstone 2006: 26–7).

I hope to contribute a deeper dimension to the feminist and historical study that has already been done on nuns as a neglected category of women, and to enrich the cultural study of their religious and institutional roles through the addition of my literary, psychoanalytic, and theological perspective to the analysis of how the screen nun's desires traverse the boundaries separating religious life from secular, modern life, a sacred vo-

---

2006), 25, 71. Neil Sinyard discusses how this father of documentary trained and influenced Fred Zinnemann in *Fred Zinnemann: Films of Character and Conscience* (Jefferson N.C.: McFarland, 2003), 11–13.

cation from the call of the world, and agapaic from erotic love. My own scholarly work on imaginative texts, and both literary and psychoanalytic interest in the realm of the imaginary, make me receptive to Rosenstone's argument that history film can convey symbolic and poetic truths about the past that bring the emotions into past enquiry and so appeal to a wide audience (Rosenstone 2006: 8–9, 17, 22, 28, 35, 68–9; Buettner 2004: 143). However, as Margaret Miles emphasizes, what distinguishes cultural history studies is the focus on the film as "one voice in a complex social conversation, occurring in a particular historical moment" (2002: xiii). Feminist cultural, literary, and psychoanalytic critics like myself also study the film as an inventive text communicating complex meanings that do not wholly depend on the cultural context of production but arise from interpretative voices stretching from the past into the present that carry on the work of insightful viewing. This filmic text is not only a visual but sometimes a visionary medium and, like the work to which nuns felt called, can have its prophetic moments and flashes of foresight.[11]

In each chapter, I foreground one major film that offers new or unexplored insights into the fluid nature of the nun protagonist's desires. In my film analyses, I consider to what extent she is represented as both a woman and a religious, although these two designations have not always been given equal weight, particularly in feminist cultural critique. I look at how these two defining terms come into conflict or coalesce to construct her screen image; how they are accentuated by film directors and screenwriters; and more generally, how they take turns to modify one another over the sixty-year film period that I cover in this work. The research strength of my study of film nuns derives from my interdisciplinary approach as an academic and from my cross-disciplinary affiliation with English, Comparative Literature, History, Women, and Gender Studies. Indeed, I bring a distinctive perspective to bear upon

---

[11]Lora Ann Quinonez, C.D.P., and Mary Daniel Turner, S.N.D.deN., note that "in the second half of the seventies terms like 'prophetic' and 'counter-cultural' entered the vocabulary used to describe the call of sisters." Quinonez and Turner, *The Transformation of American Catholic Sisters* (Philadelphia: Temple University Press, 1992), 79. See Mary Jo Leddy's description of religious life as "a prophetic moment" and her insistence that this is a fleeting and unpremeditated experience in *Reweaving Religious Life: Beyond the Liberal Model* (Mystic, Conn.: Twenty-Third Publications, 1990), 157–63. Sister Marie Augusta Neal, S.N.D.deN., discusses how American women religious were inspired by Vatican Council II to embark upon a prophetic ministry, and the personal and political risks of this commitment, in *From Nuns to Sisters: An Expanding Vocation* (Mystic, Conn.: Twenty-Third Publications, 1990), 39–51.

the subject of women religious and the veiled desires they project on-
screen as a scholar who combines the tools of feminist literary, cultural,
historical, psychoanalytic, and theological analysis and who has written
on religious and erotic literature, Catholic and Anglican devotional art,
Freud, object relations theorists, the religious cultural imaginary, spirituality and sexuality, and on film, religion, and popular culture. My use,
in particular, of a Freudian and post-Freudian critique for analyzing religious beliefs in conjunction with my serious interest in Catholic images,
practices, and politics is boundary breaking. It has made me alert to the
cultural clash that cinematic nuns could project as women who embody
faith yet are official representatives of institutional religion. On the one
hand, it enabled me to see how they could be mouthpieces of church
ideology and its self-serving tenets, and on the other, how their deeply
held beliefs were susceptible to exaggeration or misrepresentation by uncomprehending filmmakers and critics.

I am indebted to the handful of feminist historical, cultural, and film
critics such as Brandon French, Mary Ann Janosik, and Rebecca Sullivan
who have begun the serious investigation of how nuns are represented
on the postwar screen, and to Colleen McDannell's 2008 edition of *Catholics in the Movies*, which provides an introductory survey of nun movies
and critical discussions of the appearance and depiction of nuns in the
history of film.[12] Neither Janosik's tripartite typecasting of the cinematic
nun as earth mother Madonna, eccentric aunt, and social activist sister,
nor French and Sullivan's reading of her as a non-threatening intermediary between the traditional domesticated woman and the independent,
feminist career woman, address my central concerns. These scholars have
provided thought-provoking sections, articles, or single chapters on nuns
in Hollywood film, and my book continues their work by providing the
full-length study that is currently lacking. However, Sullivan introduced
an issue at the end of her work on *Visual Habits: Nuns, Feminism, and
American Postwar Culture* that sets the scene for the subject of this book.
According to Sullivan, "the nun's status as a celibate" in a highly sexualized modern culture might suggest "alternative conceptions of female
desire and pleasure that include a spiritual as well as sexual dimension,
rather than pitting these dimensions against each other" (2005: 218). I
take up this suggestion by interpreting *The Bells of St. Mary's* as a film in

---

[12]See Brandon French's groundbreaking discussion of "Brides of Christ:
Heaven Knows, Mr. Allison (1957) and *The Nun's Story* (1959)" in *On the Verge of
Revolt: Women in American Films of the Fifties* (New York: Frederick Ungar, 1978),
121–36.

which the nun can still appreciate female desire and pleasure as a dedicated religious. I go on to argue that films such as *Black Narcissus* and *The Nun's Story* have suffered from critical readings that are based on the opposition of eros and agape, sexuality and spirituality, a religious vocation and a professional calling.

I have organized the chapters to suggest how the film protagonists cross not only the sexual/spiritual divide but the mental barrier keeping their identity as women and religious separate. While the majority of the cinematic nuns in this study are Catholic, I include films that cut across Christian divisions, emerge from England's Pinewood studio as well as Hollywood, and travel back and forth between the old and the new world. I examine the woman religious and the religious woman, the exceptional Catholic nun and proselytizing Protestant single woman, in *The Bells of St. Mary's* (1945) and *The Inn of the Sixth Happiness* (1958). I look at missionary sisters from the Irish Catholic countryside and haut-bourgeois Catholic Europe, from the Anglo-Irish gentry, the ruling class of the British empire, and the Anglican colonial communion in such films as Powell and Pressburger's *Black Narcissus* (1947), *Heaven Knows, Mr. Allison* (1957), *Sea Wife* (1957), and Fred Zinnemann's *The Nun's Story* (1959). I look at enclosed Belgian, Austrian, English, and French Canadian communities in *The Nun's Story*, *The Sound of Music* (1965), *In This House of Brede* (1975), and *Agnes of God* (1985), alongside active American orders in *The Bells of St. Mary's* (1945), *Change of Habit* (1969), *Dead Man Walking* (1995), and *Doubt* (2008).

In the ensuing chapters I will turn to a closer examination of how nuns are represented in postwar film. I will show how it is not simply critical viewers *of* the films but forces at work *within* these films that conspired to stereotype them or, as Dr. Fortunati tells Sister Luke in *The Nun's Story*, to keep them "in the mold." I will suggest how the characters accept, resist, struggle with, break free from, or succumb to the stereotypes that enclose them in a verbal and visual cloister. Whether they are expected to be the proverbial perfect nun in *The Bells of St. Mary's*; pure nun in *Black Narcissus*, *Heaven Knows, Mr. Allison*, and *Sea Wife*; obedient nun in *The Nun's Story*; single-hearted nun in *The Sound of Music* and *Change of Habit*; unworldly nun in *In This House of Brede* and *Agnes of God*; or good nun in *Dead Man Walking* and *Doubt*, all the protagonists, with the exception of Sister Therese in *Sea Wife*, indicate that they want to become something more—something that they hope to find in religious life even at the risk of losing themselves. Former religious Karen Armstrong memorably called nuns "complex beings, mind, heart, soul, and body engaged in a continuous bloody battle" (1997: 279–80). In this study, cinematic nuns will emerge from their stereotypes as more complex beings who strive paradoxically to realize the desires that will enable them to love God with the whole of their being, and to offer these desires up with an undivided heart on the high altar of sacrifice (Donovan and Wusinich 2009: 26–9; Pitts 2009 95–6; Losada 1999: 69). Figures such as Sister Benedict in *The Bells of St. Mary's*, Sister Clodagh in *Black Narcissus*, Sister Luke in *The Nun's Story*, Dame Philippa in *In This House of Brede*, Sister Helen Prejean in *Dead Man Walking,* and even postulant Maria in *The Sound of Music* will show how difficult it was to be a nun and yet how uplifting religious life could be; what collective meaning, purpose, and fulfillment women could find in religious community; and yet what hard work was required in the exercise of Christian love. These nuns enact the battle of the divided heart on-screen, torn by the conflict between their twentieth-century expectations as modern women and the traditional aspirations of religious life, and by the disparity between the Christian ideology of love expressed in agape and the emotional truth of the yearning desire known as eros.

The films covered are:

Casablanca (1942)
The Keys of the Kingdom (1944)
The Bells of St. Mary's (1945)
It's a Wonderful Life (1946)
Black Narcissus (1947)
Come to the Stable (1949)
Anastasia (1956)
Heaven Knows, Mr. Allison (1957)
Sea Wife (1957)
The Inn of the Sixth Happiness (1958)
The Nun's Story (1959)
Lilies of the Field (1963)
The Sound of Music (1965)
Change of Habit (1969)
In This House of Brede (1975)
Agnes of God (1985)
Dead Man Walking (1995)
Wide Awake (1998)
The Magdalene Sisters (2002)
The Painted Veil (2006)
Doubt (2008)

1

SELFLESS DESIRES

SACRIFICIAL AND SELF-FULFILLING SERVICE TO OTHERS IN *CASABLANCA* (1942), *THE BELLS OF ST. MARY'S* (1945), AND *THE INN OF THE SIXTH HAPPINESS* (1958)

*W*hen Ingrid Bergman appeared on-screen as Sister Mary Benedict in *The Bells of St. Mary's*, she was already a major film celebrity, but she made the film nun herself a star who "light(s) up dark lives . . . with luminous Hollywood beauty" (Loudon 1993: 16). The movie reviewers in 1945 felt that Bergman succeeded in representing the Catholic nun to a modern audience as an attractive, appealing, and admirable figure. Yet by the end of the century, actual nuns had come to take a dim view of her film performance as Sister Benedict and to lament her role in typecasting them as "perpetual little girls who combined a rarified 'Bells of St. Mary's' faith with a wide-eyed naivety" (Schneiders 2001: 234). How did Sister Benedict go from being a role model to a caricature, the charming and youthful face of the modern nun to an old and outgrown likeness?

> Today's nun is no Ingrid Bergman playing Sister Benedict to Bing Crosby's Father O'Malley in some kind of real-life version of "The Bells of St. Mary's." Today's nuns are mature and independent in ways they never were before, and they carry a heightened awareness of themselves as women and as Catholics. (Deedy 1982: 12)

18

In the post–Vatican Council II era of review and reform, Bergman's Sister Benedict became easy target practice for the exponents of "today's nun." Yet a moderate like Dominican Sister Maria Christine recalls that when religious life was shaken by turbulent change and reform in the late sixties, Hollywood classics like *The Bells of St. Mary's* sustained her conviction as a young woman that she might nonetheless have a religious vocation (2008: 51). One reason Bergman's Sister Benedict is held up as both a beau ideal and discredited screen image of a nun is that she shows how the lives of twentieth-century women religious were shaped by the tension between the beliefs of traditional religion and the progressive assumptions of modernity. How, to cite a venerable paradox, was the nun to work in the modern world but give witness to spiritual values that were not of this world? Following on from this paradox, I will explore how and why *The Bells of St. Mary's* is ambivalent about its nun protagonist, uncertain whether Sister Benedict's vivid lifeforce is an impediment or boost to her religious life, and whether her vows call her to choose between self-sacrifice as a religious and self-fulfillment as a woman.

For the traditional nun, a vocation does not arise as a result of her personal efforts, merits, and achievements. It is a mysterious gift from on high prompting the answering gift of self-surrender and "obedience to God, without any thought of reward" (Nygren 1953: 95). The Church exalted this whole-hearted offering of self as a divine expression of love and as the most perfect realization of the religious call to follow Christ. In theory, a life consecrated to the vows of poverty, chastity, and obedience frees the nun "to love God with an undivided heart" (Donovan and Wusinich 2009: 26, 29, 36). However, film nun Sister Benedict dramatizes the heartache that a modern woman religious could experience as she struggles to reconcile her commitment to agape as pure, selfless love and service for God with desires traditionally deemed more worldly, self-seeking, and stirring, which go by the name of eros. An early scene of *The Bells of St. Mary's* illustrates the implicit conflict between agape and eros. Father Chuck O'Malley introduces himself to the nuns in his new parish. His tone is light but his intention is solemn. He expects to edify, console, and uplift an appreciative convent audience.

St. Mary's has been here a great many years and has seen the labors of a good number of the sisters of your order and I know that the work hasn't been easy. In the eyes of the world, very few even take notice of us, but earthly honors and rewards are not for you.

You've sent forth generations of pupils who have been a credit to the teachings inculcated here. St. Mary's has grown old doing good.

As the priest warms to his homily on agape and the centrality of unseen and unappreciated service in the lives of teaching sisters, there is a reaction shot of the convent superior, Sister Benedict. It registers the faint quiver of her lips in amusement when O'Malley moralizes that "earthly honors and rewards are not for you," and wry exchange of glances with her fellow sisters when he concludes that "St. Mary's has grown old doing good." As he proceeds to discuss the work of a parish priest, the nuns begin to titter until they are all laughing outright at what he says. O'Malley looks disconcerted rather than affronted. While he speaks, the camera lets the audience in on the joke with a medium shot that takes in the convent cat playing with his straw boater on the mantelpiece behind him. He cannot see either visually or metaphorically why the nuns might find him funny. Other than the fact that he is upstaged by a cat, do they think it rich that a priest who is still something of a man about town, who had contact with his old girlfriend in *Going My Way*, and who did not renounce his love for jazz or popular music when he became a Catholic priest should be lecturing them on the virtues of self-sacrifice?[1] Are they entertained by his tacit message that they—like St. Mary's—are antiquated and old-school? If the priest is oblivious to the fact that he has compared them to old girls, the nuns show a sense of humor that makes him look like a maladroit schoolboy. The mise-en-scène establishes the fact that the women religious who serve St. Mary's may espouse the traditional belief that submission to God and Church-appointed superiors "exemplifies an interior freedom born of mature self-surrender" (O'Brien and Schaumber 2009: 200), but this does not make them submissive pushovers. It also suggests to film viewers that they should look with greater acuteness than the priest at how the sisters regard themselves, their work, and their calling in *The Bells of St. Mary's*.

Introduction

The priest's theme of noble sacrifice and selfless service animated Christian worship, motivated religious vocations, and justified missionary

---

[1] Rebecca Sullivan points out that there was a traditional Catholic hostility to jazz. Sullivan, *Visual Habits: Nuns, Feminism, and American Postwar Popular Culture* (University of Toronto Press, 2005), 162.

evangelism and expansion. However, the ideology of self-sacrifice has been influential not only in the construction of the Christian ideal of love and the core purpose of religious life but in the institutional definition of femininity. It was the natural duty of Christian women to subordinate their personal desires to the needs of others. It was the God-given imperative of women religious to efface themselves in service so that "few even take notice of us," and to deny the "earthly honors and rewards" that not only fund churches and schools but build self-worth and a sense of achievement. Religious thinkers now question the fundamental contrast that theologian Anders Nygren drew in the thirties between agape and eros, and argue that it led to a false dualism in which selfless altruism is valorized while personal desires are denigrated as selfish and egotistic. Nygren's comparative study would later make the self-sacrifice and the self-giving sanctified in religious life and the self-knowledge, self-development, and self-fulfillment promoted in secular feminism seem contrary ideals (Nelson 1979: 110–17 and 1992: 34–5; Miles 1998: 125). His theological representation of agape as wholly opposed to eros certainly did not make it easier for nuns in the mid-twentieth century to resolve the conflict they felt between traditional religion and progressive modernity. The question I pursue through an examination of Ingrid Bergman's portraits of devoted service to others in *Casablanca*, *The Bells of St. Mary's*, and *The Inn of the Sixth Happiness* is to what extent women with a religious calling are presented as gaining power through and over the ideology of self-sacrifice to achieve their own desires (Hunter 1984: 36, 89).

The theme of sacrifice for a higher cause also resonated with "the homefront heroine(s)" who flocked to the cinema to see Bergman in the wartime film *Casablanca* (Orsi 1996: 55). At the end of the war, American Catholics would be captivated by her portrait of religious devotion to an inner-city parochial school in *The Bells of St. Mary's* even though they were moving out of the old parishes in urban immigrant neighborhoods. In the late 1950s, a cold war audience, pondering the fate of Christian missionaries who disappeared in communist China, would be inspired by her spirited interpretation of the altruistic reformer Gladys Aylward in *The Inn of the Sixth Happiness* (Sanders 2008: 137–9). Ingrid Bergman, radiant in her renunciation of romance, sexual fulfillment, native home, or natural family in this film triad, reflects an ideal of untiring, selfless femininity that appealed to the popular imagination not only of the Catholic immigrant community with its ethos of sacred lowliness and sacrifice, but war-scarred America from the 1940s through to the end of the 1950s (Burke Smith 2010: 6; Gordon 1994: 592; Gandolfo 1992: 3–4,

47; McLeer 2002: 83–4). Furthermore, the spiritual maternalism that she brought to the role of Sister Benedict as school principal and teacher also had the official approval of Church authorities who later defined the nun in the modern world as someone who "ha(s) given up the possibility of a family of (her) own in order to be at the disposal of all families and to devote to them (her) most loving care and solicitude" (Suenens 1963: 16, 127).[2]

Father O'Malley believed that the world took little notice of nuns' work at St. Mary's. Historically, however, women religious had left a visible trail across America in the Catholic schools, hospitals, social agencies, convents, and mother houses they had founded and operated since the nineteenth century. More often than not, it was the priests in charge of the parishes and the fundraising that financed brick-and-mortar Catholicism who took their services for granted and did not recognize them as the pillars of the working Church (Weaver 1995: 36). As movies shaped the national consciousness in the twentieth century, the women religious who helped build the service infrastructure of America also began to appear on-screen, first in silent pictures such as *Pieces of Silver* (1914), *The White Sister* (1915), *Naked Hearts* (1916), *The Worldly Madonna* (1922), and a celebrated remake of *The White Sister* (1923), starring Lillian Gish, by the Catholic director Henry King. In 1933, a sound version of *The White Sister* debuted for the third time, featuring Helen Hayes who would later play opposite Ingrid Bergman in *Anastasia* (1956) (Weisenfeld 2008: 39–40; Butler 1969: 89). These films recycled nineteenth-century Romanticism's trope of the nun as a beautiful, trapped figure of erotic pathos (Mourao 2002: xviii, 1–2, 53–5). Even Henry King's 1943 film *The Song of Bernadette*—which honored Catholic popular belief in the intercession of the saints and the apparition of the Virgin Mary at Lourdes—continued to stereotype the nun as a tragic victim by depicting the young visionary Bernadette Soubirous as coerced into entering the convent and cruelly treated once there. Only a year afterwards, however, *The Keys of the Kingdom* (1944) broke this mold and looked forward to Bergman's more affirmative film representation of a religious calling by giving a supporting part to a missionary nun who works in partnership with a priest in early twentieth-century China during and after the republican revolution.

[2] Cardinal Leon Suenens originally published *The Nun in the World* in 1961, but the first English edition did not appear until 1962.

Ingrid Bergman

Ingrid Bergman brought Sister Benedict alive on-screen as a nun of great energy, deep feeling, warmth, and charisma, a woman who became a religious because she desired something more in life. Those who now dismiss her performance as that of a "luminous Hollywood beauty" miss the brilliance that the first film critics saw in her as a young actress. Again and again they marveled at how she lit up a part from within. *The New York Times* reviewer Frank Nugent put his finger on her mystique when he described "that incandescence about Miss Bergman, that spiritual spark which makes us believe that Selznick has found another great lady of the screen" (October 6, 1939: 31; Spoto 2001: 91). Cultural critics who have recently studied Bergman's star image note the contradictory way in which both movie fans and critics attributed spiritual qualities to an on-screen persona that often exuded sexuality, and how the actress suffered after her extramarital behavior off-screen exposed these contradictions to public scrutiny and censor (Damico 1991: 244–52; McLean 1995: 38–49). The underlying binary assumption of these perceptions is that sexuality and spirituality are in conflict with one another. Yet Bergman used her beauty—which critics invariably referred to as shining, radiant, or luminous—to express an ardor that dissolved this opposition and pointed to the indivisibility of the body and soul. Indeed the source of Bergman's brilliance as a performer lay in her talent for plumbing erotic depths, what Audre Lorde called the capacity to "live from within outward, in touch with the power of the erotic within ourselves, and allowing that power to inform and illuminate our actions upon the world around us" (1984: 58). As my study of Bergman's performances in *Casablanca*, *The Bells of St. Mary's*, and *The Inn of the Sixth Happiness* will show, her characters brought this erotic radiance to their relationship with others whether it was through love-making, service, self-sacrifice, prayer, or devotion (Beattie 2006: 15). Indeed when Sister Benedict speaks of the "complete understanding" that is necessary for a young woman to have before she can say whole-heartedly "I want to be a nun," she is intimating that a religious vocation understood as agape is incomplete without knowledge and appreciation of other forms of desire.

In 1939, Ingrid Bergman was a popular Swedish film actress who had just arrived in Hollywood to reprise a role that would bring her international attention as Anita Hoffman in *Intermezzo*. Bergman's new Hollywood boss, David O. Selznick, later remarked that "the minute I looked at her, I knew I had something. She had an extraordinary quality of purity and nobility and a definite star quality that is very rare" (Feld-man and Winter c. 1991), qualities that would make her perfect for the leading role of Sister Benedict. However, Bergman refused to undergo the radical studio makeover or change of name that turned actresses into screen goddesses, but that ironically required an obedience to the Hollywood star system parodying that of a postulant in a strictly run convent. Selznick artfully capitalized on her initial resistance by crafting a natural image for the actress that emphasized the unspoiled and wholesome impression she first made. She later recalled, "I looked very simple, my hair would blow in the wind, and I acted like the girl next door" (Spoto 2001: 70).

Bergman made her first appearance in Hollywood just before the start of World War II, when film actresses were one of the few groups of women who—like nuns in active service—had a profession and prospects. The star dedicated herself with characteristic single-mindedness, application, and stamina to her acting career but in doing so, did not conform to the socially approved gender ideal of primary devotion to marriage and motherhood. As she later admitted with an unflinching honesty that reflects a brutal capacity for self-examination, "My whole life has been acting. I have had my different husbands, my families. I am fond of them all and I visit them all, but deep inside me there is the feeling that I belong to show business" (Spoto 2001: 397). Bergman's workaholic drive informs her film portrayal of Sister Benedict and will characterize other nuns on-screen such as Sister Clodagh in *Black Narcissus* (1947), Sister Luke in *The Nun's Story* (1959), Sister Michelle in *Change of Habit* (1969), Dame Philippa in *In This House of Brede* (1975), and Sister Aloysius in *Doubt* (2008). Her comment that "deep inside" she felt she belonged to show business is an insight into someone who had a consuming desire to be an actress. As theologian David Carr rightly points out, "There can be a deeply erotic dimension to work that coincides with what is deepest in ourselves" (2003: 35). Unfortunately, Bergman's indefatigable careerism would not always be viewed sympathetically by a conventional film audience. Her Hollywood rise to stardom coincided with a war period when society was ambivalent about the need for women to work. On the one hand, the war effort and the conscription of male breadwinners into the armed services required young married women and mothers to join the labor force. On the other hand, wartime separation put a strain on marriages, as we shall see dramatized in *Casablanca*, and the working woman could be haunted by the guilt of being a "bad mother" or taking a job that belonged rightfully to a man (Orsi 1996: 51–5). In effect, women were torn by conflicting calls to service and sacrifice on behalf of the nation and war effort, and for the sake of their husband and family.

Casablanca (1942)

With the outbreak of full-scale war in Europe, Bergman decided to pursue a film career in Hollywood and tried to settle down with her husband, Petter Lindstrom, and daughter, Pia, to live a nuclear-family dream in middle-class America. Her movie audience would be charmed by the artless beauty that she projected on-screen and brought to the film that made her a major star, that of the love-torn Ilsa Lund in the wartime classic *Casablanca*. The film was directed by Michael Curtiz who had valorized male devotion and sacrifice four years earlier in *Angels with Dirty Faces* (1938). The role of Ilsa Lund in *Casablanca* showcased another element of Bergman's film charisma—what fellow actress Angela Lansbury admiringly called "her extraordinary ability to convey a tremulous, transparent vulnerability on-screen" (Feldman and Winter c. 1991). It also reflected Bergman's ability to communicate erotic yearning, that is to say, a desire for more to life than Ilsa's passionless union with Victor Laszlo (Paul Henreid) or indeed, as we shall see shortly, her own bourgeois marriage to the dull dentist Lindstrom. This idealization of transparency as a sign of the connection between inner and outer beauty and as an indicator of purity of purpose features in both the ideology of the virtuous white woman and the hagiography of the chaste nun. Moreover, it persists in the pseudo-religious film lighting of the movie star (Dyer 2005: 122–6). When Ilsa walks into Rick's Café, the incorrigible ladies' man and wily police chief, Captain Louis Renault (Claude Rains), calls her "the most beautiful woman ever to visit Casablanca." Bergman herself was aware that this was far from true, and that with her tall and sturdy frame, broad features, and high forehead, she had the fresh-faced good looks of a strapping country girl. Indeed, a former lover later called her "a big Swede" (Kurth 1997).

Yet film viewers have never quarreled with Captain Renault's appraisal of the first impression she gave as Ilsa. Bergman projected a soulful beauty in *Casablanca* through her acting instinct for languorous stillness, which was enhanced by many long, lingering takes of the actress (Spoto 2001: 126). She also perfected a technique that had been devised to compensate for the fact she was not a classical beauty—of looking down as if lost in thought about her conflicted past, before glancing back up to study the face of the man she loves in an intent way that conveyed touching vulnerability (Ebert 2003; Damico 1991: 245). This body language allowed the accomplished actress to profile her good left side, while at the same time communicating depth of feeling and interiority as well as high regard for the two men who love her. These qualities of inner loveliness set Ilsa apart from the bleak and cynical inhabitants of Casablanca, make her the light shining in their *film noir* world, and are the underlying source of her great attraction to others.

Casablanca was made as America went from neutrality to war after the 1941 attack on Pearl Harbor. Its romantic message—that idealism, heroism, and self-sacrificing love can save lives and redeem those who have lost heart and need reminding of their own surprising capacity for altruism—was good for wartime morale. The idea that one should be a good soldier, even away from the battlefront, was nothing new to actual nuns who practiced a theology of paramilitary obedience and ran their religious institutions along army lines (Chittister 2005: 30; McDannell 1995: 24). As Rebecca Sullivan explained, "Nuns were identified as the feminine equivalent of war heroes, embodying patriotism, adventurism, and moral courage while also exhibiting the innocence and placidity appropriate to their gender" (2005: 70). They would continue to be defined in these terms in the postwar 1957 films *Heaven Knows, Mr. Allison,* and *Sea Wife.* In fact, Bergman's resigned heroine Ilsa Lund falls more squarely into this category than her feisty Sister Benedict who teaches schoolboys "the manly art of self defense" in *The Bells of St. Mary's.*

Casablanca is set in French Morocco on the borders of the European front where refugees, black market profiteers, Vichy government officials, French Resistance fighters, soldiers of fortune, and Nazi officers all meet and conduct an improbably civilized minuet. Its establishing shots dramatize the psychological predicament of the civilians back home who cannot fight and have no choice but to go on "waiting, waiting, waiting." Indeed, the fog-enshrouded and morally shady world of Casablanca, where characters are stuck brooding on their past mistakes and end up each night back in Rick's Café, is a wartime limbo. The film fiction that the Nazis will honor the letters of transit signed by General Charles de Gaulle, leader of the free French, is as spurious as the line that corrupt pardoners peddled to gullible souls in the Middle Ages—that indulgences could shorten penal time for their sins and buy their release from purgatory. Yet an audience does buy this fiction because it is responding to the film's Western ideology of quasi-religious romance where spiritual salvation is embodied by a Caucasian woman who is as pure of heart as she is beautiful (Marchetti 1993: 8, 45, 59).

As if to underline this point, Ilsa makes her second, solo entrance into Rick's Café dressed all in white, the color of bridal purity and unsullied virtue (Dyer 2005: 72–3). Her diaphanous head scarf glimmers in the search light that enforces the nighttime curfew but cleverly doubles as a movie spotlight. The strobe light capturing her close-up momentarily turns the transparent veil framing her face into an aureole. This halo of light was the visual symbol of the martyr, consecrated virgin, or saint in their ultimate victory over the world and the flesh. Ilsa's glistening tears, seen in intimate shot / reverse shots, where she intercedes with the wounded and embittered Rick Blaine (Humphrey Bogart) on behalf of her husband, Victor Laszlo, also underline her likeness to the Madonna's wartime face as the Lady of Sorrows. However, the play of light and shadow across her face and her mysterious Mona Lisa smile hint that she has a secret other life.

Bergman gives a remarkable, double-edged performance in *Casablanca*. Her plea for her husband is replete with hero-worship as she explains to Rick in the third person how, as an impressionable girl, she met this "great and courageous man" whom she "looked up to" and to whom she was forever indebted for introducing her to a world of lofty knowledge and noble ideals, a world reminiscent of the book-lined cloister. The quasi-religious connotations of her language communicate a sense of eros as "the soul's upward longing and striving towards the heavenly world, the world of Ideas" (Nygren 1953: 177). They also strongly suggest that her relationship with the great Victor Laszlo can be compared to that of a daughter to a father, a pious woman to the pillar of her faith, or a celibate nun to her mystical bridegroom Christ Victorious, triumphant leader of a militant, patriarchal Church. "Everything she knew or ever became," she tells Rick, speaking like my fair lady, "was because of him." Her pure white screen image, however, hints that hers is a "mariage blanc," or unconsummated union, with Laszlo (Dyer 2005: 75). At the time *Casablanca* was made, Bergman did not realize that Ilsa and Victor's unequal relationship was a simulacrum of her own unhappy marriage. Years later, she realized that the personal problems she had with Petter Lindstrom stemmed from the fact that she, too, had married a father figure:

> [Petter] trained and organized me . . . I had always been managed by men—first by my father, then (when she was orphaned) by Uncle Otto, then by my directors. And then by Petter, who exercised a very strong control over me . . . by doing everything for me, making all the decisions for me. (Spoto 2001: 51)

In *Casablanca*, the Catholic family romance with the saintly mother and devoted son in the *pieta* is reconstituted as that of the dutiful daughter who kneels at the feet of the noble father protector and whose sacrificial abasement to "the great man" neutralizes the dangerous sexuality and desires of young women (Orsi 1996: 73–85). Real-life nuns also recall how proud, pious fathers influenced their religious vocation and fostered their desire to give themselves to God and others (Rogers 1996: 112–13, 141–3, 158–9, 275). Former Benedictine Sister Martin Weber, who was a nun from 1957 to 1969, recollects a father who "was strong-willed . . . and liked to control, but he also loved life and was quick to laugh. It was Daddy's influence, in large measure, that led me to Saint Benedict's" (1998: 84). Identification with the father who was lovingly remembered as "my teacher and companion" (Hunter 1984: 33) would also motivate Protestant single women to continue the family tradition of missionary work and to obtain the professional training for service overseas. The evident fact that Ilsa looks up to her husband like a holy father and holds his political mission sacred (while downplaying her own role in the resistance) not only sanctifies but desexualizes her marriage, and explains how she can love two men at the same time, one platonically and the other passionately. This split is given emotional credibility by the fact that the normally dashing actor Paul Henreid plays the part of Victor Laszlo as a humorless and lackluster stiff (Ebert 2003). Like Milton's God who is aloof from the agonized human predicament of Adam and Eve on his high celestial throne in *Paradise Lost* (3: 56–9), Laszlo speaks ponderously and seems oddly detached and obtuse about the psychosexual drama swirling around him. "Is there anything you wish to tell me, my dear," he asks his wife in the role of earnest father confessor, only to conclude, to Ilsa's and the film audience's profound relief, better not to know.

If Victor will always have Ilsa, Ilsa and Rick will "always have Paris"—the city a clear code word for *l'amour* with its frisson of romance and a furlough from duty, and with the sexual chemistry between Bergman and Bogart palpable on-screen. American Catholic censors objected to any suggestion in the film's flashbacks that the pair had an affair, though Ilsa's appearance in a shimmering satin dressing gown in one scene with Rick clearly reads as the morning after (Ebert 2003). Sex or no sex, Ilsa is technically guilty of committing what Jesus called adultery in her heart (Matt. 5:28), for her husband could only be assumed dead when she and Rick fall in love in Paris. Later, Rick taunts Ilsa as a proverbial fallen woman and brings tears to her eyes a second time when he wonders

whether she prostituted herself to get where she is now. This is an interesting feminist cultural moment that shows how swiftly the sorrowful
Madonna figure can be turned about-face into a remorseful Magdalen.
It also suggests how easily the aggrieved male can revert to misogyny
with his "age-old equation between feminine beauty, sexuality and sin"
(Haskins 1993: 3). But then, even a reasonably enlightened Catholic cardinal would later invoke the traditional duality between female sexuality
and spirituality, and issue the following warning to the modern nun who
ventured out into the real world beyond the convent enclosure:

> Woman has the awe-ful choice of being Eve or Mary: she is rarely
> neutral. Either she ennobles and raises man up by her presence, by
> creating a climate of beauty and human nobility, or she drags him
> down with her in her own fall. (Suenens 1963: 13)

It is left to Rick to help Ilsa up the steps that put her on a pedestal
by escorting her onto a plane to Lisbon with her husband. Although Ilsa
goes unwillingly, he reminds her that like the nun's spousal union with
Christ, she has made final vows to Victor, and from their implicit poverty, chastity, and obedience there is no release: "Inside we both know
you belong with Victor."

The Bells of St. Mary's (1945)

Casablanca made Bergman a major star but also typecast her as a luminous
presence who embodied the grace she emanated on-screen. She would
start to feel trapped in this Hollywood image and would complain in
1947:

> I had a beautiful house and a swimming pool. I remember one day
> sitting at the pool and suddenly the tears were streaming down my
> cheeks. Why was I so unhappy? I had success, security. But it wasn't
> enough. I was exploding inside. (Spoto 2001: 230)

The role that left her isolated on the pedestal and sealed her image
as the "Virgin Mary of films" was that of Sister Benedict in *The Bells
of St. Mary's* (Feldman and Winter c. 1991). This film was released in
December 1945, in the flush of postwar victory, when women were
under social pressure to withdraw from the workforce in order to make
room for returning male veterans and war heroes, and retreat back into
a stifling domestic world or take the suburban route to social conformity

described so well later by Betty Friedan in *The Feminine Mystique* (1963).[3] Bergman's recollection of sudden depression at the poolside was a presentiment of the confusion, emptiness, and discontent experienced by women who wanted more from life than the American "house beautiful" dreams of the 1950s (Rosen 1995: 314–18). Bergman was the main provider for her own family and one of the highest paid film actresses in Hollywood at the time, but she was also under contract to the controlling producer David Selznick. She thus understood first-hand how difficult it could be to find work that did not immure the spirit but allowed free expression of talents and interests. Bergman's performance is generally thought to have stereotyped the film nun as "the good sister" whose "holiness smacks of Hollywood" (Crowther, *The New York Times*, December 7, 1945: 26). I will suggest how the star strove within the limitations of the plot and characterization to bring Sister Benedict alive on-screen as a flesh and blood woman, and as a religious who illumined the self-giving service of agape with flashes of personal desire.

Bergman had already been considered for the supporting role of a missionary nun in the film version of A. J. Cronin's popular novel *The Keys of the Kingdom* (1944). When she was chosen to play the sister principal in the sequel to *Going My Way* (1944), the director Leo McCarey suggested she visit his much admired aunt, Sister Mary Benedict, at the Hollywood convent run by the Immaculate Heart of Mary (IHM) Sisters, in order to understand how a modern woman could "want to be a nun" (Paietta 2005: 17; Spoto: 2001: 175; Burke Smith 2008: 110).[4] Cardinal Leon Suenens would remind nuns in the early 1960s that "two world wars mobilized millions of women behind the front where they successfully replaced men" (1963: 11, 33–4). Women's large-scale entrance into the mid-twentieth-century workforce during the Second World War, where they did indeed successfully replace men, contextualizes the gender politics in *The Bells of St. Mary's* and provides a historical backdrop to Sister Benedict's independent and active persona in the film. Suenens would also concede that "female emancipation has yet to be felt fully in

---

[3] As Robert A. Orsi has noted, however, the economic reality of an American consumer society was that many married women had to go on working, and "their participation in the labor force went from (an already high) 13.8 percent in 1940 to 30.6 percent in 1960." Orsi, *Thank You, St. Jude: Women's Devotion to the Patron Saint of Hopeless Causes* (New Haven: Yale University Press, 1996), 63.

[4] Leo McCarey's aunt, Sister Mary Benedict, was not a teacher, although the Immaculate Heart of Mary order was highly regarded for its work in education; and she died of typhoid, not tuberculosis.

the organization of religious life" (1963: 41). However, more conservative churchmen would grow increasingly hostile to the influence of second wave feminism and the women's liberation movement in mobilizing
American nuns to demand reform of outdated structures and practices
in their religious life (Quinonez and Turner 1992: 107, Briggs 2006:
152–87). The progressive IHMs would be dismissed in the late 1960s as
liberal "Hollywood types" (Bernstein 1976: 165).

The Bells of St. Mary's was the first Hollywood film in which the nun
emerges in a lead role as a charismatic protagonist who has known the
heady culture of dances, dating, and romance and freely chosen the religious life with "complete understanding" of why she desires to become
a nun. When it premiered at the end of the Second World War in 1945
as a sequel to the smash hit Going My Way (1944), it became one of
the highest grossing movies of its day at over US$ 21,300,000 (Gordon
1994: 592). Indeed, even though it won only one Oscar in comparison
to Going My Way's seven Academy Awards, it made five million more
at the box office, thanks largely to the added pulling power of Ingrid
Bergman. The corny tagline of the film alludes to the joie de vivre and
playfulness she brought to the role of Sister Benedict: "Your heart will
be wearing a smile." Enchantment with Bergman as the picture-perfect
nun, a picture enhanced by her beauty, idealism, and humanity, reflects
that "movie infatuation with Roman Catholicism" that Anthony Burke
Smith analyzes in American popular culture during the mid-twentieth
century period.[5]

The first movie reviewers of The Bells of St. Mary's found it "pleas-
antly entertaining" but no match for its predecessor Going My Way.
While they bemoaned the absence of the character actor Barry Fitzgerald
who played an old Irish pastor in the 1944 film, they felt the best thing
about the sequel was Ingrid Bergman who, in the opinion of Commonweal's Philip Hartung, looked "lovely" as a nun, succeeded in portraying
"the human side of the religious," and gave "another of her outstanding
performances" (December 28, 1945: 288). Time magazine appreciated
Bergman's dedication and versatility as an actress, noting that she "visited
parochial schools to see how nuns actually behave," wore no make-up
but nonetheless brought "beauty, great good humor and saintly dignity"
to the role of Sister Benedict, "even while swinging a baseball bat,"
and was equally strong and convincing in her other two hits that year

[5] See Anthony Burke Smith, The Look of Catholics: Portrayals in Popular Culture
from the Great Depression to the Cold War (Lawrence: University of Kansas Press, 2010).

as a "New Orleans cocotte in *Saratoga Trunk* and the lady psychiatrist in *Spellbound*" (December 10, 1945: 97). There was also the occasional touch of spice to the "sugar and everything nice" being said about her performance as a nun. James Agee observed sternly in *The Nation* that the film was exploiting "the romantic-commercial values of celibacy" with the crass promotion heard on radio: "Ingrid Bergman has never been lovelier, hubbahubbahubba" (January 5, 1946: 24). On September 18, 1945 the star was the cover girl on *Look* magazine—photographed in the habit that she wore as Sister Benedict in *The Bells of St. Mary's* (Spoto 2001: 181).

Today, as I have already suggested, her Sister Benedict is more likely to get bad press, and is cited as the iconic film nun who does a disservice to modern women religious (Kuhns 2003: 12). While progressive nuns tend to dismiss Sister Benedict as a girlish and sugar-coated figure, religious cultural historian Mary Ann Janosik sees her as an intelligent, nononsense "Earth Mother Madonna" cast in the image of strong women prominent in the thirties and forties, such as Eleanor Roosevelt, Dorothy Day, and Katherine Hepburn (Janosik 1997: 81–3). These polarized perceptions of Sister Benedict as winsome pin-up girl in a habit and a goody-two-shoes, or wise earth mother and strong female leader, point to the volatile significations that the film nun assumed when she was played by Bergman as a desirable and ardent woman and yet represented in a position of redoubled religious authority as sister superior and school principal. Remembered fear, defenselessness, and resentment of the all-powerful mother figures from childhood may account, in part, for the need to cut Sister Benedict down to size and reduce her—contrary to the evidence in the film itself—to "a perpetual little girl" (Schneiders 2001: 234). The same play of emotions will later lie behind the impulse to belittle or vilify the nun in twenty-first century films like *Sister Mary Ignatius Explains It All* (2001), *The Dangerous Lives of Altar Boys* (2002), and *Doubt* (2008) (Neal 1990: 68, 74; Fialka 2003: 180). In *Wide Awake* (1998), M. Night Shyamalan's affectionate tribute to his Catholic education, two schoolboys wonder whether nuns and mothers are wholly human. The feeling of magical otherness and awe that powerful and influential women can also inspire surfaces not only in positive estimations of Sister Benedict but in the appreciative recollections of those who actually had sister teachers at parochial school in the forties: "They were kind, they were omniscient, they were present, they were beautiful people" (Chittister 1987: 4).

Intertextual Links with It's a Wonderful Life *(1946)*

Despite the lukewarm reviews of movie critics, *The Bells of St. Mary's* was a smash hit with an audience that liked the frisson of chaste romance—with its undercurrents of sublimated eros—present in the working relationship of a beautiful nun and an affable priest. Catholic director Frank Capra alluded intertextually to its "feel-good" drawing power by showcasing it as the Christmas feature film at the Bedford Falls movie house in his 1946 classic *It's a Wonderful Life*. In *The Bells of St. Mary's,* an American audience's love affair with Bergman coalesced with Catholic immigrant devotion for the nuns who gave them the prospect of a better life by educating their children and facilitating their upward mobility into the suburban middle class (Sullivan 2005: 107). St. Mary's dilapidated school is symbolic of an American Catholicism rooted in old urban neighborhoods but undergoing modernization and expansion. At the time that the film was made, the Catholic parochial school system itself was on the verge of a phenomenal growth spurt, fed by the postwar baby boom. At its heyday in the 1950s and 60s, parochial schools educated around 11 percent of all American students and constituted the largest private school system in the world. Ninety-five percent of the teaching and administration was done by nuns who worked long hours, sometimes to the point of exhaustion and illness. Historians of Catholic education have often focused on the remarkable success story of the parochial school system, which, despite limited financial resources and large class sizes, produced high achievers from the inner cities and motivated student cohorts from diverse economic, social, and ethnic backgrounds (Fialka 2003: 3, 172–4, 184–5, 193, 230, 243). Its sister teachers not only made certain that the next generation of Catholics kept the faith but ensured the survival of their own communities by inspiring their girl students to consider a religious vocation (Reed 2004: 232). Feminist historians of nuns, however, have drawn attention to the hidden underside of their extraordinary achievement: that "the church used women for virtually all ecclesiastical tasks that men did not care to perform while underpaying them, denying them all access to power, and leaving them totally dependent on the good will and tolerance of male power figures" (Schneiders 2004: 33). By the end of *The Bells of St. Mary's,* Sister Benedict finds herself in this position of total dependency although Bing Crosby's easy-going charm as Father Chuck masks the fact.

Capra referenced *The Bells of St. Mary's* because it contains a pointed Christmas message central to an understanding of the film's protagonist

George Bailey (Jimmy Stewart). This message is one of self-giving that both thwarts and enlarges the individual's core hopes and dreams. It derives from the Christian paradox of strength in weakness and is conveyed more compellingly by Sister Benedict than by Father Chuck O'Malley who wields priestly authority over her in the Church power structure. Indeed, the nun's life of unrewarded service to St. Mary's holds the mirror up to George's nobility of heart in privileging self-sacrifice over self-serving interests; poverty of spirit over love of the almighty buck; duty to family, friends, and neighbors over the ruthless ambition of Henry Potter (Lionel Barrymore); and sacred *communitas* over robber-baron capitalism. Yet the film did not disguise the loss of personal freedom and death of private aspirations that these civil achievements cost. It dramatized the hero's frustrated longing to escape the insularity of a small town existence and see the world. Insularity could also make religious community life exceedingly difficult for real-life nuns. Those strictly enclosed might find that their world did not expand but shrink in the convent, that their mobility and initiatives were blocked, and that their aspirations were buffeted by the same "talent-stripping" environment George Bailey suffers in Bedford Falls (Campbell-Jones 1978: 82; Coburn and Smith 1999: 80–1, 186–7). The psychological toll of an enclosed life from which there seems to be no escape is illustrated by George's mounting sense of loneliness, isolation, depression, and despair. As we have already seen, Bergman too felt trapped as a film star on studio contract in the insular world of Hollywood.

For a film that is generally regarded as pleasant but light entertainment, *The Bells of St. Mary's* begins and ends incongruously—in darkness, like an old-fashioned picture that is framed by a black border of mourning and melancholy. Father Chuck O'Malley first appears as a dim figure walking at night to his new parish assignment past a church that is shrouded in shadow. The old crone who greets him as housekeeper of the rectory is dressed in the lace jabot and brooch of the Victorian period. She loses no time in assuming the role of informer on the convent next door, betraying the intergenerational tension among the women on whom priests depended to maintain the parish. Glad bearer of bad tidings, she welcomes O'Malley with the news that the previous pastor has just been carted off in a wheelchair to a nursing home with the ominous name of "Shady Rest," mumbling that the nuns "wanted their way in everything." Her dark hint that the nuns were driving the priest to an early grave is another jarring note to a film that was billed as being cheerful and heart-warming holiday fare (*Senior Scholastic*, December 10,

34

1945: 36). It can certainly be argued that the mood of doom and gloom that hangs over the opening sequence was a heavy-handed means of creating false, laughable apprehension in the priest and dramatic high relief to the light-filled convent and attractive women religious he finally encounters. The film's dark, oddly menacing beginning, however, is also a momentary projection of ancient and irrational thoughts that have been re-activated at night and that the sunny narrative which follows will dispel: Catholic misogyny and fear of female sexuality—of the body of woman and women as a body—anti-Papist fear of the convent as a sinister space of dread spinsters, and combined Protestant-Catholic fear of the strength and vehemence of women's veiled desires.[6]

Thus, while *The Bells of St. Mary's* has been criticized for its sentimental valorization of female self-sacrifice, its initial tenebra points to deeper themes, which are a source of male anxiety about the assertiveness of women religious, the intimidating corporate power of an all-female community, and the insidious political influence that a nun may come to wield through the range of her services to the Church. A later scene economically makes this last point: Sister Benedict is in an apron, fitting the servile work of an unpaid domestic into her hectic professional schedule of teaching, running the parochial school, acting *in loco parentis* to the odd boarder like Patsy Gallagher (Joan Carroll), and heading the convent at St. Mary's. Priests such as O'Malley had the luxury of behaving as though they had just strolled off the golf course and did not have a care in the world because they could rely on a cheap, plentiful, all-purpose labor force of women religious behind the scenes (Coburn and Smith 1999: 224). However, as the multitasking Sister Benedict also suggests, nuns in active orders are everywhere and have their finger in every pie. Indeed, the housekeeper explicitly warns the priest that he has no idea "what it means to be up to your neck in nuns."

Mrs. Breen, the housekeeper (Una O'Connor), disappears from the film after putting O'Malley on his guard, for her only function as a minor character is to be the admonishing voice that recapitulates a longstanding institutional power struggle between Catholic nuns and priests (Fialka 2003: 15, 331). When the priest does pay his first call on the nuns, straw boater in hand like an anxious suitor, he does not find a house full of

---

[6]Anthony Burke Smith argues that *Going My Way* exorcized these dark fears of Catholicism's hidden religious spaces. Burke Smith, "America's Favorite Priest: *Going My Way* (1944)," *Catholics in the Movies*, ed. Colleen McDannell (New York: Oxford University Press, 2008), 111.

harridans but one that is home to cats. These domestic pets paradoxically convey the housebound and free spirit of their mistresses. They code the convent as a cozy, chintzy, and just possibly catty female domain. While they exorcize it of the Gothic darkness that will reappear in *Black Narcissus* (1947), *Agnes of God* (1985), and *Doubt* (2008), they also carry the faint reminder that the cat was once regarded as the witch's familiar and warn that nuns may be women with secret powers. With the steady arrival of one sister after another in this scene, O'Malley's sense of discomfort visibly mounts as he faces a female assembly who studies him silently but intently. A medium shot of the priest seated back to the camera and surrounded by a sea of women religious faces illustrates the historical fact that American nuns greatly outnumbered male clergy, with a postwar boom in vocations leading to an increase of over eleven thousand between 1945 and 1950 alone (Ebaugh 1993b: 5, 82). Their sister superior, Sister Benedict, makes her entrance behind the priest in a medium long shot that captures her grace and beauty in the habit. The nun's headpiece accentuated Bergman's natural height (5 feet 10 inches) and enhanced her imposing authority as both head of the convent and the school.

The actress was nearly thirty when she made *The Bells of St. Mary's*. Although she may appear too young to have assumed a role of major responsibility, brick-and-mortar Catholicism would result in the rapid expansion of the parochial school system and the fast-tracking of capable nuns into the post of school principal at an average age of thirty-three, much earlier than in the public school system (Wittberg 1989: 531). Father O'Malley's position relative to Sister Benedict in this entrance shot conveys his vulnerability to her more dominant personality. He sits nervously fiddling with the rim of his straw boater while she stands unseen behind looking down at the priest. The fact that the nuns stand to greet her—which the priest misinterprets as a signal to start his homily—is a mark not only of their deference to her leadership but her precedence over him in the all female domain of the convent. Although they square off as equals in subsequent scenes, the camera periodically registers the nun's commanding presence and authority, notably in St. Mary's classroom where the priest sits as a visitor and she stands as the homeroom teacher in the center of the frame before her students.

From the Irish housekeeper, O'Malley had learned that the previous pastor locked horns with the nuns on "runnin' the school (and) the raisin' and educatin' of children." It is hard to take this clash seriously when it is presented by a gossipy old woman, but real differences between priests and nuns could escalate into grave conflict. One of the most un-

fortunate examples was the later ugly and destructive showdown between the IHM Sisters and Los Angeles Cardinal James McIntyre when
their community wanted to move from parochial school teaching into
other forms of service.[7] *The Bells of St. Mary's*, however, deflects the expected gender confrontation between priest and sister superior through
the well-worn contrivance of romantic comedy—an "I can do anything
you can do better" contestation over St. Mary's school and its student
body. Sister Benedict's competitive instincts begin to get the better of
her Christian precepts after she sees the good-natured Eddie (Richard
Tyler) knocked down in the playground when he ill-advisedly turns the
other cheek in an unguarded moment. She becomes determined to teach
the boy "the manly art of self defense" after her own verbal battle of the
sexes with O'Malley:

SISTER BENEDICT: We don't tolerate fighting in the school.

FATHER O'MALLEY: Naturally I like to see a lad who can take care of
himself. On the outside it's a man's world.

SISTER BENEDICT: How are they doing, Father?

FATHER O'MALLEY: They're not doing too good. But you know what
I mean. Sometimes a man has to fight his way through.

SISTER BENEDICT: Wouldn't it be better to think your way through?
That's pure conjecture, of course, from someone on the *inside*.

FATHER O'MALLEY: Don't you think sometimes in raising boys a
woman's influence can be carried too far?

SISTER BENEDICT: You mean they may become sissies, Father?

Unlike her hapless male pupil, Sister Benedict is a natural fighter who
knows how to "bob and weave," and delivers a few good "left hooks" if

---

[7] In 1968, Los Angeles Cardinal James McIntyre opposed the IHM community's proposals for Vatican II inspired renewal and reform of their religious life. He
ordered this pontifical institute to return to their traditional habit and teaching work
or withdraw entirely from the Catholic schools in his archdiocese. As a result of this
ultimatum, the majority of the community asked to be dispensed from their vows,
were dismissed from the schools they served, and eventually formed a non-canonical
community not answerable to male church authority. This confrontation has been
extensively discussed. See, for example, Marcelle Bernstein, *Nuns* (London: Collins,
1976), 162–8; Mary Jo Weaver, *New Catholic Women: A Contemporary Challenge to
Traditional Authority* (Bloomington: Indiana University Press, 1995), 93–4; and Ann
Carey, *Sisters in Crisis: The Tragic Unraveling of Women's Religious Communities* (Huntington, Ind.: Our Sunday Visitor, 1997), 184–91. I refer to this confrontation again
in Chapter 4.

not an outright "payoff" in her charged exchange with the priest. Their
dialogue bristles with political and institutional differences over the social
organization of gender: the emotional separation of boys from mother
figures and fear of their emasculation in a female dominated world, the
sexual division of labor and consequent inequality between men and
women, the human cost of World War II and male military aggression,
and the historical resentment of nuns confined by canon law "inside" the
convent at the greater freedom, mobility, and know-how priests have
"on the outside." Sister Benedict's sporting instincts also allow McCarey
to return to the successful formula of *Going My Way* and demonstrate
the nun's all-American enthusiasm for baseball despite Bergman's slight
foreign accent. In his 1998 film *Wide Awake*, M. Night Shyamalan would
both celebrate and update Bergman's projection of the nun as a woman
who remains physically active and does not let the habit hinder her game-
ness for life. His personal homage to Sister Benedict is Sister Terry (Rosie
O'Donnell), a passionate Philadelphia Phillies fan who sports a baseball
cap over her modified veil and who uses the World Series to teach basic
theology in the classroom.

Critics were charmed by the sight of Bergman's Sister Benedict
swinging the baseball bat and getting a sock in the kisser after successfully coaching Eddie in boxing techniques. Indeed, if O'Malley made
the priest an all-round Joe in *Going My Way*, Sister Benedict made the
nun a good sport in *The Bells of St. Mary's*. Both would be used as positive reference points for later filmic representations of religious figures
in authority (Burke Smith 2010: 86; 2008: 108, 119–20). In the view of
the London *Times*, which was culturally immune to the enchantment of
Roman Catholic religious in America, "Miss Bergman nearly succeeds in
making a person out of Sister Benedict, but Mr. Crosby has lost his way"
(March 22, 1946: 6). It is certainly true that Sister Benedict outshines
Father O'Malley in the demonstration of gender role reversal, but this is
not the fault of the actor but his reduced role. While Bergman can steal
scenes coaching baseball and boxing, Father O'Malley is left to show that
priests are not from Mars and that he has a feminine side without raising the suspicions of a conventional postwar audience that men in long
cassocks are "sissies." What he can safely teach the class numskull, Patsy,
product of that feared Catholic calamity—"the broken home"—is EQ,
which he does by helping her with an essay on the five senses. He also
plays the role of "soft cop" to Sister Benedict's "hard cop" in a variation
on the gender politics of the omnipresent mother who must be a disciplinarian in the home and the absent father who can afford to be indulgent.

While the nun insists that Patsy must be failed because she did not meet her high academic standard of 75 percent for a passing grade, the priest argues that bending the rules is "better than breaking a child's heart."

The question is whether Father Chuck breaks Sister Benedict's heart in this film. Critics remain sharply divided. Anthony Burke Smith believes that the priest does "gently and barely concealed romantic battle" with the strong-willed nun, while Jeffrey Marlett maintains in the same collection of essays on *Catholics in the Movies* that *The Bells of St. Mary's* "contains not a whiff of romance" (2008: 108, 167).[8] I, for one, see no physical chemistry between them, nor the sexual tension evident later in the charged relationship between Sister Clodagh and Mr. Dean in *Black Narcissus* or Sister Luke and Dr. Fortunati in *The Nun's Story*. Bing Crosby's Father O'Malley has the Teflon affability of a Ronald Reagan but does not convey that intensity of interest that signals erotic attraction to Sister Benedict. In the religious press, Crosby was lauded as the good Catholic who did not feel he was worthy to play a priest in *Going My Way* (Orsi 1996: 92). On the film set of *The Bells of St. Mary's*, he was pleasant but aloof, and in private life he was a petty tyrant (Spoto 2001: 178–9). Yet his Father O'Malley is willing to get involved in the messy lives of St. Mary's parishioners. He is non-judgmental when he learns that Patsy's mother, Mrs. Gallagher, is supporting her daughter by her night-time work, euphemistically referred to as that of a "cocktail hostess." She tells O'Malley that Patsy is "beginning to think that I'm no good. I want her put in your care before she finds out she's right." While he arranges for the thirteen-year-old to board at St. Mary's, he quietly uses his contacts in the music industry (dramatized earlier in *Going My Way*) to track down her father, a wayward piano player with a traveling band. He delivers no sermon to the man who abandoned his wife and child, or the mother who survives on immoral earnings, after the Gallaghers are finally reunited as a family. In his sensitive handling of the Gallagher

---

[8] Mary Gordon argues that "the romantic dance between priest and nun is as exquisitely choreographed as the most formal minuet. They are witty and attractive, with a charge between them as man and woman, but no boundaries are ever crossed." Gordon, "Father Chuck: A Reading of *Going My Way* and *The Bells of St. Mary's*, or Why Priests Made Us Crazy," *The Southern Atlantic Quarterly* 93.3 (1994): 600. David Kehr concludes in his 2003 online review of *The Bells of St. Mary's* for the *Chicago Reader* that "the film (is) so subtle in its romantic exposition that it's halfway over before you realize what it's about: a priest in love with a nun." See http://www.onfilm.chicagoreader.com/movies/capsules/008.html (accessed July 2, 2006).

case, Father O'Malley shows a characteristic that ultimately draws nun and priest together, despite their differences, and that is sexual humanity.

Father O'Malley and Sister Benedict demonstrated that celibates could have a healthy, relaxed, and positive attitude to sexuality. It will become clearer to what extent this constitutes a breakthrough in the filmic representation of religious life when I examine how *Black Narcissus* (1947) dramatizes the psychosexual strain of chastity and the loneliness of celibacy in Chapter 2.[9] However, I have already argued that Crosby's screen personality as Father O'Malley was one of nonchalant geniality smoothly deflecting any overtures of intimacy. If the film suggests that celibates are not asexual and that the energies of the sexed and sensuous body find different forms of outlet in the religious life, this is largely owing to Bergman's screen talent for suggesting passionate longings that cannot be satisfied by lovemaking alone, a talent she displayed earlier in *Casablanca* (Carr 2003: 149–50). She did not make O'Malley but a film audience fall in love with Sister Benedict. Or to be more precise, she gave *The Bells of St. Mary's* its romance by portraying the nun as a woman who takes the vow of chastity with full consciousness of the power, the importance, and the remembered pleasure of eros.

This intimate portrayal occurs near the end of *The Bells of St. Mary's* and does not take place between the nun and priest, but the nun and the problem student who came between them. The scene makes it clear that Father O'Malley and Sister Benedict have not only been gender and religious competitors but rival "father" and "mother" in the Catholic family romance, which can compensate celibates for the sacrifice of an active sexual and reproductive life. Sister Benedict has already lost her institutional battle with the priest when this scene takes place. Father O'Malley has recently informed her that she will be replaced as convent superior and school principal of St. Mary's and will no longer work with children. "Not to be with children," as even O'Malley recognizes in dismay, is to deny the nun a desire central to the agapaic ideal of the religious life: to nurture and provide maternal service not only to other people's children but to all the children of God. Her spiritual motherhood, however, is

---

[9] A. W. Richard Sipe notes that "before the 60s, celibates were presumed to have no sexuality." Sipe, *A Secret World: Sexuality and the Search for Celibacy* (New York: Brunner/Mazel, 1990), 4. Sister Joan Chittister, O.S.B., supports this view by recalling that before Vatican II, the nun "had a religious life that was working *against* the flesh, to put it mildly." Chittister, "Sister Says," *Once a Catholic: Prominent Catholics and Ex-Catholics Reveal the Influence of the Church on Their Lives and Work*, ed. Peter Occhiogrosso (New York: Ballantine Books, 1987), 10.

now triumphantly reaffirmed in medium close shot as she takes the confused adolescent Patsy into her arms and holds her against her wimpled bosom. O'Malley may have won the battle, but the final victory belongs to Sister Benedict. In her hour of need, Patsy turns to her and not him, confides in the nun and not the priest that she deliberately failed her final exam, and shyly expresses the wish to "be with you" and become a nun like Sister Benedict.

This scene transforms the conservative Catholic ideology exalting the "Mother Church" and the sacred maternalism of the celibate nun (Finnegan 2004: 18–19; Gandolfo 1992: 3). The mothering sister chose a religious life of sexual abstinence, which bore spiritual fruit; the natural mother chose sexual life, which perpetuated the cycle of original sin, suffering, and death (Beattie 2006: 188–9; Dinnerstein 1991: 127, 148–9). Given the ancient association of the sexed female body with the fall into corruption and mortality, one would therefore expect the nun to warn the teenager about the dangers of her awakening sexuality. Given the

Figure 1-1. This iconic portrait of Sister Benedict as a surrogate mother to forlorn schoolgirl Patsy is replayed in *In This House of Brede* (1975) (see Figure 5-1), and is used as an intertextual indictment in *The Magdalene Sisters* (2002).

fact that Catholic schools were prime sources for new vocations, one would also expect her to encourage Patsy's jejune desire to enter the convent. However, Sister Benedict shows sexual humanity in intuiting that the young adolescent's idealization of the religious life and her spiritual motherhood as "so clean and so good" originates from the unconscious wish to punish and demonize her natural mother as "no good."

Like Father O'Malley in *Going My Way*, the nun also sympathizes with the desires of youth in *The Bells of St. Mary's*, even if she left them behind when she entered the convent (Burke Smith 2008: 114). Her romantic litany of the first prom, party dress, waltz, and date that await Patsy is spoken with tender feeling. Sister Benedict's celebration of budding female sexuality lifts the veil on her own capacity for *jouissance*. In an earlier scene, she sang a Swedish love song that might well have been censored, if translated, as too risqué for the hearing of her fellow sisters and a respectful Catholic film audience. However, the lyrics contain a subtextual message that is important in the film: "Spring breezes whisper and caress loving couples. Streams rush by, but they are not as swift as my heart" (Spoto 2001: 180). They suggest that the celibate nun could remember the springtime of love with pleasure and gratitude as a swiftly flowing current that carried her erotic longings toward God. In drawing attention to the fact that the vow of chastity was not taken as a denial of love, desire, and embodiment, the film is gently nudging an American audience toward a more mature understanding of the religious life.

While Bergman brought out the full humanity of the nun in her film performance, later movie fans and critics would turn her Sister Benedict into a popular religious icon, and the star would feel suffocated by the nun's aura of sanctity. What would be forgotten was the more complicated energy of desire that Bergman brought to the role of a woman religious. However, as I shall now show, the plot development of *The Bells of St. Mary's* invites this stereotyping by reducing Sister Benedict from a vibrant character to a holy cipher. At the time of its release, reviewers cited the denouement of the film as a major shortcoming. *Commonweal's* Hartung articulated a general sense of letdown: "I couldn't help feeling that the picture's climax, in which the ailing Sister Superior is to be sent away without being told about her illness, is pure hokum and dishonest" (288). This critical disappointment is perfectly justified. Sister Benedict is changed overnight from a dynamic leader into a consumptive invalid. It is as though screenwriter Dudley Nichols and director Leo McCarey took fright at the magnificent personality they had created: a woman who was not held back by the religious habit and convent; whose desires were not dimmed by the vow of chastity or diminished by the call of agape to selfless service; who loved children, teaching, and St. Mary's. In the scenes I have touched on, Sister Benedict demonstrated the vital élan of eros in her appetite for work and zest for life, her charisma, gregariousness, and compassion, her droll humor, sense of fun, and ready laughter. She also showed qualities that will be black marks against other film nuns in this study—will, determination, tenacity, fighting spirit, and stubborn integrity. Her rapid decline from a figure of robust health and vigor to a weakling suggests that a woman religious who forcefully expressed her own desires through willing service of her time, talent, and energy was a threatening ideal for Catholic male filmmakers and had to be sacrificed.

Significantly, the enfeeblement of her character begins when Sister Benedict and Father O'Malley quarrel over whether to fail or pass Patsy: "Sister, you and I have had our little differences of opinion . . . but this is serious." Ironically, Sister Benedict's insistence on upholding St. Mary's rigorous academic standards is what, in actuality, made Catholic parochial school students stand out as high achievers (Fialka

Figure 1-2. Sister Benedict is visually cut down to size and submits to the higher priestly authority of Father O'Malley.

2003: 184). While the priest asserts that he is not going to undermine the nun's authority as school principal and "order you to do anything," the mise-en-scène suggests he doesn't need to. As he says this, O'Malley stands in the right-hand side of the frame while a high-angle shot looks down over his shoulder to where the nun is sitting. The high angle of the camera erases her authority as school principal at her desk and gives the impression that she is lower, kneeling in a quasi-confessional mode and looking up in a beseeching manner at the priest. When she finally falls ill, Sister Benedict gently chides O'Malley for using his higher priestly authority to pull rank: "You've been writing to Mother General, going over my head." In an idealized scene near the end of the film, she will once more look up, this time at the crucifix on the altar, and implore Christ to "remove all bitterness from my heart." Father O'Malley's holy orders and his sacramental power as Christ's anointed minister to "bind on earth (what) will be bound in heaven" (Matt. 16:19) are thus visually reaffirmed. The 1944 film *The Keys of the Kingdom* presents a contrasting but illustrative shift of religious power between nun and priest. There the aristocratic Mother Maria-Veronica (Rosa Stradner) stands looking down at the man she has dismissed as a "peasant priest." Father Francis Chisholm (Gregory Peck) sits below, seemingly at a disadvantage like Sister Benedict. Yet as Mother Maria begs forgiveness for her arrogance, it becomes apparent that this priest is hearing confession from a position of sacred lowliness rather than O'Malley's clerical superiority. Mother Maria extols "the magnificence of (his) faith and the courage in (his) heart," virtues that Sister Benedict also displays in *The Bells of St. Mary's*.

O'Malley recognizes these qualities in Sister Benedict, too, but thanks to the contrivance of the film script, they are downplayed in the very act of being acknowledged. After the nun is diagnosed as having "a touch of tuberculosis," the priest and doctor note her exceptionality—the fact that "she has a mind of her own," is "such a remarkable woman," "has a wonderful vitality" and "natural optimism"—as though her real malady stems from the core desires that make her unforgettable in this film. They discuss with patronizing wonderment her unconditional faith that God will persuade the cantankerous tycoon, Horace Bogardus (Henry Travers), to convert his modern headquarters into a new school for St. Mary's:

> Does she really believe that Bogardus is going to give her that building? . . . Well, I've heard of such things but I've never come across it before, not since I was a little boy and I wished for what I wanted for Christmas and got it.

44

Belief in the power of prayer resides at the heart of religious life, yet the conversation between the doctor and priest devalues it as symptomatic of feminine childishness and social-economic powerlessness. In one fell swoop, the fear of the powerful mother figure who makes men feel like "little boys" is neutralized by reducing the sister superior to a naive little girl; and thus Sister Benedict's diminution as a film nun begins.

The plot proceeds to cut Sister Benedict down to size with ruthless and petty efficiency. It is the priest and not the nun who has a diagnostic consultation with Dr. McKay (Rhys Williams) and is given privileged knowledge about her medical illness and treatment. The patently false argument for not informing her that she has tuberculosis is that it will depress her spirits and "delay her recovery." The hidden motive driving the plot is the wish to make her docile and obedient. Similarly, a thinly veiled view that a nun with "a mind of her own" should learn to do what she's told "without question" lies behind the man-to-man decision not to explain to her why she is being transferred from St. Mary's to Arizona. Sister Benedict is consigned to the same fate as the hapless pastor she allegedly opposed at the beginning of the film.

Yet at the same time that the film systematically diminishes the nun, it uncannily anticipates what would become clear in the 1960s: that the postwar baby boom and consequent growth of the parochial school system had fueled a building expansion that taxed not only the supply but the health of serving sisters. The real risk of tuberculosis among young teacher nuns was exacerbated by overcrowded classrooms and the mounting after-school pressure to obtain further educational qualifications and professional accreditation. The stress of overwork would also produce higher than average incidents of mental breakdown among women religious (Wakin and Scheuer 1965: 36–9). Not only individual nuns but religious orders would begin to collapse under the strain, and 42 percent of the parochial schools they staffed would eventually close, many in poor, inner-city neighborhoods like St. Mary's (Fialka 2003: 203–4, 230, 243).

At their parting, Father O' Malley calls Sister Benedict "perfect." It was a misfortune not only for the actress, Bergman, but for *The Bells of St. Mary's* that his final words are what people remember about her representation of the nun on-screen. Praise for Sister Benedict as the perfect nun is predicated, as Dr. McKay remarks, on her obedience "without question" to higher religious authority and it smoothes over that complex mix of self-will and self-surrender, of eros and agape, that makes Bergman's performance not only in this film but *The Inn of the Sixth Hap-*

piness so interesting (Hunter 1984: 51). As I shall suggest in Chapter 3, the struggle of the woman religious protagonist to perfect automatic and unthinking obedience may account for the critical aversion of feminist cultural analysts to *The Nun's Story*. In actuality, the vow of obedience was never easy for modern nuns, but in the postwar period, it would increasingly become a source of vocational angst, conflict, and crisis.[10] While Sister Benedict's final beatific submission to unquestioning obedience might not win the sympathy of later and more reformist-minded sisters, it would still be regarded with approbation by more traditional nuns. For when she raises her luminous, tear-stained face to the crucifix above the altar, she is reconfigured as the suffering servant of Christ and reaffirms the sacrifice of self intrinsic to agape and indeed all three religious vows (Miller 2009: 74; Pitts 2009: 93–6, 100, 103–6). At the same time, the "why" that she cries as she looks up at the cross articulates the questioning, the yearning, and the consciousness of need integral to eros and the belief that there is "more" that God alone can answer (Nygren 1953: 175–6).

Rather than conclude this discussion of *The Bells of St. Mary's* on a pessimistic note, let us remember Sister Benedict's "natural optimism" and consider where the nun is going as she disappears into the engulfing darkness. She is heading West—into the professional wilderness, but also into the desert, which was the historical birthplace of Christian monasticism and symbolic site of spiritual renewal, and which Jeffrey Marlett called "the place of the possible" (2008: 151). Her journey yonder to the American Southwest can thus be read as a potential re-opening and expansion of the desires that she reached out for in *The Bells of St. Mary's*. It seems particularly apt that she is heading to Arizona where Mother Maria

---

[10] Cheryl L. Reed notes, and actual nuns have confirmed, the sacrifice of freedom and autonomy inherent in obedience made it the hardest vow for modern women religious. Reed, *Unveiled: The Hidden Lives of Nuns* (New York: Berkeley Books, 2004), 50. However, as Sister Sandra M. Schneiders, I.H.M., pointed out, chastity would prove more difficult than obedience for male religious. Schneiders, *Finding the Treasure: Locating Catholic Religious Life in a New Ecclesial and Cultural Context* (New York: Paulist Press, 2000), 25–6. Patricia Wittberg, S.C., explained that up until the 1990s, chastity was "a source of great spiritual meaning" for women religious, although with the sexual revolution in the 1960s, there was increased recognitions of the psychological challenges that this vow could pose. Wittberg, *The Rise and Fall of Catholic Religious Orders: A Social Movement Perspective* (Albany: The State University of New York Press, 1994), 249–50. Chapter 2 will look at chastity, and Chapter 3 will consider the issue of obedience in greater detail.

and the sisters of *Lilies of the Field* (1963) will get a chapel built with the same energy, determination, and guile that Sister Benedict exerts to save and redevelop St. Mary's school.[11]

With her success as Sister Benedict, Ingrid Bergman could do no wrong in the eyes of her many film fans. To the star's annoyance, Catholic women began to stop her in the street to say they hoped their daughters would follow her example on-screen and take the veil (Spoto 2001: 181). The popular influence that she exerted as a result of her film role as Sister Benedict bears out Anthony Burke Smith's view of "movie depictions as themselves constitutive of religious identity" (2010: 39). Her forgotten achievement in *The Bells of St. Mary's* was to show that the celibate nun did not have to sacrifice her sexuality and to give an ardent film performance, which suggested how women religious could regard chastity as "the most meaningful and the least difficult" of the three vows (Wittberg 1994: 249–50). Bergman would burnish her unblemished screen image when she took on the 1948 film role of St. Joan of Arc, the patron saint of virgins. However, she gave sensational evidence a year later that ordinary women did not live without sex or sin when she became pregnant by her lover, the Italian director Roberto Rossellini, while working with him on the 1949 film *Stromboli*. When her extramarital affair became public, Bergman would be pilloried in the American press. "Having been so loved, I was now deeply hated," she said in dismay and disbelief, as though uncomprehending of the binary logic behind the defamation of her character (Spoto 2001: 285). She had hoped to reinvent herself with Rossellini. She did—through her dramatic metamorphosis in the eyes of her movie fans from a wartime Madonna into a postwar Magdalen, and from a "perfect" wife and mother into a modern-day Eve. Her affair was messy and unseemly. She divorced her dentist husband a week after the birth of her son Robertino in Rome on February 2, 1950, and married Rossellini by proxy in Mexico several months later, but her "love child" cost her Pia, her daughter by Lindstrom. In Ireland, women were still being confined in magdalen asylums for bearing children out of wedlock. Stateside, Senator Edwin Johnson denounced Bergman on the floor of the American Senate in March 1950 as "one of the most powerful women on earth today—and,

---

[11] *The Nation*'s film reviewer, James Agee, remarked that he was "just plain horrified by the way in which the sisters hound an old nabob into beneficence" (January 5, 1946: 24). *Theatre Arts*, January 1946: 49, criticized "the alarming concept of morality" displayed by "these reverent folk (who) think nothing of dunning . . . Bogardus."

I regret to say, a powerful influence for evil" (Spoto 2001: 296; Damico 1991: 242–4). The role of Sister Benedict had made her the model face of the nun; but her iconic status as the Virgin Mary of films made her fall into adultery unconscionable.[12] Mary Gordon recollects how Bergman's notoriety blighted her mother's enjoyment of their annual family Christmas screening of *The Bells of St. Mary's*: "Why that bitch thought she had the right to be a nun while all the time she was planning to run away with that Italian, I will never know" (2002: 60).

Anastasia (1956)

At the time that the actress was under attack as a scarlet woman, China had gone "Red," America was on the brink of involvement in the Korean War, and Catholic Senator Joe McCarthy had just launched a cold war crusade to hunt down communist infiltrators of the state. The face that Bergman now began to project on-screen was that of a world-weary and wounded heroine approaching middle age, and the films that she made over the next five years with Rossellini were certainly a departure from her Hollywood star image. However at another level, they were a continuation of the spiritual journey that she dramatized as a beautiful young fugitive in *Casablanca*. The two films that would redeem her American reputation and prompt her sardonic comment—"I've gone from saint to whore and back to saint again, all in one lifetime" (Freitas)—were *Anastasia*, for which she received her second Academy Award in 1956, and *The Inn of the Sixth Happiness* in 1958. In *Anastasia*, she played an amnesiac who impersonates and increasingly feels that she actually *is* the sole surviving member of the Russian imperial family butchered by the Bolsheviks during the Russian Revolution in 1918. It was

---

[12] Adrienne L. McLean argued that "there is broad evidence of support, rather than censure, for Bergman's actions, as well as evidence which suggests that she remained an audience favorite throughout her 'banishment' from American films." McLean, "The Cinderella Princess and the Instrument of Evil: Surveying the Limits of Female Transgression in Two Postwar Hollywood Scandals," *Cinema Journal* 34.3 (1995): 37. In contrast, James Damico argued that the star's ardent spiritual film image lost her popular sympathy in "Ingrid from Lorraine to Stromboli: Analyzing the Public's Perception of a Film Star," in *Star Texts: Image and Performance in Film and Television*, ed. Jeremy G. Butler (Detroit: Wayne State University Press, 1991), 240–53. Bergman herself remarked that "nobody could have lived up to that unreal image people had created of me." See Donald Spoto, *Notorious: The Life of Ingrid Bergman*, repr. (Cambridge, Mass.: Da Capo Press, 2001), 265.

a role that matched her own ironic philosophy that "happiness is good health and a bad memory" (Freitas). It was also a part that resonated with her lost years on the continent when she felt abandoned by a formerly adoring American audience. During the 1950s while she was abroad, American Catholics were encouraged to say "Prayers for the Conversion of Russia." Although *Anastasia* is not a religious movie and did not make a direct contribution to the screen fight against godless communism in the fifties, it nonetheless dramatized the miraculous return of Czar Alexander's daughter from the dead to give white Russian émigrés momentary hope that their homeland might eventually be restored to Christian and monarchal rule (Burke Smith 2010: 37–8). The film opens in Paris in 1928 where Bergman's character goes by the name of Anna Koreff and is living rough as a homeless person, despised and rejected, but drawn instinctively to the half-remembered consolation of the Russian Orthodox Church and its Easter liturgy of promised resurrection. Bergman played Koreff as a suffering Christa or female Christ-figure who is acquainted with the deep grief of the Russian people displaced and deranged by the horrors of civil war. Though she has fallen on hard times and the regal beauty of her youth has been eroded, she convinces a cynical Russian émigré class of her imperial identity by the authenticity of her memories and emotions. In the end, her film character makes a major sacrifice, not of her life, but of her blood ties to her closest living relative, her beloved grandmother, the Dowager Empress Maria Feodorovna (Helen Hayes). She forfeits her rightful inheritance in order to be with a man it is hard to believe she can love, General Sergei Pavlovich Bounine (Yul Brynner), a cold martinet rather like Bergman's domineering first husband. When she disappears with her lover, any forlorn hope of the salvation and conversion of Russia dies.

The Inn of the Sixth Happiness (1958)

Two years later, Bergman returned to the screen in *The Inn of the Sixth Happiness*. The film was based on the life of the Englishwoman Gladys Aylward who in 1930 journeyed alone on the Trans-Siberian Railway and braved Sino-Soviet conflict on the Manchurian border in order to work as a Christian missionary in China. It was thirteen years since Bergman had played Sister Benedict in *The Bells of St. Mary's* and ten years since she starred in *Joan of Arc*. "I swore that I wouldn't play any more saints or nuns, so now I'm playing a missionary!" she bantered when preparing for the role of the Protestant Gladys Aylward (Spoto 2001:

345). Although *The Inn of the Sixth Happiness* made it clear that her heart no longer belonged to St. Mary's, film reviewers had no problem with her change of religion on-screen. Jack Moffitt of *The Hollywood Reporter* deemed that "while its protagonist is a Protestant, its message will be moving to every Catholic who has read the Sermon on the Mount" (November 18, 1958: 3). Indeed the headline of this review—"Adler-Robson Film Remarkable Story of a Modern Saint"—publicized *The Inn of the Sixth Happiness* as a welcome return to the films, which led to Bergman's canonization in the pre-Rossellini era. Other movie critics called attention to the religious persona she projected as Gladys Aylward and, in particular, the agapaic qualities of "implacable self-sacrifice," "selfless idealism" (Belmont, *Films in Review*, January 1959: 36), and "a burning desire to be of service" (Crowther, *The New York Times*, December 14, 1958: C2). These were qualities that she had exemplified before as Sister Benedict. The only person who did not think she was suitable for this role was Gladys Aylward herself who was extremely upset to be depicted by a notorious divorced woman and who tearfully complained to *Life* magazine, "what have they made me out to be?" (January 12, 1959: 45; Nicholson 2007: 212).

Historically, both Catholic nuns and Protestant women missionaries had been active in China since the second half of the nineteenth century and engaged in the same work of establishing a school system for girls, abolishing footbinding, providing medical care, and evangelizing in the countryside. Single women groomed for mission work abroad by "protestant nunneries" such as Mount Holyoke College came in increasing numbers in the 1880s and 90s. Like Gladys Aylward who went to Yangcheng in northeast Shanxi province, they were prepared to work in the most remote and inhospitable regions of China. Although they took no vows, they often had a strong sense of religious calling and committed themselves for life to missionary service in China. As single women grew to be a prodigious workforce, they formed "ladies houses" which did not bind them to a particular community like Catholic nuns but which did provide the surrogate family structure and female autonomy characteristic of the Anglican sisterhoods that arose in the mid-nineteenth century. By 1919, Protestant single women staffed 13 percent of all American missionary stations in China (Hunter 1984: 12–22, 35, 52, 62, 81–2; Mumm 1999: 138–9, 183). Even for Catholic nuns, however, the far reaches of China offered scope for freedom, adventure, and enterprise not available to women religious in more regimented and enclosed communities, and linked them in spirit with pioneering Protestant women missionaries.

For instance, when the American Maryknoll Sisters were formally approved as a missionary congregation in 1920, the founder, Mary Josephine Rogers, advised sisters heading for China that they should travel in pairs and live among the people as Aylward did in the remote regional inn for muleteers to which the film title refers (Chu 2007: 2–17, 38).

With this feminization of the missionary workforce went a zeal to improve the social plight of Chinese women. *The Inn of the Sixth Happiness* depicts this as one incentive—the other is financial—for Aylward to agree to become a district "foot inspector." In the film, the "very old custom" of footbinding is supported by the local mandarin overlord but outlawed by the KMT government intent on building a modern China and so prepared to tolerate Western missionary help in achieving greater health and productivity in the female population. In reality, male church leaders feared that missionary work would promote the women's rights movement. However, while both Catholic and Protestant women missionaries had a strong social conscience, they were largely conservative reformers. They were committed to more equality for women but not the radical change of the so-called "new woman" (Hunter 1984: xv, 87).

While the Maryknolls wore the distinguishing habit of the Catholic nun, other religious congregations established by European orders like the Presentandines and Sisters of Loretto showed greater latitude and identification with the population they served by dressing as Aylward did in Chinese peasant clothes. All these communities respected the regional culture, tried to retain its traditions, and recruited local women as fellow workers and sister companions (McNamara 1996: 583–7). Their efforts to efface themselves and walk humbly among the people of God attested to religious ideals of service and self-denial. Yet paradoxically, the work of missionary reform also required exceptionalizing qualities of ambition, drive, and single-mindedness. As I will show, Bergman's Gladys Aylward combines the strong personality, sacrificial spirit, and progressive desires that made both Catholic and Protestant missionary women such protean figures. However conservative their religious rhetoric and demeanor, their missionary work in China contributed to a "radical transformation" in the conditions of women (Hunter 1984: 21).

Dressed in the drab coat and hat of the indigent English servant class, the actress first appears on the screen looking like a hard-up Mary Poppins. Critics of the time were too polite to observe outright how much Bergman had aged. She was forty-three when the film premiered and playing a woman who was twenty-seven. *The New York Times* film reviewer Bosley Crowther felt obliged to note, however, that "the lovely

Miss Bergman (had) grown a bit matronly and plump" (C2), while *Variety* remarked that the actress's big physique made her an odd choice for the film adaptation of Aylward's life as *The Small Woman* by Alan Burgess (November 19, 1958: 6). Yet all agreed that she imbued the character she played with great dignity by showing a single woman face life with faith alone to comfort, shelter, and support her. Both unmarried Protestant missionaries at the turn of the twentieth century and Anglican sisters active in the second half of the nineteenth century had been derided as superfluous spinsters and sexually withered old maids (Hunter 1984: 52; Mumm 1999: xi, 171). However, in actuality, Aylward's social predicament was more acute because she was born in 1902 and grew up as one small statistic among nearly 1.75 million "surplus women" who had little or no choice but to remain single after World War I wiped out an entire generation of eligible men. Aylward was doubly disadvantaged by gender and class. With her working class background and basic education, she became part of that army of over 1.6 million women in domestic service in 1930 when the film opens (Nicholson 2007: 123–4). *The Inn of the Sixth Happiness* is not a great movie. What saves it is Bergman's performance, as film reviewers in 1958–59 were the first to appreciate (Alpert, *Saturday Review*, December 13, 1958: 26; Belmont, 36).[13] The actress interpreted Aylward as a single woman who refused to be trapped in a dead-end job or be typecast as a failure.

At the beginning of the film, Bergman is barely recognizable; but she used the fact that she had visibly aged to portray her character as a careworn domestic without job security or social support to keep poverty and despair at bay. The real-life Aylward had no shortage of work as nanny, parlormaid, and housekeeper. However, Bergman played Aylward as an anonymous figure in the London crowd whom no one "even take(s) notice of." One of the cruelest prejudices against the surplus woman was the suspicion that she had a stunted capacity for love and therefore somehow deserved the loneliness and invisibility she was forced to endure.

---

[13] Film reviewers also singled out Robert Donat's performance as the mandarin of Yangcheng. The distinguished actor was dying when he made *The Inn of the Sixth Happiness*, and *Newsweek* noted "the genuine agony of Robert Donat's final performance. Visibly suffering from pain and mental failure, (he) . . . needed off-screen blackboards" to help him remember his lines. *Newsweek*, December 15, 1958: 114. Not only *Newsweek* but *Films in Review*, January 1959: 36, and *Monthly Film Bulletin*, January 1959: 3, caught the brief moment where he looks directly at the camera as he says to Jen Ai, "Farewell. We shall not see each other again, I think."

Although the nunnery continued to be stereotyped crudely as a refuge for the unwanted and abnormal, there was also more enlightened understanding of how consoling religion could be for women, especially those in soul-destroying jobs (Nicholson 2007: 29, 44–6, 123–4, 185–6). Critics once again praised the glowing "warmth," "sincerity," "tenderness and spunk" Bergman brought to the role of Aylward (Hartung, *Commonweal*, December 19, 1958: 317; Crowther, C2). These commendations register the actress's talent for expressing the deep longings of eros—not always fully intelligible to the woman character herself in *Casablanca*, *The Bells of St. Mary's*, and *Anastasia*. They now convey Aylward's personal conviction that she has been called by God to be a Chinese missionary and despite insufficient education and training, can make a success of this life. Aylward's determination touches on a subject I will explore in more detail in the next chapter. This is how sublimation features in a life dedicated to religious service. Christian speakers urged Aylward's many superfluous sisters to channel their sexual and maternal desires into Christian care for the great family of humanity (Nicholson 2007: 43). From a single life that seemed destined to be wasted, Bergman showed Aylward blossom as she traveled to a new life of iron-willed purpose and willing sacrifice. *The Inn of the Sixth Happiness* dramatizes how much she accomplished through a "condition of complete simplicity / costing not less than everything" (T. S. Eliot, "Little Gidding," 253–4).

The 1958 film articulated the Cold War desire to turn back the clock by romanticizing a period in the 1930s when China was not yet Red but ruled by an emergent nationalist Chinese government that could do business with capitalist and anti-communist America. It portrays China's birth throes as one country and deep suspicion of the "foreign devils" who were agents of Western colonial power. The Western presumption that the Chinese are heathens who need to be civilized and Christianized is repudiated in no uncertain terms by the male lead and love interest in the film, the proud nationalist Captain, and later Colonel, Lin Nan (Curt Jurgens), who bluntly tells Gladys that the white missionary is "the most frightening type of foreign devil." Several film reviewers shrewdly picked up on the fact that *The Inn of the Sixth Happiness* does not specify the Protestant denomination Aylward represented and is vague about her religious motivation for becoming a missionary in China (Hartung, 317; Alpert, 26; Crowther, C2). *Hollywood Reporter* Jack Moffitt's persuasive explanation for this is that "she, intuitively, emphasized the spirit rather than the forms of Christianity" (3). Indeed, the film is quick to play down her proselytizing role, and so protect her from detraction as a missionary head hunter. The woman evangelist whom she joins at the inn of the sixth happiness in Shanxi province, Jeannie Lawson (Athene Seyler), dies soon after her arrival; and in order to survive alone in Northern China, Gladys turns from preaching the gospel to living it through her social work across the countryside.

Bergman had been branded as Hollywood's "apostle of degradation" (McLean 1995: 37) in the furor over her affair with Rossellini. However, in playing an active missionary she not only shed the remnants of the sackcloth and ashes that she had worn for the last decade as whore personified but also recuperated Mary Magdalen's positive role in the gospels as Christ's female disciple. As Gladys Aylward, Bergman represented all that was most noble in Mary Magdalen's apostolate—her loyalty, love, hope, and persistence in the teeth of death itself (Haskins 1993: 10, 15, 31, 40, 55, 67, 85, 365). Film reviewers were not sure "what makes the heroine tick" (Crowther, C2). It was what motivated earlier Protestant women missionaries in China as well as Anglican sisters active in nineteenth-century philanthropy: a longing to be fully, usefully, and meaningfully employed; to seek God's kingdom and righteousness; and not only to grow in goodness but to do good (Hunter 1984: 42; Mumm 1999: 15). Indeed Protestant women missionaries were successful in China because they led by example, disseminating the message of the gospels not by what they said, but how they devoted their lives to others. This strategy empowers Gladys Aylward in the film after she is turned down by the China Missionary Society because she is not "qualified" or fluent in Chinese. Undeterred she travels as a lone apostle—one who is not given much credence—to China. Both Captain Lin Nan and the mandarin of Yangcheng (Robert Donat) district observe her feminine faith in action as Gladys proves her missionary competence and dedication in a range of social services from running a hostel, a food kitchen, a school, and an orphanage, to overseeing rural health, the end of foot-binding, and prison reform. She assumes the spiritual and social motherhood that both Anglican and Catholic nuns claimed in justification of their work and vow of chastity (Mumm 1999: 95, 183, 208–9). In an uplifting finale that looks forward to the sentimental close of *The Sound of Music* (1965) and that, as *Monthly Film Bulletin* pointed out, glosses over the suffering and hardship (January 1959: 3), she leads the orphaned children in her keeping to safety over the mountains "whence cometh their salvation" (Ps. 121).

Gradually the male principals in the film move from a position of polite contempt for a woman who arrives in the most isolated region of

China with no money, no friends, and no knowledge of the country, culture, or language, to grudging respect, admiration, and finally love. The mandarin will be so moved by her charitable deeds and spirit of altruism that he eventually becomes a Christian convert. Of course, Gladys does not come to China as a member of the British ruling class but its servant underclass. Captain Lin Nan is impressed, despite himself, by her missionary spirit because it is closer to the communitarian and indeed communist ideal of early Christianity. Moreover she shows a very post-colonial respect for cultural difference and religious pluralism in China, and certainly does not possess the white missionary's imperious sense that Christianity should supersede indigenous beliefs and dominate through mass conversions. "Being a Christian," she memorably affirms, is "making each man know that he counts—whether he believes in Christ or Buddha or nothing." In this respect, Aylward resembles Father Francis Chisholm in *The Keys of the Kingdom*, a Chinese missionary who also insisted that "all atheists are not godless men" and whose conscience was a rebuke to the postwar Catholic ideology that communists were a godforsaken people (Sanders 2008: 140–1; Burke Smith 2010: 141–3).

In real life Gladys Aylward was called either Ai weh-deh, "the small woman," or Ai weh-te, "the virtuous woman," but her honorary Chinese name in the film is changed to Jen Ai, meaning "the one who loves people."[14] Love of people goes hand-in-hand with a love of work that also distinguishes Catholic screen nuns such as Sister Benedict in *The Bells of St. Mary's*, Sister Luke in *The Nun's Story*, and Dame Philippa in *In This House of Brede*, as well as the Anglican sisters in *Black Narcissus*. Gladys's Chinese name in the film frees her from a European identity that has been defined in terms of gender and class limitations. Like female saints and nuns, she breaks the gender rules of both European and Chinese society by an independence that was coded male and a public visibility and mobility that had once been the mark of the prostitute (Coburn and Smith 1999: 83; McNamara 1996: 3; Mumm 1999: 96). Both the surplus woman between the wars and the Protestant missionary spinster at the turn of the century were vulnerable to stigmatization as mannish (Hunter 1984: 53). In *The Inn of the Sixth Happiness*, Gladys directly addresses this historical suspicion of the single woman and speculates to Captain Lin Nan that the life of a solo female missionary suits her because she is "like a man" herself. By this she does not mean a lack but

---

[14]I have drawn on Catherine Swift's account of *Gladys Aylward* (Minneapolis Minn.: Bethany House Publishers, 1989) for the factual details of her life history.

an excess of the desires that have been the prerogative of men: for travel, adventure, emigration, betterment of self, rewarding work, and a life of active service. Her growing public authority enables her to stand up to the mandarin of Yangcheng and teach the concubines in his household to read. In contrast to Sister Benedict, she is not bound by the religious vow of obedience "without question" to follow the orders of male superiors: "Did you not tell them . . . that to obey any man unquestioningly was old-fashioned?" Her passionate energy for work hints of other emergent desires. Indeed, she transgresses racial and sexual taboos when she unexpectedly finds an erotic love, which was denied to most surplus women and which was taboo to the missionary nun and the white woman of empire.

The film's original tagline refers to her "love for this Eurasian soldier who now pressed his earthy, Oriental skin against her own." This lurid description is a gross distortion of a very sedate, middle-aged film romance but it plays on an interracial sexual fantasy calculated to excite the interest of a Hollywood audience. Lin Nan's conflicted relation to his Eurasian identity with his shame, rejection, and ultimate acceptance of miscegenation through his own love for Gladys when she becomes Jen Ai are the most interesting and progressive aspects of this film. Captain Lin Nan's dilemma is that of Hollywood itself, which was fascinated by and at the same time fearful of the theme of miscegenation. Sensitive to social disapproval of interracial marriage, Hollywood handled this transgressive subject by giving most Eurasian characters a Caucasian father, synonymous with the Western blood line, and an Asian mother identified with Orientalist sensuality and sexual excess (Marchetti 1993: 67–9).[15] Lin Nan's identification not only with the suffering but the sensibility of his abandoned Chinese mother is complicated by guilty suspicion that he gave her further pain because he "didn't look very Chinese as a child." His remark conveniently naturalizes the fact that the German actor Curt Jurgens plays the Eurasian Lin Nan and also suggests a strong if abhorrent physical resemblance to his Dutch colonial father.

Lin's racial consciousness of inferiority as a "half white" seems more inescapable than Gladys's class and gender consciousness of being a second class citizen in Britain. His xenophobia is a displacement of the

[15] As Susan Haskins notes, nineteenth-century Romantics conceived Mary Magdalen as a type of the oriental woman who seduced the white man with her exotic alterity and erotic mystery. Haskins, *Mary Magdalen: Myth and Metaphor* (London: Harper Collins, 1993), 352–3.

self-hatred he internalized from his father—"it is my own mixed blood which offends me since I believe China should be for the Chinese." He deals with the psychic conflict of his hybrid Eurasian identity by setting up a fierce and false opposition between his mind and body: "My heart and my mind are Chinese, only my blood is mixed." The fear of further rejection and humiliation haunts his later proposal to Jen Ai: "Would it offend you to be loved by a man of another race?" As the one who loves the Chinese people and has come to love this "man of another race," Jen Ai demonstrates the benevolent desire that impels individuals to make sacrifices for others. In returning Lin Nan's love, she is assuming the role of the good mother and redeeming a man who has been harmed by the parents of real life (Klein 1994: 311–12). Thus the film presents miscegenation positively as a marriage of her faith in God, his belief in his (mother)land, and their mutual love, pride and commitment to China. The odds were heavily stacked against single women born between 1885 and 1905 finding a life partner, especially by the 1930s (Nicholson 2007: xi, 44). Indeed, the actual Gladys Aylward never married, although she had the emotional fulfillment, like Jen Ai, of adopted children. While Jen Ai's marriage to Lin Nan clearly reflects Hollywood's need to romanticize the spinster missionary's life, it also shows that not only Catholic nuns but Protestant religious women could be "used to explore the changes occurring between the races and the genders" (McDannell 2008: 24). Together the lovers face a barbaric decade of war in which both soldiers and missionaries would suffer hardship and horror. The pair is thus unlikely to find the traditional happiness that is wished for—wealth, longevity, good health, virtue, and peaceful death in old age. However, the film presents their interracial and intercultural union as the source of the sixth happiness—a happiness that is not skin-deep and that springs from the power of the erotic within.

Conclusion

As a missionary in *The Inn of the Sixth Happiness*, Bergman once again brought sexual humanity to the spiritual ideals she embodied on-screen. However, Jen Ai was a mature role resistant to binary split, one that was developed so that she could find room in the inn for both agape in her selfless love for the Chinese people and personal eros in her longing for communion of mind, heart, body, and soul with another, and so have the power to heal her divided lover Lin Nan. The film plot did not require Ilsa Lund's sacrifice of love and happiness to a higher wartime cause in

Casablanca. It did not clip her wings, pathologize her signs of exceptionality, or send her off alone into the darkness like Sister Benedict in *The Bells of St. Mary's.* Instead, *The Inn of the Sixth Happiness* suggested how religion could activate rather than stifle the potential of women (Mumm 1999: x). Bergman's character finds freedom from domestic servitude through Christian service of others. In following God to the world's end, she discovers and lives out her deepest desires. The virtuous woman is ultimately a keeper of the status quo in *Casablanca.* The religious woman is a conservative rather than radical change agent in *The Bells of St. Mary's.* In *The Inn of the Sixth Happiness,* Aylward is represented as a woman of faith who is indifferent to the tenets of institutional religion but is moved to become a missionary by the spirit of foolhardy, audacious, dynamic, and superabundant love that gave Christianity its revolutionary edge.

2

SEXUAL DESIRES

REPRESSION AND SUBLIMATION IN *BLACK NARCISSUS* (1947), *HEAVEN KNOWS, MR. ALLISON* (1957), AND *SEA WIFE* (1957)

Introduction to *Black Narcissus*

Michael Powell and Emeric Pressburger's 1947 film *Black Narcissus* dramatized the vocational crises of five Anglican sisters who struggle to establish a missionary foothold in the Himalayas, and the tragedy that unfolds when the neurotic Sister Ruth disintegrates under the strain, forsakes her vows, and runs amok. The shocking finale of *Black Narcissus* and the over-the-top performance of Kathleen Byron as the deranged Sister Ruth have left a powerful impression on film viewers.[1] That said, they have diverted attention from an important feature of the film: its examination of the psychosexual pressures of the religious life, an examination, which, I argue here, is not salacious but serious, thought-

---

[1] See Craig McCall's documentary on Jack Cardiff's cinematography, "Painting with Light," which is an extra feature on the *Black Narcissus* (1947) DVD, the Criterion Collection, 2000. Byron herself saw Sister Ruth as "quite sane," although she certainly did not play her that way, and was at loggerheads with Michael Powell who wanted the nun played raving mad. See Sarah Street's British Film Guide on *Black Narcissus* (London: I. B. Taurus, 2005), 82. Brian Case details the "endless fights" between Byron and Powell over this issue in his review of *Black Narcissus* for *Time Out*, March 8–15, 1995: 153.

provoking, and visionary. At the time *Black Narcissus* was made, chastity was a vow that both Anglican and Catholic nuns took for granted and indeed was a norm for all respectable single women (Mumm 1999: 32). Twenty years later in the 1960s, the sexual revolution, second wave feminism, and the Second Vatican Council would prompt nuns to study this vow more closely and consider how they could live it out faithfully without ignoring their own sexuality or stunting their capacity for friendship, love, and intimacy (Schneiders 2000: 247; 2001: 133, 160–6). In the decade following Vatican II, Catholic and Protestant theologians began to study the sacred and unitive value of sexuality and to appreciate, as Benedictine monk Sebastian Moore opined, that "the task before us is not to subject sexual passion to the will, but to restore it to desire, whose origin and end is God" (2002: 164, 168). This marks a radical departure from Anders Nygren's theological view earlier in the 1930s that God is pure agape and the yearning desire of eros is totally contrary to his divine nature (1953: xiii, 199, 212, 479). Although *Black Narcissus* would be vilified by American Catholic censors for bringing the subject of religion and sex uncomfortably close, it was far-sighted not only in asking sexual questions about religious life but in visualizing the sacred dimension of such questions (Nelson 1979: 14–15). I will begin by examining how the psychosexual pressures of religious life are unveiled in the heated scene between Sister Ruth and her superior near the end of *Black Narcissus*.

In the Gothic prelude to this scene, the religious superior, Sister Clodagh (Deborah Kerr), descends a dark and narrow staircase, holding a candle, which illuminates the ghostliness of her pale face and habit, and enters the convent sleeping quarters, which are off-limits to profane eyes. A trespassing camera trails her as she pauses at one cell door after another, and eavesdrops as she listens for sounds that are characteristic of each sister. She hears the spiritually distracted Sister Phillippa (Flora Robson) pray for protection from the evils of the night: "Drive from us all the snares of the enemy and may Thy Holy Angels dwell herein to keep us in peace." She hears sobs from the tender-hearted Sister "Honey" (Jenny Laird) who is distraught by the death of a native baby whom the nuns were unable to save. She hears the reassuring snores of the sensible and unflappable Sister Briony (Judith Furse). When she reaches Sister Ruth's cell, the camera pans down to the light shining through the bottom of the doorway, a light that does not dispel the darkness but is an ominous sign of unwelcome and uncanny revelations. Sister Clodagh stands on the threshold of what Freud called the "*Unheimlich*," that is "everything . . . that ought to have remained secret and hidden but has come to light." The medium shot of Clodagh entering Sister Ruth's underground cell captures not only her horror at an *unheimlich* sight that is alien and disorientating but her shock that the aura of "*Unheimlichkeit*" veiling the divine has been violated.[2] Sister Ruth has removed the sacred veil and habit of a nun and, in the light of Clodagh's candle, glares triumphant and defiant, auburn hair primped, complexion rouged, dressed in dark crimson the color of congealed blood.[3]

This melodramatic scene was wholly the invention of Powell and Pressburger and does not exist in Rumer Godden's 1939 novel, which they adapted to the screen. It shows their cinematic instinct for uncanny effects that create uncertainty whether the camera is recording a real world or the delusions and fantasies of the film characters (Freud 1919, *SE* 17: 230). The moment that won their film both notoriety and acclaim occurs when Ruth sit downs opposite Clodagh. The confrontation between these two women was staged as a conflict that raged within and was projected by the mind, one mirrored in the dramatic contrast of their two faces—that of the defrocked sister florid with sexual desire, anger, and jealousy, and that of the habited nun blanched with exhaustion, fright, and the strain of maintaining *sang-froid*. The Anglican view of the vow of chastity as a corrective to sensuality is melodramatically deconstructed in this scene (Mumm 1999: 30). In a gesture that is both a sexual and religious taunt, Ruth slowly—flagrantly—applies deep red lipstick. Garish lipstick on a woman who has not yet shed the nun's stainless aura is an *unheimlich* spectacle calculated to cause offense; and it made *Film Comment*'s Henry Sheehan call this scene "one of the most depraved . . . in . . . personal cinema" (1990: 39). Yet what first appears *unheimlich* to Clodagh is unnervingly familiar and "leads back to what is known of old" and has become alienated from the mind through the process of repression (Freud 1919, *SE* 17: 220, 241). Ruth has become a lurid exaggeration of Sister Clodagh's past, concealed self, the young Irish red-head called "Clo" who was once madly in love. A reaction

[2] See Freud's "The 'Uncanny'" (1919), *SE* 17: 224–5.

[3] See detailed descriptions of characterization and camera shots for each scene of *Black Narcissus* in the Bound Screen Script, Michael Powell Special Collection, Box 4, item S-68A, British Film Institute (BFI) Library.

shot of Clodagh picking up a Bible after Ruth has applied lipstick suggests how the literal truths of scripture can be used as the defenses that fortify repression. These protect the ego from the mental anguish of ambivalence inherent in the uncanny. As Freud pointed out, the *unheimlich* and *heimlich* illustrate the human capacity for "doubling, dividing and interchanging of the self" (1919, *SE* 17: 234). In her English Bible, the nun seeks the reassurance offered by institutional religion that good can be clearly distinguished from evil and love kept separate from anger and aggression, and by colonialism that the world is black-and-white, not murky and confused.

Black Narcissus has been called "one of the greatest works of art about repression yet made" (London *Times*, August 4, 2005, T2: 17); and readers of the scene I have just discussed recognize Ruth as Clodagh's double or split self, acting out the return of her repressed and forbidden desires, arising as a figure from the unconscious, which knows no negation.[4] Yet while Freudian and psychoanalytic concepts have been incorporated into the postcolonial critique of this film and identification of Ruth as the void at the heart of the colonial narrative, they have not been used to address the question of how sexuality functions in the reli-

---

[4] Celestino Deleyto regards Sister Ruth as both Clodagh's rival and double, "the embodiment of those desires which the protagonist nominally represses." Deleyto, "The nun's story: femininity and Englishness in the films of Deborah Kerr," in *British Stars and Stardom: From Alma Taylor to Sean Connery*, ed. Bruce Babington (Manchester: Manchester University Press, 2001), 127. Michael Walker famously called her "the monster from the id," but still concluded that she was a psychologically complex character. Walker, "*Black Narcissus*," *Framework* 9 (1978–79): 11. As evidenced by the fact that I discuss her only in relation to Sister Clodagh, I do not think Ruth is given any character development or credible motivation at all. I agree with Philip Gillett who argues that "it is hard to understand why she became a nun, and no explanation is forthcoming. She is a dramatic device rather than a real person." Gillett, *Movie Greats: A Critical Study of Classic Cinema* (Oxford: Berg, 2008), 74. Priya Jaikumar suggests that she is "the vortex that absorbs the other Sisters' weaknesses." Jaikumar, "'Place' and the Modernist Redemption of Empire in *Black Narcissus* (1947)," *Cinema Journal* 40.2 (2001): 67. Marcia Landy contextualizes this problem by underlining the fact that "melodramatic characters are not fully rounded, and they are not psychologically complex. They are identifiable by their polarized nature, their representation of specific moral qualities, their likeness to the split figures in dreams, and their relation to fantasies." Landy, *British Genres: Cinema and Society, 1930–1960* (Princeton: Princeton University Press, 1991), 197.

gious life of these Anglican missionary sisters (Jaikumar 2001: 57, 66–7; Deleyto 2001: 124, 128; Stone 2004: 268). Even when the characters of *Black Narcissus* have been discussed as nuns and not British colonial agents, the critical presumption has usually been that celibacy requires the repression and not the understanding or appreciation of sexuality (Walker 1978–79: 10). The first film critics registered their hostile view that the religious life was unnatural and the renunciation of sexual activity unhealthy. James Agee of *The Nation* expressed the strong personal opinion that "celibacy is of itself faintly obscene" (August 30, 1947: 209). *Variety* reduced *Black Narcissus* to "the story of two sex-starved women, and a man. And since the women are nuns, there can be no happy ending, except perhaps in the spiritual sense" (May 7, 1947: 18). Philip Hartung of *Commonweal* warned that "if seen by the uninformed a film like 'Black Narcissus' could do great harm" (August 22, 1947: 455). These perceptions surface again forty years later in Jeffrey Richard's film review for *The Daily Telegraph* where he argues that Powell and Pressburger saw "the nuns' celibacy as a denial of their essential femininity" (October 19, 1987: 13).

Binary representations of nuns are the legacy not only of sensationalist and anti-religious fiction but patriarchal and imperialist Christianity. In their face-to-face encounter, Clodagh and Ruth embody the duality of the chaste and the scarlet woman, the pure spirit and the carnal flesh, sacred and profane desire, "higher" and "lower" orders of life (Deleyto 2001: 125–6; Stone 2004: 265–6). These divisions gain additional force from the assumption reflected in Richard's film review: that the nun must split herself in two when she enters the convent, and that in becoming a religious, she forfeits her identity as a sexed woman. Yet as I have argued, the uncanny tension inherent in this scene stems from the effort to maintain polarity and fend off awareness of identification with the opposite, the awareness in the final analysis that the nun is both a religious and a woman.

In fact, Powell wanted to make a film that used a spectacular Indian setting but told a story that "was intimate and dramatic and depended upon . . . the interplay of passion and devotion" (2000: 559). This play of passion and devotion takes different forms in the film. It leads to the doubling and dividing that we have seen in the confrontation between Clodagh with her Bible and Ruth with her red lipstick, but it eventually provokes Clodagh, the lead nun character, to radically alter her view of herself and others, for *Black Narcissus* is not only a film about sexual repression but also about sublimation, or how desire is internalized, channeled, and transformed in the religious life.[5] Repression and sublimation were intrinsic to the nineteenth-century dispute over whether celibacy was abnormal and deleterious for the first English women to become Anglican nuns, or liberated them from sexual servitude in Victorian marriage and its compulsory cycle of reproduction. Repression and sublimation have also informed feminist debate over whether entrance into the convent was a defensive or desirous action, institutional claustration or escape from confinement in the home, a retreat from the world or advance toward it. As we saw in Chapter 1, the arguments in this debate were similar whether the women in question were Catholic nuns, Anglican sisters, Protestant solo missionaries, or self-supporting spinsters (Mumm 1999: x–xii, 166–9, 196–9; Nicholson 2007: 54–5).

Powell imagined Sister Clodagh as thirty-six in *Black Narcissus*, and the Rumer Godden novel, which he adapted to the screen, is set around 1938 before the outbreak of World War II and near the end of the British Indian empire.[6] This means that, like Gladys Aylward, the film character belonged to the post–World War I generation of surplus women who battled with secret loss, grief, loneliness, and yearning. They were haunted by social accusations of inadequacy because they were spinsters struggling to survive on their own, living a celibacy that was not freely chosen but ordained by the catastrophic male mortality rates of the Great War. If they elected the religious life, they were derided for seeking the last refuge of undesirable women or becoming "unhinged old maids" (Nicholson 2007: 29, 40).[7] Failure . . . failure . . . failure is a repeated

[5] See Freud's essay on "Leonardo Da Vinci and a Memory of his Childhood" (1910), *SE* 11: 78, which argues that "the sexual instinct is particularly well fitted to make contributions of this kind since it is endowed with a capacity for sublimation," and Hans W. Loewald, *Sublimation: Inquiries into Theoretical Psychoanalysis* (New Haven: Yale University Press, 1988), 19, who elaborates by explaining that "sublimation comes about . . . by an internalizing transformation of passion or desire."

[6] There is no specific indication of how old Sister Clodagh is in Godden's novel *Black Narcissus*. However, Michael Powell was emphatic that she was thirty-six when he began casting for his film, and for this reason initially discounted Deborah Kerr at twenty-six, even though Emeric Pressburger regarded her as perfect for the role. Powell had to eat his words. See his highly entertaining autobiography, *A Life in Movies* (London: Faber and Faber, 2000), 576–7.

[7] As Susan Mumm notes, even in the nineteenth century women outnumbered men, but male emigration led to an increased public concern about the problem of "superfluous women." Mumm, *Stolen Daughters, Virgin Mothers: Anglican Sisterhoods in Victorian Britain* (London: Leicester University Press, 1999), 170–1.

critical charge leveled against the Anglican sisters in the film *Black Narcissus* (Deleyto 2001: 124–5). Yet what shines through in Virginia Nicholson's moving historical account of surplus women between the two world wars is how those "doomed" to remain single withstood repression by asserting the power of sublimation in making a success of their lives. Christian feminists urged them to "transmute the power of sex and 'create' in other ways. He (Christ) did it supremely for the world. You and I can do it for our village, our city, for England, for the world, for anything you like" (Nicholson 2007: 43).

Sublimation is crucial to understanding Audre Lorde's influential essay on the "Uses of the Erotic: The Erotic as Power." As theologian David Carr suggested in his discussion of Lorde's essay, repression is not about the sexual abstinence defining celibacy, but the inhibition of libido or its restriction to a narrow aspect of life (2003: 9). Lorde's vision has a majestic Pauline breadth, length, height, and depth (Eph. 3:19) in its conception of eros as "those physical, emotional, and psychic expressions of what is deepest and strongest and richest within each of us," passions that she describes as becoming most meaningful when they are shared, whether they find intense expression in human friendship and intimacy, or magnanimous outlet in social service or cultural contributions to humanity (1984: 56). Lorde's expansion of eros to include passions that find non-sexual outlet not only enhances Freud's study of sublimation in his extended essay "Leonardo Da Vinci and a Memory of His Childhood" (1910), but is an important corrective to this essay in insisting that women's capacity for sublimation is not inferior to that of men (Van Herik 1985: 20, 84, 110). In tandem with Lorde, I will employ Freud's sublime view of eros as "the divine spark which is directly or indirectly the driving force—*il primo motore*—behind all human activity" (*SE* 11: 74) to explore Powell's own claim as director that *Black Narcissus* is "one of the most subtly erotic films ever made" (2000: 623), and to argue that it is not just another crypto-pornographic representation of nuns (Mourao 2002: 75–7). Moreover, my reading of the protagonist Sister Clodagh and her antagonist Sister Ruth will bear in mind Freud's conviction that sublimation was a skill crucial to mental well-being: "Not every neurotic has a high talent for sublimation; one can assume . . . that they would not have fallen ill at all if they had possessed the art of sublimating their instincts."[8] This "high talent" required a vitality, drive, imagination, and

[8] See "Recommendations to Physicians Practicing Psycho-analysis" (1912), *SE* 12: 119.

creativity that were beyond the capacity of many (1910, *SE* 11: 136; Loewald 1988: 8, 38–9).

Deborah Kerr

Although a decade younger than the character Powell conceived, Deborah Kerr combined an outer austerity and inner longing in the role of Sister Clodagh that captured the religious tension of rigidly maintained repression and an instinctual capacity for sublimation. The first reviewers of *Black Narcissus* thought she was, in fact, "too beautiful to be altogether believable" as a nun. Yet in the same breath they conceded that she "subtly registered" the tribulations of the religious life by the friction between her delicate appearance and her strength of character (O'Hara, *The New Republic*, September 15, 1947: 38). As Celestino Deleyto observed, this "outward delicacy and inward strength" were the foundation of Kerr's screen identity and projected a Victorian stereotype that was still admired in the immediate postwar period—that of the well-bred, dignified and autocratic English lady (2001: 121). The star's neo-Victorian gender persona made her perfect to embody traditional convent culture, which Cardinal Suenens would later describe as the "last stronghold of the very studied manners of the middle-class woman of the nineteenth century" (Suenens 1963: 18). Powell, who had a conflicted, and ultimately thwarted, courtly love affair with the actress, celebrated her as "both the ideal and the flesh-and-blood woman whom I had been searching for ever since I had discovered that I had been born to be a teller of tales and a creator of dreams" (Powell 2000: 413). Kerr's Tudor combination of alabaster skin and auburn hair was a striking visual emblem that enhanced the director's romantic perception of her beauty as both spiritual and sensual, and which encouraged critics to lyricize the fire-and-ice in her screen performances (Denby 1994: 43). Moreover, it matched the male protagonist's intuition of Sister Clodagh's character in Rumer Godden's novel:

> He looked ... to her face in its narrowing wimple, the forehead and cheek-bones beautiful and intelligent, the mouth fastidious. She looked cold, almost severe, and yet he thought, "I believe you're sensitive. Sensitive and warm." (Godden 1963: 52)

In a post-colonially inflected reading of *Black Narcissus* that was inspired by Richard Dyer's study of how Western imperialism and Christianity culturally constructed racial whiteness, Deleyto argued that Kerr both represented and subverted the binary exaltation of the pure, white spirit over the lower sexual and subaltern body (2001: 123–7). Yet Hollywood would still typecast the actress in the 1950s as the personification of a higher and more refined English femininity—which in Powell's view "gave her no chance for real acting" (1995: 161). Fred Zinnemann rescued Kerr from this stereotyping as "the Virgin Queen of England . . . a very cold, remote sort of person" (2005: 101) when he chose her to play a promiscuous army officer's wife who surrenders her voluptuous body to passionate lovemaking in the famous beach scene of *From Here to Eternity* (1953). Four years later, the star would be back playing women pure in spirit when she starred opposite Robert Mitchum as a sexually innocent Irish nun in John Huston's *Heaven Knows, Mr. Allison* (1957). In *The Sundowners* (1960), Zinnemann once again dispelled her ice-maiden image by casting her as the earthy and sexually fulfilled wife of Mitchum's Australian drover (Nolletti 2005: 132). However, *Black Narcissus* anticipated this image shift by showcasing Kerr's erotic doubleness and her forte for both concealing and revealing a passionate nature (Denby 1994: 43; Deleyto 2001: 128).

Sublimation is central to my own reading of the film and Clodagh's character because it does away with the perceived opposition between base desire and the fastidious spirit by regarding erotic passion as the promethean fire that can be channeled creatively not only into high cultural activities such as art and religion but, as Lorde said more simply, into the ordinary events of "our loving, our work, our lives" (1984: 55; Loewald 1988: 19, 21). Although Kerr appeared to be a more delicate, fastidious, and reserved screen personality than the robust and ardent actress Ingrid Bergman, both stars made the film nun come alive with very mortal longings. Bergman radiated eros outward in *The Bells of St. Mary's*, but Kerr makes it "a *deus absconditus*, a hidden or concealed god" (Jung 1989: 151) in *Black Narcissus*. This god is symbolically unveiled at the close of the film as Kerr's Sister Clodagh sheds the illusion that she can hold her mind aloof from the sexed body, and not only assert her spirit over the wind-swept Himalayas, which soar above her, but over the subterranean desires that are a reminder of her embodiment (Dyer 2005: 14–18, 74–7; Goldenberg 1993: 75–6, 90–2). Her vain and ultimately calamitous attempt to convert the remote mountain palace of Mopu into a convent mission station prompts a revaluation of her religious vocation and a painful, remarkably forward-looking recognition for 1947 that women religious are not a cut above lay people. As the male lead Mr. Dean (David Farrar) sarcastically remarked, she is not the "superior being" she thought herself to be at the beginning of the film. In acquiring the wisdom and humility to let go of her sense as an Anglican missionary nun of being a breed apart, groomed to lead the civilizing mission of a religious elite, Sister Clodagh abandons the Christian hierarchy that not only ranks the soul above the flesh but the sacred and divine as distant from the sexual. By the end of *Black Narcissus* she has begun to redefine her religious life as a pursuit of holiness that must accept and transform—not repress—the passionate energy of the body. Her arrogant colonial understanding of religious transcendence as ascendancy over others is replaced by a quasi-mystical awareness of diminishment and enhancement (Hunter 1984: 51).[9] As Freud marveled in his study of sublimation in the life of Leonardo Da Vinci, she has begun to have an inkling of a world in which she may no longer be destined to do great things but in which "the small is still no less wonderful and significant than the great" (1910, *SE* 11: 76).

Powell and Pressburger's 1947 Film, Black Narcissus

The Powell and Pressburger film *Black Narcissus* was based on a best-selling novel by Rumer Godden, a migratory daughter of the waning British Raj, who lived in India on and off from 1907 until 1945. As a writer, she explored the vivid and eclectic impact that this colonial home had on her identity, her creative imagination, her vision of life, and her spiritual sense of the invisible reality behind it (Lassner 2004: 70–4; Dukes 1991: 18–22). In her memoir, *A House with Four Rooms*, Godden recalled the epiphany she experienced on reading a quotation from the *Bhagavad-Gita* that her sister Jon sent her: "The god Krishna says: However men approach me, even so do I welcome them, for the path men take from every side leads to me" (1989: 240).

The path that the British filmmakers Michael Powell and Emeric Pressburger took in bringing her 1939 novel to the screen in 1947 was very different from the one she had envisaged. She thought the film, shot in Pinewood Studios and the sub-tropical Sussex garden of Leonardslee

---

[9]This is made explicit in Godden's novel where Sister Clodagh looks out at the mountain as she prays in the chapel and reflects: "How could the years she had given to God be small and petty? She tried to think how, to Him, the mountain was as infinitesimal as the sparrows; instead she thought how the eagles, filled with His life, were beaten down before it." See Rumer Godden, *Black Narcissus* (New York: Dell Books, 1963), 59.

rather than on location in India, was a tawdry "counterfeit" redeemed only by Jack Cardiff's magical cinematography (Godden 1989: 52; Powell 2000: 559–62; Street 2005: 13–14). She was particularly indignant that Powell "saw the book as a fairy tale, while for me it was utterly true. . . . There is not an atom of truth in the film of *Black Narcissus*—famous as it has become" (Godden 1989: 51). Godden herself followed a winding path to enlightenment, dabbling with Hinduism, returning to the Anglican cultural roots of her childhood, and finally converting to Catholicism in later life. Yet the fact that the nuns she imagines in her early novel, *Black Narcissus*, are members of an Anglo-Catholic order at the High Church end of Anglicanism with Romanist trappings of Marian devotion suggests that she was in religious passage years before her conversion.[10] In Chapter 5, I discuss *In This House of Brede* (1975), a made-for-TV film based on her second novel about women religious, in this case Catholic cloistered Benedictines, and one that gives credence to Powell's tongue-in-cheek remark that "nuns are always box-office" (2000: 623).

Despite the author's chagrin at Powell and Pressburger's fabulist interpretation of her story, it would be the film and not the novel *Black Narcissus* that would be recognized as a masterpiece. Its circle of admirers grew to include influential Catholic filmmaker advocates such as Martin Scorsese and Francis Ford Coppola who responded to the fantasy, magic, and mystery of the film (Scorsese 1995: ix–xi; Christie 1985: 111). Not only did Powell perceive *Black Narcissus* as the most erotic film he ever made, but he saw the art of filmmaking as "the child of sex and religion," implicitly drawing on the deep, passionate energy of eros. He approached the role of director with the attitude that he was "a high priest of the mysteries" (1995: 19–20). Both the uncanny, dreamy mystery that Freud saw at work in Da Vinci's most celebrated painting, the *Mona Lisa* (1910, *SE* 11: 108, 112), and the strange, disorientating dreamscape that Powell and Pressburger created in *Black Narcissus*, bear out Hans Loewald's conclusion that the great work of art is also a great work of sublimation in which there is a "return, on a higher level of organization, to the early magic of thought, gesture, word, image, emotion, fantasy" (1988: 81).

Black Narcissus explodes the pious assumption that celibate nuns are asexual, with no awakening to sexuality before entering the convent and no awareness of it afterwards, and so addresses an area of religious life

---

[10] Mumm (*Stolen Daughters*, 137) notes that most Anglican sisterhoods "tended to cluster at the Anglo-Catholic end of the Anglican spectrum."

that did not become a subject of serious theological discussion until after Vatican II. The film uncannily pursues the connection between sex and religion by scrutinizing the efforts of a small band of Anglican nuns, led by Deborah Kerr's Sister Clodagh, to establish a convent mission base in Mopu palace, a derelict Indian harem from bygone days of pleasure. In christening this former "House of Women" as the "House of St. Faith," the nuns do not erase but simply modify its past name carrying the reminder that they are women as well as religious. They unknowingly resurrect an "old, discarded belief" (Freud 1919, *SE* 17: 247–8), which generates uncanny disquiet in the film: that God's House is built on sexual foundations. Indeed the word "harem" stems from the same Arabic root as "haram," which refers to the sacred, the taboo, and the enclosed (Tromans 2008: 17). Freud speculated in his study of sublimation that religious worship arose from primitive awe and exaltation in the power of sexuality: "In the course of cultural development so much of the divine and sacred was ultimately extracted from sexuality that the exhausted remnant fell into contempt" (1910, *SE* 11: 97). Although the nuns fill the House of St. Faith with Christian iconography and talismans, the ghostly enchantments of the harem still seep into their prayer life and color their missionary work with a strange *jouissance*.[11] For they have not reckoned with the stirring power of the erotica decorating the harem walls. The fluid movements of the figures who dance and make love there blur the distinction between the sexual and the sacred, the human and divine. The disturbing inference of these murals is that as veiled brides of Christ the nuns bear a perverse polygamous resemblance to the Indian potentate's wives and concubines.[12]

Mopu has often been read from a Christian cultural perspective as an evil place that takes malevolent possession of Sister Ruth (Jaikumar 2001: 62, 66, 68), or as the "exceeding high mountain" where the devil

---

[11] See continual evidence of this in Godden's novel, 82, 88, 125, 139.

[12] Mary Daly would later quip in her feminist, postchristian introduction to *The Church and the Second Sex* (Boston: Beacon Press, 2002), 29, that in designating nuns as brides of Christ, convent life is imagined as "a sort of Divine Harem." Not only traditional Catholic but Anglican nuns thought of themselves as brides of Christ because, as Mumm points out in *Stolen Daughters*, 192, Anglican "sisterhoods often borrowed openly from Roman Catholic models." Manuela Mourao notes that the comparison of the convent to a harem was an established literary trope. Mourao, *Altered Habits: Reconsidering the Nun in Fiction* (Gainesville: University Press of Florida, 2002), 68.

tempted Jesus and Sister Clodagh falls from her high perch of pride.[13] Even though the nuns are initially inspired to attempt an assault on Mopu by interpreting the Himalayan site as the stairway to heaven, they try to impose the Christian topography of the transcendent white spirit on the colorful, voluptuous, embodied past of the old House of Women.[14] Yet as the film reviewer Herb Lightman was the first to appreciate, Alfred Junge designed the film sets of *Black Narcissus* to give not one but three points of view on Mopu. These show how the interiors were once enjoyed by the "natives" and have reverted back to nature; how the nuns have endeavored to whitewash this past; and how the old ways compete with the new and gradually creep back to take possession of Mopu again (*American Cinematographer*, December 1947: 456).

At 8,000 feet altitude, Mopu faces the peaks of Nanda Devi in the great Himalayan range at the top of the world. As the nuns walk the cliffs in prayer, they can look across at the dramatic, snow-capped, twin-peaked massif, which is revered by the locals in the film as "the Bare Goddess," and in reality, was also known as the "Bliss-giving Goddess." In Godden's novel, the indigenous people worship Kanchenjungha, the third highest mountain in the world, on the Indian-Nepalese border (Godden 1963: 85). In changing the location of Mopu, Powell and Pressburger drew attention to the mountainous and feminine sublime.[15]

[13] As he worked on corrections to the *Black Narcissus* screen script, Pressburger jotted down from memory the biblical passage where "the devil taketh him (Christ) up unto an exceeding high mountain, and sheweth him all the kingdoms of the world, and the glory of them." See the Michael Powell Special Collection, Box 4, item A-S-68, BFI Library.

[14] Richard Dyer argues that the mountain is a perfect symbol of Caucasian ascendancy in its "sublime, soul-elevating beauty (and) . . . greater nearness to God above." Dyer, *White* (London: Routledge, 2005), 21. The novel bears out this view. In response to Mr. Dean's complaint on 33 that Mopu is "no place to put a nunnery," one of the nuns cries, "Oh, how can you say that? . . . It might be Heaven . . . Who can live here and not feel close to God." *Staircase to Heaven* was the alternative title of the 1946 Powell and Pressburger film *A Matter of Life and Death*.

[15] While John Stone notes that Mount Kanchenjungha is on the Nepal–India border, it is, in fact, on the border of the Indian state of Sikkim. Stone, "Gothic in the Himalayas: Powell and Pressburger's *Black Narcissus*," *The Gothic Other: Racial and Social Constructions in the Literary Imagination*, ed. Ruth B. Anolik and Douglas L. Howard (Jefferson, N.C.: McFarland, 2004), 281n.14. See Mark Rawlinson's fascinating essay in which he discusses how and why Powell and Pressburger relocated *Black Narcissus* from the then unconquered Kanchenjungha to Nanda Devi, which was first climbed in 1936. Rawlinson, " 'Far more remote than it actually is': Rumer

Rumer Godden complained that "in the film the snows were white muslin blown up on bamboo poles" (1989: 52). As several critics have suggested, however, the English filmmakers were deliberately creating the visual impression that Mopu Palace is swathed mysteriously in layer upon layer of veils (Lassner 2004: 82; Stone 2004: 282n.21). As long as the nuns cannot recognize their own veiled desires—as long as sexuality is an aspect of religious life "shrouded in secrecy, denial, and mystery" (Sipe 1990: 4)—they will peer with uncomprehending eyes through the diaphanous veils of gauze, mist, wind, and snow that flash like will-o'-the-wisps past the camera and swirl around and through Mopu.

As he worked on the film script, Pressburger jotted down a quote from Swinburne—"Dead dreams of days forsaken, / Blind Gods that snows have shaken"—and the lines suggest how he visualized Mopu in his mind's eye.[16] A Christian and orientalist reading of these lines would be that the animistic spirits the locals revere, the Hindu deities decorating Mopu palace, and the pagan idols worshipped in India are the "blind gods" that the Anglican missionary must vanquish. Yet compared with the sunnyasi or holy man in the film who sits in rapt silence contemplating the majestic peaks opposite, the nuns are blind, worshipping their Christian God but unable to see the many sides of divinity in the mountains and people around them. Because one of their first tasks at Mopu was to conceal the nude figures adorning the interior walls, they are not disposed to discern the body of "the Bare Goddess" in the contours of Nanda Devi. Nor can they imagine its twin peaks as a pantheist projection of the breasts of the bliss-giving mother goddess whose body is the earth and whose lifeforce cascades down, like the great river sources of the Himalayas, into the human body and sexuality (Jantzen 1998: 265–6).

While these Anglo-Catholic nuns call themselves "the Servants of Mary" and give a family of holy women including the Blessed Mother and St. Elizabeth an honored devotional place in Mopu, they are not receptive to other cultural conceptions of sacred femininity.[17] Yet feminist and postcolonial theologians who engage in comparative religious

---

Godden's *Black Narcissus* and 1930s Mountain Writing," *Rumer Godden: International and Intermodern Storyteller*, ed. Lucy Le-Guilcher and Phyllis B. Lassner (Farnham U.K.: Ashgate, 2010), 39, 44–50.

[16] Michael Powell Special Collection, Box 4, item A-S-68, BFI Library.

[17] In the novel (56), the Blessed Mother has an extensive female court of attendants, which includes Saint Elizabeth, Saint Catherine, Saint Teresa, Saint Helen, and Saint Faith.

study have been inspired by the Hindu vision of Shakti as divine mother, dynamic feminine principle of the universe, and source of all cosmic energy (Gnanadason 1993: 351–3, 358–60). Godden herself was alive to this mystery and explained:

> India is always spoken and written of as "she" . . . the Indian "she" has something of the quality of her own great universal Goddess, Durga or Kali; she has many different aspects and many other names because she is manifold and has the feminine attributes of "shakti" or energy. She is the wife or female aspect of Shiva. (1989: 289)

During the final years that Godden lived in India, stretching from the publication of *Black Narcissus* in 1939 until 1945, the year before the film version was shot, she came to feel with increasing urgency that "I must have something; something, far beyond myself to hold to. For a long time I had thought it would be Hinduism" (1989: 70). Even after her return to England and Anglicanism, and subsequent conversion to Catholicism, Godden continued to look toward the far horizon, to respect the religious pluralism she grew up with India, and to remain drawn to Hinduism (Jenkins 2010; 183). Indeed, she asked the Jesuit bishop of Bombay, Thomas Roberts, who became her spiritual adviser, "what about all the holy spiritual people I have known . . . in India for instance . . . Hindus, Muslims, Buddhists, Zoroastrians? Are they to be shut out?" Reassured that this was not the case, she was reminded of the Jesuit poet Gerard Manley Hopkins's poem in which "Christ plays in ten thousand places, / lovely in limbs, and lovely in eyes not his" (1989: 242).

Yet the film represents colonial missionary sisters as not acculturated to search for Christ in the face of the other so much as to make the other see them as the face of Christ. When Sister Clodagh complains to Mr. Dean that the local holy man is squatting like a vagrant on convent grounds, he raises the uncomfortable possibility that she not only lacks charity but needs saving by pointedly asking, "What would Christ have done?"[18] It would be twenty years before Trappist monk Thomas Merton's writings, promoting respect for religious alterity, inter-faith dialogue, and belief that the wisdom of spiritual systems in the East could enrich Christian theology, began to take root and spread. As actual missionary nuns

---

[18] In the novel (62), Sister Clodagh dismisses the sunnyasi as "a dirty, ragged old man." Interestingly, Melanie Klein saw the house-proud domestic as giving sublimated "expression to her aggression in destroying the enemy, dirt, which in her unconscious mind has come to stand for 'bad' things." See *Love, Guilt and Reparation and other works* 1921–1945 (London: Virago Press, 1994), 311–12 n.1.

became conscious of their Christian participation in colonialism, their Eurocentric insularity and unthinking assumption of both Western and religious superiority, they would ask themselves the questions that begin to trouble Sister Clodagh and make *Black Narcissus* far-sighted: "Was the church required to convert these people, to control them, to ban them, or to learn from them?" (Chittister 2005: 38,75–6).

None of these questions initially occur to the nuns in *Black Narcissus* as they busy themselves covering up the Hindu statuary and erotic murals of Mopu. It is through the transgressive eye of the camera and Mr. Dean's close inspection of the Blue Room frescoes that we can see what the sisters studiously ignore: the exuberant nudity, dancing, and love-making, which blur the distinction between the sacred and profane, and shift focus from the Christian valorization of the soul to the Hindu appreciation of the sexual body as a dwelling place of the divine. A crucial moment of *darshan*, or Hindu glimpse of divinity, occurs as Ruth escapes her convent cell at Mopu. As she runs toward the camera along a narrow corridor, gossamer material can be detected fluttering from a figure obscured in the background. In her flight, she has accidentally dislodged the veil that the nuns used to hide a statue of Shiva, the god of destruction and transformation, and the male consort of the divine feminine. Michael Walker and Sarah Street read this unveiling as a signal of "the forces which will destroy the convent" (Walker 1978–79: 13; Street 2005: 50). However, Shiva was also revered as Nataraja, Lord of the dancers who are depicted on the frescoed walls of Mopu. Shiva Nataraja's cosmic dance of bliss (ananda tandava) within an arch of flames destroys illusion, begets wisdom, and simultaneously recreates life as it consumes the old order. Thus, the old Hindu beliefs, which the nuns have attempted to obliterate, make an uncanny return at the end of the film. These beliefs celebrate the human intimation of the divine through eroticism (Brown 2007: 37–8, 71–6; Carr 2003: 80, 145). Shiva is literally the *deus absconditus*, the hidden or concealed god in *Black Narcissus*, and his unveiling alludes to the repressed link between sex and religion.

In his study of Leonardo Da Vinci, Freud argued that such sacred symbols as the male *lingam* and the female *yoni* can be interpreted as relics of an early stage of human development when "the genitals were the pride and hope of living beings" and, through a fundamental process of sublimation, "were worshipped as gods." He concluded that with the advance of culture and civilization, divine meaning was drained from sexuality and official religions lost touch with their libidinal roots, leading to the diminishment of both sex and the sacred (1910, *SE* 11: 97;

Loewald 1988: 11). Indeed, Godden recalled her delight in informing her daughter's prudish headmistress that the family had "lived in India where the lingam—the phallus, in erection—is holy; it, and the yoni, the hole in the ground, symbol of the female organ, are sacred and worshipped" (1989: 80). The tantric play of Shiva and his faithful wife, Parvati—commemorated by the graceful dalliance of the figures in the Mopu murals—restores sacred significance to eroticism and exults in the union of the sexed body and the godhead.[19] At the same time, the intricacy of the dancers' moves suggests that sublimation does not recover an original unitary oneness but rather achieves what Loewald calls a new, manifold, and "differentiated unity" that reconciles polarities but preserves difference (1988: 23–4). The polygamous couplings on the harem wall gesture that divine love is pluriform and extends to many people and religions (Carr 2003: 174–5).

While the ithyphallic symbol was important in the worship of Shiva, at the same time this Hindu deity was venerated as "the great ascetic," and thus has affinities with both the celibate nuns who occupy Mopu and the sunnyasi who has made his hermitage on their grounds. Shiva's identity as both a phallic and an ascetic god is not a sign of the mind-body dualism that has racked Christianity, but rather of sublimation in which celibacy and eroticism become congruent as Shiva's intense sexual desire for Parvati is alchemized into pure divine energy and power (Abbott 2000: 164–70). Shiva is a reminder to celibates that religious disconnection from sexuality can lead to extreme asceticism and to repressive practices that Elizabeth Petroff rightly calls "dangerously erotic. For the attempt to deny the body through certain bodily practices turns the smallest act of physical gratification . . . into a stunning sensual experience" (1979: 34). Mopu and its Indian inhabitants—from the young Indian General (Sabu) wearing the heavy musk cologne named "black narcissus" to the meretricious slave

[19] Parvati is the daughter of the mountains and a female avatar of Shakti. Madhu Khanna notes that while Parvati and Shakti are often represented as long-suffering goddesses in patriarchal and Brahmanical Hinduism, in heterodox Tantra Hinduism, Shiva, the male principle, is static and requires dynamic union with Shakti, the active, female principle, for "the potent energy of the goddess is the source of empowerment of her male consort." Khanna, "The Goddess–Woman Equation in Sakta Tantras," *Gendering the Spirit: Women, Religion and the Post-Colonial Response*, ed. Durre S. Ahmed (London: Zed Books, 2002), 35–6, 38–40. Stone notes that Mopu is located along the transmission route of Tantric Buddhism and that the embracing figures in the Blue Room of Mopu may illustrate tantric practices. Stone, "Gothic in the Himalayas," 282n.22.

girl Kanchi (Jean Simmons)—virtually bombard the nuns with sensual experiences that are as potent as mind-altering drugs. Indeed, the native girl Kanchi was played by a heavily bronzed Jean Simmons, an actress who was noted, like Deborah Kerr, for her English beauty and refinement. This hidden resemblance suggests that the sultry Kanchi was not the polar opposite of the ascetic Sister Clodagh but another embodiment of the sexual desire that the nun believes she has surmounted.[20]

A colonial "can-do" mentality has led this sister superior to believe that she can stifle her own sexual nature, stamp her authority on Mopu, and impose order on the surrounding wild. Yet in a later confession of missionary failure and powerlessness to Mr. Dean, Sister Clodagh will finally admit, "I couldn't turn out the holy man; I couldn't stop the wind from blowing and the air from being as clear as crystal; and I couldn't hide the mountain." Queer theorist Stephen Bourne rightly describes these lines as "sheer poetry . . . central to the film . . . telling us what is natural cannot be contained, or restrained. It has to flow" (1996: 86).[21] Rather than regard the mountain winds of Mopu as the forces disrupting her prayer, work, and sleep, she can go with the "flow" that expresses the fluid nature of her own longings. From a polarized Christian perspective, this wind may symbolize the distractions that hinder the single-hearted pursuit of religious life.[22] However, from a psychoanalytic point of view, it can also indicate the stirring of sublimatory power (Loewald 1988: 38). Going with this flow might lead to epiphanies: that the "Wild air, world-mothering air, / Nestling me everywhere" (Gerard Manley Hopkins, "The Blessed Virgin compared to the Air we Breathe," 1–2) is the sacred breath of the Blessed Virgin Mary this nun serves, or the cosmic energy of the Hindu gods and goddesses the locals worship, or the Holy Spirit, which blows where it wishes (John 3:8).[23]

---

[20] One of the few things Rumer Godden liked about the film version of *Black Narcissus* was the casting of Jean Simmons who "perfectly fulfilled (her) description of Kanchi . . . 'like a basket of fruit piled high, luscious and ready to eat.'" See Godden's memoir *A House with Four Rooms* (New York: William Morrow, 1989), 52, and the discussion of Street, *Black Narcissus*, 24–5.

[21] See Street's discussion of how lesbian and feminist directors have been inspired to read *Black Narcissus* in her chapter on revival and appropriation of the film, 75–84.

[22] In Godden's novel, Father Roberts, the nuns' chaplain, worries, "to-day, I somehow felt I'd lost you. You're none of you as single-hearted as you were" (130).

[23] Rita M. Gross suggests that just as in the past "the goddesses of the ancient world became the Virgin Mary," so the present global migration of religious symbols

Catholic Censorship of the Film

Despite its broad-minded study of the psychosexual strains of the religious life and the cultural disorientation of missionaries in an alien environment, vocal interest groups in the American Catholic community joined forces with their film censorship watchdog, the Legion of Decency (LOD), to condemn *Black Narcissus*. In explicitly linking religion and sex, the film left an audience in no doubt that nuns were not plaster-cast saints but flesh-and-blood women. The profane, Freudian, and sexual symbolism embedded in a film about women religious was a cause of particular distaste to the LOD (Street 2005: 69–70). Even before filming began, Joseph Breen, Catholic Head of the Hollywood Production Code Administration (PCA), anticipated serious trouble from the LOD. After seeing an early draft of the narrative in 1945, he worried that, "the slightest implication of sex sin or sexual longings or desires on the part of the women consecrated to religion, would give great offense to religious-minded folk in this country" (Street 2005: 65–6). However, the measured reviews of the American secular press do not suggest disapproval of the film, but rather of Catholic narrow-mindedness, puritanism, censorship, and blacklisting of *Black Narcissus*. *The New Republic*'s Shirley O'Hara noted that "this picture has been objected to by religious organizations on the ground that . . . it is offensive to show women in whose heads and hearts there sometimes exist doubts or desires or worldly confusion." She countered that *Black Narcissus* was "a most superior British film," honest in its depiction of the interior trials of the religious life, and deemed it "a notably virtuous picture" (September 15, 1947: 37). *Newsweek* was similarly surprised by "the storm of protest registered against this sensitive study of missionaries in the Himalayas by more than 300 Roman Catholic nuns and priests in conference last month at Notre Dame University," and maintained that apart from Sister Ruth, "the nuns . . . are represented as splendid, steadfast women." The critic concluded that "whatever its minor faults, this is a strangely disturbing film, full of subtle antagonisms, and adult and sympathetic in treatment" (August 18, 1947: 77–8). *Life* magazine was likewise puzzled by the vociferous Catholic objection to *Black Narcissus* when "the film's preface . . . carefully points out that these are Anglican nuns who are sworn to their vows for only

---

across cultural borders may lead to a counter movement in which Asian goddesses are revered in Western Christian and post-Christian religion. See her essay on "Feminist Theology as Theology of Religions," in *The Cambridge Companion to Feminist Theology*, ed. Susan Frank Parsons (Cambridge: Cambridge University Press, 2002), 72–3.

a year at a time." The review slyly alluded to the fact that Powell and Pressburger had dispensed with the deferential, "kid gloves" treatment that *The Bells of St. Mary's* gave American Catholic nuns only two years earlier in 1945 by dramatizing the turbulent desires, longings, and regrets that Anglican missionaries kept hidden beneath their veil and habit: "The film's treatment of religion is so unlike Hollywood's honeyed, idealized portrayals that the Catholic National Legion of Decency has condemned it." It noted without comment in closing that "the Anglican Church has made no statement," as if to say, why then did Catholics play their Protestant brethren's keeper (September 1, 1947: 55).

Black Narcissus obtained a PCA certificate of approval after Breen wrote a foreword reassuring an American audience that the subjects were not Catholic nuns who took perpetual vows but Anglican sisters who renewed them annually and worked far away in the remote reaches of the British Indian empire (*Variety*, July 8, 1947: 3; Street 2005: 66–7). This did not placate the LOD, which defiantly gave the film a *C* rating on the grounds that it was "an affront to religion . . . ignores the spiritual motivation which is the foundation and safeguard of religious life, and offensively tends to characterize such life as an escape for the abnormal, neurotic, and frustrated" (*Variety*, August 14, 1947: 4). In a rare political showdown with the PCA, American Catholic censors succeeded through this pressure in obtaining crucial cuts to the American release of *Black Narcissus* that defaced Powell and Pressburger's artistic achievement and mangled the core meaning of the film.[24] Ironically, in the severity they showed toward *Black Narcissus* and the zeal with which they lobbied to suppress its creative vision, they demonstrated the reaction formation consistent with repression (Loewald 1988: 39–40). As the film itself shows, extreme repression can lead to irrational prejudice, neurotic fixation, or unhealthy vigilance with regard to sexuality, and outbursts of anger, aggression, and anxiety in people who pride themselves on being good and virtuous (Carr 2003: 86).

In a Powell and Pressburger retrospective held in 1980 at New York's Museum of Modern Art, William Everson argued that the cuts made to the American release of *Black Narcissus* exemplified "the idiocies of

---

[24] I thank Professor Thomas Doherty for not only discussing the censorship issues raised by this film, but also forwarding the 1947 film report, which indicates that the PCA and LOD were at odds. *Variety* noted on December 8, 1947 that "British-made 'Black Narcissus' made . . . hasty concessions when confronted with a Catholic thumb-down; and while the shears were at work and a new finale being tacked on, Universal-International withdrew the J. Arthur Rank film from release" (7).

American censorship some thirty years ago" (November 20, 1980 – January 5, 1981). These cuts were directed at the moments that explicitly reveal what *The Bells of St. Mary's* was careful only to intimate—that the nun has a sexual past and erotic memories. The result was the ruinous decision to eliminate all of Sister Clodagh's vivid flashbacks to a youthful romance in Ireland. Detachment from such personal memories was a spiritual objective in traditional religious formation, as my discussion of *The Nun's Story* (1959) in Chapter 3 will show. It could thus be argued that Catholic censors were only respecting this established practice when they eradicated all visual traces of the nun's former life from the film. Everson reasoned that the flashbacks also "raised the possibility that some nuns might recall the past wistfully, and question whether their choice had been the right one." Yet when the Legion of Decency insisted that these be removed, they not only cut the heart out of the main character but out of *Black Narcissus*. For only through the film flashbacks can Mopu be seen as the bridge between the nun's past and present life. They reveal that Sister Clodagh has taken vows in order to disavow an old love affair. Until she acknowledges the house she once occupied as a woman, she will never find rest in the house of faith as a religious. The flashbacks thus hold the key to Sister Clodagh's conversion experience from repression to sublimation in the religious life.

Preface to the Film Flashbacks

In an opening film scene of surprising harshness, Sister Clodagh is told by her Reverend Mother that she has been promoted to superior only to be bluntly informed that she is too self-important to lead a community of nuns to Mopu. Mother Dorothea (Nancy Roberts) reminds Sister Clodagh that while she may be the youngest sister superior in the Order of the Servants of Mary, "the superior of all is the servant of all." It is often assumed that this chastisement reflects the paradox I examined in Chapter 1: that women religious in leadership positions—whether portrayed as school principals like Sister Benedict or representatives of British colonial power like Sister Clodagh—were expected to conceal their personal pride behind a feminine facade of subservience and subsume their career ambitions under the religious ideology of self-sacrifice (Deleyto 2001: 124–5; Hunter 1984: 38, 89). However, this account does not give the whole picture. The flashbacks later in the film flesh out the emotional truth behind Clodagh's exceptional rise in her order. They show Con (Shaun Noble), the man she loved, dreaming of a career abroad and not marriage to her, and indeed questioning her own lack of ambition. They show further that her sense of self-importance and superiority as a nun originated as a defensive gesture to protect herself from the social stigma of personal rejection and humiliation by leaving him "first"—before he could leave her—for the convent.[25] Mother Dorothea's prediction that the young nun will be "lonely" seems especially astute. She is warning Sister Clodagh that a lust for power is the special temptation of religious celibates who have repressed their feelings and find compensatory pleasure in the religious discipline and control of subordinates (Sipe 1990: 84).

Over the course of the film, Sister Clodagh must thus come to terms with the fact that her motives for entering the convent were far from pure. Her hauteur in rising through the ranks of a religious class elevated above common people and aloof from their demeaning lives helped to distance her from a love affair that ended unhappily. Her privileged social status as an Anglican colonial missionary, joining the chosen few who would help rule the empire, enabled her to save face in a small, close-knit, Anglo-Irish community expecting news of Con's marriage proposal. As she finally admits to the disreputable British agent Mr. Dean—a man she first treated with cool contempt—her religious life has been founded on repression of the past and denial of its enduring influence: "I had forgotten everything until I came here. The first day I came, I thought of him for the first time in years. I went back to the first time I loved him when we were children." Yet the film suggests this disclosure is not a spiritual defeat but a breakthrough. In an interview with Powell, Everson marveled at the warmth that suddenly lights up Kerr's Sister Clodagh from within as she tremulously talks about her past (2003: 103). In suppressing the painful memory of a formative love affair, she has actually stifled her passion for life itself. Her unconscious defense mechanism reflects what Lorde sees as the grave danger of separating the spiritual from the erotic and so "thereby reducing the spiritual to a world of flattened affect, a world of the ascetic who aspires to feel nothing" (1984: 56)—and to forget everything.

Sister Clodagh's Flashbacks

In his audio commentary on the film, Scorsese described Sister Clodagh as a "character burning inside," a description that is visually borne out by

---

[25] The novel makes clear that she is deeply ashamed of the "secret unworthy reason" (159) she had for entering the convent.

Deborah Kerr's fire-and-ice persona. Fear of this fire within accounts for the nun's coolness and priggishness, especially toward the pleasure-loving Dean, and for her projection of angry emotions onto Ruth. Yet Mopu excites passionate and irrepressible memories, and the mysterious forces at work in this place beckon her to see them as erotic illuminations of the religious present. The vibrant, joyous, and quasi-mystical quality of Sister Clodagh's four flashbacks makes it difficult to read them as spiritual failings in the nun. Their seamless incorporation into the text through the editing device of dissolves intensifies the impression that they are not distractions, but rather pathways to interiority. Powell and Pressburger created visual memories that capture the sense of "flow" in conveying the nun's rapt and ecstatic absorption in the past. In eliding the distance between her past youth and the present, her sexual feelings as a woman and her spiritual life as a religious, the dissolves illustrate how flow does away with the awareness of duality and division. The rapid fade out of one scene or image into another defines this inner state further as one in which "action follows action according to an internal logic, with no apparent need for conscious intervention" (Turner 1978: 254). These shimmering memories suddenly transfigure the pale, impassive face of Sister Clodagh and shed light on the mystery of her deep forgotten self. Walker rightly observed that "from all points of view—timing, relationship to the present psychological implications, visual beauty, emotional resonances—they are among the most stunning flashbacks in the cinema" (Walker 1978–79: 10; Sheehan, *Film Comment* 1990: 38–9).

These stunning flashbacks convey the erotic vitality and enjoyment that shine through in sublimation (Loewald 1988: 38). All four show how radiant, passionate, and unprepared for rejection Sister Clodagh was as a young woman. However, sublimation requires the removal of repression. The admission of fellow missionary Sister Phillippa that she can no longer "forget everything in chapel," but "remember(s) things before I joined our order, things I wanted to forget," precipitates Clodagh's first recollection.[26] As the convent horticulturalist, Sister Phillippa is most alive to the elemental power of the mountainous landscape, and she struggles to explain how the vista mysteriously heightens sensibility, amplifies memory, and extends vision outward by exclaiming helplessly

[26] Jo Ann Kay McNamara notes that nuns were trained to forget their history. McNamara, *Sisters in Arms: Catholic Nuns Through Two Millennia* (Cambridge: Harvard University Press, 1996), 632. Jaikumar observes that "amnesia becomes a necessary part of serving in the colonies." Jaikumar, "'Place' and the Modernist Redemption of Empire in *Black Narcissus*," 72.

to Sister Clodagh, "I think you can see too far." Her intriguing suggestion that Mopu gives strange, new, and unsettling powers of sight acts as
an exegesis on the flashbacks that follow.

Sister Clodagh's first recollection occurs as she kneels before the altar
and is transported into the past by the sunlight streaming through the
chapel window. The dramatic shot on this book's cover shows the cross,
which casts a shadow on her face. The shadow of the cross is a powerful visual reminder that, historically, nuns accepted celibacy as a "little
crucifixion" and "white martyrdom," but it also underlines the sacred
quality of her remembrances (Bernstein 1976: 111; Wright 1996: 87).
The camera pans from her face to the chapel window, which is given
a pre-Raphaelite quality by the flowers hanging down against the sky.
This is indeed a moment richly layered with Anglo-Catholic symbolism
because traditional nuns schooled to death of the self were told to think
of themselves as glass that would eventually break and be replaced by
an identical pane (Bernstein 1976: 350). The sexless mystery of the Annunciation, in which Mary conceived a divine son while remaining *virgo
intacta*, was compared to light passing through a clear windowpane without piercing it (Warner 1990: 44). However, Powell and Pressburger's
flashbacks are magic casements that do not alter the laws of nature, deny
women religious a sexed body, or sacrifice the personal identity of nuns.
While Clodagh's face is pinched and pale in a wimple, the flashback
opens up her countenance and captures the visage of her youth, hair
blowing, complexion blooming, expression warm and animated. It visualizes a time that Bergman's Sister Benedict dreamily alluded to in *The
Bells of St. Mary's*—when the nun had not yet taken the veil and was a
desirable and desiring female.

As prayer segues into the recollection of the first flashback, the voice
of Sister Clodagh's younger self is heard exclaiming, "Oh, isn't it a grand
day," and the light-flooded chapel window dissolves into the dazzling
waters of the Irish lake where "Clo" is seen happily fishing in long shot.
This scene economically conveys Clo's blind love for the self-centered
"Con" who sulks indifferently by the shore, although she is as fair as
the maiden Echo in the myth of Narcissus. It is also a vivid reminder of
her "Irishness"—her auburn-haired, country-girl beauty, her deep, soulful affinity with nature, and her love for her homeland—which will be
whitewashed by the habit of Anglican colonialism. Her spiritually restless
and dissatisfied boyfriend will join the tide of male emigration that left
many women high and dry between the Wars (Nicholson 2007: 13, 23,
82–3). However, Clo treasures her roots and regards settling down to

married life in Ireland as her natural and desired fate: "No, I don't want to go away. I want to stay here like this for the rest of my life." Powell's camera also endows this enchanting scene with a mythopoeic character. As she stands knee-deep in water, Clo faintly resembles a Botticelli Venus at the same time that her sport foreshadows the fact that she will not follow Con to America but Christ to India: "Follow me, and I will make you fish for people" (Matt. 4:19).

A close shot dissolve of Clo's happy face back into the pensive, pained face of a nun underlines the total involvement that characterizes the flow of her memories. The first memory then runs on into a second and even more exultant flashback, with a fast tracking shot of a rural hunt, two figures on horseback galloping across the Irish countryside, rider and horse as one, leaping together for the sheer joy of being alive. This is a scene that conveys indescribable *jouissance*. As she relives the moment, an involuntary smile of corresponding bliss lights up and transforms Sister Clodagh's face, revealing this religious overachiever as a beautiful woman still in her prime. Yet again, the nun's green memory has a mythopoeic richness—suggesting Clo's likeness to Artemis-Diana, the goddess of chastity who is depicted "windblown and free, surrounded by hunting dogs" (Doody 1997: 447), but perhaps also alluding to the hound of heaven who will capture her for his kingdom.

The third flashback occurs later in the film and is occasioned by the sisters' idle gossip about the sumptuous dress and jewelry of the spoiled Indian princeling whom they reluctantly agree to tutor. It reinforces a cumulative sense of oceanic feeling as Sister Clodagh lets the past come flooding back into her mind and so discovers "far other Worlds, and other Seas; / annihilating all that's made / to a green Thought in a green Shade (Marvell, "The Garden," 6.43–8). In this green saturated scene, Clo materializes in a mint evening dress, auburn hair curling on her milky shoulders, lips deep pink and sensual. She tries on a suite of emeralds that her grandmother has promised her when she marries Con, and admires her appearance in the mirror as she awaits the arrival of the man who is planning to leave her behind. However, the emeralds are another symbolic reminder of her attachment not only to Con but to the emerald isles. They are also a prefiguration of the Anglican vocation in which she will forget her Irish identity, for the emerald is the green stone of chastity and spiritual aspiration (Doody 1997: 471).[27]

[27] I'm grateful to Professor Kevin Rockett of Trinity College, Dublin for suggesting that I emphasize Clo's Irishness.

In the much-admired conclusion of this scene, she hears Con whistle for her to come outside—as if she is his horse or hound. The camera tracks her as she runs eagerly through the front door into a frame of "black nothing," calling: "Where are you Con?" (Powell and Scorsese: 2000). Her cry in the dark betokens the hollow heart of her lover, her future depression after rejection, and the erotic vacuum that she tries to fill by joining a religious "order of workers."[28] However, the capacity for sublimation depends on a core passion that disappears down a black hole in Clodagh's life. Sister Ruth begins her slow, monstrous gestation in the closing darkness of this flashback, and will come to personify the psychosexual void in the nun's life (Jaikumar 2001: 67). As John Stone cleverly concluded, it is not the Indian native or the white male but the Anglican nun who becomes "the unknowable Other, the site and source of Gothic horror" (2004: 269, 276).

Repression is a defense against the strain of mental conflict and contrariety, a defense well suited to colonial rule because it involves the domination and exclusion of disturbing or disruptive instincts. Sublimation requires a new type of mastery—not of the other but of the otherness in the self—a coming to terms with what has been hidden and defended against, a reconciliation of what has become separated or split (Loewald 1988: 13, 41). The fourth and final flashback is the most significant, but gets no discussion in Walker's Freudian analysis of "the return of the repressed" (1978–79: 10), and only cursory mention by Sarah Street in her British Film Guide study of *Black Narcissus* (2005: 45). Yet it is a crucial step toward sublimation's work of reconciliation because it explicitly links Dean to Con, and connects Sister Clodagh's tense, tight, and touchy persona as a nun to the personal and sexual disappointment she suffered in the past.

Once again, Sister Clodagh drifts into reminiscence while in chapel, this time during a Christmas carol service. There could be no more suitable location for such a commemorative event since the set designer, Alfred Junge, conceived the chapel as the room the nuns converted from a disused stable (Lightman, *American Cinematographer*, December 1947: 456). Faint traces of Clodagh's Irish rural past thus pervade this place of worship and carry evocative significance at Christmas in their allusion to the sacredness of the lowly flesh. Dean drunkenly gate-crashes this

---

[28] Freud argued in his 1910 essay on Leonardo Da Vinci (*SE* 11: 77–8) that "most people succeed in directing very considerable portions of their sexual instinctual forces to their professional activity."

charming scene and, like the ox and the ass, disturbs the peace by his loud but spirited singing of the carol "Lullay my Lyking." This tender lullaby—in which the Blessed Mother croons the baby Jesus asleep with rhythmic endearments—is an appropriate hymn for the Servants of Mary who have brought the maternal icons of their faith to Mopu. The lullaby is a reminder of the semiotic origins not only of language but of the Incarnation in the body that must be cradled, caressed, and cared for. Like the Freudian uncanny, the lullaby is also a reminder that past needs live on in the present. As Elizabeth Grosz commented, the subject may be most affected by the semiotic in "moments of crisis and psychical upheaval" (1992: 195).

The semiotic melody of "Lullay my Lyking" thus serves as a medium for deep and inexpressible feelings. These suggest the original unity of the sacred and the sexual, for although the lyrics are sung by the Virgin Mary to the Christ Child, they have the tenor of a passionate love song and show that Christian devotion is a response not only of the spirit but of the sensuous body desiring to be in intimate touch with the divine. This is why Dean's fine voice stirs erotic sentiments that the nun thought were dead, particularly those associated with her last memory of her lover. A close-up of Sister Clodagh singing the refrain "Lullay my dere heart, myn own dere darling," her face alight with happiness, dissolves to a medium long shot in which she and Con are singing this same carol together in the snow. What makes this last flashback particularly poignant is that it has all the hallmarks of a proposal scene. Con slips a jewelry box into Clo's hand. She opens it by lantern light and inspects the brooch that he has given her with obvious delight. A dissolve back to the chapel registers the nun's smile of *jouissance* in recollecting this moment before a look of severity clouds the sister superior's face once more—for the box did not contain an engagement ring, and only later will Clo realize that the brooch was Con's parting gift to her.

The shock, crushing disappointment, and humiliation of this realization have been rigorously repressed but return with sudden, irrational fury when the chapel scene dissolves to the external courtyard after the carol service. As Freud so insightfully pointed out, the acquaintances of later life can inherit our feelings for the objects of primary love and hatred. Their hapless lot is to "encounter sympathies and antipathies to the production of which they themselves have contributed little."[29] Thus,

[29] See Freud's "Some Reflections on Schoolboy Psychology" (1914), *SE* 13: 243.

85

Dean now bears the brunt of Sister Clodagh's anger, and an offhand reference to Christ triggers a sharp rebuke—"We don't speak of *Him* so casually." Dean retorts by reminding her that the Lord's Prayer emphasized the holy quality of the here-and-now and the presence of the divine in the basic matters of everyday life: "He should be casual and as much a part of life as your daily bread." However, Sister Clodagh does not heed the call for forgiveness at the heart of this prayer that Jesus taught his followers, and proceeds to berate Dean for his drunkenness: "You are unforgivable." Her holier-than-thou attitude in this scene is a displacement of deep-seated bitterness over Con's "casual" affection and "unforgivable" dalliance with her deep love. In response, Dean mocks her self-righteousness by serenading her with the vaudeville lyrics—"No, I won't be a nun! No, I cannot be a nun! For I am so fond of *Pleasure*! I cannot be a nun!"—as he makes his own rowdy exit from Mopu on pony. His irreverent humor probes the fault line in her vocation. The religious renunciation of desire is never simple, and repression itself can provide "covert forms of pleasure of which the consciousness is kept blissfully ignorant" (Miles 1989: 77).

Postcolonial critics of *Black Narcissus* have interpreted this sarcastic male figure as a cynical colonial agent who has gone native. He is also, however, the provocative agent of Sister Clodagh's spiritual transformation. Through her unlikely and unorthodox friendship with this man, the nun comes to decipher the core message of her flashbacks—that, as Rowan Williams, Archbishop of Canterbury, advised, "all those taking up the single vocation must know something about desiring and being desired if their vocation is not to be sterile" (2002: 317). In a confessional scene that is reminiscent of *The Keys of the Kingdom* (1944) and that occurs near the climax of the film, Dean sits down on the outer terrace wall of Mopu, face sensitively averted, and assumes the posture of sympathetic listener and adviser. Sister Clodagh stands tall and proud as she confides in him. Both Anglican and Catholic communities were alert to the dangers of close friendships, whether within or outside the convent (Mumm 1999: 75–6; Campbell-Jones 1978: 86). It would therefore have been seen as a grave breach of chastity for a sister superior to make intimate disclosures to such a profane man, especially when they raise the possibility that she could have lost her virginity to her lover, and it is a miracle that the scene survived the Catholic censors' cuts.[30] Yet this scene is

---

[30]Street speculates that this scene escaped censorship because its verbal dialogue was not feared to have the same impact as the visual images in the flashbacks

crucial in resolving the impasse in her religious life. She acknowledges her present failure to gain control—over Mopu, convent life, the native people, the natural environment, or indeed her own nature. She lets down the celibate's impregnable guard and painfully acknowledges what her flashbacks have made her see—that her entrance into the convent was a flight from passionate vulnerability: "In a little place like that, I'd shown that I loved him and couldn't stay." Her readiness now to expose herself to Dean's possible derision or seduction is a significant spiritual advance. She has begun to understand the sacred meaning of the summit the locals revere as the "Bare Goddess." On Dean's part, we see a new respect for the nun as a person, a surprising capacity for emotional intimacy and tenderness, and the stirrings of genuine friendship that run counter to his reputation for the sexual pursuit of women.

Conclusion to Black Narcissus

When Sister Clodagh makes the hard decision to abandon Mopu, she is learning that the soul cannot make headway in the journey up the holy mountain without a corresponding movement downward and deeper into embodiment. Her desperate fight with the murderous Ruth at the climax of the film can thus be read as a decisive struggle with the sexual past and tenacious desires that she has tried to split off from her religious vocation. In a film suffused with ambiguity, Ruth's fatal plunge off the steep cliff of Mopu recapitulates the original fall and at the same time, collapses the distinction between the higher existence of the spirit and lower life of the body. In a handwritten script note, which seems both strangely out of place and fitting to the tragic close of Black Narcissus, Pressburger quoted a passage from Isaiah that Handel celebrated in his Messiah.

> Every valley shall be exalted, and every mountain and hill shall be made low: and the crooked shall be made straight, and the rough places plain: and the glory of the Lord shall be revealed, and all flesh shall be revealed together: for the mouth of the Lord had spoken it. (Isa. 40:4)[31]

(Black Narcissus, 45–6). I am especially indebted to her comprehensive account of the history of the film's censorship in her chapter on reception.

[31] The quotation is followed by a single exclamation—"Wow!" See Michael Powell Special Collection, Box 4, item A-S-68, BFI Library.

Black Narcissus is more than sixty years old, but the film examines a subject that is still regarded as prurient, improper, and disrespectful today, which is the place of sexuality in the religious life (Boswell 1994: 372n.2). Sister Ruth's melodramatic hysteria, madness, and death have allowed critics to evade this uncomfortable subject by analyzing sex as a psycho-pathological force among the nuns of Mopu. However, this emphasis does not do justice to the film's valiant heroine Sister Clodagh, or to the profound way in which her flashbacks and charged exchanges with Dean open up the definition of sexuality and advance a vision of eros that will alter the direction of her religious life. In a final scene that was regrettably deleted from the film, Mother Dorothea's interview with the nun after her return to Calcutta makes it clear that she has undergone a spiritual metamorphosis: "I seem to find a new Clodagh, one whom I had long prayed to meet."[32]

How, in the final analysis, can we read the bond that develops between this nun and layman? When asked by an interviewer why he chose to make a film of *Black Narcissus*, Powell did not make the expected reply. What interested him was not the East / West dichotomy that postcolonial critics have focused on, but something more old-world and chivalrous. He saw *Black Narcissus* as "a very beautiful love story. In an unusual setting" (Lacourbe and Grivel 2003: 53). This answer plays with, but also subverts, the romantic expectations of a mainstream film audience. Although there is no future for this love story and no question of actual lovemaking between Sister Clodagh and Dean, this does not mean, as Walker argues, that there is no "recognition of on his part love and on hers sex" (1978–79: 10). The common assumption of such a reading is that sexual attraction can only lead to a desire for physical intercourse and cannot bring two people together in other ways, and conversely, that all sexuality has been filtered out of the religious life making it impossible for a nun to "show" someone she loves them. However, Sister Clodagh learns that eros cannot and should not be wholly repressed in the religious life and Mr. Dean demonstrates by his uncharacteristically honorable behavior in the film that sexuality is not always genitally expressed. Thus, *Black Narcissus* raises issues that are crucial not only to religious, but all walks of life: how the sexual body can be affirmed without being seduced; how sexual desire can be sublimated; and how individuals can keep their passion and energy as sexed women and men alive while re-

[32] Michael Powell Special Collection, Box 4, item S-68A, BFI Library. See also Powell's discussion of his regrets over deleting this scene in *A Life in Movies*, 623–4.

Figure 2-1. With this parting gesture, the nun is no longer untouchable as Sister Clodagh acknowledges her emotional intimacy with Mr. Dean.

maining faithful to their calling and commitments (Brown 2007: 20, 54, 420; Carr 2003: 34–5).

Roy Stafford sees male colonial rule affirmed over emotional susceptibility to women at the end of the film: "The price Dean pays for maintaining his control is the loss of Clodagh; and the measure of this loss is evident in the final understated scene."[33] I see the power of erotic sublimation affirmed in the sensuous but non-sexual intimacy that is finally depicted between Sister Clodagh and Dean. They have come to accept each other for who they are and are reconciled to the fact that they will follow very different paths in life. If hers eventually leads to what Godden later called "the greatest love story in the world" (1989: 279)—between the nun and God—it will be because her chaste but charged relationship with Dean has helped her find that path. The only intimacy that is open to them is "closeness-in-distance" (Loewald 1988: 58), which illustrates sublimation's dynamic synthesis of connection and

[33] National Film Theatre Programme Notes, BFI Library, n.d.

divergence. The central gesture that expresses the discovery of this bit-tersweet intimacy is their final farewell in the film. In what Powell called a "High Romantic" close (2000: 624), Sister Clodagh does not shake hands with Dean but rather lays her hand palm up in his and allows it to rest there. Sister Clodagh's graceful gesture is the eloquent body language of tactile connection (Walker 1978–79: 12). It mimes the spoon position of sleeping lovers—as well as that primary need to be cradled by and feel close to another—and is her way of saying how deeply he has touched her (Milhaven 1994: 85–90; Timmerman 1994: 100–1). If *Black Narcissus* ends by representing the celibate nun as no longer untouchable, the final moments of the film are reserved for Dean who, as Powell envisaged it, strains through the sudden downpour of the rains "for one last look of his beloved Sister Clodagh" (Powell 2000: 624). This straining to see in parting is a perfect visual metaphor of sublimation's striving for "unity in the act of separating" (Loewald 1988: 24).

Introduction to *Heaven Knows, Mr. Allison* (1957) and *Sea Wife* (1957)

The persistent fear of the postwar Catholic Church in the late 1940s and 50s was that vocations were dwindling and defections from the convent were increasing. This concern was unfounded in America but justified in Europe where *Black Narcissus* was produced (Curran 1989: 133, 145, 155; Ebaugh 1993b: 38; Sullivan 2005: 126–7). Was the film seen as spreading contagion to American shores by using Anglican nuns as a thinly veiled parable of the decline and fall of modern convent life, and was it feared that the dramatic collapse of these Anglican sisters would demoralize Catholic nuns in active service? Certainly the conveners of a confer-ence on religious vocations at Notre Dame University in July 1947 were worried enough to write a letter not only to the PCA but partner film distributors, the Rank Organization and Universal-International. They warned that the film was bad publicity for their cause and furthermore, that it traduced the heroic image nuns had earned in the Second World War and on the missionary frontier.

> To imply that this isolated series of incidents is a typical instance of what goes on in convents and of what happens when Sisters are sent by their vow of obedience, freely made, to the foreign missions, would be diametrically opposed, for example, to the first-hand observation and experience of innumerable G.I.s, many of whom

were … nursed, helped, cheered, comforted, and edified by the nuns themselves. (Street 2005: 69)

The two films that close this chapter were only too happy to cheer and edify a popular audience by dramatizing nuns as the comrades-in-arms of men in the theater of war. Although John Huston's *Heaven Knows, Mr. Allison* and Bob McNaught's *Sea Wife* were made a decade after *Black Narcissus*, they fall back on the assumptions that Powell and Pressburger so evocatively deconstructed—that celibacy is a state devoid of sexuality and religious life is maintained through rigorous repression of desire (Boswell 1994: 363). Both films tease an audience with their respectful, restrained, romantic depiction of the nun's vulnerability to male sexual overtures and temptation in wartime, without the living cloister of the habit and convent to protect her. The British-made *Black Narcissus* was a marked departure from Hollywood's penchant for "honeyed, idealized portrayals" of nuns with proven box-office appeal (*Life*, September 1,1947: 55). Only two years later, however, the 1949 film *Come to the Stable* reverted to type when Loretta Young and Celeste Holm played sisters positively coated in corn syrup who belong to the French "Order of Holy Endeavour." Like Sister Clodagh, they are Trojan workers, and like Sister Benedict, they never take no for an answer. An awe-struck bishop echoes Father O'Malley's view that they are "an irresistible force against which there is no defense and hasn't been for two thousand years." At the same time, this postwar film heralded the heroic recasting of the cinematic nun as the soldier of Christ who is armed with the secret spiritual weapons of prayer and chastity in the 1957 films *Heaven Knows, Mr. Allison* and *Sea Wife*. *Come to the Stable* represented Young's Sister Margaret and Holm's Sister Scholastica as courageous women who refused to abandon a children's hospital in France when it was caught in the crossfire of World War II. They kept it miraculously safe from destruction through the power of their intercessions to St. Jude, a popular saint of American Catholics, a favorite among women from European immigrant backgrounds, and the patron of hopeless causes.[34] *Come to the Stable* also used the nun to eulogize the nobler qualities that were shown in war but that the male veterans had selfishly forgotten and needed to recall in peacetime. Inherent in this insipid film is a message that will be

---

[34]See Robert A. Orsi's brilliant religious, historical, and cultural study of this popular American saint's cult in *Thank you, St. Jude: Women's Devotion to the Patron Saint of Hopeless Causes* (New Haven: Yale University Press, 1996).

central to the war setting of *Heaven Knows, Mr. Allison* and *Sea Wife*: that women religious can bring out the best in men.

Heaven Knows, Mr. Allison and *Sea Wife* also stand in somewhat incestuous relationship to *The Bells of St. Mary's* and *Black Narcissus*, the two films earlier in the 1940s that for very different reasons made the nun unforgettable. Ingrid Bergman's notoriously temperamental second husband, Rossellini, had agreed to direct *Sea Wife* but was abruptly dismissed, leaving the Associate Producer Bob McNaught to take his place (Spoto 2001: 322–3). It later became evident that Rossellini must have had other things on his mind at the time when Bergman divorced him in 1957, the year *Sea Wife* was released. *Heaven Knows, Mr. Allison* would provide a star vehicle for Deborah Kerr in her second leading role as a nun. Mary Wickes, Rosalind Russell, and Whoopi Goldberg would also play nuns more than once in frothy film numbers such as *The Trouble with Angels* (1966), *Where Angels Go, Trouble Follows* (1968), *Sister Act* (1992), and *Sister Act 2: Back in the Habit* (1993). Diana Rigg would take the commanding role of an English Benedictine dame in a TV film adaptation of another Godden novel, *In This House of Brede* (1975), and a supporting role as a French missionary nun in *The Painted Veil* (2006) over thirty years later. However, only Kerr would have the distinction of two serious lead performances as a nun with major filmmakers like Britain's Powell and Pressburger and America's John Huston.

When Kerr made *Heaven Knows, Mr. Allison* she was nearly thirty-six, the age she was meant to be in the role of Sister Clodagh ten years earlier. In Fred Zinnemann's 1953 film *From Here to Eternity*, Kerr had broken Hollywood typecasting but come nearer to her complex characterization in the Powell and Pressburger film *Black Narcissus*. She played an unfaithful officer's wife (Karen Holmes) who, like Sister Clodagh earlier, looks "colder than an iceberg." She thaws to reveal a troubled woman in great need of love, one who has found temporary comfort in a string of army affairs. Her parting comment—"You're already married to the Army"— is a reproach to her lover Sergeant Milton Warden (Burt Lancaster). In Huston's wartime drama, however, it becomes the basis of a sympathetic identification between her character Sister Angela, who is married to the convent, and Robert Mitchum's Corporal Allison, who is married to the Marines. This time, however, Kerr was not playing an Anglican sister superior with a cut-crystal English accent and ruling class authority from the Anglo-Irish gentry, but a simple Irish Catholic country girl with a brogue who had not yet taken the final vows binding her permanently to religious life.

As the military officer George Stewart remarked in his history of American Catholic nuns, "war has a way of creating unusual friendships" (1994: 405). The first film reviewers of *Heaven Knows, Mr. Allison* duly noted the film's odd coupling of a nun and a marine and likened it to the World War I partnership of a riverboat captain and a spinster missionary in *The African Queen* (Murphy, *Films in Review*, April 1957: 176; *Commonweal*, March 29, 1957: 661). The shifting fortunes of the Second World War on the Asian and Pacific front furnish the extraordinary circumstances that occasion *Heaven Knows, Mr. Allison* and *Sea Wife*. They provide a dramatic pretext that temporarily releases cinematic nuns from the religious community where they put on a corporate identity, and from the habit, which veiled their personal and sexual identity. War throws up a possibility of romance hitherto inconceivable by bringing them into sudden, close, physical contact with highly attractive alpha males played by Robert Mitchum and Richard Burton. The shared dangers of war generate intimate friendships characterized by professional or gender equality and chaste foreplay; but rescue provides a narrow escape from romance back into the mother arms of the Church when the friendships acquire an explicit erotic dimension, and become too strong and sexually dangerous. In this respect *Heaven Knows, Mr. Allison* and *Sea Wife* touch on but do not fully engage the question of such central importance in *Black Narcissus*—which is how a celibate woman religious can come closer to others in love without becoming sexually intimate or denying the power of sexual attraction and physical attractiveness (Schneiders 2001: 62, 98; Brown 2007: 20, 54).

Heaven Knows, Mr. Allison (1957)

The recollections of Hollywood censor Jack Vizzard certainly suggest that the Church was on the lookout for any sleight of hand by which the subject of sexuality was smuggled into films that ostensibly gave an uplifting portrait of religious life. Vizzard represented the PCA on the movie set of *Heaven Knows, Mr. Allison* in Tobago and presumably was in a special position to understand the affinity between the religious and military life after "sixteen long sequestered years" with the Jesuits whom he described as "the Marine Corps of the Catholic Church" (Vizzard 1971: 5; Black 1998: 82). The crux of the problem for him as censor revolved around the sexual temptation—what the Catholic conscience might call the near occasion of sin—implicit in the plot of *Heaven Knows, Mr. Allison*. Film reviews written in 1957 diverged in their interpretation of this erotic subtext. *Film Daily* saw it as an edifying and spiritual story "of moral strength of character played against the uncertainties of war" (March 15, 1957: 6). *The Hollywood Reporter* admired the "chaste approach" the film took to "a subject that has been taboo, the possibility of romantic love for a nun" (March 15, 1957: 3). Yet other reviews were not so respectful. *Time* magazine bluntly dismissed *Heaven Knows, Mr. Allison* as "one more theological striptease," citing Deborah Kerr's performance a decade before in *Black Narcissus*" (March 25, 1957: 106). *Monthly Film Bulletin* was uncomfortable with the "near-blasphemous contrivance" that precipitated the film events taking place in 1944 when the tide of war was turning in the Allies' favor (May 1957: 55).

In the opening of the film, intense fighting between the Americans and Japanese for control of the South Pacific carries a shipwrecked marine on a life raft to a deserted atoll. There he encounters an Irish Catholic missionary sister who has been stranded alone after the elderly priest she was to accompany to relative safety in Fiji dies. Both *Heaven Knows, Mr. Allison* and *Sea Wife* maroon a beautiful young nun and a handsome man on an island paradise where they can, and indeed may have to, survive on their own for years, and so quickly bring the sexual tension inherent in their predicament to the surface. The *Time* magazine reviewer sarcastically asked of Huston's characters, "Will they be able to resist temptation? Will the honor of the corps be upheld? Will the vows of the spirit hold firm against the fevers of the flesh?" (106). Or as Corporal Allison asks Sister Angela, "what's the point you're being a nun, if we're all alone. . . . It's just you and me. . . . All we got is it (the island) and each other. Like Adam and Eve. Like we was the first two people on earth and this is the garden of Eden." *The New Yorker* acerbically reassured film viewers prepared to be offended by the impropriety of the subject that the serpent and all his phallic works had been banned from this particular film paradise (March 23, 1957: 103). Thus, while *Heaven Knows, Mr. Allison* heightens the sexual tension by forcing the nun and marine to hide together in a small cave when the Japanese turn the atoll into a base camp, the *Time* reviewer is right to conclude that there is no real suspense about the outcome: "Will Hollywood knowingly offend millions of Roman Catholic moviegoers and throw $2,500,000 down the drain?" (106). Nonetheless Vizzard found himself in a delicate position. For as a *Variety* reporter remarked, there were potentially two audiences for this film, one secular and the other Catholic. The first might be drawn to the erotic "implications inherent in throwing the marine together with the nun on a lonely and dangerous island." The second, he assumed, would find pleasure in the nun's goodness, in her "steadfast rejection of the ma-rine's (verbal) advances and in the glowing description of her firm faith" (March 20, 1957: 6).

Vizzard's fellow censors had a paternalistic view that nuns were frag-ile and defenseless and needed to be protected by big, strong "fellas" like Corporal Allison: "I'd rather die for you." *The Hollywood Reporter*, for one, echoed this sentiment by falling back on the stereotype that the nun was a luminous spirit unhampered by a sexed body with her immaculate white tropical habit symbolic of her innocent and unsul-lied state: "It is natural that Mitchum (Corporal Allison) would love this glowing woman and his love is tenderly, solemnly presented. Miss Kerr, stripped of makeup, incandescent in her pledged purity, makes her nun a figure of unassailable credibility" (3). In actual fact, only the most resilient, resourceful, spiritually mature, and emotionally well-adjusted women religious were chosen for missionary work. They went to their post knowing full well they could remain there for life, be cut off from the outside world in time of war and revolution, die in the job, or end up in a lone grave on a remote mountainside, like the one that inspired Godden's portrait of Sister Ruth (Bernstein 1976: 242–3).[35]

Stewart's historical account of the valor of missionary sisters in war-time complicates the neat and tidy feminist cultural reading of nuns as women with an unusual but strictly limited degree of independence, shackled by a long chain to the patriarchal high command of the Church. Oblivious to the exigencies of war, Vizzard thought it would be an im-propriety for the film to suggest that Sister Angela had no sister chaper-one and worked alone with an ageing missionary priest whose only vice and phallic activity seems to have been pipe smoking (1971: 193). In reality, mission stations in China and Japan were ransacked and destroyed during the fighting, and nuns were left on their own to face the constant threat of rape, capture, internment, infectious disease, death, slaughter, or execution. Despite efforts to evacuate all American Catholic missionary nuns from China in 1941, 160 sisters were still stranded there after Pearl Harbor. Some evaded capture by joining the swelling mass of refugees who were fleeing the Japanese, or made their way on foot, and often

[35] Godden described her discovery of "a grave . . . marked only by a small headstone in the shape of a cross with a name, 'Sister . . .' and two dates; she had died when she was only twenty-three" as the seed that later mushroomed into her novel *Black Narcissus*. Godden, *A Time to Dance, No Time to Weep* (New York: William Morrow, 1987), 129.

under cover of darkness, to mission bases deep in the interior. Others hazarded the perilous overland journey to India, as a badly injured and scarred Anglican nun is depicted doing in Godden's novel *Black Narcissus* (Godden 1963: 144–5). During the battle to take Saipan in 1944, an American Air Force chaplain found seven Spanish missionary sisters hiding with civilians in a local cave. One nun had already been killed by shellfire and was later buried in a mass grave. This band of Mercedarian Missionaries stayed on Saipan in fidelity to their fourth vow: "I will remain in the mission when there would be danger of losing my life if the good of my sisters and brothers so demands" (Stewart 1994: 400–1, 405). These wartime events make Sister Angela's account of how she has been marooned in *Heaven Knows, Mr. Allison* dramatically credible.

While Vizzard had his own suspicions that Huston's screenplay was designed as a romance though disguised as religion, he also conceded that Catholic censors had a "Jansenistic imagination" leading to unrealistically high expectations of human behavior: "Does the Code say a nun cannot be *tempted?*" He softened the initial stance of the PCA by pointing out that the plot of *Heaven Knows, Mr. Allison* was based on "a true story"—a historical incident in which the bodies of a nun and marine were found on a beach in an American Army mop-up exercise. They were dressed in stolen Japanese uniforms and it was concluded that they had been killed by friendly fire as they ran toward their rescuers (Vizzard 1971: 166–8). The film further allayed the suspicions of the censors by suggesting that despite Kerr's delicate appearance, her nun character was not entirely a soft touch or utterly defenseless against a virile male, even in uncharted sexual waters. The admiration of Allison grows when he discovers that the convent is run like the army or navy, that they both belong to a "pretty tough outfit," and that Sister Angela has been subject to the hard discipline and regimentation that produces crack troops willing to follow orders without question. The giant turtle that the nun and marine cooperate in catching for a "gourmet" meal is a good symbol of the protective carapace that the military uniform and the religious habit might offer a vulnerable woman or wounded man. Abandoned as a baby in a crate, raised in an orphanage, and in and out of reform school, Allison can keenly appreciate the fact that the military and religious life offer different forms of salvation, inspire intense corporate loyalty, and foster the pride of belonging to an elite: "Then I see the light and I started being a Marine. . . . Other guys . . . got homes, families. Me, I got the Corps, like you got the Church."

Vizzard's self-flattering recollections of his interventions on the set of *Heaven Knows, Mr. Allison* are not borne out by other members of the film crew who remember him as "a pain in the neck" with a talent for reading the "salacious" into the inconsequential, and whose name was rhymed, in comic revenge, with "buzzard" (Grobel 2000: 440).[36] Although the Catholic Church began to lose its iron grip over Hollywood censorship in the late 1950s, it clearly retained a proprietary interest in the image of nuns, a body of women whom it subjected to the internal censorship of enclosure and habit (Black 1998: 184). Neither film masterpieces such as Powell and Pressburger's *Black Narcissus* and Fred Zinnemann's *The Nun's Story* nor lesser films by equally respected directors such as Huston's *Heaven Knows, Mr. Allison* escaped its often presumptuous scrutiny until the LOD was reconstituted as the National Catholic Office for Motion Pictures (NCOMP) in 1965 (Black 1998: 220–9; Sullivan 2005: 76, 105–7). Vizzard recklessly remarked that Mitchum had "bedroom eyes" (1971: 196). If there were nothing he could do about the scopophilia or male film gaze inherent in how Mitchum's character looked at Sister Angela—and, by extension, the subtle and complex visual ways in which humans communicate desire—he stepped up his surveillance to ensure that Allison's hands did not "profane" the "inviolable person" and "sacrosanct" body of the nun on-screen (1971: 197, 201). As a result of this vigilance, *Variety* rightly saw that "the character and motivations of Miss Kerr remain shrouded in mystery and she reveals very little of herself" (6). This will be even more true for Joan Collins's Sister Therese in *Sea Wife*. Perhaps the need to project the nun as *virgo intacta* also explains why Sister Angela appears so naive and indeed clueless in this film—asking Allison why a "big handsome fellow like you isn't married"; acting like the little wife: "I woke up and you weren't there. . . . Promise you'll never go again without telling me"; and giving him the bottle of sake, which makes him drunk, arouses his sexual desire, and provokes the clumsy embrace that prompts her flight from sexual responsibility into the jungle.

However, another cultural explanation is that nuns could give mixed messages—especially to men without faith like Allison who had no pre-

---

[36] Kerr got comic revenge with a prank on the set that left Vizzard speechless. She feigned a violent struggle with Mitchum after he made a lunge for her, kicked him in the balls, and cried, "Let go of me, you sonofabitch." Vizzard told the joke against himself in *See No Evil: Life Inside a Hollywood Censor* (New York: Simon & Schuster, 1971), 202.

vious exposure to women religious—signaling, on the one hand, their sexual non-availability, and on the other, their altruistic availability to all. A pious female character who grew up in the conservative Catholic climate of rural Ireland and who probably entered the convent directly from school could not be expected to know the sexual score and understand the cues that indicate the boundaries of desire in a developing heterosexual friendship (Ebaugh 1988: 115). Traditionally, young women who consecrated their virginity to Christ, as Sister Angela tells Allison she has done in "giv(ing) my heart to Christ out Lord," imagined the convent as a cloister of the heart, and as Sister Jeannine Gramick, S.L., remarked, they did not "really think of themselves as sexual beings" (Rogers 1996: 156; Reed 2004: 114). *Black Narcissus* envisaged how this uncritical assumption of an asexual identity could constitute a form of premature repression and block the sublimatory channeling of desire in the religious life.

Ironically, experienced novice mistresses were on the lookout for candidates with a profile resembling the desirable screen nun: "someone who could have been married and would have made a good wife" (Campbell-Jones 1978: 77). Indeed, in her 1957 defense of the American Catholic censors who had Sister Clodagh's flashbacks cut from *Black Narcissus*, an LOD spokeswoman gave prudish and preposterous expression to the feminine domestic ideal that nuns were praised for embodying through service and sacrifice. She argued that instead of showing Clodagh energetically leaping hedges during a fox hunt, it would have been altogether more appropriate for Powell and Pressburger to place the future nun indoors, "in a nice kitchen with her mother . . . in a nice gingham apron . . . drying dishes" (Black 1998: 178; Vizzard 1971: 211–13). Perhaps her film exemplar was the "perfect" Sister Benedict happily cleaning St. Mary's from top to bottom with a large apron over her black habit.

Yet *Black Narcissus* showed how genuine service to others could only "flow" if the film nun resolved the tension between the psychosexual restraints of celibacy and the emotional need to love and be loved. By the time real-life nuns who entered the convent as school-leavers in the 1940s and 1950s became more cognizant of their own sexuality and aware of the personal cost of chastity, they were often in their mid-thirties—the age Powell envisaged Sister Clodagh—and contemplating the end of their sexual and reproductive prime (Schneiders 2001: 133). It is no wonder that poor Mr. Allison "don't get it" when *America*'s Moira Walsh rightly characterized Sister Angela as "deeply religious and unsophisticated" (March 23, 1957: 716). It is not the actress Deborah Kerr who "is properly sexless," as Anne Murphy of *Films in Review* concludes (177), or lacking "spiritual depths" as *Monthly Film Bulletin* argues (55), but the nun character she plays. Her religious training has not equipped her to read the marine's signals of sexual attraction or to see how reasonable it is for him to conclude that the perfect nun would make him the perfect wife.

For Catholic censors, sexuality was the proverbial elephant in the room, lurking in the cave where the marine and nun hide, ready to go on the rampage when Allison strips the delirious Sister Angela of her soaking wet clothes, and unveils the curled, auburn hair against the pale skin that makes hers a chaste and erotic spectacle. But this red-blooded male with bedroom eyes does not have his wicked way with her, nor do I think there is any suggestion in the film that he is an "evil young man" with rape on his mind and in need of the nun's "moral regeneration" (Sullivan 2005: 70). This film script, like *The Bells of St. Mary's* earlier, limited the main character development rather than risk giving offense to the Catholic hierarchy and losing their main target audience, and kept well clear of the deep, dangerous waters of eroticism that *Black Narcissus* plumbed. Generally, film reviewers praised Robert Mitchum for the restraint, fundamental decency, and above all "tenderness" that he showed in the role of Corporal Allison (Knight, *The Saturday Review*, April 6, 1957: 27; *Commonweal*, 661; Crowther, *The New York Times*, March 24, 1957: sec.11:22, *Film Daily*, 6). This tenderness does evoke a response from Sister Angela and brings feelings quivering to delicate life in this film that elude the heavy-handed detection of the censors.

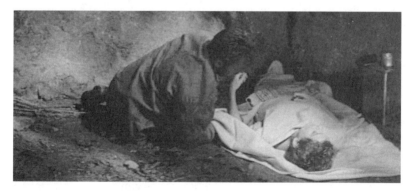

Figure 2-2. Stripped of her veil and habit, Deborah Kerr's Sister Angela is a chaste and erotic spectacle that attracts and commands the respect of the marine Mr. Allison.

Thrown into each other's company, the pair intimate that they may be giving each other what they've never known and need for their personal development. Precisely because they are an odd couple, they are forced by circumstances to engage in sublimation's dynamic work of reconciling their contrariety. Her Irish sociability awakens in the monosyllabic loner marine his capacity for love, for self-awareness, and for an interiority that might lead in time to prayer: "I never loved anything or anybody before. I never even loved before . . . inside." His respect and romantic interest remind her that she is both a woman and a religious (*Variety* 6). His tender care in removing her habit, wrapping her in a pure white blanket that he has stolen from the Japanese, and nursing her back to health require her to revaluate the severe warning that was given to novices: "Touch no one, and do not allow yourself to be touched by anyone without necessity or evident reason, however innocent" (Kaylin 2000: 174).

Far from objecting to the film's express violation of this religious rule against touch, the LOD awarded *Heaven Knows, Mr. Allison* its highest A-I rating, indicating it could offend no one—except Sister Angela whose first trained instinct is to fly when Allison puts his arms around her (Vizzard 1971: 203). Her wiser instinct when she has recovered is to question a religious vocation that has left her so sexually naive: "Dear Mr. Allison. Perhaps God doesn't want me to take my final vows." While the film does not probe beneath the surface, it does move gingerly toward the same conclusion as *Black Narcissus*, one memorably articulated by John Boswell in his review of lesbian desire among nuns: "Most of the drama of sexuality in any individual's life has to do with nonphysical aspects of human interaction: affection, attraction, devotion, jealousy, passion, restraint, desire, sublimation, transformation" (*The New Republic*, January 6, 1986: 36). Like Sister Clodagh, Sister Angela has begun to recognize her sexual self and the otherness of those who have touched her life.

In a closing scene of intimacy reminiscent of the unity achieved by Sister Clodagh and Mr. Dean in the act of separating, the nun not only affirms but redefines the importance of the unusual friendship she has discovered with Mr. Allison on a South Pacific atoll. When he says in farewell, "We're coming to the end of our time together," her response contains an implicit religious correction, one that it may take him many years to work out: "Goodbye, Mr. Allison. No matter how many miles apart we are, whether I ever get to see your face again, you will be my dear companion always, always." Film history seems to be repeating itself as she paraphrases the sentiments that another Sister Angela spoke in a pre-war nun film, *The White Sister* (1933), when she told her ex-lover she would think of him every day.[37] However, Kerr's Sister Angela is not reaffirming the formulaic words of film romance. She is avowing a fundamental reason why real women become nuns—their belief in the power of prayer to touch and change human lives. Prayer puts the nun in communion with God and with his Church Militant on earth. Thus, prayer empowers the transformative work of sublimation that closes the distance between people, however "many miles apart," and keeps them united as intimate comrades in that invisible corps known as the mystical body of Christ. In the nun's inter-connected faith system, heaven does indeed know Mr. Allison.

Sea Wife (1957)

"Heaven forbid" would be the likely reaction now to the idea of Joan Collins in a serious dramatic role as a nun. Like Deborah Kerr in *From Here to Eternity*, Collins was cast against type in *Sea Wife*. Collins was more than a decade younger than Kerr in 1957 when she starred in a film on the rival theme of a nun's transgressive wartime friendship and embryonic romance. Both films were produced by Twentieth Century Fox but *Sea Wife* had the disadvantage of being released later in the year than *Heaven Knows, Mr. Allison*. Early reviewers were quick to see the "superficial resemblance" (*Film Daily*, August 6, 1957: 8) between the two films and were divided over the merits of *Sea Wife*. *Monthly Film Bulletin* dismissed it as "inconsequential" (May 1957: 56) and *The New York Times*, interestingly, complained that it had no flesh on its bones (December 5, 1957: 45), but *Film Daily* ranked it "high above the general run of film" (8), not least for its excellent acting, and *Motion Picture Herald* admired its "touching and moving, if somewhat familiar story" (August 17, 1957: 489). While the subject of romance hangs in the air between Sister Angela and Corporal Allison, it ultimately provided the language to imagine a theology of mystical community where they can remain spiritually close and supportive of one another. For the marine, it is the very particularity of his romantic regard for the nun—her "big blue eyes," "beautiful smile," and above all, her "freckles"—that is a gateway to interiority, to a world that has suddenly come alive "inside"

[37] Ivan Butler briefly discussed the two silent and one talking picture version of *The White Sister* that were made in 1915, 1924, and 1933 respectively. Butler, *Religion in the Cinema* (New York: A. S. Barnes, 1969), 89. In 1960, there was one final, Mexican remake.

him (Haughton 1981: 55). However, while *Heaven Knows, Mr. Allison* and *Black Narcissus* explore the entanglement of romance with religion, *Sea Wife* bears out the polarized claim that "story-lines in films about nuns are often fairly limited, with romance rather than religion forming the substance and impetus of the plot" (Jones 1995: 44). The romancing of a nun is made tenable in *Sea Wife* by the simple device of keeping her religious identity a secret. The uncomfortably intimate presence of a handsome bachelor causes her to become less single-hearted in her vocation, pray to heaven for renewed strength of purpose and succor, and be miraculously restored in the end to the safety of her habit and convent.

When Collins took the female lead in *Sea Wife*, she was trying to make it big in Hollywood. She had been spotted by the J. Arthur Rank organization in England, and signed up by Twentieth Century Fox as a sultry rival to Ava Gardner. In 1955 alone, she appeared as an Egyptian temptress in Howard Hawks's *Land of the Pharaohs*, a lady-in-waiting to *The Virgin Queen*, and a mistress at the center of a sex scandal and murder in *The Girl in the Red Velvet Swing*. This sensational role would have her swinging like a star on the September 12, 1955 cover of *Life* magazine. Collins's siren image made it hard for *Monthly Film Bulletin* to accept her "synthetic modesty" in the role of a nun (May 1957: 56). However, other reviews were kinder with *Films and Filming* recognizing the serious promise in the starlet: "If Joan Collins had had more experience in screen drama, she might completely have convinced us; as it is, she gives a performance of sufficient intensity and control to almost steal scene after scene from the veteran Basil Sydney" (May 1957: 26). *Motion Picture Herald* declared that the actress was "becoming more popular with each film (and) effect(ed) a welcome change of pace as the soft-spoken, thoughtful nun" (August 17, 1957: 489).

Collins's hopes of becoming a major Hollywood star eventually faded when she missed out on the role of *Cleopatra* (1963). Although it went to Elizabeth Taylor, Collins already had the satisfaction of starring opposite Richard Burton as his love interest in *Sea Wife*. The tagline of the film tantalizes an audience with the suggestion of rough, oceanic sex between the two—"what happened out there . . . in the surging vastness of the India Ocean"—and then puts a pious lid on the prurient imagination by billing *Sea Wife* as "one of the most challenging Stories of Faith ever told." If anyone had the dramatic power to make it seem he could part the waters of the Indian Ocean in two like Moses, and deliver a prim nun from her vow of chastity, it was Richard Burton. In 1957, Burton was approaching the height of his fame as a stage and screen actor. He had magnetic good looks, the great classical actor's presence, and the mesmerizing voice of a god. He had conquered the epic genre with starring roles in *The Robe* (1953) and *Alexander the Great* (1955), and made heroic war films a specialty with *The Desert Rats* (1953), *Bitter Victory* (1957), and now *Sea Wife*, a World War II drama with a hint of biblical epic and a religious twist to romance.

The plot of *Sea Wife* was compared to Hitchcock's 1944 *Lifeboat* in dramatizing the social, psychological, and sexual tensions that build up amongst the four survivors of a refuge ship torpedoed by the Japanese during the evacuation of Singapore in 1942, but *The New York Times* lamented the fact that Bob McNaught did not measure up as a director (December 5, 1957: 45). Mythopoeic allusions to the book of Job, the story of the Flood, and even Coleridge's "The Rhyme of the Ancient Mariner" are also interwoven into a plot in which the survivors float for almost fourteen weeks at sea, as food, water, patience, hope, humanity, and finally sanity run out. An element of suspense is injected into the film by the fact that the survivors are stripped of their normal social identity and go by the nicknames of Biscuit (Richard Burton), Bulldog (Basil Sydney), Number Four (Cy Grant), and Sea Wife (Joan Collins). Only Number Four, the longsuffering black bursar on the ship, knows Sea Wife's secret: that she is a missionary nun called Sister Therese. The ostensible reason that Sea Wife gives for not wishing to disclose her religious identity is that it will further exacerbate the hate-swollen bigotry and white man's prejudice of Bulldog. He has already made himself objectionable by his racist bullying of Number Four, his braying role as Job's comforter, and his cynical Darwinian view that every man is out for himself. Another reason is the sea change the nun undergoes when she dives overboard dressed only in her nightgown. She is given the nickname "Sea Wife" because she swims like a mermaid. Buoyant in the water, and no longer weighed down by a heavy habit, she is made disturbingly aware of the fact that nuns are not asexual beings, as the body she was trained to discipline floats free and the naked feeling of being a woman washes over her (Campbell-Jones 1978: 175). Yet so ingrained is her religious formation in detachment that Biscuit will later wonder how she can remain "so calm, so removed. Don't you have any feelings, any emotions?"

Sea Wife's reluctance to tell Biscuit she is a nun makes this film a romantic tease. It also upholds the cinematic stereotype of the nun as a holy mystery who ultimately remains unfathomable to others. Indeed her outward calmness makes Biscuit question her emotional knowledge of herself and her erotic capacity for deep feelings. In J. M. Scott's bestseller

Sea Wyf, which was adapted to the screen, the nun's identity remains a suspenseful mystery until the novel's denouement. Film reviewers were disappointed that the audience knows her secret from the start and understands why she passively resists the attention of the leading man (*The New York Times*, 45; *Newsweek*, August 26, 1957: 98). However this privileged information does win sympathy for Biscuit. Burton portrays him as the perfect English gentleman, one who would never be so dishonorable as to woo a woman he knew was a consecrated nun, or so disrespectful as to think of sex when faced with a representative of religion. We are never told to what order of nuns Sea Wife belonged as Sister Therese. If she was a Catholic sister, entrance to the convent was still regarded an "an almost irrevocable decision" (Ebaugh 1988: 100). If she was Anglican, given her missionary work in British colonial Singapore, her vows may be renewable like those of the nuns in *Black Narcissus*, but many sisters still regarded them as a binding commitment for life (Mumm 1999: 33–5). Biscuit is oblivious to Sea Wife's veiled identity from the start to the end of the film. This "he'll never know" stance not only gives him tacit permission to romance the nun but generates the pathos that frames the film story as Biscuit sends Sea Wife ardent newspaper messages to contact him after the war: "Home at last. Please get in touch." "Am certain you are alive. Are you afraid of past or me?" "If I have a rival, so much the worse for him." And the final provocative message that prompts the film's continuous flashback to how they were thrown together by war— "Intend to find you publishing story of 14 weeks and No. 4."

Neither Biscuit nor, indeed, the distrustful, sharp-eyed Bulldog ever suspect that Sea Wife might be a nun, despite the fact that she has the habit of saying her prayers aloud; fervently declares that they are "all in the hands of God"; ministers like an angel of mercy to the wounded Biscuit; and exemplifies extraordinary Christian charity and forbearance. Both men think it odd that they "never noticed her on the ship"—an irony that is not lost on the audience as they look at the eye-catching beauty of Joan Collins. However, as Number Four rightly replies, they "would not have recognized her then," for a traditional nun was dressed like a remote figure from the distant past, and in her strange garb was as much a *rara avis* as a mermaid. The full habit made her stand out as a religious role model and sacred icon, but pass unseen as a person in public (Kuhns 2003: 158–9). When Biscuit asks Sea Wife: "what's your name . . . your real name?" her reply is a revealing statement of how convent training and dress effaced individual and augmented corporate identity (Briggs 2006: 89): "I'm not a real person here."

If Sister Therese feels at sea after being re-christened "Sea Wife," unsure of her identity as either a religious or a woman, she has also been given a rare wartime opportunity for personal development. Susan Michelman later remarked that "gender and sexuality, obscured by wearing the habit, became evident when the women came forth as visible females" (1998: 169). However, this historic move out of the habit and religious-run institutions and into secular clothes and jobs, only came in the mid 1960s. It would not only change actual nuns' perception of their gender and sexuality but their understanding of how men treated ordinary women. Nuns had grown accustomed to automatic deference to their spiritual status and respect for their sexual unavailability. When their religious identity was no longer apparent or respected, they too began to encounter sexual discrimination and harassment in the workplace (Wittberg 1989: 530, 532, 534). As the only woman on the lifeboat, Collins's Sister Therese suddenly finds how a nun's interactions with men can dramatically alter when she removes the habit. Bulldog watches her lasciviously as she sleeps in innocent unawareness on Biscuit's protective arm. Biscuit defends her gender rights when she insists on her participation in keeping night watch: "Did you never hear of the equality of women?" Number Four takes it upon himself to act as her moral guardian and reconnoiter her walks with Biscuit on the tropical island where they land: "Sea Wife, what's happened to you? Why don't you tell him you're a nun?"

Collins did not give a great performance as a nun, but then, she was not given as good a part, script, or director as Deborah Kerr. However, she does convey the old-fashioned, neo-Victorian persona of modesty, gentleness, attentiveness, and serenity that nuns routinely cultivated up until the sixties, and convincingly suggests that this maidenly persona might enhance rather than detract from Sea Wife's erotic appeal for an inherently chivalrous man like Biscuit. Read conservatively, the film reaffirms a non-threatening, traditional religious femininity. One answer to Biscuit's question—"Why are you running away from things, running away from life, from yourself?"—might be that, as in *Heaven Knows, Mr. Allison*, neither Sister Therese herself nor a general film audience was quite ready in 1957 to hear about "equality of women" for nuns or what it implies, that she must confront the mystery of her own subjectivity and sexuality. However, Biscuit himself asks a rhetorical question near the end of the film that yields a more moving answer: "Why shouldn't I love you? You're young and brave and beautiful and good. When I was sick, you nursed me. If ever we get out of this alive, it's because of you.

Figure 2-3. Sister Therese complains that "no one ever looks at the face of a nun," and Joan Collins's wistful gaze here suggests how the screen nun was confined by religious stereotyping and cried out for recognition as a woman.

You held us together." Ironically, he loves the woman she has become as a nun; he unwittingly loves how religious consecration has made her put agape or selfless love and care for others above her own desires (Donovan and Wusinich 2009: 26–32). When Sea Wife herself tries to explain how she feels without betraying her identity as a nun—"There's no faith anymore. It's as though the springs have dried up"—she indirectly voices the religious argument for chastity: that service flows from the primacy of her love for God and from the dedication of a whole and undivided heart to this relationship (Pitts 2009: 95–6).

The best moment of the film is the end where Biscuit, still in hot pursuit of Sea Wife, visits Bulldog, fighting insanity in a London asylum over his responsibility for Number Four's hideous death in a shark attack. Bulldog brings Biscuit's romantic quest to an end with the formulaic trope of ill-fated lovers: "She's dead. Her last thoughts were of you. She said, 'tell Biscuit that I loved him.'" Biscuit walks out silent and numb with grief, and as he does so, lifts his hat in his habitual courtesy to two nuns who are entering the grounds of the asylum. One of them, of course, is Sea Wife: "What's wrong, Sister Therese?" asks her religious companion, reminding us that, in ordinary circumstances, nuns never went out unaccompanied. "Just someone I once knew." "He didn't seem to recognize you," her religious companion replies. Then Sister Therese says the line that encapsulates the paradoxical position of nuns on-screen: "No one ever looks at the face of a nun." They look, but as I have shown in this chapter, there is much they overlook. The looks exchanged in parting between Sister Clodagh and Mr. Dean in *Black Narcissus*, and to a lesser extent by Sister Angela and Corporal Allison in *Heaven Knows, Mr. Allison*, conveyed the prospect of an emotional intimacy beyond lovemaking (Jones 1995: 53). Sister Therese now looks longingly after Biscuit, and then lifts her eyes in silent thanks to God. What has God saved her from—Biscuit, herself, sexuality, or the arduous but rewarding human task of sublimation? While both *Black Narcissus* and *Heaven Knows, Mr. Allison* close with a farewell scene in which the nun and the layman not only lovingly face one another but bravely face up to their life choices and the limits of their relationship, *Sea Wife* retreats from this final encounter. Sister Therese's failure to call after Biscuit, look him in the eye, or correct the lie that she is dead, is an act of cowardice and dishonesty that sullies her wartime heroism. Sublimation, as Loewald concludes, is the hard work of "understanding ourselves, our fellow beings, our world" (1988: 82). By letting Biscuit go away in ignorance, the nun has evaded the very work that can make religion and her missionary calling most meaningful. Sister Therese was a better person out of the habit than in it.

Conclusion

In this chapter, I have examined *Black Narcissus* as a daring and dramatic study of repression and the emerging counter dynamic of sublimation. In so doing, I have expanded the scope of film analysis from the postcolonial question of how gender and religion operate in imperialism to consider how sexuality functions in the religious life. Sister Clodagh's flashbacks address the disconnect between her sexual past and her present religious life, and facilitate the move from repression to sublimation where the passionate desires energizing the body flow into more intense and heightened forms of living through religion, work, and non-sexual intimacy. Her flashbacks would be the precursor to another film scandal when Scorsese was inspired to give Jesus sexual daydreams, longings, and regrets in *The Last Temptation of Christ* (1988).

While *Heaven Knows, Mr. Allison* is a much lesser film achievement than *Black Narcissus*, there are nonetheless glimpses of sublimation's transformative process in the tender understanding that develops between the nun and marine, in the interest that Allison shows in Sister Angela as both a woman and a religious, and in the way they profoundly touch each other's lives. This involves the nun's flickering recognition of the need for further psychosexual development as she approaches her final vows. However, given the religious censorship in place at the time, this insight is never pursued with anything like the same depth or complexity as in *Black Narcissus*. In both of these films, the erotic dilemma faced by the woman religious leads to greater self-understanding, but in *Sea Wife*, the nun remains a mystery to herself and others. Although literally thrown into the arms of a man who comes to love her, and cast on a sea of stormy emotions, there is little indication of how the awareness of embodiment or desire might lead to a more meaningful assessment of her religious life. In Chapter 3, I discuss *The Nun's Story* (1959), which examines the scope for personal and professional desires in a strictly observed religious life, and which validates Freud's insight that absorbing work is the most common form of sublimation.

SUBJECTIVE DESIRES

THE ROLE OF THE CATHOLIC FAMILY
ROMANCE IN *THE NUN'S STORY*
(1959)

Introduction to *The Nun's Story*

When Audrey Hepburn appeared on-screen in 1959, looking immaculate in a black-and-white habit, the nun was still a figure veiled in mystique. This mystique derived its power from the traditional religious view that she "binds herself to *a state of perfection*, which requires a striving toward holiness that is . . . life-long" (Donovan and Wusinich 2008: 39). In *The Nun's Story*, film director Fred Zinnemann showed his respect for the heroic entrants, endurance runners, and dropouts in the arduous spiritual marathon to become perfect as "your heavenly Father is perfect" (Matt. 5:48). He appreciated the ancient beauty of this ideal and at the same time grasped the new tribulations that it would hold for twentieth-century women religious who desired to serve God with not only their heart and soul but mind and strength. Through his Catholic nun protagonist, Sister Luke, he dramatized the conflict that the call of agape would increasingly pose for religious aspirants who were asked to become humble, obedient, and "willing slaves" for Christ but who had longings aroused by modernity—for self-actualization and self-affirmation—longings that would be condemned as the self-regard and superbia of eros (Nygren 1953: viii–ix, 472–3; Pitts 2008: 100). In her religious memoir *Through the Narrow Gate*, which she subtitled *A Nun's Story* in an intertextual nod to the influence of Zinnemann's film, Karen Armstrong articulated the question that the postulant still asked herself in 1962 when John XXIII convened the Second Vatican Council: "Is she prepared to deny herself all self-fulfillment by laying aside her own selfish desires to lose them in that close relationship with God to which the nun aspires" (1997: 91).

The Nun's Story is the melancholy account of an earnest young Belgian woman who slaves away for seventeen years to become "a perfect nun" only to realize finally that her intractable will and consequent struggles with utter obedience mean she can never live up to the religious ideal of her strict, semi-cloistered order. Zinnemann's film was an adaptation of a 1956 bestseller written by Kathryn Hulme. The author had met ex-nun Marie Louise Habets while she was working as a nurse in the postwar ruins of Nazi Germany. In a refugee camp where former lives were routinely told and traced, Hulme heard an oral history out of the ordinary—of a woman who was a displaced person from religious life— which she fictionalized into *The Nun's Story*. Prior to Vatican II, the decision to leave the convent after taking perpetual vows was a grave and exceptional course of action. While the transgressive nun had long been a popular subject in sensational, libertine, and anti-religious literature, the faithful and long-serving sister who obtained a canonical dispensation from her vows was a new figure who would become commonplace after the Second Vatican Council closed in 1965. However, even then there was still a lingering belief, as a former nun recollected, that the renuncia-tion of sacred vows was "the ultimate disgrace . . . absolutely unforgive-able. . . . I had a terrible sense of failure" (Bernstein 1976: 317).

This "terrible sense of failure" hangs over Sister Luke's final leave-taking and is made more poignant by the fact that she entered the convent as a young woman who believed that she could succeed with exertion and determination. She did not understand how little her own efforts would count in a traditional belief system based on agape—the wholly unmerited gift of divine grace, which requires the nun's loving surrender to God without thought of reward or satisfaction (Nygren 1953: 213–18). She did not appreciate the historical legitimacy of her father's warning that once enclosed, her "personal wishes cease to exist." Zinnemann's film begins in the 1920s at the onset of a "great repression" of desire for Catholic nuns.[1] This was the decade in which cloistral rules

---

[1]Some readers and critics think Sister Luke entered the convent in 1927. However, Kathryn Hulme indicates in her novel that she enters in 1926, finishes her

were tightened in response to the extensive codification of canon law in 1917. Particular friendships of affinity with other nuns were discouraged within the convent, and the collaborative working relationships that nuns once had on the outside with men who helped them succeed became taboo. As religious historian Sister Mary Ewens, O.P., observed, "sisters were pushed back behind their cloister walls and were no longer so free to respond to contemporary needs" (1979: 272–3). When the film debuted in 1959, it was perceived by sisters in both Europe and America as an attack on their current religious life even though it was set in the prewar period, and there was concern about the adverse effect its Catholic departure narrative would have on new vocations (Sullivan 2005: 109–17).

American sisters who saw *The Nun's Story* at a special premiere shortly before its general release gave film critiques in the Jesuit periodical *America* that reflected the disjuncture between their progressive and "new world" view of religious life and the traditional and "old world" views frozen in time by early twentieth-century canon law (Coburn and Smith 1999: 225). An Ursuline nun acknowledged that *The Nun's Story* was "the most beautiful Hollywood-produced film" she had ever seen but thought the nun characters were "terribly out-of-date (not to say medieval), and marble statues living most inhuman lives in ivory towers." A Sister of Charity noted Zinnemann's documentary-like accuracy in presenting the minute "externals of religious life," but felt he did not capture the spirit of joy, vibrancy, and heightened reality that pervades authentic community life. She paid the film a back-handed compliment by hoping that it would discourage "unstable, confused or slightly neurotic girls" like Sister Luke from entering the convent. A Sister of Notre Dame agreed that Sister Luke's religious training was deficient in its emphasis on tedious and repressive regulations, and worried that non-Catholic viewers, in particular, would regard it's "grim, friendless" and cold representation of the motherhouse as a realistic picture of "religious life in America." She echoed the underlying vocational concern that it would be "difficult to conceive how a girl could be drawn to religious life as a result of seeing this film."[2] In fact, *The Nun's Story* would join

---

novitiate in 1927, and goes to the School of Tropical Medicine in Antwerp in 1928. See *The Nun's Story* (Boston: Little, Brown, 1956), 54–5, 80.

[2] See "'The Nun's Story'—A Symposium: Views of Three Nuns," *America*, June 27, 1959: 470–1. See also "Reactions to *The Nun's Story*," *America*, January 26, 1957: 482–3, for a range of lay, religious, and clerical views on Hulme's book. Nuns

the list of Hollywood classics that moved and inspired young women to consider whether they might have a vocation. Karen Armstrong and Deborah Larsen, who became entrants soon after the film release in the early sixties and both significantly subtitled their convent memoirs *A Nun's Story*, register the impact that Audrey Hepburn's performance as Sister Luke made on them. They found that *The Nun's Story* helped them make meaning of their own personal experience in the convent. They saw this film nun as a pathfinder and explanatory guide for their spiritual journey in and ultimately out of religious life (Campbell 2003: 130, 194). Larsen, for example, would conclude her departure narrative by remarking that "Sister Luke and I in the end were not so different. I saw that all the way back to the first days at Mount Carmel, I had mentally asked questions. . . . Her thought had become mine: 'What I do from now on is between me and God alone.' I would leave now" (2005: 209).

The Nun's Story evoked these contradictory reactions of alienation and identification among women with experience of religious life because it is a Janus-faced film. It looks back at a noble and exalted calling, a religious institution that was enclosed and otherworldly, and traditional practices that derived from medieval monasticism and were increasingly incompatible with modern life. It dramatizes the nun's continual struggle not only of conscience but intellectual and professional integrity with the vow of obedience that binds her to the "holy rules" of the cloister. It thus suggests the historical dilemma of progressive thinkers in the convent who were ahead of their time but tragically out-of-step with a more conservative and restrictive religious culture. Finally, its departure narrative looks forward to the conflicts of "new nuns" in the 1960s, the era of Catholic modernization and second-wave feminism, who set out to reform but sometimes ended up forsaking the religious life. *The Nun's Story* was also Janus-faced because it appeared at a momentous turning point as the Church geared up for the Second Vatican Council. Vatican II's spirit of change and renewal would transform the face of Catholicism so that it bore little resemblance to the religion that is practiced so rigor-

---

had more positive things to say about the book than the film adaptation, with one nun commending it as a "simple and profoundly moving story of Gabrielle Van der Mal, who knew only too well what it meant to be a flesh-and-blood nun." Yet another complained that the book presented a caricature of religious life.

ously in Zinnemann's film.[3] Sister Sandra Schneiders, I.H.M., remarked on "the incredible speed and the radicality of the transition Religious made from an enclosed medieval institution to a fully modern one . . . perhaps the most painful evidence of which was the departure of tens of thousands of Religious" (2000: 104).

As a result, *The Nun's Story* can be seen as a visual landmark of the great divide that would separate those who grew up with the rituals of the Tridentine Church and those who came after Vatican II reforms (Gordon 2002: 66, 80). Older Catholics have as much difficulty eradicating the ancient rhythms of the Tridentine Church from their heart as Sister Luke had getting the drumbeats of the Congo out of her blood. Later Catholics are more likely to be bored, baffled, or estranged by their solemnity. While the first hour of the film registers both the director and protagonist's fascination with "the mysterious otherness" (Leddy 1990: 14) of traditional Catholic observances, it is also troubled by the presentiment that lies at the core of this nun's anguished story and prompted increasingly urgent ecclesiastical calls for reform. The presentiment is that the cloister preserved a venerable and beautiful way of life, but one increasingly hard and anachronistic for modern women to follow, and traditional religious life must adapt and bend, if it was not, like Sister Luke, to break.

Indeed, well before the film premiere of *The Nun's Story* in 1959, religious directors on both sides of the Atlantic had fears about a shortage of vocations. In Europe, it was concern over the increasing number of "Sister Lukes" who were leaving the convent and the steep decline in new entrants. In America, it was anxiety that the institutional demands of a growing church would outstrip the supply of able-bodied nuns represented by Sister Benedict and her religious community in *The Bells of St. Mary's*.[4] In 1952, Pius XII advised religious superiors to "make sure

---

[3] Sister Joan Chittister, O.S.B., recalls the personal impact of Vatican II reform: " 'I'm not leaving religious life,' I told my parents when I announced after months of turmoil that I would not be staying in the community much longer. 'Religious life is leaving me.' " In fact, she did not leave. Chittister, *The Way We Were: A Story of Conversion and Renewal* (Maryknoll, N.Y.: Orbis Books, 2005), 49–50.

[4] Sister Marie Augusta Neal, S.N.D.deN., believes that "the increase in numbers of (American) religious leaving congregations actually began in 1953, when systematic degree programs were introduced . . . as well as newly initiated theology programs." Neal, *From Nuns to Sisters: An Expanding Vocation* (Mystic, Conn.: Twenty-Third Publications, 1990), 32.

that nothing in your customs, your manners of life, or your ascetical practices raises a barrier or causes loss of vocation . . . for a good girl with courage" (Curran 1989: 134; Weaver 1995: 81–2; Ebaugh 1993b: 38). For "a good girl with courage," 1960 would prove to be a watershed as religious congregations in America came to terms with the fact that young entrants with a mind of their own were no longer the exception to the holy rule, and that its latest intake had begun to openly question the exacting practices that regulated convent life with a military-like precision.[5]

In 1961, Cardinal Leon Suenens, who had been involved earlier in 1957 studio negotiations to film the convent scenes of *The Nun's Story* on location in Belgium, published his landmark work *The Nun in the World* (Vizzard 1971: 230–1; Sullivan 2005: 109). The book registered his concern over the number of religious houses that had closed down in Belgium for want of new vocations, his disapproval of bleak insider accounts by popular writers such as Kathryn Hulme and Monica Baldwin, and his general conviction that religious life urgently needed to move with the times (1963: 28–9, 32–3). Although he had earlier opposed Zinnemann's making of *The Nun's Story* as further bad publicity for convent life, Suenens now, ironically, articulated a plea for reform that was intrinsic to the equivocal close of Zinnemann's 1959 film. He challenged nuns to reject the religious siege mentality that closed them off from the world, vow to live as women who would no longer "passively accept (their) fate," and strive to be seen as modern women (1963: 11, 17–18, 33–4). Suenens confidently predicted that the reform of religious orders with active ministries would lead to an increase in vocations (1963: 177).

Four years after the publication of *The Nun in the World*, the cardinal's optimism appeared to be justified when the number of American Catholic nuns reached an all-time high of approximately 180,000, making them the largest group of women religious in the world. However, only a year later in 1966, a sharp decline would begin and gather momentum. By 1970, the number of nuns had fallen to 161,000, as religious congregations responded with alacrity to Vatican II reforms only to go into freefall institutionally (Burns 1994: 132; Ebaugh 1988: 100, and 1993b: 46–51; Schneiders 2000: 155, 380n.23). Ironically, traditional communities that remained socially and symbolically cohesive and contemplative orders that did not become radical change agents had the best chance of long-

[5] Sister Patricia Curran, S.N.D.deN., regards "1960 as the definitive year when convent culture lost its hold on the religious aspirant." Curran, *Grace Before Meals: Food Ritual and Body Discipline in Convent Culture* (Urbana: University of Illinois Press, 1989), 135–6.

term survival, and in some cases, even went on to experience a resurgence of vocations as the century came to a close (Carey 1997: 290–4, 327; Campbell-Jones 1978: 24–6, 192–210).

The Nun's Story functioned not only as a premonitory text of the convent departures that would escalate in the second half of the 1960s, but as a requiem for the passing of what author Kathryn Hulme called the "meaningful beauty" from Catholic religious life (Hulme, *America*, June 27, 1959: 468). Zinnemann linked a love of beauty with the love of God by showing the aesthetic grace of the cloister liturgy, music, rituals, and bodily symbols. Through the eyes of his admiring protagonist, we see that this beauty has the power of the erotic: to direct her desires toward God, elevate her spirit, and inspire upward striving—toward a religious state of perfection that will ultimately prove beyond her reach (Nygren 1953: 172–4, 223; Miles 1985: 142–50). So successful was the director in capturing the visual and spiritual drawing power of the convent's beautiful practices that a first screening of *The Nun's Story* had an "overwhelming" effect on Belgian ex-nun Marie Louise Habets who had not only told Kathryn Hulme her life story but become her life partner.[6]

> I'm never going to see it *again* because if I do I'm going to run right back to the convent. When you see the chapel, all those nuns . . . I could just sit there and cry my eyes out, not with regret or anything, but because of the beauty of it. It is a beautiful life, the religious life, if you really are a religious person. (Zeitlin, *Life*, June 8, 1959: 144)

Karen Armstrong recalled the sorrow of a postulant who realized she did not have a religious vocation and must leave "the most beautiful life in the world" (1997: 118).

When Zinnemann first tried to interest Hollywood in a film on Hulme's 1956 bestseller, he met the studio response, "who wants to see a documentary about how to be a nun?" (Phillips 2005: 45).[7] Indeed,

---

[6] The distinguished film critic, Stanley Kauffmann, astutely titled his influential review of *The Nun's Story* "A Use of Beauty," *The New Republic*, June 29, 1959: 21.

[7] Alexander Walker documents Warner Brothers' initial reluctance to proceed with such a super-sensitive cultural subject for the Catholic Church as a nun's renunciation of her perpetual vows, and their subsequent fear at a preview screening that such a film would leave a popular audience cold. Walker, *Audrey: Her Real Story*, rev. ed. (London: Orion, 1997), 200, 210–11. Barry Paris quotes the director Zinnemann: "To say that Warners were not entirely happy with the film would be an understatement. They thought it would flop." Paris, *Audrey Hepburn* (London: Weidenfeld & Nicolson, 1997), 151.

the film project might never have gotten off the ground had not Audrey Hepburn, then at a standstill in her star career, been keen to shed her gamine screen image and tackle the testing role of Sister Luke (Spoto 2006: 119–20; Walker 1997: 206). Even after Warner Brothers acquired the movie rights, they had serious doubts about an audience's interest in the private and muted subject Zinnemann chose—the largely silent and interior life of a nun in the prewar period. At the risk of alienating his audience, Zinnemann incorporated Hulme's viewpoint that "nuns are *not* like other people" (*America*, June 27, 1959: 469), and then complicated it by emphasizing from the very start of his film that Sister Luke is *not* like other nuns. Certainly the sisters who first saw the film could not identify with his heroine, despite the respect and awe he shows for her religious community. Movie critic, Moira Walsh, was surprised that Zinnemann's "wholehearted tribute to women in religious life" should be regarded with such hostility by actual nuns, and wondered if this could be because the film probed the fault line in modern religious life, which was "the conflict between the old rules and new obligations" of professional life (*America*, June 27, 1959: 471).

The Vow of Obedience

Although religious spokeswomen of the time protested that *The Nun's Story* gave a false picture of religious life,[8] later nuns who looked back at the enclosed world that women religious inhabited before Vatican II acknowledged that it resembled a "total institution" (Curran 1989: 125–7; Wittberg 1994: 253; Chittister 2005: 19–32). This is how Zinnemann visualized the cloister in *The Nun's Story*, and it may be another reason why nuns in 1959 reacted not only with "coolness" but "outright indignation" to his film (Walsh, 471). Two years after the film's premiere, Erving Goffman defined the total institution as an encompassing organization that isolates members from the outside world and sets up barriers to departure.[9] Indeed, he illustrated how it managed the lives of large

---

[8] Even though she appreciated the fact that auto/biographical texts mix fact and fiction, Sister Mary Augustine, S.M.S.M., first woman president of the Catholic Press Association, tried to demystify *The Nun's Story* by nailing down the book's distortions and inaccuracies in an unpleasant article called "Cross My Heart: NUN'S Story JUST THAT!" *Marist Missions* May–June 1958: 24–8.

[9] As Sister Luke's religious struggles show, and as Suzanne Campbell-Jones conceded in *In Habit: A Study of Working Nuns* (New York: Pantheon Books, 1978), 27, "an active religious congregation can never be totally isolated from the world outside."

groups of people and imposed ideological conformity and group socialization by citing the exercises of personal mortification and collective
training in Hulme's bestseller (Goffman 1991: 15, 18, 24, 30, 32, 37–8,
41, 109, 111, 188–9). As a German Jew whose Viennese parents died in a
concentration camp, Zinnemann would have seen the disturbing resemblance between the drills of automatic obedience in religious formation
and the tests of absolute loyalty in political indoctrination (Campbell-
Jones 1978: 94–5; Goffman 1991: 27; Sinyard 2003: 168). Against a film
background of rising totalitarianism in Europe during the 1920s and 30s,
it is impossible to ignore the potential for authoritarian abuse in Sister Luke's vow of unquestioning obedience, especially when Nazi war
criminals would later claim at the Nuremberg trials that they were simply
obeying the orders of their military superiors (Neal 1990: 85).

Women religious in 1959 were not the only ones to react negatively
to *The Nun's Story*. While later feminist cultural critics have shown interest in its gender themes, they have tended to ignore, misconstrue,
or be dismissive of its religious significance, with Rebecca Sullivan recently arguing that both Hulme's book and Zinnemann's film "verge
on the tedious" and have not "survived the test of time."[10] The vow
of obedience is depicted as the great stumbling block to Sister Luke's
vocation in *The Nun's Story*, but it is also an impediment to contemporary appreciation of the film. The convent pressure exerted on Sister Luke to cultivate unthinking obedience carries the implication not
only of political submission to authoritarian rule but resigned acceptance
of an anti-intellectualism especially repugnant to feminist scholars who
value the role that liberal education has played in modern women's social
advancement and autonomy. The nun's running battle of conscience
with her congregation's exacting definition of this vow and her refusal
to compromise her professionalism might have earned the sympathy and
admiration of more feminist critics but it has not yet proved to be the
case. The films in Chapter 2 showed how the vow of chastity could be

---

[10] Rebecca Sullivan devotes a chapter to the making of *The Nun's Story* rather
than a critical analysis of the Zinnemann film or Hulme's book after concluding that
both were boring and passé. See "Whose Story Is *The Nun's Story*?" in *Visual Habits:
Nuns, Feminism, and American Postwar Popular Culture* (Toronto: University of Toronto Press, 2005), 95–123, esp. 96. Arthur Nolletti Jr. was surprised that *The Nun's
Story* "lends itself to feminist criticism but that there has been so little attention paid
to the film using this extremely vital approach." See "Spirituality and Style in *The
Nun's Story*," *The Films of Fred Zinnemann: Critical Perspectives*, ed. Nolletti (Albany:
State University of New York Press, 1999), 120–1.

tested in the religious life and acquire different and richer meaning from past, forgotten, or repressed desires. I want to suggest in this chapter how *The Nun's Story* probes the vow of obedience and redefines it within the history of desires that is created by the family and that is configured by a daughter's indelible love for her father.

At the time *The Nun's Story* was made, obedience was regarded as the pre-eminent vow of the religious life. Contrary to the popular belief that is exploited in *Black Narcissus*, chastity was less onerous and more spiritually meaningful for women religious than obedience (Wittberg 1994: 241–2, 250). Before Vatican II began in 1962, American nuns were generally held up as Catholic paragons in their devotion to lives of service and their loyalty to ecclesiastical authority (Schneiders 2000: 350–1). After the Council ended in 1965, obedience became the most difficult vow for nuns to follow, and they would come to be regarded as "the most rebellious group in the U.S. Church" (Burns 1994: 131; Neal 1990: 82–90).[11]

In the old world and authoritarian church culture of the 1920s and 30s, Sister Luke appears almost entirely alone in questioning the vow of obedience. Janus-faced in this respect as in others, *The Nun's Story* critiques the "blind obedience" that was the subject of occasional protest by exceptional women religious in the past.[12] It also looks forward to the time when nuns would be free to embrace Vatican II's *Declaration on Religious Liberty*, emphasizing that the individual was bound to obey the dictates of her own conscience, especially in religious matters (December 7, 1965). However, Zinnemann fully comprehended that the traditional convent was a house that survived because it was built upon the rock of institutional obedience, and that this vow assumed such importance because it compelled observance of the regulations canon law prescribed for religious life, and so maintained the institutional infrastructure of women's communities. This is why he devoted so much initial time in his film

---

[11] Sister Patricia Wittberg, S.C., points out that articles singling out obedience rather than chastity for discussion began to appear in U.S. religious journals during the 1950s. See *The Rise and Fall of Catholic Religious Orders: A Social Movement Perspective* (Albany: State University of New York Press, 1994), 127, 230, 241–3, 250.

[12] In *Singled Out: How Two Million Women Survived Without Men after the First World War* (London: Viking, 2007), 248, Virginia Nicholson quotes an English women who left her Anglican order in the 1920s because she realized she was "far too individualistic, far too independent, far too disinclined to blind obedience to fit into the Religious Life"—the dilemma of Sister Luke in Zinnemann's film.

to a documentary-like depiction of how impressionable young entrants were conditioned to this vow. He showed how it was defined in military and quasi-mystical terms as "obedience without question, without inner murmuring," and how it is the counsel of perfection that comes close to breaking the health and spirit of his conscience-torn nun heroine.

In carving out a place for themselves as women religious in the modern world, American sisters would take the lead in interpreting obedience with greater latitude and spiritual discernment as a non-hierarchical vow of responsiveness to God (Burns 1994: 141–2; Chittister 2005: 30, 143; Ebaugh 1993b: 65). Those in active apostolates would become sensitive to how psychologically debilitating petty rules could be, especially for community members with considerable professional responsibility. It became inconceivable that a highly intelligent nun would even contemplate deliberately failing an exam on the rash recommendation of an unwise superior, as Sister Luke is pressured to do in the film (Gordon 2002: 62). Yet stories abounded in the pre-Vatican convent of how unique talents were buried in the name of undisputed obedience to incompetent religious leaders who were mystified as having "the grace of office" (Curran 1989: 76; Campbell-Jones 1978: 82).[13] However, in thinking for themselves, nuns not only undermined the religious chain of command that gave institutional life its backbone but embarked on the initial questioning that Helen Ebaugh identified as the first stage in the process of exiting the convent (1988: 105–6). As I shall show in an alternative argument, which further suggests how this film looks forward and backward in time, ontological inquiry is also the first phase of the psychological formation that can lead to lifelong belief in God.

The question that the first critics of the film repeatedly asked was why the protagonist Gabrielle Van der Mal became a nun in the first place. Moira Walsh was unsure in *Catholic World* whether the "heroine ever had a true vocation" (July 1959: 315) as was Philip Hartung of *Commonweal* (July 17, 1959: 374). Henry Hart of *Films in Review* felt "the secular reasons that contributed to Gabrielle's becoming a nun should have been presented" (June–July 1959: 354). Hollis Alpert of the *Saturday Review* had no answer for why she entered the convent but concluded

---

[13] Carol L. Reed interviewed older nuns who recounted stories of "abusive and malicious superiors who held them back professionally (by) assigning those who wanted to become doctors to become housekeepers under the guise of instilling humility." Reed, *Unveiled: The Hidden Lives of Nuns* (New York: Berkley Books, 2004), 50.

that "Sister Luke was essentially a Protestant in a Catholic realm of world and spirit" (June 27, 1959: 24), a view echoed by *The Nation*, which applauded "the great, terrible, emancipating cry of Protestant" conscience that finally made her leave: "What I do from now on is between *You* and me alone" (July 4, 1959: 20).[14]

Zinnemann's camera moves from the exterior mystery of Catholic iconography deeper into a mystery of the self that baffled the first reviewers. Later critics debated whether the film should be seen as one that systematically distanced itself from Catholic religiosity or as one that moved toward a new and enhanced conception of spirituality (Sullivan 2006: 98, 109, 117, 121; Kauffmann, *The New Republic*, June 29, 1959: 21; Nolletti 1999: 121–5). I will focus on the psychological drama that precedes this debate, however, and show how the film deftly depicts the emotional origins of Sister Luke's religious vocation and her special difficulty with the vow of obedience. Although obedience was considered second nature for dutiful daughters who were deferential to paternal authority (Wittberg 1994: 127), the exceptional women who stood out in Protestant missionary accounts, Anglican community memoirs, and the testimonials of Catholic nuns were often "strong-willed, active and intelligent girls" (Mumm 1999: 57) like Gabrielle Van der Mal, "given a boy's education by proud fathers."[15] Indeed, Dr. Van der Mal (Dean Jagger) warns her on the brink of her admittance to the convent that obedience will be the most difficult vow for her to follow. "Gaby, I can see you poor, I can see you chaste, but I cannot see you, a strong-willed girl, obedient to those bells."

The obedience that the film heroine has learned from her diagnostic father is closer to the post-Vatican II definition, which drew on the Latin root word, *ob-audiere*, accentuating the obligation in the vow to listen attentively not only to conscience but to others in order to hear and discern the will of God (Wittberg 1994: 243; Burns 1994: 150–1).

---

[14] This is an astute critical observation as Hulme herself saw something in Sister Luke's religious life that "seemed to merit communication to a readership predominantly Protestant" and felt her story would bridge the gaps in understanding "between members of the Christian family." See "'The Nun's Story'—A Symposium: Author's View," *America*, June 27, 1959: 468.

[15] See Helen Rose Fuchs Ebaugh's discussion of "traditional nuns as unwitting feminists" in *Women in the Vanishing Cloister: Organizational Decline in Catholic Religious Orders in the United States* (New Brunswick, N.J.: Rutgers University Press, 1993), 133–8.

In this respect, the film departs very significantly from Hulme's book where "old-fashioned obedience to a parent's wishes" leads Gabrielle to the convent after her father has refused to let her marry her boyfriend, Jean (Hulme 1956: 9). For Zinnemann's film protagonist, the conflict is not between obedience to her father and following her heart. The mis-en-scène in her bedroom on the day she enters the convent emphasizes her free and happy choice of the religious life—symbolized by the large photo of a Congo missionary nun on her bedroom wall—over marriage to Jean who is pictured in a small frame on her dressing table. For the obedience she has internalized from her father instructs her to listen to her heart. Obedience to the loving, accepting, approving, encouraging voice of the father will be the cause of her disobedience in the convent.

The reading of Hulme's 1956 bestseller *The Nun's Story* was "a major emotional experience" for Zinnemann (*America*, 469). The moral conflict at the heart of the nun's story, between the individual's loyalty to an institution and fidelity to conscience, was a subject that had not only personal but artistic importance for Zinnemann. He had refused to take the loyalty oath prescribed by the pro-McCarthy board of the Screen Directors Guild earlier in the fifties (Deveau 2005: 139–41). He heroicized the individual's conflict with the military system in *From Here to Eternity* (1953) and with the royal and legal court in *A Man for All Seasons* (1966). However, this signature film theme was given an interesting twist in *The Nun's Story* (1959) because he was examining a corporate religious body that encompassed within itself other institutional models. The nun's life in the convent is a series of passages from one enclosed system to another: first, the motherhouse, which resembles a female penitentiary, a boarding school, and a boot camp; then, her first assignment to a padlocked mental asylum, followed by her journey to the colonial compound of the white hospital, a leper's colony and private TB sanatorium in the Congo; and culminating in her return to the mother/prison house, internment of sorts during the German occupation of Europe in World War II, and eventual release from her long sentence to institutional life. In tracking the nun protagonist as she undergoes one punishing incarceration after another, Zinnemann suggested that her powers of resistance derived from the enduring importance of her home world. As Goffman pointed out, "Whether a particular total institution acts as a good or bad force in civil society, force it will have, and this will in part depend on the suppression of a whole circle of actual or potential households" (1991: 22). The obedience Gaby has learned in her father's household is never wholly suppressed in the convent, and the strength of her familial formation is an internal defense against religious institutionalization.

Audrey Hepburn

Audrey Hepburn's own personal history gave her interpretative insight into the events that are recounted in *The Nun's Story*. She grew up in Holland during World War II and knew Sister Luke's experience of deprivation and suffering during the Nazi occupation. Her aristocratic Dutch mother was an imposing matriarch, undemonstrative, hard to please, and with a natural proclivity for "talent-stripping," like some religious superiors (Campbell-Jones 1978: 82). When her daughter was recognized as a star, she marveled, "Considering that you have no talent, it's really extraordinary where you've got" (Paris 1997: 372). Hepburn would later explain poignantly that her mother "had a lot of love *within* her, but she was not always able to show it" (Paris 1997: 7), a realization that she worked into Sister Luke's strained rapport with the mother superiors, strict disciplinarians and "living rules" of her religious congregation.

By all accounts, Hepburn's Anglo-Irish father was a disturbing mix of the romantic and the right wing in his penchant for adventure and fascist causes. Yet although he deserted his wife and six-year-old daughter, Hepburn admitted that she "worshiped him" as a child and that his abrupt departure was a "tragedy" (Paris 1997: 9) from which she never fully recovered. In the films that propelled her to stardom in the 1950s such as *Sabrina* (1954), *Funny Face* (1957), and *Love in the Afternoon* (1957), she played the adorable daddy's girl who falls in love with such Hollywood father figures as Humphrey Bogart, Fred Astaire, and Gary Cooper (Walker 1997: 147). In *Roman Holiday* (1953), the first film that brought her fame, she instinctively began to channel her emotional vulnerability into her screen performances. As she later explained: "Actors, directors, technicians . . . there's something in some of them that makes you open up to them. . . . I was born with an enormous need for affection . . . even when I was small. And a terrible need to give it, like every child" (Paris 1997: 375–6). Hepburn perfected the art of pent-up need in her thwarted role as Sister Luke. In her character's relationship to Dr. Van der Mal, she could at last play out her longing for the father who loved and believed in her, who would never willingly desert her, and whose sudden, barbarous death leaves her utterly desolate.

Like Deborah Kerr, Hepburn projected a Victorian gender ideal in *The Nun's Story*, one that was preserved in the old-fashioned manners of the traditional convent (Suenens 1963: 18). Indeed, this ideal was still culturally approved for respectable women in both the old and new world who grew up between the two World Wars, especially those from a conservative Catholic background. She played a devoted daughter from an affluent and socially prestigious family who could afford to be high-minded. Gaby's chaste idealism is also the mark of a girl who lived in the shadow of the motherhouse and had prolonged contact with nuns extending from childhood up through late adolescence when she enters the cloister. Her sexual naivety is first shown in her blithe insensibility to the fate of her boyfriend, Jean, whose life is involuntarily shaped by her vows as a nun, and later in her obtuseness about the erotic feelings that arise between her and the Congo surgeon with whom she works closely.

In private, Hepburn endorsed this sheltered image by privileging the security of marriage, motherhood, and a comfortable home over her film career. While the nuns who first saw the film were hostile to her portrayal of Sister Luke, American Catholic lay women such as Moira Walsh were moved by "her extraordinarily sensitive and well-modulated performance" (*Catholic World* 315). This may be because the actress made her female viewers conscious of parallels between the hidden lives of religious in the convent and their invisible lives in the home (Chittister 2005: 18; Campbell 2003: 86). Hepburn's stricken face as Sister Luke registered the quiet unhappiness and despair of middle-class women in the fifties who "chafed against their restricted spheres" (Rosen 1995: 313–21). Betty Friedan traced their unhappiness to a false gender belief system that she called *The Feminine Mystique* in 1963. These housebound women communicated a non-verbal message of frustration and disappointment that is also conveyed through the nun's body language of dejection, weeping, exhaustion, and illness.

Although *The Nun's Story* was a serious departure from the romantic comedies that made her a star, paradoxically the restrained role of Sister Luke elicited hidden talents from Hepburn as an actress (Vineberg 1999: 232; Sinyard 2003: 82). She felt a strong professional affinity with the nun protagonist: "I am like Sister Luke in many ways" (Spoto 2006: 121, 137). As a perfectionist, she understood the nun's neurotic pursuit of a religious state of perfection. As a highly disciplined performer, respected for her stamina and composure on set, she admired "the show-must-go-on" courage and calm exercised by the nuns in this film. While Hepburn was criticized for her impeccable good looks in the habit of a nun, ordinary women "wept openly" (Young 1959: 16) because her youthful beauty called dramatic attention to the sacrifice of female sexuality and embodiment that Gabrielle was required to make but was not wholly aware of herself. Zinnemann's camera took custody of Hepburn's large, expressive eyes and made them the windows through which the audience gains insight into "the heroic demands" of the religious life (Zinnemann, *America*, 469), and beholds the nun's "never-ending struggle for self-perfection." In *The Nun's Story* Hepburn gave her most moving and consummate screen performance, bringing to the role of Sister Luke a conviction born not of Catholic faith but a sad, compassionate understanding of character.

The Catholic Family Romance

The role of Sister Luke also made heroic demands on the actress because she features in almost every scene of the film. Indeed, she first appears in the opening credits, standing as Gabrielle Van der Mal on a bridge near her home and gazing down into the canal waters at her own wavering reflection, symbolic of her later religious identity crisis. As she silently reflects on the radical step she is about to take, the voiceover of a nun mature in faith is heard quoting Christ's counter-cultural counsel to the apostles: "He that shall lose his life for me, shall find it" (Matt. 10:39). This paradoxical precept summons the nun to practice the self-emptying, self-giving, and self-forgetting love, which is a response to God's own outpouring of love in agape and which lies at the heart of religious life (Nygren 1953: 213, 232). Yet there is no corresponding recognition that the young and immature candidate cannot lose her life unless she has first found herself, cannot offer her life up to the service of God if she has not developed the desires and gifts of the self known as eros. Thus, at the very outset, the film adumbrates the interior dilemma that Gabrielle will experience in the convent, a dilemma arising from the traditional opposition between self-sacrificing agape and self-regarding eros (Brock 1988: 34). Even after Gabrielle has entered her family house, a brooding camera continues to stare into the canal as it flows past the imposing Belgian motherhouse that will rule her life. As film critics have noted, the initial impression is that of an upside-down world (Rapf 1999: 239; Fitzpatrick 1983: 382). This is a world where Gabrielle's hopes and longings will be overturned and her obedience as a daughter inverted into disobedience as a nun.

Zinnemann's film reflects a close and intelligent reading of Hulme's book. One feature of the doctor-daughter's character formation assumes great visual meaning in his film interpretation. Gabrielle Van der Mal has been trained to be observant and inquiring, and it is through her watchful eyes that the hidden world of the cloister is first opened to the film viewer. This habit of intent looking will also contribute to her disobedience in the convent. However, it is a crucial feature of early mirror bonding in which the young child sees herself in the face of the primary caretaker and seeks reassurance there that she is wanted, cherished, and loved (Winnicott 1992: 111–18). The human need for recognition and approbation, in turn, gives rise to the family romance where the child both seeks and creates an alternative family in the imagination. The psychic function of this imagined family is to continue the mirroring process, provide other forms of belonging, and satisfy the desires for self-affirmation and aggrandizement that cannot be met by the real parents (Rizzuto 1981: 186, 198). Freud saw this family romance at play in those make-believe narratives where the child fancies that she is an "orphan" and invents eminent figures who bestow some special sign of their grace upon her. On closer inspection, these figures replace, magnify, and finally re-create the original parents (1909, SE 9: 238–41).

Freud regarded God as the "exalted father" who was the supreme creation of the child's grandiose imagination (1910, SE 11: 123). Some religious and psychoanalytic thinkers have concluded that a mature faith requires the deconstruction of this childish father God (Schneiders 2000: 192; Bingaman 2003: 17–19). However, others have seen the beauty and truth in the Freudian theory that faith in God shows the lifelong hold of the family romance over the human mind. They have noted the benevolent role that both the mother and father can play in the child's early creation of a God image as well as in the later development of a mature and vibrant faith (Erikson 1993: 115–119; Rizzuto 1980: 121, and 1981: 194).[16] They did not agree with Freud that the family romance is a wish-

---

[16] Ana-Maria Rizzuto also conceded that the religious sublimation of parents sometimes had a deleterious as well as beneficial effect on the spiritual development of her adult patients, but "was a rich, variegated phenomenon, with such complex impacts on psychic life, that to take any single point of view would be reductionist." See The Birth of the Living God: A Psychoanalytic Study (Chicago: University of Chicago Press, 1981), 88. Rizzuto's study remains a landmark work in its respect for the psychical complexities that produce a representation of God and for the private experience that underlies individual faith. Rizzuto's beautiful appeal in her epilogue is to the Freud of "Family Romances" (1909) who understood the heart and not only the head, "the Freud of object relations, the Oedipus complex, family relations" (212). One of the few women writers on spirituality to recognize its "profound" implications is Joan Wolski Conn, "Dancing in the Dark: Women's Spirituality and

fulfilling story that must be altogether outgrown. Indeed, for Melanie Klein, this romance could be spun out over a lifetime, begetting not only religious belief but the child's enduring faith in herself, loved ones, and other people, and so become:

> a benign circle, for in the first place we gain trust and love in relation to our parents, next we take them, with all this love and trust, as it were, into ourselves; and then we give from this wealth of loving feelings to the outer world again. (1994: 340)

For Klein, this ever-turning and unfolding romance is "like a rock which withstands the blows of circumstance" because it gives the child the permanent assurance, even when the parents are no longer present, that she is inherently good, loveable and loving (1994: 341).

Actual nuns have certainly testified to the influence that loving mothers and fathers had in their vocational calling and in their belief that God took a passionate interest in their lives. Sometimes it was the lost and longed-for parent who led them to the convent. For example, Sister Gloria Perez, P.B.V.M., gave a candid personal interview, which may shed light on what puzzled the first film reviewers—namely, why Gabrielle Van der Mal became a nun:

> My mother died when I was four and a half years old. And that to me is a very significant reason why I entered religious life. I did not enter religious life for all the most wonderful holy reasons. What I really did was, I entered to find a mother. . . . My father . . . put me in a Catholic high school (in the 1950s). And I met the nuns. And I fell in love with them. They were wonderful teachers; they were caring women. I think it was the first time in my life that I looked at women as women. They were just so good at everything they did. I wanted to be just like them. (Rogers 1996: 7–8)

As Hulme herself made clear at the beginning of *The Nun's Story*, "Gabrielle saw the outlines of a great family" in the Belgian congregation that she joined (1956: 31–2). As Zinnemann's film shows, it is this Catholic romance of a great and good family of caring women that draws Gabrielle to the convent.

To begin with, Gabrielle seems "sure" of her religious vocation; indeed her calm resolution to enter the convent contrasts dramatically with

---

Ministry," *Women's Spirituality: Resources for Christian Development*, ed. Conn, 2nd ed. (New York: Paulist Press, 1996), 13.

the distress and disquiet she causes her family, the well-to-do offspring of an eminent Belgian surgeon. When she tells Dr. Van der Mal that it would perhaps be better if she went in alone, he tellingly replies: "you're not an orphan, or going without your father's consent." The not-said is her missing mother. In Hulme's book, Gaby reflects inwardly as a new postulant on how this half-orphaned state determined her role in the Catholic family romance: "She had never been a child. . . . She had been the replacement for the mother who had died so early that only she could remember her clearly" (1956: 22). The early scenes in the film reflect Zinnemann's perceptive reading of these lines. They simmer with the tension of a family who now feels abandoned by their surrogate mother and are suffused with the intense, incestuous tenderness of a father who has made his daughter a substitute companion for his dead wife. Entrance into the convent is a backward-looking search for a mother substitute who will call her "my child"—and often treat her like one. The more forward-looking foundation of her vocation is devotion to her doctor father and wish not only to emulate him professionally but become like Sister William (Patricia Collinge), the nun who worked by his side as a surgical nursing sister.[17]

The Motherhouse

Once behind the grilled and locked door of the cloister, Gabrielle learns that she must repress the family romance, which facilitates the enlarged play of feelings in the personality and creates the widening circumference for later beliefs and loves. She is drilled by the Mistress of Postulants (Mildred Dunnock), a cool and aloof personality like Sister Clodagh, in the necessity of "detachment," not only from her "family and friends" but from "things and memories" that call up her former life. Film cinematographer Franz Planer conveyed the interior culture of emotional mortification and impersonal charity that the postulant now encountered by using pale and subdued colors in the motherhouse (Nolletti 1999: 124). Church officials who monitored the making of *The Nun's Story* were understandably concerned that the director was visualizing the religious life with too much severity (Vizzard 1971: 231). In point of fact, radical separation from family was routine and enforced through such

[17]Zinnemann emphasized the influence of this minor character in the convent entrance scene where Sister William and Gabrielle violate protocol by talking together privately apart from the other new postulants.

practices as censorship of personal mail and curtailment of visiting rights (Schneiders 2001: 208–9).

Yet Gaby's personal God was largely created in the image of her loving doctor father; she worships the one and imitates the other as healer, comforter, and saver of lives. She must forfeit her maiden name in the convent but cannot forget her kinship and identification with her father when she is given the religious name of Luke, the patron saint of doctors. Indeed, the ideals of her singular family romance unconsciously dictate the moral choices she makes throughout *The Nun's Story*. Although she does not realize it when she first becomes a nun, her holiest desire is "to become a good nurse." Over the course of the film, she repeatedly fails the tests of obedience that inculcate spiritual perfection, and her faith in God is shaken to the core by the death of her father. However, her desire to be a good nurse remains adamantine. Only when she has a last interview with her Superior General, Reverend Mother Emmanuel (Edith Evans), does it become fully evident to either woman that she entered the convent seventeen years before for the wrong reasons: "You entered the convent to be a nun, not to be a nurse. The religious life must be more important than your love of medicine." The religious contract between the nun and her congregation was founded on a tragic misunderstanding. Both parties underestimated the psychic indestructibility of the original family romance, with its replay of love for the father and his medical legacy. All the molecules of Sister Luke's character, which the film takes as samples and subjects to the scrutiny of the laboratory microscope— her "real spirit," "stubbornness," "strength," "ferocious will," tenacity of purpose, and powers of concentration—derive from this bedrock source.

Women religious now look back with astonishment at the fact that prior to the 1960s, communities paid so little attention to the family history and personal upbringing of their candidates. *The Nun's Story* is thus remarkable to focus on the complex psychological origins of vocational motivation. After the Vatican Council call to review religious life, congregations began to examine the unhealthy emotional aspects of the pseudo-family convent culture that replaced primary relationships in the home (Schneiders 2001: 210–11). Yet with a characteristic even-handedness as a director, Zinnemann also saw the romance of this surrogate religious family. Fittingly, Sister Luke catches her first glimpse of her adopted family in Christ when she is first ushered into the gallery overlooking the motherhouse chapel below. As film spectators, we sense her awe as she beholds an inner sanctum, which is veiled from the outside world and which evokes the womb of the desired and idealized

good mother (Riviere 1991: 325). Zinnemann captured the stark black-
and-white beauty of this oratory with nuns ranked in stalls running the
length of the chapel. He emphasized the grace and synchronism of this
corporate religious body by choreographing this scene with the help of
the ballet corps from the Rome Opera. His intention was not simply to
stage a magnificent spectacle of Movie Catholicism.[18] He was visualizing
the analogy that Hulme made explicit in her book. If the nun's life looks
beautiful, it conceals a story of discipline, pain, grit, and sacrifice that is
comparable to the training of a prima ballerina (Hulme 1956: 52).

Yet despite the "great beauty and reverence" that impressed the first
film reviewers (Hartung, *Commonweal*, 374), there is something chilling
and disembodied about this family whom Gaby formally embraces while
prostrate on the floor, a family that greets her in the chapel with their
backs turned, their faces resolutely averted, and whose mother superior
sits ramrod straight, her back never touching her chair. Gaby is instructed
by the Mistress of Postulants that "we do not engage in useless conversations. We use a kind of sign language. We never touch another sister,
of course." She is taught to hug the walls of the convent corridor and
adopt abject body language, minimizing movement, when she walks.
She is trained in the "culpa" and "penance," which promote self-con-
demnation and corporate punishment of any familiarities with her new
female family. She publicly confesses before them that she and another
novice have been "seeking each other's company"—early warning sign
of the "particular friendships" that were regarded as socially and sexually
dangerous (Loudon 1993: 82–3). She is instructed by Reverend Mother
Emmanuel to "ask God to help you to overcome this attachment" and
to beg her bread and kiss the feet of her fellow sisters like a prisoner in
a poor house.[19] A convent cell replaces the comfortable bedroom she

---

[18] In fact, Zinnemann was emphatic that he did not want to make a "Catholic"
film: "One of the things I wanted to do on the film was not to have any Catholics,
not the writer or the actors, because I was worried about getting an 'in' film—a film
that would be very meaningful to Catholics but that nobody else would want to look
at." See "Dialogue on Film: Fred Zinnemann," as well as Arthur Nolletti's "Conversation with Fred Zinnemann" in *Fred Zinnemann Interviews*, ed. Gabriel Miller
(Jackson: The University Press of Mississippi, 2005), 99, 125.

[19] Karen Armstrong recalled the contrast between the scene where Sister Luke
gracefully begs her bread and kisses the feet of her fellow nuns in refectory in *The
Nun's Story* and "the prosaic nature of the whole penance: the squashed peas under
the table, the taste of boot polish, the bunions" when she was in the convent. Armstrong, *Through the Narrow Gate: A Nun's Story* (London: Flamingo, 1997), 153.

had in her father's haut-bourgeois home. It resembles the curtained-off cubicle in the public ward of a hospital. This cell prefigures the sickness of body and spirit she will cure as a nurse but suffer periodically as a nun in her futile attempts to detach herself from primary "family and friends," "things and memories," "wishes (and) desires."[20]

Reverend Mother Emmanuel's uncompromising advice to her incoming postulants in Hulme's book was that the life of a nun is "a life against nature" (1956: 26)—in other words, one of renunciation, and requiring, as Pope Paul VI later counseled, the "sacrifice of the human love experienced . . . in family life" (Pitts 2009: 93). Not surprisingly, this line was an ideological sticking point between Zinnemann and the Catholic authorities who policed this sensitive film project. They wished to see the religious calling exalted as a "life *above* nature" with ascetic denial leading to spiritual transcendence. Harold Gardiner, the literary editor of *America* and Jesuit adviser on the making of the film, suggested a compromise wording that Edith Evans would improvise on-screen as "*in a way*, it's a life *against* nature" (Paris 1997: 143; Zinnemann 2005: 99; Nolletti 2005: 126–7). Indeed one reason why critics of *The Nun's Story* find Sister Luke a character who "both attracts and repels" (Hartung, *Commonweal*, 374; Kauffmann, *The New Republic*, 21), and why they remain divided over the film, is that her undertaking seems so unnatural, at once inhuman and superhuman. The religious aspirant is systematically stripped of her individuality and, as traditional nuns explain, "any status gained from family background, education, worldly achievements, or possessions" (Donovan and Wusinich 2009: 27).

However, Zinnemann also showed his appreciation in this and other ceremonial scenes of the role that renunciation and sublimation have played in religion's high cultural achievements (Van Herik 1985: 18–19, 57, 84). Like a Gothic cathedral, the life of the cloistered community not only defied the laws of nature but celebrated the human elevation of spirit through union in prayer with God. The daily rigors of obedience were the flying buttresses of this cathedral, and while these supports appeared graceful feats of construction, in reality they had to withstand enormous pressure. For his close-ups of the nuns who personify Reverend Mother Emmanuel's advice, Zinnemann chose faces from the old Roman aristocracy (Paris 1997: 144). He conveyed Gaby's startled im-

---

[20] Curran, *Grace Before Meals*, 144, observed that "dis-ease was present even in the first quarter of the century," when Gaby became a nun, "but by 1960 candidates were highly stressed."

pression in Hulme's book that she is staring at "a family of statues" (1956: 8) by giving their visages the austere, weathered and burnished look of the saints on a cathedral portal.

Zinnemann will go on to show how the religious life that the mother superior recommends is the height of heroic folly for Sister Luke because it runs contrary to her *better* nature. As a result, renunciation will require continual repression of her core desires and will block the sublimation of the erotic into the activities of scientific inquiry, nursing care, surgery, and missionary service. Mother Emmanuel concludes her address to her new recruits with the caution that "if you question these exercises in humility, these steps towards a closer unity with our crucified Lord, you do not belong with us." Yet one of the early signs of cognitive maturity is the child's growing fascination with causality and reliance on her parents for the answer to her first questions. The child's ceaseless musings help to spin not only the superior beings of the family romance but a God who is *living* and not made of stone. This God begins existence as an idealization of the parents and grows, evolves, diminishes in importance, or dies in response to the vicissitudes of life and the developmental history of the individual (Rizzuto 1981: 44–53). In the convent, however, questioning is culpable, along with the past attachments, associations, and aspirations that give rise to the family romance and give flesh for Gaby to a personal God.

Psychic Mirroring

In an insightful, Protestant-inflected commentary on the "abasement before God" that is required of Gaby in the convent, the reviewer of *The Nation* saw that what distinguished her from the other nun aspirants was her desire to see God face to face (20). This need is encoded in Paul's assurance to the Corinthians—"Now we see through a glass darkly, but then we shall see face to face" (I Cor. 13:12). He poetically expressed here the hope of finding God in the psychic mirror that is first formed when the baby looks at her mother or father and perceives herself through the responses on their faces. This early mirroring establishes the need for meaningful eye contact throughout life, and the exchange of intimate glances is used by the child not only to understand herself and her relationship to her parents and significant others, but to reflect on what God is like (Rizzuto 1981: 122, 184–6; Erikson 1993: 115; Winnicott 1992: 111–12). In the second hour of *The Nun's Story*, Sister Luke is often shown peering into the medical microscope that reflects back the proud paternal eye and constantly reminds her that she is loved and admired. In the first hour of the film, however, she is locked into what Hulme described as the "mirrorless world" of the motherhouse (1956: 34), where she is instructed to exercise "custody of the eyes" and not look directly at her fellow sisters or commit the sin of vanity by viewing her own reflection. Although Zinnemann depicts the novel enjoyment Gaby takes in putting on her hat without a looking glass when leaving home for the convent, he gradually shows the psychological danger of not being seen—which is to lose sight of herself.

From her first moments in the motherhouse, Gabrielle is singularized from the ordinary rank and file of nuns by her reflexive "upward disobedient glance" (Hulme 1956: 8). In the chapel gallery she will be mesmerized by a ritual that is unfamiliar but that, ironically, will hold the mirror up to her future religious life. It is that of a nun abasing herself in apology before the mother superior for being late to chapel. As she will confess seventeen years later to this same superior, "I'm late every day for refectory or chapel or both." When the new postulants later prostrate themselves before Reverend Mother Emmanuel during their formal admittance ceremony, a medium close-up captures Gabrielle stealing another disobedient glance up at the majestic "Gothic face" (Hulme 1956: 316) of her new spiritual mother. There is a brief flicker of acknowledgement in close-up that subtly suggests a mysterious recognition of exceptionality on both sides. It is followed by a formal question that has great personal significance for Gabrielle: "What do you ask, my children?" What she asks of this exalted figure is her maternal notice. Although she is instructed that the desire for personal recognition is wrong, she is impelled by a need for the psychic mirroring that will not only allow her to reflect upon who she is as a daughter in the religious life but will give her a more complete likeness of God. Her disobedient glance upwards stems from the wish to look into the eyes of Reverend Mother Emmanuel and see her as she is described by the Mistress of Postulants—as the one who "represents Christ among us and as such, she is loved and obeyed by us."

Obedience, Work, and Love

At the beginning of the film, the nun's father raised the question that perplexed the first film reviewers—why "a strong-willed girl" like Gabrielle Van de Mal would become obedient to the bells of the convent. Her answer brims with desire—"In the Congo, Father, they'll be calling me to work I love"—and echoes the view Freud later expressed in his

1930 essay on *Civilization and Its Discontents*: that love and work are the foundation of civilized humanity (*SE* 21:101). However, her father warns her that "your personal wishes cease to exist when you enter that door" and that she is gambling with her life—with her very subjectivity—to assume she will ever be sent to Africa. Yet one of the few respectable ways that a young, single, white woman from a reputable Belgian family could aspire to work in the Congo in the late 1920s was as a missionary sister (French 1978: 133). Canon law prohibited missionary nuns from becoming doctors or doing surgical and obstetrical work until 1936, so nursing was the only option open to Sister Luke despite her desire to follow in her father's footsteps and evident talent for surgery (Bernstein 1976: 247–8; Weaver 1995: 33–4). Today, Sister Luke would no longer have to content herself with being a nursing sister and might well work for a secular, humanitarian organization such as *Medicins sans Frontieres*, which still trains its physicians at the School of Tropical Medicine in Antwerp where she is sent in 1928 after completing her novitiate. This was also the symbolic first step taking her out of the female cloister and into a modern, scientific, and masculine world where her real-life counterparts "were exposed to ideas that frequently challenged the very existence of the God they worshipped" (Ebaugh 1988: 107) and that in the long run, made them question their religious vocation. After Vatican II, it would become evident to religious orders that as nuns became better educated and received more professional training, there was a correlative danger that they would leave the convent as Sister Luke finally does in the film (Ebaugh 1993b: 24).

Training in tropical medicine was only open to nuns in the 1920s, so when Sister Luke is sent to the School of Tropical Medicine in Antwerp, she assumes it is the first stage of her desired journey to the mission stations of Africa (McNamara 1996: 625). Hulme described this posting as "a homecoming into the world of medical thought" (1956: 81), but Zinnemann dramatized the conflict of interests that arises in the familiar world of the class laboratory. First, proud memories of her distinguished surgeon father intrude. The doctor who teaches the course on tropical diseases will allow neither her nor the class to forget that she is her "father's daughter—excellent!" and was raised to take a professional interest in medicine: "She was brought up looking through a microscope while most of you were playing with kaleidoscopes." Second, the simmering, sibling rivalries of her adopted convent family surface when another student nun, the slow learner Sister Pauline (Margaret Phillips), shows jealous resentment of Sister Luke's distinction as a medical student and confides her grievances to their local mother superior. Her antagonism reflects the tension that talented and well-educated nuns such as Sister Luke could cause within a small and parochial religious community, especially one headed by an unwise superior (Coburn and Smith 1999: 80–1, 186–7; Kennelly 1996: 62–5). Mother Marcella (Ruth White) suggests that Sister Luke has been given a God-sent opportunity to become what her order desires—a "perfect nun . . . obedient in all things unto death." In a distortion of the religious ideal of agape, she is called upon to sacrifice her intelligence, her aptitude and her learning to God and "fail" her medical exam in order that the mediocre Sister Pauline may "succeed." Her superior's proposal violates the religious principle that true obedience should not repress, dehumanize, or diminish the dignity of the nun (Pitts 2009: 107). Sister Luke's desire to be a missionary nurse in the Congo is the deepest and most authentic expression of the commandment to love God with all her heart, soul, mind, and strength.

Zinnemann staged the film scene of Sister Luke's final oral examination in tropical medicine as an agonizing conflict of conscience in which she has been harried into choosing between the spiritual perfection of the professed nun and the skilled perfectionism of the professional nurse. Hepburn's face is white with the stress of this inner drama, her eyes the windows of a soul torn in two, her hand clutched to her throat as she gags on right answers, which are a secret test of pride and recalcitrance. Her concerned professor unwittingly increases her suffering with his words of encouragement: "I promised I would call your father immediately after the exam." In the name of the father, Sister Luke fails the spiritual test in radical humility she has been set and instead distinguishes herself in her public exams by coming fourth in a class of eighty. Because she has donned the habit of mute obedience, heavy with many previous lifetimes of sisters who "did good and disappeared," Sister Luke never learns which rule she has broken in Antwerp—whether it was failing her first religious trial as a nun or passing her medical finals with flying colors. Even as a novice she realizes that she is temperamentally in a no-win situation: "The more I try, the more imperfect I become. When I succeed in obeying the rule, I fail . . . because I have pride in succeeding." Her pursuit of excellence in everything she does is perceived as spiritual egotism and leaves her prone to the pathological spiral of guilt, fault-finding, and exacting conscience that is known in the religious life as scrupulosity (Ricoeur 2004: 425; Kaylin 2000: 133). There is a terrible irony in the disciplinary action that is taken against Sister Luke for openly demonstrating how much she loves her medical work. She is sent to a mental sanatorium near Brussels, while the other nuns in her class, including the incompetent Sister Pauline, are given coveted postings in the Congo.

Mental Incarceration

Sister Luke's spell at this mental sanatorium furnishes some of the most harrowing moments of *The Nun's Story*. Despite her outstanding nursing abilities, she is assigned the grim duty of assistant warden and locked for up to ten hours at a time in the bathhouse where the most violent lunatics are kept immobilized. The deafening cacophony in this room is the antithesis of the choral harmony in the motherhouse chapel. In this Marat-Sade setting, she has nothing to contemplate but the meaning of bedlam, and in a medical era that had not yet discovered the merciful release of anti-depressant drugs, she finds that she is not a nurse so much as gate-keeper at the howling mouth of hell. Although Sister Luke is unaware of the danger, the locked cell of the madhouse reflects her own isolation in the cloister. With the habit muffling her body language as an actress, Hepburn now made her own eyes the eloquent mirrors to the desolation of being disregarded and passed over (Paris 1997: 150–1; Walker 1997: 206). These eyes take on a trapped look in the asylum, and become prone to what Lacan would call *méconnaissance* or misrecognition arising from the flawed views of others.[21]

Sister Luke becomes fascinated with one of the most dangerous patients in the Brussels asylum, a woman schizophrenic who believes she is the Archangel Gabriel (Colleen Dewhurst), and who makes prolonged eye contact with the nun when they first greet each other at the grilled window of her cell. The solitary confinement of this patient poignantly reminds her of the loneliness of the enclosed and incommunicado self. The deluded belief that "one might be able to get through to someone like her" will put this nun's life at risk and proceeds from her own disobedient desire for recognition and understanding. Although forbidden to open the door to the Archangel's cell without another sister present, Sister Luke breaks another rule of her order and responds to the basic

[21] Unlike Winnicott, Klein, and Rizzuto, Lacan did not think either parent could be a reliable mirror of identity for the child. Ellie Ragland-Sullivan explains: "Each of us tries to become whole or ideal in the eyes of others on the basis of a desire to be thought of in certain ways, which others can never validate as fully true." See her discussion of Lacan and the imaginary in *Feminism and Psychoanalysis: A Critical Dictionary*, ed. Elizabeth Wright (Oxford: Blackwell, 1992), 174.

human need of this patient—"I am so thirsty! . . . a terrible thirst!" This request is irresistible because it is a complicated appeal to both her nursing and religious instincts, in which she hears not only the cry of a sick and helpless patient, or a fitful child who cannot sleep at night, but Christ calling to her in his extremity of thirst on the Cross. In reaching out to this inmate, the horrified Sister Luke finds herself caught off guard as she is yanked into the padded cell. The film viewer is drawn with her into a dramatic vortex staged by Zinnemann to suggest the nun is wrestling in the night with the angel of death. The uneven character of this contest is underlined by Colleen Dewhurst's menacing size and muscularity as the demented Archangel, and by the fact that when she rips off the holy veil and exposes the white coif that sculpts Sister Luke's head, Hepburn resembles a rag doll. The nun's desperate struggle to escape is given an interior thrust and intensity by the fact that it occurs in almost complete silence and is only punctured by a trinitarian cry which we realize at once is wrenched from her very soul, "God . . . God . . . God."

When she later makes her *culpa* to her new superior, Mother Christophe (Beatrice Straight), Sister Luke confesses to maverick pride and a "sense of heroism." Sister Luke's confession of faults, however, is flawed by *méconnaissance*. She does not recall that before the Archangel called out

Figure 3-1. Sister Luke's distorted mirror reflection is a symbol of her tortured religious identity in the strict cloister.

to her, she was momentarily distracted by the sight of her own wimpled face in a highly polished metal inkstand on the warden's desk. The face that stared uncannily back at her was one she barely recognized.[22] The metal surface has shrunk her reflection and made it as distorted as the wavering images that open the film—of the cross, the church, the convent, and the solitary self in the canal waters. Her spiritual dilemma is that she is required to engage in scrupulous examination of conscience but at the same time is forbidden to look at herself or scrutinize others.[23] This may explain why she never seems to realize that the woman who thirsts in the cell reflects her own spiritual aridity. Nor can she see that the madwoman calls herself by a name that bears secret resemblance to her own. That name is a hieroglyph of her conflicted desires as an enclosed nun—for deliverance, for flight, and for freedom in the sight of God.[24] Above all, she has a need to be known not solely as the cipher Sister Luke but as Gabrielle, that spirited sub-personality who is held prisoner in the nun's cell. Gilbert and Gubar's famous description of the madwoman in the attic as Jane Eyre's dark double, her angry secret self, explains the forbidden attraction that the Archangel Gabriel has for Sister Luke (1979: 360). When she responded to the entreaty of this patient, she was hearing her own *cri de coeur* as a religious. In vainly imagining that she might help this other Gabriel, she was trying to save herself. It is left to her father to ask her superiors "an angry question" on behalf of this secret self—why has her order sent her to a madhouse and not the missions in the Congo?

The Father Figure

In Catholic Belgium, Sister Luke's "father is a very great man," and it is evident from Gabrielle's first interview as a new postulant with Reverend Mother Emmanuel that his patriarchal influence reaches inside the cloister. Very great men have not had great track records for empowering the women close to them, although they have inspired the adoration that is the foundation of early religious belief or fascist hero worship. Brandon

---

[22] In his 1919 essay on "The 'Uncanny,'" Freud recalled how he was disturbed by a stranger while alone in a train compartment, only to discover "to my dismay that the intruder was nothing but my own reflection in the looking-glass on the open door." See *SE* 17: 248n.1.

[23] Hulme described this dilemma as that of "the inner awful mirror of the mirrorless convent world" in *The Nun's Story*, 91.

[24] Rizzuto suggests that the fantasy of the twin or the angel can function as an alter ego and an embodiment of unfulfilled desires in *The Birth of the Living God*, 198.

French saw an incestuous male trinity at work in this film, comprising three gods who are competing influences in Sister Luke's religious life, starting with Christ and her father, and followed by Dr. Fortunati in Africa. In her brilliant but wholly secular feminist analysis, Dr. Van der Mal is the earliest representation of the triune male supremacy "which she worships but cannot obey" (1978: 133; Nolletti 1999: 120–1). My object relations interpretation suggests an alternative film dynamic in which the empowering natural father and the strict adopted mother offer competing views of how God is to be worshipped and served, and how obedience should be written on the tablets of the human heart (2 Cor. 3:3).

I see no evidence in *The Nun's Story* of the paternal coercion and domination that run through Freud's theories of gender, culture, and religion, but in the next chapter, I examine films that reflect his ideas of how the Oedipus complex shapes the patriarchal family. Van der Mal's love for his daughter is not conditional on her submission to his authority or on the unquestioning obedience that her spiritual mothers ask. Rather, it is characterized by respect for her freedom to choose and think for herself—a right that later women religious would claim but which is still not fully recognized by a patriarchal Church. Despite the profound misgivings he has about her temperamental suitability for an order that requires her to offer up her liberty, memory, and will to God—tragically proven right seventeen years too late—he gives his "father's consent" to her entrance. When she promises to try and make him proud, his response is: "I don't want to be proud of you. I want you to be happy." His letter of protest is not an assertion of patriarchal pique so much as paternal advocacy of her deepest desire, which is to do the work she loves in the Congo.

Nonetheless, French's analysis of *The Nun's Story* raises the important question of how the first love for parents, caretakers, and siblings develops away from exclusive attachment and leads to more mature libidinal bonds. As French suggests, Sister Luke's religious dedication to God does reify her daughterly devotion to a father who is "a very great man." Freud thought that women, Christian believers, and especially Catholics were predisposed to lifelong reliance on a paternal protector for wish fulfillment—which would seem to make nuns triply prone to religious illusion. Yet Gabrielle embarks on a path of renunciation, detachment, and sacrificial excellence that he equated with ideal masculinity.[25] Indeed

---

[25] For Freud, the desire for consolation, protection, and fulfillment from an external father figure is associated with femininity, while the renunciation of wishes and

her entrance into an order that maintains strict rules of enclosure and her fierce desire to serve far away from Belgium in the Congo suggest the need for distance from the omnipotent and omniscient-like influence of the father. Even the spiritual difficulties she now encounters in her religious life and the obstacles her community seems to put in her path to Africa can be interpreted constructively as providing both the internal and external frustrations that she did not have in her personal relationship with him. These can motivate the individual to discover a world that is greater than the influence of the parent (Rizzuto 1981: 94–5, 106–7).

Dr. Van der Mal's intervention appears decisive, for shortly after leaving the sanatorium and taking her final vows, Sister Luke embarks on a symbolic rite of passage to Africa. The *bon voyage* scene at the sea port of Antwerp is imbued for this bride of Christ with a happy sense of release from inner tension and with an air of excitement and expectancy associated with a long-awaited holiday or deferred honeymoon. As Sister Luke shakes confetti out of the folds in her veil, the first notes of Cherubino's joyful aria from *The Marriage of Figaro*, "Voi che sapete," are heard on the sound track. She is replaying the melodic line that her father idly fingered on the piano as he waited to escort her to the convent: "You ladies who know what love is, see if this is what I have in my heart." The music airs his unspoken question—whether she can ever learn to love the religious life, even when doing the work that she loves in the Congo.[26] Her parting words to him run with this melody through her mind: "Don't be proud of me, Father. This is really flight. It will be so much easier in the Congo. There will be no worldly associations in the bush station, in the jungle." She does not realize that her "flight" follows the trajectory of the family romance, or that Cherubino's aria prefigures her encounter

---

attachments through the internalization and gradual depersonalization of this figure is characteristic of mental masculinity. He believed that Mosaic and Judaic monotheism enforced instinctual renunciations, while Christianity, and especially Catholicism with its feminine and maternal features, were the religions of wish fulfillment. I will discuss these issues in the next chapter. See the helpful discussion and critique of this complicated process with detailed reference to Freud's writings by Judith Van Herik, *Freud on Femininity and Faith* (Berkeley: University of California Press, 1985), 5, 79–80, 103, 107, 138, 143–5, 150–5, 195–9, and by Kirk A. Bingaman, *Freud and Faith: Living in the Tension* (Albany: State University of New York Press, 2003), 123–9.

[26] I am indebted to Donald Spoto for suggesting how the lyrics of this aria reflect on Gabrielle's relationship with her fellow sisters, and how its joyful melody is heard at key moments in Franz Waxman's film score. Spoto, *Enchantment: The Life of Audrey Hepburn* (London: Hutchinson, 2006), 142–3.

with the erotic desire that is inchoate in her relationship to her father, formally subject to the religious vows of chastity and obedience, partially sublimated into her nursing work, but not fully transmuted into love of the religious life (Nygren 1953: 223).

Voyage to a Dark Continent

In 1926, the year Sister Luke entered the convent, Freud notoriously confessed that the "sexual life of adult women is a 'dark continent' for psychology" (1926, *SE* 20: 212). Sexuality could be a dark continent for the young virgin who entered the convent straight out of school in late adolescence, and *Black Narcissus* showed that this subject was unchartered terrain for a general film audience. *The Nun's Story* raises questions about the degree to which Sister Luke's identificatory love for her father, channeled into religious life, has arrested her psychosexual development. If we look back at the first half of the film, her postulancy focused exclusively on the importance of obedience and was conspicuously silent on how the vow of chastity featured in the interior formation of young women religious. Her boyfriend, Jean, does not appear to have been an object of erotic longing or regret. An early domestic scene in the film depicts the ease with which she turns his photo, in its heart-shaped frame, face down on her dressing table in a symbolic act of emotional closure. She never gives him another moment's thought, even when her father brings up his name years later. This strongly contrasts with the way Dr. Fortunati will dominate her mind and give her no rest on her cell bed after her return from the Congo. What is striking about the intimate scenes at home is how intense, exclusive, and incestuous her relationship with her father appears to be. The rest of the family only serves as a backdrop for the eldest daughter who is what every child oedipally strives to become, which is the parent's favorite, preferred companion, "number one" in affection and esteem (Rizzuto 1981: 195–6). French reads this oedipal attachment as "Gabrielle's neurotic fixation on her father" (1978: 135). Yet Freud argued that "fixation" is not only normal if parental bonding is successful but crucial in laying down the emotional pathway for all later attachments:

> The nature and quality of the human child's relations to people of his own and the opposite sex have already been laid down in the first six years of his life. He may afterwards develop and transform them in certain directions but he can no longer get rid of them. The people

to whom he is in this way fixed are his parents and his brothers and sisters. All those whom he gets to know later become substitute figures for these first objects of his feelings. (1914, *SE* 13: 243)

If Gabrielle suffers from fixation, it is a condition she shares with those fortunate members of the human race who have been raised in a loving family. The second half of the film shows how she develops and transmutes these formative feelings, and how the so-called "dark continent" of Africa stimulates the psychosexual development that has been dormant.

African Missionaries

In her two thousand year history of Catholic nuns, McNamara paid tribute to missionary sisters as "the extraordinary women who have pressed forward along the social and spiritual frontiers" (1996: 599). Missionary nuns in Africa were recognized as the most progressive thinkers in their religious order and were known to return from abroad with the qualities of leadership and exceptionality that distinguish former missionary Reverend Mother Emmanuel.[27] Belgian priests in the Congo had a reputation for being liminars who lived on the edge of Catholicism and adapted native rituals or dangerously crossed boundaries like the film character Father Vermeuhlen (Niall MacGinnis), ad/minister of the leper colony (Campbell-Jones 1978: 116, 168, 187). In traveling across cultural borders, the missionary nun could well discover that the protective barriers of enclosure began to dissolve, and that she was being called to transform "her understanding of self: spiritually, psychologically, socially, emotionally, sexually" (Burns 1994: 140).[28] Reverend Mother Emmanuel gives Sister Luke a sound hint on all of these levels when she cautions her that only the strongest nuns are chosen for the congregation's African mission stations. A rigorous selection process determined these overseas postings because the missionary sister did not simply serve God but Caesar—

[27] In Hulme's book, the exceptional life history of this religious leader is unfolded. She "served as missionary in India, as teacher in Poland, as supervisor in the psychiatric institutions of the Order." She "held degrees in philosophy, the humanities, and was a diplomaed nurse besides, and . . . every six years when she visited the missions of the Order all the way from the Great Wall of China to the Himalayas, she could call every nun by name without prompting" (1956: 27).

[28] While this was the revised goal for new entrants in one religious community, a religious critic dismissed it as more suitable to a self-help group. See Wittberg, *The Rise and Fall of Catholic Religious Orders*, 235–6.

namely Belgian colonial interests in the Congo. Physical fitness was essential because the missionary sister faced overwork, dangerous living conditions, and life-threatening illnesses such as malaria, tuberculosis, and leprosy (Bernstein 1976: 247; Coburn and Smith 1999: 190). Spiritual fortitude was required because her teaching, nursing, and managerial activities brought her back into the world she had disavowed and into close touch with the white settlers who ran the colony and relied on the ancillary services of the missionaries. Her vows of poverty, chastity, and obedience, and her living rules of silence, inwardness, and corporate discipline, were the personal armor that guarded her from the temptations of the world, the flesh, and the devil (McNamara 1996: 592–3).

The Congo

The Congo is depicted as anything but a dark continent in *The Nun's Story*. In a move that is reminiscent of the vibrant flashbacks to Sister Clodagh's youth in *Black Narcissus*, expert cinematographer Franz Planer used vivid color for the exuberant environment of equatorial Africa (Phillips 2005: 45; Nolletti 1999: 129–30, 133; Walker 1997: 206). This dramatic burst of Technicolor on-screen paints the nun's voyage from the Northern European cloister to the Congo missions as a movement from intellectuality to sensuality.[29] Her religious commitment to a "life against nature" has been an exertion of will and mind but it has left her heart cold. The deepening colors of Africa set the scene for the emergence of a passionate intensity in the nun's own character, and Hepburn's wondering descent from the train that carries her into the heart of the Congo gives the impression that a sleeping beauty has finally awakened from her long frozen slumber in the motherhouse. The rich green, red, and gold of the Congo also signal the film narrative's sharper focus on the Catholic family romance, as if a faded family snapshot or memory has suddenly been restored to its original warmth and brilliance.

Klein psychoanalyzed the deeper need that colonial travel satisfied: "In the explorer's unconscious mind, a new territory stands for a new mother, one that will replace the loss of the real mother. He is seeking the 'promised land'—the 'land flowing with milk and honey.'" Sister

---

[29] I am playing with Freud's contention that the "turning from the mother to the father points . . . to a victory of intellectuality over sensuality" and represents "an advance in civilization," in *Moses and Monotheism: Part II* (1939), *SE* 23: 114, although I see it as a turning from the father to the mother and back in *The Nun's Story*.

Luke's voyage to Africa can thus also be viewed in Kleinian terms as a "wished-for restoration" (1994: 334), carrying her to a fertile country that personifies the benevolent mother she has lost, longed for, and sought in entering the motherhouse. Here she will also be reminded of her own sexed body and its maternal potential. On her arrival at Stanleyville, Sister Luke finds a more demonstrative family waiting to greet her. She is told by her traveling companion, Sister Augustine (Molly Urquhart), how "very fortunate" the local community is in its superior, Mother Mathilde (Peggy Ashcroft). Mother Mathilde subverts one of the first rules of the Belgian motherhouse—that "we never touch another sister, of course"—by extending a warm and tactile welcome to the new nun. Within minutes, the drums report that Sister Luke "held hands with Big Mama Mathilde on way back to sisterhouse, therefore esteemed. Talks little. Looks much. Young enough to bear children."

The native drums that Sister Luke hears as she travels with her new mother and sisters across the Congo River to their mission station transmit the rhythmic, sensual, semiotic message of a land that was the cradle of human life long before it became a colony. Hepburn's own sing-song cadence as an actress was an ideal vocal instrument to express the lilting melody of the semiotic—whose source for Kristeva lay in the primitive body language of the mother and child—and the nun's elation at the prospect of caring for African mothers and their children. On the way to the native hospital, she is introduced to the mission's chaplain Father André (Stephen Murray) and encounters a living embodiment of Freud's theory that Judeo-Christian monotheism arose as a primitive exaltation of the great father (1939, SE 23: 85–90, 133–6). This priest is "greatly loved" in the local community and greatly revered by the natives as an image-likeness, with his long, white beard, of a venerable Father God. Like her father, he represents the benevolent face of Christian patriarchy, and his later accident will give Sister Luke spiritual insight into the value and potential of her surgical nursing work. With her introduction to both Mother Mathilde and Father André, the Catholic family romance appears, at last, to have turned a full circle of reassurance and security. Yet as she contentedly cradles a baby in her arms, she learns from her new mother superior that the congregation has once more thwarted her deepest desire by assigning her to assist the surgeon, Doctor Fortunati (Peter Finch), in the white hospital where the European colonial class is segregated as privileged, paying patients.

This latest "disappointment" is especially hard not only because the nun has caught a tantalizing glimpse of the work she desires but because the great outdoors of the Congo has opened up her senses. Even before she steps off the train at Stanleyville, many pairs of eyes track her arrival, and she looks intently out the train window in return. Accustomed to the nun's inconspicuous gliding walk, she now sees bodies proudly and un–self-consciously on display, waving, swaying, jumping, jostling, touching, bathing, and staring at her appraisingly. Instead of convent silence, she hears a symphony of noise: tribal chanting and drum-beating; children crying, shouting gleefully, and reciting their lesson aloud; and mothers with babies calling for her attention. The Catholic nuns who saw a preview of *The Nun's Story* complained of "the entire absence of joy in Sister Luke" (*America* 470). Yet as she absorbs these sensory experiences, Sister Luke visibly relaxes and her face lights up with *jouissance*, reminding the viewer how young and beautiful she still is. She reaches down to pet the convent dog, and she reaches out to the natives she meets at the mission. "Seeing all of this," she contentedly tells Mother Mathilde, "I'm very happy to be here." In her walk up the path to the white hospital, Africa presents her with a vision of unfettered beauty. A medium shot of royal cranes squawking and preening themselves in their exotic plumage against the verdant exterior is a reminder that Africa celebrates life that is not against, or above, but an enhancement and intensification of nature. The abrupt cut from these colorful "birds of paradise" outside to the cool, monochromatic interior of the white hospital dramatizes Sister Luke's re-subjection to institutional enclosure and returning dejection. There is a final, almost unbearable, glimpse of the Congo life from which she has been shut out when Mother Mathilde make her departure. She flings wide the French doors of the operating theater to the accompaniment of a musical flourish that makes them seem magic casements leading to an Edenic world that is quickly closed from view.

The White Hospital, Dr. Fortunati, and the Return of the Repressed

In times of stunning setback such as the one that Sister Luke now experiences, the sudden memory of a family member or loved one can return with subliminal power as a form of reassurance. Mother Mathilde warns Sister Luke that she is leaving the cloister of the spirit and entering a masculine domain of science and skepticism ruled by a doctor who is "a genius and a devil. He works himself and his nurses to exhaustion. He's also a man, a bachelor and an unbeliever. Don't ever think for an instant, Sister, that your habit will protect you." Zinnemann's mise-en-scène paints a different picture, however. The cool and quiet atmosphere of the white hospital may be visually reminiscent of the motherhouse, but intellectually and emotionally this is also familiar, home ground. Thus, she instinctively responds with confidence, recalling her faith in her father—"I'm used to doctors. My father . . . I'm sorry. I forgot"— and has her inadvertent slip of the tongue completed by her mother superior: "Your father is a great surgeon, I know." This unconscious slip is one, interestingly, in which she both remembers and forgets.[30] She momentarily loses the basic memory that the nun was permitted for her work, and feels the stirrings of the autobiographical memory that she was taught to repress in the motherhouse. As Anglican film nun Sister Clodagh has already suggested, although the religious missionary was highly trained and disciplined, she was susceptible to the return of the repressed when in a more relaxed culture and more open natural environment. Like *Black Narcissus*, *The Nun's Story* calls into question the assumption that the nun can, or indeed should, suppress the autobiographical memory, which is a repository of personal history and enduring attachments to family, friends, and places, or that she should exorcize the past, like some deep-seated evil, from her heart. Klein speculated that in difficult situations we may return in our mind to our loved parents, as Sister Luke does now, so that we can be "guided by them, and may find ourselves wondering how *they* would behave, and whether or not they would approve of our actions" (1994: 338).

After shutting the French doors that symbolically keep her enclosed and while waiting for Dr. Fortunati to arrive in the operating theater, Sister Luke momentarily breaks down and cries. She recovers her composure and is discovered by the amused surgeon adjusting her veil in the glass face of the surgical cabinet: "You'll say six 'Aves' and a 'Pater Noster' for that bit of vanity, Sister." She compounds her vanity with pride by name-dropping when asked if she has ever assisted at an operation before: "My father's Dr. Hubert Van der Mal." In fact, her allusion to her father, her reminder of his great name, and her glance at herself in

---

[30]Rebecca Sullivan made the penetrating observation that "the habit marks its wearer, positions her in fields of both memory and forgetfulness: memory of the social body of women bound together regardless of distance or death as one in union with the sacred body of Christ; and, in order to maintain that memory, forgetfulness of the long history of urgent needs and spiritual longings which are invested into the habit." Sullivan, "Breaking Habits: Gender, Class and the Sacred in the Dress of Women Religious," *Consuming Fashion: Adorning the Transnational Body*, ed. Anne Brydon and Sandra Niessen (Oxford: Berg, 1998), 112.

the reflecting front of the cabinet are a complex, subliminal reaction to the shock of bitter disappointment. They reflect yet again her convoluted search for mirror-recognition, as in her earlier struggle with the Archangel Gabriel. They indicate her failure of identification with both the order and orders of nuns, and they show that she is again looking in the glass for the noble father-protector who will provide needed approval. Yet in adjusting her veil, she is also reproducing Reverend Mother Emmanuel's sacred act of straightening the black veil she was given as a vowed nun. This gesture in turn recalls the affectionate mother who comforts her child by stroking her hair (Rizzuto 1981: 56).

Sister Luke's spell in the Congo is visualized as a gradual shift in orientation and outlook from the convent to the white hospital and from Mother Mathilde to Dr. Fortunati. French saw Fortunati as the oedipal rival of the father and competitor with God—and by extension the religious community, which Mother Mathilde heads—for possession of the nun's heart, mind, and body. I will interpret the dynamic of this internal trinity more positively to suggest that Fortunati not only stands in for Van der Mal but vitally succeeds him in releasing the libidinal energy that was necessarily repressed in the nun's attachment to her father. It is evident that Sister Luke is drawn to this brilliant surgeon because of his professional resemblance to her father. With only one parent as a significant influence in her life, it is understandable that Sister Luke's representation of God and later choices of work and love will be modeled on her primary attachment to her father. However, the two doctors are temperamentally very different. One embodies Northern European composure and the other temperamental passion.[31] This difference means that Fortunati does not perpetuate the nun's relationship to her father but rather challenges, indeed continually goads her, to move on developmentally from it. In the eyes of Mother Mathilde, Dr. Fortunati is the devil incarnate. Later he will be suspect as the tempter who leads her astray from religious life. From a psychoanalytic, as opposed to religious, point of view, the devil can be seen as a split-off image of the beloved father. His psychic function is to express the defiance, the unacknowledged tensions, or the ambivalence in the child's relationship with the all-powerful parent (Rizzuto 1981: 18–22, 35–6). This is why Sister Luke's obvious hero worship of her father is an immediate source of friction with the doctor who fully lives up to his reputation as a tormentor by needling the nun about her

[31] In Hulme's book, Fortunati is described on 160 as "an Italian with hot blood."

family background. His initial promise to explain his surgical procedures ends with the sarcastic disclaimer—"though being the daughter of Dr. Van der Mal, I expect you could instruct me."

Fortunati's name, however, also hints that he will, in fact, play a providential role in the nun's life. As assistant to him in surgery, Sister Luke will have the intellectual stimulus of a professional relationship that is an expansion of the teacher-pupil bond she once enjoyed with her father. Her internship with Fortunati in this film was not pure Hollywood. For as McNamara pointed out, "nursing sisters trained on the job in collaboration with doctors who appreciated their discipline, obedience, neatness, and above all their fearlessness in the face of contagious disease" (1996: 625). Although Sister Luke does make a decisive shift from cloistered to professional life while at the white hospital, it would be wrong to conclude that her commitment to nursing implicitly becomes less sacred as she works more and more in the world. As I shall now show, the close rapport that she develops with the doctor as a surgical nurse will return her to her most authentic desire—which is to attend and heal others. As she recognizes that her deepest vocational motivation is to heal, she will gradually live out the call to holiness through her commitment to "the rehabilitation of the bodily as the very locus of . . . divine likeness" (Schneiders 2004: 81).

A Nursing Vocation

Their work together in surgery provides some of the most visionary moments of the film, and gradually unfolds as a spiritual exercise in which there is unorthodox imitation of Christ. Zinnemann makes this working relationship pivotal in the film because it calls into question the fundamental antithesis between the religious and the secular realm, and the binary split of the body and soul on which this polarity is predicated. Fortunati operates in the relatively cool hours of the dawn at the same time that Sister Luke's fellow sisters attend daily mass. She is excused from this service but receives communion from Father André at the operating theater door. She will later confide in Mother Mathilde that she felt Dr. Fortunati was "close to God in those unearthly hours when he operates." Her remark will hardly have served to reassure the mother superior that she has not fallen in love with the doctor in that limbo realm where they worked closely and intently together. Yet Mother Mathilde might also take comfort from the implication of her remark: that work can not only inspire love but become a form of prayer, indeed that doing the work we love can bring us close to one another and to God (Beattie 2006: 70–1, 76). The operating theater becomes, in effect, Sister Luke's place of worship. The operation is the sacred drama, and it is conducted in a hushed atmosphere that approximates the "grand silence" of the convent and the solemn moment of consecration. The operating table is the altar; the prone and unconscious patient a simulacrum of the lifeless body of Christ awaiting resurrection. Dr. Fortunati is the celebrant who presides at this life-and-death re-enactment.

Zinnemann included a respectful close-up of Sister Luke's head bowed in prayer to avoid any impression that her taking of communion is a perfunctory interruption of her nursing duties. But his scene suggests how the holy sacrament has been transformed and elevated from a peripheral to a central, incarnate event in surgery. Sister Luke experiences the real, active, ministering presence of Christ in the operating team that is gathered around the other "communion table." In the threshold world of early dawn surgery, the nun stands at the intersection of night and day, life and death, earth and heaven, old and new religious practices. Like other pioneer nuns who had the experience of living in-between spaces and cultures, past and future, Sister Luke is moving toward a mystical apprehension of the Eucharist as "located in the participants rather than in the bread and wine" (Campbell-Jones 1978: 168; Orsi 1996: 102). She is also advancing from the traditional female religious role of handmaiden to a position of altar acolyte that was only open to women after Vatican II, and finally to the proto-feminist office of co-worker that is still threatening to a clerical Church. When Fortunati later leaves on a weekend fishing trip, she must deputize for him during a medical emergency, operate on Father André after his leg is shattered in an accident, and take the decision to try and "save the leg." In so doing, she assumes an authority and professional competence that were the prerogative of men.

While the nun's skill reflects the belief in her own ability that her father originally inspired and Fortunati resurrected in the operating theater, it flies in the face of an unwritten clerical rule discouraging nuns from advanced training in surgical procedures and from intimate medical work that was perceived as a threat to chastity (McNamara 1996: 626). This is one reason why Sister Luke's subsequent efforts to improve the general standard of hygiene at the white hospital and train the native paramedics earn the displeasure of ecclesiastical authority. As Sister Sandra Schneiders, I.H.M., observed, women religious were continually reminded that they only "ministered by the permission of men, on male terms (and) only in those spheres permitted to them by men" (2004: 33).

Like post–Vatican II nuns, she also finds that her professional activism makes trouble for her superior. Mother Mathilde receives a telephone call from the regional Bishop who has read Sister Luke's "name" in the papers, heard on the Congo drums that she has introduced medical "innovations," and demands to know why she is trying to "singularize herself." Her flair for management reform also catches the roving eye of the local white boss who is recovering in hospital and tells Mother Mathilde that he'd "like to borrow Sister Luke to organize our boys in the textile mills." Her talented individualism attracts not only colonial and clerical but sexual attention: "No one's hands are as soft as Sister Luke's." Her close contact with her patients reminds them of the body that the nun kept well hidden beneath her habit of chaste untouchability, and is a return of the Florence Nightingale image of "the saintly yet intensely eroticized heroic nurse" (Gilbert 2003: 17). It is left to one of her black orderlies to state the erotic reality that she is blind to: "Mama Luke where are your husbands? I can understand some of the others not having husbands, but not you."

The film contrasts Sister Luke's growing sense of her medical ministry with the steady deterioration of her health. The impossible workload that she shoulders at the white hospital is the compensatory activity of the perfectionist. She takes refuge in her professional duties as her dream of being a frontline missionary fades and as her repeated attempts to become a perfect nun "obedient in all things unto death" fail. Sister Luke's predicament in the 1930s would become the norm rather than the exception for sisters active in health care over the next thirty years. In 1961, Suenens warned of the danger faced by nuns who were "snowed under by purely administrative or supervisory tasks . . . (and became) more and more like professional nurse(s) overburdened with technical duties" (1963: 19). After Vatican II came to an end in 1965, the American commentators, Wakin and Scheuer, would urgently call attention to the physical and mental toll on overworked sisters who floundered under outmoded rules of enclosure and obedience and who struggled to "balance (their) individual conscience with (their) acceptance of authority" (1965: 40). However, like *The Bells of St. Mary's*, *The Nun's Story* suggests this was a problem waiting to happen earlier in the twentieth century. Zinnemann delicately intimates that work blocks Sister Luke's conscious awareness of her feelings for Fortunati, and at the same time unconsciously allows her to grow even closer to him by her "all or nothing" approach to her hospital duties. She is driven by the desire to do the nursing work she loves in the Congo, but now learns, as Freud wisely counseled, that: "we must begin to love in order that we may not fall ill, and we are bound to fall ill if, in consequence of frustration, we are unable to love" (1914, *SE* 14: 85).

In a compact but emotion-packed scene that Arthur Nolletti has analyzed in terms of her spiritual development (1999: 132–3), the director closeted the two principles together in a small room and then dramatized Sister Luke's uptight and agitated reactions to Fortunati, reactions that somatically register his phallic presence as a devil (often depicted as priapic), a man, and a bachelor. The scene begins with a long shot of the nun standing by an open window that looks out over the Congo River. Fortunati is casually seated on a hospital bed draped in a mosquito net, watching her inspect the X-ray of Father André's healed leg. This is another threshold moment, recalling her arrival at the white hospital when the abundant life of Africa beckoned beyond the French doors of surgery. As Sister Luke moves away from the window, Fortunati indicates that he is sending her up the river to conduct a leprosy check on the legendary Father Vermeuhlen. He frankly admits that he has an ulterior motive and that he hopes the trip will be beneficial for her health. A medium close shot from Fortunati's position on the bed takes in the visible symptoms of underlying illness in Sister Luke's pale, strained face, taut posture, and defensive clutch of her throat and chest—recalling her body language during her oral exam in tropical medicine—as she realizes that she has become a patient in his eyes. It is as though Fortunati is stripping her bare for examination, and in a psychological sense he is, when he comments: "As a surgeon it's not my business to probe into the mind, but I'd say that tension is the sign of an exhausting inner struggle." Alternating close-ups underline their physical proximity in the cramped space. The white bed netting that frames them both in reverse shots alludes to an intimacy Zinnemann could not state explicitly in the film. In the novel, the "little white room" (Hulme 1956: 197) they occupy is Sister Luke's bedroom at the hospital. The veiled source of her discomfort in this scene is psychosexual.

The next scene visualizes the tumultuous impact that his words have on the nun as she is carried by canoe along the mighty Congo to Vermeuhlen's leper colony. A wide-screen frame takes in the churning waters and turbulent currents of this river and makes them a powerful metaphor for the erotic feelings that Fortunati stirs within her. Later she will recall the concerned question that Mother Mathilde asked her on this voyage: "You're not in love with him, are you my child?" and her automatic response, "No, Mother. Of course I've not fallen in love with him." If it is unthinkable to fall in love with Fortunati, the body thinks for her. Sister Luke falls ill instead with tuberculosis, an ailment common among nuns who were the workhorses of the institutional Church, and one that brings more intimate contact with the doctor. A "classic Hollywood undressing scene" (Gilbert 2003: 18) ensues. It is the logical sequence to the doctor's earlier probing in her hospital cell. He now insists that she partially disrobe for his immediate medical examination and disobey the convent rule requiring the presence of another sister. Her shy "I'm ready," when undressed, has erotic undercurrents suggestive of a virgin nervously contemplating sexual intimacy for the first time.[32] However, she is not ready for a medical diagnosis that does away with the illusion of a mind / body, woman / religious, spiritual / scientific division:

> I'm going to tell you something about yourself, Sister. You're not in the mold, Sister. You never will be. You're what's called a *worldly* nun. Ideal for the public; ideal for the patients; but you see things your own way. You stick to your own ideas. You'll never be the kind of nun your convent expects you to be. That's your illness, the TB's a by-product.

In the Belgian motherhouse, no one looked at her, but Fortunati closely watches the live theater of the nun's face (Walker 1997: 206; Kauffmann, *The New Republic*, 21). The wimple and veil were designed to "protect" Sister Luke from the intrusive glances of men such as him. In actuality, they draw attention to "the mysterious and indescribable experience of eye contact" (Rizzuto 1981: 184), which is the most fundamental way in which humans respond to one another. In the Congo, everyone looks at her, but Fortunati looks through the veil of outward religious conformity and sees a kindred spirit—a maverick and individualist. Although called "an unbeliever," he does not question or disparage the nun's faith in God, but he does challenge her to see how the religious life has distorted this faith and eroded her self-belief. In addition to corrective mirroring, he supplies the intellectual stimulus that is missing in her convent life. He needles, provokes, and champions Sister Luke by not only speaking his mind but uncomfortably reading hers: "You comfort your patients by listening to their troubles. Who listens to yours?" Although the opportunities for intimacy with a semi-cloistered nun who observes rules of silence and chastity are severely restricted, he listens as

---

[32] I am grateful to one of my students, Lucy Kinder, for this suggestion.

with the stethoscope to her hidden protests of body and soul. He hears the silent communication that takes place in that interior space where the individual first hopes to be understood by parents, later by other loved ones, and may ultimately converse in secret with a private God: "You're afraid you won't be able to stand the convent if they send you back." He shows the discernment of a gifted spiritual director. He tells her what she needs to hear in the deep, dark, depressed africa of the self: "You're the only one in the whole Congo I can work with. I can't lose you."

Catholic officials overseeing the production of the film were worried about the sexual subtext to the relationship that developed between the doctor and semi-cloistered nun (Vizzard 1971: 231–2; Paris 1997: 147). What makes this relationship erotic is not physical contact but their meeting of minds, an intersubjective attunement that Jessica Benjamin argues "can be so intense that self and other feel as if momentarily 'inside' each other, as part of a whole" (1988: 126). Indeed, this unorthodox and intense friendship is a historical throwback to the close working partnerships that early missionary nuns sometimes enjoyed with men, based on what Dominican scholar Sister Mary Ewens described as "common interests and a sharing of the deepest aspirations of the human

Figure 3-2. The charged exchange of glances between Sister Luke and Dr. Fortunati expresses a mental intimacy and intersubjective connection that are visually erotic but can never be spoken aloud.

soul" (Ewens 1978: 256–7). Fortunati has a deep and transformative impact on the nun's life and so completes a holy trinity of loving father-
doctor-God. I cannot agree with French's conclusion, however, that
by introducing an erotic dimension into this trinity, Fortunati provokes
psychic "confusion between father, lover, and God" (1978: 134), only
resolved with the end of her relationship to all three and her departure
from the convent.

French implicitly reads the trinity as a mystery of divinity divorced
from our humanity when, in fact, it celebrates the unity of the divine and
the human, the fusion of agape and eros in a God who "so loved the world
that He gave his only Son" (John 3:16) and desires human love in return.
Theologian Sarah Coakley has argued that the "messy entanglement of
sexual desires and desire for God" (1995: 74) should not be censored
out of Christian speculation on the trinity. Indeed, she envisioned this
mystery as the supreme expression of the intimacy that humans discover
across a broad psychosexual spectrum that includes moments of sudden
rapport and erotic attraction, or the surrender of the body in sex and the
spirit in prayer (Coakley 1995: 82; Coakley 1998: 230). The relationship
between nun and doctor is forged as they work on the bloody, mangled
mess of human beings on the operating table. Even saintly figures like
Father Vermeuhlen have a murky past in the bush country, which can
remind Sister Luke of the "messy entanglement of sexual desires and
desire for God."[33] Fortunati's feelings are a complicated tangle of professional faith in her as a nurse, skepticism about her religious vocation, and
respect and love for her as a person. Sister Luke's great admiration and
trust in him as a doctor are complicated by personal feelings she cannot
acknowledge, and after she is back in the Belgian motherhouse, these
feelings will return as the sexual repressed to torment her.

While Sister Luke's intense feelings for Dr. Fortunati have an erotic
dimension that she is slow to recognize, they are not the cause of her
eventual exit from the convent. Rebecca Sullivan noted that if actual
nuns experienced sexual confusion, it "often led to greater conflicts with
the vow of obedience" (2005: 99), and sexual confusion is an undeniable

[33] While it comes as no surprise now, the Catholic censors would never have
allowed Robert Anderson to mention in his screen script the fact that Vermeuhlen
"lived with a native woman and had three children by her" before renewing his
priestly vows and devoting himself to the lepers as a lifelong penance. One can only
wonder what happened to his poor family who, in effect, became social "lepers" to
him. See Hulme, *The Nun's Story*, 193–4.

element in this screen nun's intimate working friendship with the doctor. However, her religious conflict with this vow is aggravated by the professional bond that unites them in surgery, requiring that they closely attend their patients and listen carefully for vital life signs.[34] Sister Luke will later defend her decision to leave the convent by articulating her foremost fidelity to a spiritual rather than religious, and internal rather than external, rule of obedience, one that is consonant with her sacred duty as a nurse:

> When I have night duty, I break the grand silence because I can no longer cut short a talk with a patient who seems to need me. Mother, why must God's helpers be struck dumb by five bells in the very hours when men in trouble want to talk about their souls?

The Benign Circle of the Family Romance

These questions acquire not simply professional but personal importance when Sister Luke becomes a patient herself. The medical treatment Fortunati prescribes for her tuberculosis is a long holiday from the nun's life of forsaking private memories and wishes, where she has nothing better to do than "sleep . . . relax . . . live life as it comes from day to day." The convalescent home he devises is a "little pavilion where you'll be sleeping practically in the treetops." Here, her nurse, Sister Aurelie (Dorothy Alison), remembers the magic circle of childhood—"this reminds me of a tree house that I had when I. . . ."—and Sister Luke can be as carefree as a child for the first and the last time in her life: "Anything you want, you ask for, because Dr. Fortunati says you're to be pampered. Isn't it wonderful!" This includes sympathetic gifts of food from the natives and a pet monkey called Felix whose name is symbolic of an unfamiliar and spontaneous felicity. Under the watchful eye of the doctor and her fellow sisters, Sister Luke experiences a renewed spiritual perception of agape—of "each day and each night as a gift from God"—and of the divine to be found not only through living fully in the present but in our full presence to one another. However after her recuperation, it will become increasingly difficult for Sister Luke to maintain that "a nun is not a person who wishes or desires." The official reason for her abrupt transfer from the Congo is to accompany a high-ranking colonial figure

[34] On 256, Hulme described "the peculiar bond that bound them breathless over a flickering life on the operating table."

on the journey to a sanatorium in Belgium. Yet once back in her cell at the motherhouse, Sister Luke is haunted by the question that tacitly made her repatriation politic: "You're not in love with him, are you my child?" Nolletti perceptively suggested that as "her personal struggle intensifies, . . . so does her longing for God's presence" (1999: 131–2). The nun's erotically charged relationship with Fortunati, reminiscent of that other odd couple, Sister Clodagh and Mr. Dean in *Black Narcissus*, has awakened a "spirituality of yearning desire" (Coakley 1995: 77; Nygren 1953: viii) for a God of not only benevolent but passionate love, who does not ask her to renounce but to recognize and reach out for her deepest wishes and desires.[35]

Sister Luke first encountered Fortunati as a devil's advocate who way-laid her as she went about her work in the hospital and confronted her with the sickening, indeed the deadening, effect that the religious vow of obedience was having on her spirit. Yet she had made her solemn vesture into the novitiate to the stirring sound of *Veni Creator Spiritus*. In this ancient hymn, the corporate Church prays for divine aid and for the grace and creative love of agape. Its majestic melody is woven into Franz Waxman's musical score for *The Nun's Story*, where it functions as an interior summons to a new understanding of obedience—as a response to the call of the Holy Spirit and openness to divine inspiration through dialogue with others (Burns 1994: 138, 142). Grace comes to the nun's assistance later in the film when she begins to see Fortunati in the light of a Trinitarian God as not only a tormentor but the spirit of truth painfully making her face up to more authentic feelings and desires. Sister Luke is right in her intimation that this atheist is paradoxically close to God, and indeed is gifted here with the same insight of missionary priest Father Chisholm in *The Keys of the Kingdom* and missionary Gladys Aylward in *The Inn of the Sixth Happiness*. Ironically, the magnanimous pontiff John XXIII would invite Vatican II to engage in the dialogue with atheists that is both romance and anathema in *The Nun's Story* (Burns 1994: 53). His papal entreaty that the Church must join the modern world would inspire later women religious to re-interpret their ancient calling. But it is Sister Luke's fate in Zinnemann's 1959 film to be a pilgrim soul who walks alone and ahead of her sisters in Christ.

[35]Here I differ from Rebecca Sullivan in *Visual Habits*, 120, who contends that the film "remov(ed) erotic or libidinal desire from Luke's motivation," and so "curtailed her own autonomy."

The Beginning of the End

Planer shot the scene of the nun's silent arrival back at the motherhouse against a dark rain front that is not only a dismal contrast to the vibrancy of the Congo but a visual projection of her dampened spirits on return. After the warm and relatively relaxed community life of Africa, the somber and silent interior of the motherhouse appears especially forbidding. Sister Luke glides along its cheerless corridors like a wraith. The first person she encounters on her homecoming is the austere figure of her former Mistress of Postulants, Sister Margharita, who taught her the convent rule of detachment from people, memories, and places, yet whose surprised face momentarily betrays delight at seeing Sister Luke again. Reverend Mother Emmanuel greets her warmly and affectionately and as a mark of esteem for her missionary status, has her sit close by her side rather than kneel submissively as before in front of her desk. However, her kindly words—"You must have a good rest. You must not worry about anything. Simply enjoy being home again"—inadvertently echo Fortunati's soothing advice when she was recovering from TB in her treetop pavilion. They intensify her homesickness for Africa, bring pained consciousness that she no longer belongs in the pseudo-primary family of the convent, and at the same time re-awaken eros, which Nygren described as "the soul's home-sickness, its longing for what can give it true satisfaction" (1953: 235).

Where does she belong? Sister Luke's reunion with her father after her years in the Congo is stiff and inhibited—a poignant encounter in which she converses with the man who means so much to her as if he is a stranger. Van der Mal greets Sister Luke as "Gaby," the personal name that has not been heard since the beginning of the film. In addressing his daughter by her old, familiar name, her father is also appealing to that incommunicative core of her character that she has been trained to shut up inside the habit of a nun but that Fortunati released from solitary confinement. "How are you *really*, Gaby? . . . I mean in here," he adds, pointing to his heart. Only later, during the lonely hours of the grand silence, does the nun listen to her heart, in obedience to the spirit, and hear the evocative sounds of Africa and the provocative voice of Fortunati. She beseeches God to "help detach from these memories. How can I be a good nun, if I can't get the Congo out of my blood?" However, in requiring the sacrifice of her personal memories, the cloister violated a central truth of the psyche—that the people we have loved become an integral part of the internal world we carry with us wherever we go in life, and are indeed irreplaceable (Rizzuto 1981: 76–81). It is once again the voice of Fortunati, now internalized as an unforgettable imago, which brings home these truths: "I finally had to take a hand in training your successor. But she'll never replace you. She has none of your rebellion in her."

The Casualties of War

Only by leaving the verdant land of Africa behind and walking through the valley of death when Europe finds itself at war does the path becomes clear for Sister Luke. If she does not summon the courage to leave the convent, she must renounce that complex and arduous subjectivity that is not simply a secular value but a sacred gift: fruit of the thinking subject's engagement with life's experiences, relationships, and memories. As an assistant in surgery on the Holland border, she finds herself at the epicenter of World War II as Europe falls to the Germans and the Allies retreat to the sea. When her hospital becomes a casualty station for those wounded on the battle front, she finds it impossible to follow the congregation's advice of studied neutrality and detachment from a troubled world—"Our work must go on as if nothing has happened"—and effectively declares internal war on her religious vows. However, when the Germans gun down her beloved father as he gives first aid to wounded refugees fleeing the enemy, her religious life finally falls apart.

The film visualizes her alone and distraught in her cell, pacing back and forth, agitatedly fingering and folding up the letter containing news of his death. In a scene close that is reminiscent of the third flashback in *Black Narcissus* where Clodagh disappears into a dark void, Sister Luke turns to face her opaque cell window, her black habit dissolves into its black-out curtain, and a dark night of the soul consumes her (Sinyard 2003: 88; Fitzpatrick 1983: 383). The stifled cries she utters here—"Oh Father, Father, Father," heard only because of the musical outburst that punctuates them—echo not only her triune entreaty for help in the Archangel Gabriel's cell but Christ's lamentation on the Cross: "My God, my God, why have you forsaken me?" Klein asserted that "in the last analysis the image of the loved parent(s) is preserved in the unconscious mind as the most precious possession, for it guards its possessor against the pain of utter desolation" (1994: 330). The final phase of *The Nun's Story* dramatizes the pain of a nun on the brink of utter desolation, desolation more terrible for the fact that she must writhe in silent grief and agony within her cell and cannot cry her pain out loud in the grand silence. With the sudden and shocking death of her father, she must contemplate the death of the God she has called upon from early childhood, who was made in her father's supportive image and escorted her to the cloister doors. This is why, in answer to the puzzled review in *The Hollywood Reporter*, "the ending when it comes, seems abrupt and incomplete" (May 6, 1959: 3).

Yet her father's death ennobles the self-sacrifice defining religious life. He died giving Christian witness to agape as selfless care for others, and he demonstrated "obedience unto death" to the Hippocratic oath, which calls the doctor to practice medicine in "a pure and holy way." The nun's dark night of the soul is symptomatic not only of a religious crisis but a conversion experience, which now triggers a transformation of self-identity in tandem with the God representation (Bingaman 2003: 64–5; Rizzuto 1981: 50–3). Sister Luke must face her own limitations as a flawed and fallible human being who has dedicated her life to a pursuit of religious perfection. While Christ pleaded: "Father, forgive them for they know not what they do," she confesses: "when I think of my father, I can't forgive the enemy." As an actress with the talent of projecting vulnerability and sensitivity, Audrey Hepburn was particularly well-equipped to convey an emotion that is insupportable for the nun herself—implacable hatred of the enemy who killed her father, an innocent civilian and humanitarian (Paris 1994: 373; Walker 1997: 359). She remembers the pitiless reaction of a black hospital orderly to the murder of Sister Aurelie in the Congo: "If such a death happened with us, Mama Luke, we should tie the murderer to a stake and cut his body for fish bait." And she now hears the complacent and sanctimonious piety in her own reply: "But we would not. We have been taught to forgive," which mimics Christ's measured compassion, "they know not what they do." This reproachful memory brings home the disharmony between the tranquil emotions she has been trained to feel as a nun and the tormented ones she now experiences, and between her past religious ego ideals and present, deeply personal reactions (Schneiders 2001: 244; Rizzuto 1981: 55–7, 77). Sister Luke must finally contemplate the question that is integral to separation-individuation from parents and can return in the hour of their death. Has her father forsaken her or has she forsaken him as a daughter? She saved Father André in the Congo; but she never imagined that her own father's life would be in danger or that she would not be there to aid the person she loved most in the world.

Conclusion

Film critics are divided on how to read Sister Luke's final decision to leave the convent. Is it a symbolic victory or defeat of the spirit? Is she— to reiterate the opening voiceover—losing her life or finding it again after so many years?[36] And should the path she now follows be conceived as a stark and irrevocable choice between religious and professional life, the sacred and the secular world? She departs in silence but as she leaves, hears the tolling of the chapel bell, which no longer compels her instant obedience. This bell has now become a *memento mori*, tolling for the death of her father, for the end of her vocation as a nun, and for her loss of the community she had as a religious where, despite her sense of failure, "your sisters love you; the doctors trust you; and your students respect you enormously." Yet as the metaphysical poet John Donne reflected, the church bell serves an intrinsic function of religion, which is to remind us continually that we are bound to one another wherever we may go and whether we are separated by life or death: "Any man's death diminishes me, because I am involved in mankind; and therefore never send to know for whom the bell tolls; it tolls for thee" (*Devotions*, "Meditation XVII").

With the bell tolling three times in the background, Sister Luke removes her religious habit and veil, steps over the threshold of the convent as Gabrielle Van der Mal, automatically moves her hand to lift her now non-existent robes, and walks to the end of the alleyway. There she hesitates, a vulnerable figure, unsure which way to go, and then briskly turns right. While this last visual impression is of someone "completely alone" (Sinyard 2003: 147), she nonetheless takes with her Reverend Mother Emmanuel's final words of parting: "When I go from here, I shall take you with me in my heart and keep you each day in my prayers." This Living Rule of religious detachment is paradoxically expressing the psychic inescapability of attachments, and the devotional duty that stems from them. For Sister Luke has become a part of Mother Emmanuel's internal world as well as her spiritual life. Likewise Mother Emmanuel, Mother Mathilde, Father André, the community of nuns, and Dr. For-

---

[36]Spoto, *Enchantment*, 130–1, included an influential letter Hepburn wrote to Zinnemann in which she expressed concern that the character she would play, Sister Luke, "calls herself a 'failure' at the end of the story. . . . I still would like to feel the start of something new and strong at the end of the story, instead of a sense of dejection and defeat. . . . Like you, I want the final situation to be fifty-fifty, so that neither the nun nor the Order becomes a villain."

tunati join forces with Dr. Van der Mal in that "company of many" (Riviere 1991: 317) that complicated her religious life, fortified her character, enriched her experience, provided her unforgettable moments of humanity, and became at last an immortal part of her. Of course, Mother Emmanuel would not see it this way, but even she would acknowledge that Christianity is first and last a religious community called to remembrance: "Do this in memory of me."

The Nun's Story is a film that should interest more feminist cultural critics. It honors the female protagonist's subjective point of view; it reflects Zinnemann's admiration for intelligent, ardent, and strong-willed women characters; it is sensitive to how hard they have to work to come within reach of their professional goals; it recognizes that failure is a risk inherent in aspiration; and it is respectful of the nun's hidden life of striving, struggle, suffering, and sacrifice (Rapf 1999: 237–8; Sinyard 2003: 147–9). As someone who was wary of corporate culture and, as we have seen, refused to take the loyalty oath mandated by the Hollywood Screen Directors Guild, Zinnemann was particularly interested in the vow of unquestioning obedience that bound Sister Luke to the rules and regulations of institutional life. His film recognized the authoritarian potential that the vow had, if not interpreted with critical intelligence and spiritual discernment, to subject women to a religious life of subservience rather than willing service. At a time when modern women religious were about to embark on a radical reassessment of this pre-eminent vow, his 1959 film was prescient in seeing how obedience would become an issue of personal conscience, and astute in intuiting how this vow could be tied up for women with their emotional history and with the people they first listened to and obeyed. What has intrigued me about The Nun's Story is how the perpetual vow of obedience comes into conflict with the perpetual nature of these primary attachments and their evolution through the love objects encountered in later life (Rizzuto 1981: 212). In looking at the role that the Catholic family romance played in Gaby's decision to enter the convent as well as in the recurrent problems she encountered there, I have suggested that the God she worships is not principally to be found in the chapel, on the altar, in the tabernacle or within the communion wafer, but in the loving heart, faces, voices, and memories of her family, sisters, and associates.

SONOROUS DESIRES

SWEET, SPIRITED, AND STIRRING VOICES IN *THE SOUND OF MUSIC* (1965) AND *CHANGE OF HABIT* (1969)

Introduction

The Nun's Story comes to an end in solemn silence, a silence heavy with Sister Luke's sadness and regret at failing to become "the perfect nun . . . obedient in all things unto death." When she leaves the convent, she does not close the door behind her. Technically, this allowed the camera, which stays behind inside the cloister, to watch her cross the threshold and walk down the alleyway into the unknown. This wide open door is a metaphor for Zinnemann's open-mindedness as a film director and a final ironic reiteration of why the hidden life of a nun first captured his imagination: "It seemed to open the door to a new world" (Sinyard 2003: 81; Nolletti 2005: 126). When Gabrielle Van der Mal steps outside, she faces immense uncertainty. The old world has been swept away with the Second World War. Her old life is gone with the death of her father. Her religious life is now behind her. Yet she carries with her the consoling reminder of her former superiors, that whether in or out of the convent, "there is no resting place ever" from life's struggles. Like John Bunyan's pilgrim, longing beckons her onward; the search for God's dwelling place does not end: "Some also have wished that the next way to their Father's house were here, that they might be troubled no more with either hills or mountains to go over; but the way is the way, and there is an end" (*Pilgrim's Progress*, Pt. 2).

In the decade after *The Nun's Story*, there was a proliferation of Hollywood films featuring nuns: *Lilies of the Field* in 1963, *The Sound of Music* in 1965, *The Trouble with Angels* and *The Singing Nun* in 1966, *Where Angels Go, Trouble Follows* in 1968, and *Change of Habit* in 1969. These films of the sixties made nuns more familiar to a large and diverse audience that had no direct contact with them through the traditional Catholic channels of parish school and church. Indeed, one of the most charming aspects of the 1963 film *Lilies of the Field* derives from Homer Smith's surprised encounter with nuns who are refugees from East Germany, dressed like nineteenth-century prairie women, farming land of little promise in the Arizona desert (Marlett 2008: 160). The delightful ecumenical dialogue that ensues between this free-and-easy black Baptist (Sidney Poitier) and their bossy-boots superior Mother Maria (Lilia Skala) disarms the viewer with its warm and generous humor, and so diffuses the religious prejudice that makes it difficult for lay people to see habited nuns as real, "imperfect" human beings or religious traditionalists to appreciate the vibrancy of other branches of Christianity. Yet the girlish squeals of delight with which the sisters greet Homer's gift of lollipops also show why vocational directors complained that popular film too often caricatured nuns as simple, childish souls or belittled their religious lives (Rooney 2001: 12).

When considered collectively, it looks like these films wish to be "troubled no more" by nuns—not seriously at least. In their desire to serve up nuns, especially the troublesome and problematic ones, as entertainment, they dramatically deviate from the exacting standard set by Zinnemann who refused to sentimentalize, trivialize, or make light of the demands of religious life (Sinyard 2003: 87). The cinematic nuns of the 1960s often appear singing and sometimes even "swinging" where Sister Luke and her fellow sisters were silent and dignified, spontaneous where they were disciplined and composed.[1] They appear young at heart, playful, joyous, and upbeat where Sister Luke was grave, mature beyond her years, pensive, and often heavy-hearted; gregarious where she was introspective. They are unruly, rebellious, and defiant, whereas she agonized over her infractions of the holy rule and inner resistance to the vow of obedience. It is therefore no wonder that the contrast with Zinnemann's

---

[1] See Alfred G. Aronowitz's report on "The Swinging Nuns," January 4, 1964: 66–7 in *The Saturday Evening Post*.

"earlier thoughtful, subtle film" was too much for film critic Pauline Kael who reviewed *The Sound of Music* and *The Singing Nun* together as one big lump of sickly sweet sugar that gave a general audience a "feel-good" high and addicted them to cheap rushes of sentiment (1970: 176–8). Even reviewers who were plugged into Catholic popular culture, such as Moira Walsh writing for the Jesuit magazine *America*, could find little to say about *The Sound of Music* after noting "the presence of silly, stereotyped nuns and the absence of any real religious feeling" (March 13, 1965: 375). Bosley Crowther of *The New York Times* saw a chorus line of "twittering nuns" (March 3, 1965: 34) while Judith Crist of *The New York Herald Tribune* sarcastically described them as "great big super-screen nuns singing cutely about their naughty, naughty novice" (March 3, 1965). *Esquire* regarded them as a cross between Sister Benedict, Saint Teresa, and the Wife of Bath in their "gutsy, going-my-way" behavior, "full of beans under those great costumes" (August 1966: 20). Indeed, the superficial, silly, and saccharine stereotypes that were fixed in place by these films of the sixties seemed to have become applied with a broad brush retrospectively to *The Nun's Story* with Rebecca Sullivan beholding a "cast of blithely happy-go-lucky nuns" supporting Sister Luke like those in *The Sound of Music* and *The Singing Nun* (2005: 119). What I aim to do in this chapter is to focus on the serious elements that have been lost to stereotyping in *The Sound of Music*. These are captured in the most memorable songs of the film, "The Sound of Music" and "Climb Every Mountain," and affirm Bunyan's view that there are no shortcuts on life's arduous pilgrim way but hills and mountains for everyman and woman to go over. I also intend to explore *Change of Habit* from a different angle by considering Elvis Presley's performative presence in this film and by suggesting how his history of musical embodiment and expressiveness affected the representation of the three nun characters.

The Background to *The Sound of Music* (1965)

The Nun's Story premiered only four months before Rodgers and Hammerstein's musical *The Sound of Music* opened on Broadway. Like Zinnemann, Rodgers and Hammerstein showed a serious and respectful interest in women religious and their world. Rodgers consulted the nun who headed the Music department at Manhattanville College on the Nonnberg Abbey music that is heard in the "Preludium." Hammerstein corresponded with Sister Gregory Duffy, O.P., head of drama at Rosary College and good friend and of Mary Martin who starred as Maria, on his representation of the convent. "Why," he asked, "did young women choose the religious life?" Sister Gregory's response was that like everyone else they were looking for answers: "What does God want me to do with my life? How does he wish me to spend my love?" (Wilk 2007: 18, 54; Hirsch 1993: 30; Wolf 1996: 59, 62–63n.37). Although these are the same questions that Sister Luke asks herself in *The Nun's Story*, there is a cultural chasm between the *zeitgeist* of Zinnemann's 1959 film and that of both Rodgers and Hammerstein's hit musical, which ran from November 1959 until June 1963, and Robert Wise's 1965 film version of *The Sound of Music*, which began production work in earnest after the musical finished its major run (Wilk 2007: 57; Hirsch 1993: 16–17). One obvious reason for this is that *The Sound of Music* does not make the same demands on an audience as *The Nun's Story*, which focuses relentlessly on the austere interior drama of the religious life. Instead it lightens and popularizes its representation of nuns through the appealing tropes of children, family life, and romance, to the accompaniment of Rodgers and Hammerstein's uplifting music. The film further enhanced the elements of *wanderlust*, adventure, heroism, and suspense by its Technicolor shoots on location in Austria, against the backdrop of stunning Alpine and Salzburg scenery (von Dassanowsky 2003: 7). However, another reason was that the 1960s was a decade of profound social change not only for nuns and the Catholic faithful but also for the American public who ignored the carping critics and made both the stage musical and the film phenomenal hits. The film's director, Robert Wise, suggested that the timing of the release of *The Sound of Music* in 1965 was serendipitous, and that the film assuaged social anxieties in the collective unconscious of its audience and answered their longing for vicarious escape to a better world (Grace 2009: 3–5; Ostwalt 1995: 155).

> Nineteen sixty five was a volatile year in the United States and throughout the world. Newspapers carried headlines of the war in Vietnam, a cultural revolution was beginning to spread throughout the country, and people needed old-fashioned ideals to hold on to. The moviegoing public was ready, possibly even eager, for a film like this. Besides an outstanding score and an excellent cast, it had a heartwarming story, good humor, someone to love and someone to hate, and seven adorable children. (Hirsch 1993: x)

Scholars in religious, cultural, and historical studies have all shown interest in "how clusters of films made in certain periods could serve as windows onto an exploration of particular ideologies or climates of opinion" (Rosenstone 2006: 21). Rebecca Sullivan has provided a particularly comprehensive and cogent account of the social conditions in the turbulent sixties, era of the counterculture of youth, the sexual revolution, second-wave feminism, civil rights, and the peace movement, out of which the cluster of Hollywood films about nuns emerged. She has concluded that the religious protagonists continued to represent a safe and stable compromise between idealized and liberated, traditional and progressive, selfless and self-assertive, domesticated and careerist femininity. While I would agree that, in the films of the 1960s, "the role of the nun is rarely fleshed out into a complex character," I hope to show nonetheless that *The Sound of Music*, which premiered in the middle of this decade, makes a more complex appeal to an audience than many of its critics have perceived (Sullivan 2005: 64, 93). Indeed, unlike the dismissive East Coast reviews that first greeted this film, cultural and historical readings of *The Sound of Music* over the last two decades have shown a greater willingness to look at the film more closely, consider if there is anything more serious going on beneath its glossy surface, and reassess the assumption that it simply panders to a passive, popcorn-eating audience.

In 1992, Richard Dyer situated the film musical in the tradition of the inspirational woman's picture, which helped a bourgeois female audience to manage the tensions arising from rapidly changing gender roles, sexual mores, social opportunities, and expectations in the sixties (1992: 45, 58–9). Jacqueline Vansant and Reinhold Wagnleitner, writing in 1999, argued that *The Sound of Music* was an American *heimatfilm*, or "homeland film," projecting a wholesome and uncomplicated world where an audience had a holiday abroad from deeply troubling American foreign policy in the 1960s—the escalating war in Vietnam, the military draft, and agitated student protests. In identifying with "the absolute loyalty and unquestioned patriotism of the Trapp family," they found comfort from the social instability of the times and placed their trust in rock-solid values such as love of country, family, father, and God (Wagnleitner 1999: 13; Vansant 1999: 180–3). However, Ruth Starkman read *The Sound of Music* as propagator of an end-of-war myth stemming from the Moscow Declaration signed in 1943 by the Allies. This represented Austria as "the first free country to fall a victim to Hitlerite aggression." Rodgers and Hammerstein's sentimental folk song "Edelweiss" reified the Alpine country as a "small and white" mountain flower offering bright but short-lived resistance to Nazism (Starkman 2000: 68–9).

Indeed, some American tourists assumed from the pivotal emotional and political importance the ballad has in the film plot and from the closing line—"bless my homeland forever"—that "Edelweiss" was the Austrian national anthem (Wagnleitner 1999: 13n.6; Vansant 1999: 179).

Anne McLeer offered an interpretation in 2002 that recognizes Julie Andrews's centrality in making the film such a success. Even the film critics who originally lambasted *The Sound of Music* when it opened in 1965 paused in their sarcastic set-downs to commend her performance. Judith Crist called her "a trouper all the way" (March 3, 1965), while *Esquire* marveled at how she energetically threw herself into her part (20). Moira Walsh praised Andrews as "a remarkably skilled and winning singing actress" (375), while Bosley Crowther admired the "air of radiant vigor . . . plain-Jane wholesomeness . . . and Mary Poppins logic and authority" she brought to the role of Maria (34). McLeer, picking up on Andrews's typecasting as the English nanny sporting her magical umbrella, argued that she played Maria as a transitional figure who soothed a 1960s American audience's conflicted view of the sexual division of labor and women's changing social role in society. She embodies proto-feminist and egalitarian principles but devotes them to the gender task of saving the von Trapp family, displacing her love from the convent to the children, and reforming the authoritarian patriarch Captain von Trapp (2002: 80, 84, 94, 98). Robert von Dassanowsky challenged the widespread view that *The Sound of Music* is a de-politicized and de-historicized fairy tale set in the Alpine never-never land of "Salzburg, Austria in the last Golden Days of the Thirties" by reading the film as "an allegory for the *Standestaat*" or Catholic and authoritarian state rule in Austria between 1934–38. He saw the union of the postulant Maria and Captain von Trapp as a romantic and nostalgic expression of its Austro-fascist social mission: to promote sovereignty with historic pride in the old Habsburg empire and in the glittering achievements of Viennese cosmopolitan society, but embracing Alpine folk culture and traditional Catholic values (2003: 3–4).

On the whole, these readings suggest that Americans, who flocked to *The Sound of Music* in 1965 and made it the top box office hit of the year and the number one grossing film of all time until the seventies, could not bear too much reality (Wilk 2007: 80; Hirsch 1993: 208–9; Starkman 2000: 64). The film built not only castles but mountains in the air, which offered fantasy escape from a tumultuous and threatening postwar world, and fashioned a storyline and musical numbers, which affirmed clear, constant, and conservative ideals in confusing times. Gone is the ambivalent ending that characterized *The Nun's Story* and underlined the existential courage of the protagonist who leaves the convent and possibly the Catholic Church. Instead, as the von Trapp family flees their country and evades their Nazi hunters after the *Anschluss*, the audience has the unambiguous satisfaction that the director Wise publicized of "someone to love and someone to hate."

Vatican Council II and the Renewal of Religious Music

In 1958, the year before *The Nun's Story* was released, Angelo Giuseppe Roncalli was elected as a kindly, grandfatherly, caretaker pope, but as John XXIII took the Church by surprise when he announced the bold and vigorous plan characteristic of a much younger man to call the Second Vatican Council. On his return from this ecumenical council held in Rome, Archbishop John Charles McQuaid reassuringly told the "good people of Ireland . . . Do not fear. Nothing has changed" (Chittister 2005: 79). In fact, Vatican II, lasting from 1962 until 1965 when *The Sound of Music* premiered, engaged in the thorough overhaul of a seemingly immutable Tridentine edifice built on Peter's rock and carved from Roman marble. The Second Vatican Council was a summons to review and renew the Church so that it no longer presented a stony face to modernity. The ensuing conciliar sessions opened up the doors and windows of this Church to the winds of change. When Maria leaves the secure gates of Nonnberg Abbey to take up the post of von Trapp governess, she consoles herself with a thought in keeping with the ecumenical spirit of the times—"When the Lord closes a door, somewhere he opens a window." Like Maria, the Church ventured out from behind its thick institutional walls and endeavored to make a fresh start. The Catholic faithful would greet with jubilation this new openness to the world, to *aggiornamento* or updating, and to the Holy Spirit as the wellspring of pure possibility. As Jeffrey Marlett has so eloquently stated, the "elemental joy" in the 1963 film *Lilies of the Field* emanates from the optimism of the early sixties but "also bubbles up from the deepest wells of Christianity" (2008: 150, 170).

The "down-home-go-to meeting" rendition of "Amen," which Homer Smith teaches the nuns in this film as a replacement for their plainsong Vespers hymn, "Ave Maris Stella," suggests how Catholic piety would become open to other Christian voices of praise. The Council call to renewal would encourage the development of popular religious music, which found inspiration not only in black spirituals and Protestant hymns but folk ballads and pop song. The guitar would no longer be denigrated as the profane and phallic extension of youth rock idols like Elvis Presley and Jimi Hendrix but would become a sweet accompaniment to Homer Smith in *Lilies of the Field*, Maria in *The Sound of Music*, and Dr. Carpenter in *Change of Habit*. The Belgian Sister Luc-Gabrielle, who became known as "The Singing Nun," strummed her 1963 hit song "Dominique" on a guitar she called her companion, "Sister Adele." The joy of singing, which permeates the sixties, not only filtered down into sacred music but the convent. American sisters publicized and subsidized their good works by recording choral albums that included pop tunes and Broadway songs, had covers featuring the nuns in natural settings such as those lyricized in *The Sound of Music*, and had titles such as "Joy" or "Joyfully Yours."[2] Recording company executives would crow that the singing nun was not only a swinging nun but a miracle worker who "reviv(ed) the whole industry. It's a miracle" (Aronowitz, *The Saturday Evening Post*, January 4, 1964: 66).

The Sound of Music (1965)

The Sound of Music certainly worked miracles for Twentieth Century Fox, saving the company from near bankruptcy after making the mega-expensive and grandiose epic *Cleopatra* (1963). It won five academy awards, including an Oscar for best picture and a second Oscar for Robert Wise as best director. It was nicknamed *The Sound of Money* as its phenomenal earning capacity became evident (Wilk 2007: 57–8, 64, 80–2; Kael 1970: 176). Critics were less kind in calling it *The Sound of Muzak*, and its lead actor, Christopher Plummer, derided it as *The Sound of Mucus* (*Esquire* August 1966: 21; Wilk 2007: 79–80). Yet it has remained in the list of top-ten most popular films ever made—except in Austria and Germany, where it was an unhappy historical reminder of the *Anschluss*, the Nazi past, and the postwar victory of American political and cultural imperialism.[3] Its remarkable success derived from an unprecedented repeat

[2] I am greatly indebted to Rebecca Sullivan's fine chapter on "Sacred Music and the Feminized Folk Scene," which she did not bring into her discussion of *The Sound of Music*. Sullivan, *Visual Habits: Nuns, Feminism, and American Postwar Popular Culture* (University of Toronto Press, 2005), 157–89.

[3] Julia Antopol Hirsch recounts the history of the two German hit films that were inspired by Maria von Trapp's *The Story of the Trapp Family Singers* (1948). German-Austrian director Wolfgang Liebeneiner made *Die Trapp Familie* in 1956 and its popular sequel, *Die Trapp-Familie in Amerika*, in 1958. Paramount bought the film

business. In several US cities, the box office ticket sales outnumbered the entire population (Hirsch 1993: 179, 208). Taking these figures into account, Reinhold Wagnleitner ironically concluded that "it is a revealing indication for the 'revolutionary' character of the 1960s that this film is the single most important and successful product of popular culture of the decade and not, as some would have it, Jimi Hendrix's 'Star Spangled Banner'" (1999: 13).

Both the extraordinary and the enduring popularity of *The Sound of Music* has motivated interpreters in feminist, film, historical, and cultural studies to revaluate the original critical estimates of the film. The fact remains, however, that there was a dramatic divide between the first film reviewers who panned *The Sound of Music* and an American audience who loved it. Their national enthusiasm was soon shared by global fans who were drawn to the film by a colorful range of culturally translated titles—*Love and Tenderness* in Egypt, *Music in the Heart* in Portugal, *Smiles and Tears* in Spain, *Charms of the Heaven-Sound* in Thailand, *The Rebellious Novice* in Argentina, and *Fairy Music Blow Fragrant Place, Place Here* in Hong Kong (Hirsch 1993: 180). Pauline Kael asked: "What is it that makes millions of people buy and like *The Sound of Music*?" and decided that it could only be that "the audience for a movie of this kind becomes the lowest common denominator of feeling: a sponge" (1970: 176–7).

Kael illustrates the initial critical reaction to the popularity of *The Sound of Music*, which was to bad-mouth not only the film but the mass audience that derived such vulgar enjoyment from it. This critical despair at the lowbrow tastes of an enthusiastic audience can be heard in Judith

---

rights to the first film in 1956 as a star vehicle for Audrey Hepburn but eventually let it go. Twentieth Century Fox purchased the film rights to *The Sound of Music* in 1960 but protected its investment by exercising a six-year option on the American release of the two films. It combined them into one film, dubbed that film in English, and released it to little note in 1961. See *The Sound of Music: The Making of America's Favorite Movie* (Chicago: Contemporary Books, 1993), 4–8, 181–82. Reflecting on this prior film history, Ruth A. Starkman argued in "American Imperialism or Local Protectionism? *The Sound of Music* (1965) fails in Germany and Austria" that Liebeneiner's two films represented Austrians in a more flattering light than *The Sound of Music* as heroically resisting the Nazis, and thus gave a German audience a "sense of ownership over its own history." See *Historical Journal of Film, Radio and Television* 20.1 (2000): 63–78. Robert von Dassanowsky challenges Starkman's reading by arguing that it is *The Sound of Music*'s depiction of the authoritarian Austrian *Standestaat*, not discomfort with the anti-Nazi theme, that made the film unpopular with a German audience. See "An Unclaimed Country: The Austrian Image in American Film and the Sociopolitics of *The Sound of Music*," *Bright Lights* 41 (2003): 1–10.

Crist's concluding remarks on *The Sound of Music*: "Film, however, is a great leveler. The movie is for the five to seven set and their mommies who think their kids aren't up to the stinging sophistication and biting wit of 'Mary Poppins'" (March 3, 1965). It baffled the *Esquire* film reviewer how both *Psycho* and *The Sound of Music* could break box-office records: "Is it possible to enjoy both the *Marquis de Sade* and *Rebecca of Sunnybrook Farm*? Perhaps we have *two* mass audiences like the offensive and defensive teams football coaches alternate" (21). Fans who subsequently read Bosley Crowther's "offensive" review for *The New York Times* online saw *The Sound of Music* as a symbol of the disparity of taste "between professional critics and the general public." They defended the film against the "highbrow film critics" who dismissed it, noting that none had mentioned the political dimension—which later interpreters would indeed explore—and maintained that screenwriter Ernest Lehman and director Robert Wise had "transform(ed) a mediocre (stage) script into a cinematic marvel."

In order to make a case for *The Sound of Music* being more complex than it first appeared to film columnists, I wish to give more serious attention to the question of why a general audience appreciated the film, and why, nearly fifty years after its release, they still say: "I've loved this movie my whole life." I will now address this split between the film's reviewers and fans. Indeed, I will argue that the long-standing disagreement between its detractors who, as *America*'s Moira Walsh accurately observed, "will be likely to call it vulgar, sentimental and phony," and its admirers who "will talk about its artistry and describe it as charming, wholesome, delightful, inspirational, clean" (375), results from *The Sound of Music*'s volatile blend of the beautiful, the sublime, the kitsch, the playful, and the sacred.

The Beautiful

The film's critics and fans were in agreement on one feature of *The Sound of Music*—the stunning beauty and visual impact of the aerial opening. It was the end result of an adroit decision that talented screenwriter Ernest Lehman took soon after being hired: to switch the order of the first two songs from the stage musical to the screen and start with Maria singing "The Sound of Music" on an Alpine hillside rather than open with nuns chanting "Dixit Dominus" in their Salzburg cloister nestled below (Hirsch 1993: 23). It could be surmised that his intention was to play down the importance that Nonnberg Abbey, with its sacred music and religious aspirations, has in Maria's life, and substitute a soaring landscape that exhilarates a general audience and gradually comes alive with the natural sounds leading into the title song. In notes sketching his vision of the opening film sequence, he described the feeling that he wanted the initial establishing shots to convey:

> We are floating in UTTER SILENCE over a scene of spectacular and unearthly beauty. As far as the eye can see are majestic mountain peaks, lush green meadows, deep blue lakes, the silver ribbon of a winding river. . . . As we glide in silence over the countryside, we see an occasional farm, animals grazing in the meadows, houses nestling in the hills, the steeples of churches, a castle surrounded by water. And now something is subtly happening to us as we gaze down at the enchanted world. FAINT SOUNDS are beginning to drift up and penetrate our awareness . . . And with this, we are aware that the ground seems to be rising. The treetops are getting closer. Our speed seems to be increasing. Without knowing it, we have started to approach a mountain. A MUSICAL NOTE is heard, the first prolonged musical note that leads to "THE SOUND OF MUSIC". Faster and faster we skim the treetops. And then suddenly we "explode" into . . . (Hirsch 1993: 35)

The Sacred

The film opening is hushed and reverent like the cloistered interior of Nonnberg Abbey; the spaces Lehman imagines are awe-inspiring; the mood he wished to create was one of transcendence in which viewers are transported from their mundane life into a more beautiful and exalted realm. For disparagers of *The Sound of Music*, this other world is nothing more than a puerile fairy tale and fantasy, but for fans, it answered the longing that lies at the heart of religious film "for something beyond the world we know" (Grace 2009: 3). A daredevil helicopter pilot and intrepid cameraman achieved the high panoramic shots that gave the impression of "floating" over the top of the Alps (Hirsch 1993: 83). This floating has a spiritual equivalent: the sense of uplifting prayer that is cultivated in the religious life through utter silence and through the contemplative practice of total absorption. As Richard Dyer has observed, the lyrics of "The Sound of Music" reiterate the fact that "the music of nature is a form of religious experience" (1992: 48). In Maria's song of praise, the mountains are implicitly a natural cathedral in which the birds on the wing hover, swoop, and soar like holy spirits. The pealing church bells shot as a backdrop to the opening credits of *The Sound of Music* accompany their flight through the air. The lark is a little postulant who is just "learning to pray" like Maria. This birdsong assures Maria that the singing she loves can be a form of worship and moves her to join her hands together in prayer near the end of her solo rendition of "The Sound of Music." Indeed, the nun protagonist of Rumer Godden's 1969 novel *In This House of Brede*, which I discuss in the next chapter, will describe the monastic chant of the divine office as "the nearest thing to birdsong she had ever heard, now solo, now in chorus, rising, blending, each nun knowing exactly when she had to do her part . . . rising up and up, until it seemed no human voice could sustain it" (1969: 60).

The message then of the first musical number is that the natural world offers another religious gateway to God. Indeed, Maria will later captivate her Mother Abbess (Peggy Wood) with a life story reminiscent of *Heidi* in which the Alpine mountain with its daily plainsong of creation led her to the sacred "birdsong" of the abbey. The Reverend Mother's reply, however, indicates that the convent may only be a way station and not a permanent "home" for her spiritual desires: "Maria, when you saw us over the abbey wall and longed to be one of us, that didn't necessarily mean that you were prepared for the way we live here." Maria is sent forth into the world to seek God's loving purpose for her life. The message that made a general audience feel good was the goodness of the world outside and the holiness of ordinary life.

The Sublime

Mountains are also a metaphor for the uphill struggle of religious life and appeared twenty years before as a dramatic backdrop and psychogeography in the nun film *Black Narcissus* (1947). Mountaineering imagery features significantly in Kathryn Hulme's 1956 *The Nun's Story*. The Mistress of Postulants, Sister Margarita, is likened to a seasoned mountain guide who leads her charges safely over the first "alpine peak" of religious discipline (1956: 36, 38). In *The Sound of Music*, it is not Maria's indulgent Mistress of Postulants, Sister Margaretta (Anna Lee), but her Mother Abbess who teaches her that mountain climbing represents not only religious life but all purposeful existence as *per ardua ad astrea*. Rumer Godden's 1939 novel *Black Narcissus* critiqued white Christian imperialism by suggesting how the local population mocked the Anglican nuns in their pale veils and topees and saw their resemblance to the Himalayan snow-capped peaks, "tall and white, over-topping everything" (Godden 1963: 6; Rawlinson 2010: 46). In Powell and Pressburger's *Black Narcissus* (1947), the Himalayas represented a mountainous alterity that beckons the Anglican sisters at missionary base camp to change their cultural perspective and expand their religious vision. As the convent gardener exclaimed after working in this landscape, "I think you can see too far."

In contrast to these colonial nuns, Maria does not fear losing her way or want to conquer the mountain but rather "be a part of it." As she strides across the hillside and toward the swooping camera, she whirls round in delight, holds her arms wide, and commences singing "The Sound of Music." Both her body and vocal language extend a deeply appealing invitation to a popular audience—to "be part of it," too, to join her as she merges quasi-ecstatically with nature. Late for Vespers because this landscape is so blissful, she confesses to her Mother Abbess that "the *Untersberg* kept leading me higher and higher as though it wanted me to go right through the clouds with it."[4] On the one hand, Maria is articulating the concept of the mountain as a beacon of salvation lyricized in the psalms. On the other hand, she is expressing the tradition of the mountainous sublime visualized in the *bergfilm* or "mountain film" genre and captured in the vertiginous dives of the opening aerial shots (von Dassanowsky 2003: 3).

It is these first moments that I now wish to focus on more closely. For the aerial opening of *The Sound of Music* is reminiscent of the start of that other cult nun film, Powell and Pressburger's *Black Narcissus*. Maria's hillside performance communicates the reassuring message of the nineteenth-century Romantic poets, that "the lark's on the wing . . . God's in his heaven—all's right with the world" (Robert Browning, "Pippa Passes"). However, the airborne camera that glides like an eagle over the Austrian mountain peaks and sheer precipices above her scans a landscape that is more alien and hostile to humans. Wild winds whip and whine around the Alpine summit as they do around Mopu, the palace perched precariously on a Himalayan cliff side that the Anglican nuns in *Black Narcissus* make their disastrous convent base. If God is in his heaven in *The Sound of Music*, he seems remote and distant at first, a veiled mystery that only abstract theologians can explore, but hidden from the naked eye behind the dense clouds that hang over the highest peaks. This sublime panoramic opening was certainly devised to astound an audience,

---

[4] Vespers is known as Evensong in the Anglican Communion, and brings Maria's day to an end with one last, time-honored song.

but its moaning winds also stir uncanny wisps of disquiet. Moreover, its gathering clouds and treacherous rock faces give an ominous intimation of a world on the brink of the Second World War where the *bergfilm* would be appropriated for Nazi ideology (Wilk 2007: 88).

Drawing on Edmund Burke's 1756 treatise *On the Sublime and Beautiful*, philosopher Roger Scruton distinguishes between landscapes of natural beauty, which evoke feelings of affinity and love, and those which strike amazement and fear into the heart of the observer:

> When we are attracted by the harmony, order and serenity of nature, so as to feel at home in it and confirmed by it, then we speak of its beauty; when, however, as on some wind-blown mountain crag, we experience the vastness, the power, the threatening majesty of the natural world, and feel our own littleness in the face of it, then we should speak of the sublime. (Scruton 2009: 72–3)

His distinction perfectly illustrates how *The Sound of Music* takes an audience on an emotional ride of thrilling visual contrast in which the airborne camera embarks on a rapid descent from the imposing Alpine mountain range to the picturesque Austrian countryside in the valley below where Maria first appears as a small dot on the horizon. While filming on location in Salzburg, Julie Andrews would recall her own response to the sublimity of the Alps: "You're surrounded by a ring of mountains. It's a private, magical place, and I adored it, but it does give you a lonely feeling" (Hirsch 1993: 137).

The Kitsch

While hostile critics conceded that *The Sound of Music* was visually captivating and made the natural beauty of the Alps and the Austrian countryside a dramatic foil to the historic and architectural beauties of Salzburg, they could not overcome their dislike for the film's kitsch, especially its kitschification of the von Trapp children and prewar Austria (von Dassanowsky 2003: 8). In fact, *kitsch* was originally an Austro-German word associated with the cheap sentiments of twentieth-century mass culture and defined as a simulacrum of art in which emotion is counterfeit, and there is no underlying meaning (Scruton 2009: 188–9). *The New Yorker's* film reviewer, Brendan Gill, savaged *The Sound of Music* for its sanitation of the *Anschluss* and fraudulent representation of the Austro-German era immediately preceding it as "the last Golden Days of the Thirties" when preparation was already underway "for that happy day when the two hundred thousand Jews of Vienna could be liquidated" (March 6, 1965: 96). *Esquire*'s critic poured scorn on the "paper-tiger Nazis" in the film who allow "the whole family (to) walk over a sunny mountain meadow to the nearest border and Freedom" (20).

Scruton regards the kitschification of history as a defensive reaction to the modern horrors of two world wars, weapons of mass destruction, the Holocaust, and global-wide outbreaks of genocide in which real and acute feelings of love, loss, and sorrow become too painful. Because it hides such horrors behind a screen of pretense and prettiness, kitsch is a useful tool of totalitarian regimes: "The world of kitsch is . . . a heartless world, in which emotion is directed away from its proper target towards sugary stereotypes" (Scruton 2009: 191). This is the world that the cold and nasty martinet, Captain von Trapp, inhabits along with his "seven adorable" offspring who in the binary logic of kitsch are both nauseating toy soldiers and super-cute performing poppets. *Esquire*'s critic suggested that *The Sound of Music* is like one of those complicated Alpine cuckoo clocks that the children mime in their goodnight party piece: a "man-made product that approaches perfection of its kind," an "exercise of supreme professional skill," and "pure, unadulterated kitsch" (21). The perfectly unreal, gingerbread fantasies of kitsch can be addictive, as is evident from the habit-forming effect *The Sound of Music* had on some viewers. A widow from Wales showed the devotion of a regular church-goer and not only attended every Monday matinee screening of the film, but watched it religiously from the same seat during its entire 940 day run, earning mention in the *Guinness Book of Records*. She was outdone by a Denver truck driver who not only watched the film every Sunday for three years, but bought his seat after the film theater closed (Wilk 2007: 79; Hirsch 1993: 207–8).

Nuns and Religious Life

Compared to the opprobrium heaped on Plummer and the young actors who impersonated the von Trapp family, both Julie Andrews as Maria and the nuns who constitute her only other "family" escape relatively lightly. Yes, the sisters do twitter like songbirds when considering "How do we solve a problem like Maria." However, Peggy Wood's Mother Abbess gives them gravitas, and together, as a body of good women, they humanize and leaven the sugar spun stereotypes in which they are cast. In fact, I will argue now that they not only save the von Trapp family but save the film from unremitting kitsch. Maria's opening scene on the mountain joyfully proclaimed that the grandeur, the vibrancy and the sheer beauty of the natural world can elevate the spirit, open the eyes and heart to a sense of the sacred, and inspire quasi-religious devotion and thanksgiving (Dorsky 2007: 407–11). The Vespers service that follows in the abbey is a more solemn, canonical expression of the same faith. The choir's hallelujah swells the sounds of Maria's earlier rejoicing. The female trinity of Mother Abbess, Mistress of Postulants, and Mistress of Novices (Portia Nelson) who kneel at the altar give a glimpse of the mystery of a three-personed God who made female and male in the divine image. The Mother Abbess's final benediction confirms Maria's earlier sense of being blessed.

It is clear in this chapel scene that *The Nun's Story* established a formal style for the representation of nuns at prayer (Sullivan 2005: 118). Wise draws directly on Zinnemann's presentation of the contemplative nun as a still life, his focus on the face, eyes, and hands as they reveal the beauty and the hardship of the religious life, and his May–December pairing of the spiritual neophyte and the lifelong nun (Nolletti 1999: 127–9). The orchestrated beauty of this Vespers service illustrates Scruton's view that what distinguishes real art from kitsch is its "appeal to our higher nature, an attempt to affirm that other kingdom in which moral and spiritual order prevails" (2009: 192). Although Wise's chapel scene is a brief interlude in this film musical, it extends the insight of the opening song, "The Sound of Music," by suggesting how religious perception can transform

Figure 4-1. The Trinitarian tableau of Mother Abbess, Mistress of Postulants, and Mistress of Novices subverts the religious stereotype associated with *The Sound of Music* of silly, singing nuns, and recalls the sacred solemnity of *The Nun's Story*.

the way we see not only the natural world but other human beings (Miles 1985: 2).

Neither Julie Andrews's tomboyish Maria nor Peggy Wood's venerable Mother Abbess could be called beauties, especially in comparison with earlier Hollywood nuns such as Ingrid Bergman's Sister Benedict, Deborah Kerr's Sister Angela, or Audrey Hepburn's Sister Luke. Yet like the modern-day saint Mother Teresa, they project inner beauty outward in *The Sound of Music*.[5] Maria's generous and exuberant spirit and the Mother Abbess's magnanimous and invincible soul shine through onscreen, and indeed lie at the heart of this film's general appeal (Kemp 2002: 3). Scruton argues that sacrifice is the only remedy for kitsch, redeeming art, reminding us of the pain of feeling and the cost of love, and so making us look with admiration (2009: 193). Both women display that selfless love for others, which is known as agape and considered the noblest ideal of religious life. They cement their mother-daughter bond with one another in Rodgers and Hammerstein's great woman's song of self-sacrifice, "Climb Every Mountain" (Dyer 1992: 58).

Maria and Agape

Maria was a charismatic figure not only for a general audience but for Catholic clergy and religious in the sixties. Mary Martin, the star of the Broadway musical, would receive many religious accolades for her stage performance and indeed would travel to Rome for a special blessing from Pope John XXIII (Wilk 2007: 43). A former nun, Kathleen J. Waites, would recall how the figure of Maria inspired her religious vocation:

> My older brother and I had grown up watching *The Bells of St. Mary's*, *The Nun's Story*, and *Heaven Knows Mr. Allison* on late night television, so it wasn't unusual to see a motion picture about a Catholic nun. But Maria, the singing nun, was special. Pure and passionate, beautiful and happy, she embodied what I aspired to be. (2006: 15)

---

[5] I am paraphrasing Audre Lorde's assertion in "Uses of the Erotic: The Erotic as Power" that "when we begin to live from within outward, in touch with the power of the erotic within ourselves, and allowing that power to inform and illuminate our actions upon the world around us, then we begin to be responsible to ourselves in the deepest sense." See *Sister Outsider: Essays and Speeches by Audre Lorde* (Freedom Calif.: The Crossing Press), 58.

When Maria opens her arms wide to the natural world on the mountainside and sings how the hills fill her heart and make it blessed with the sound of music, she is expressing key characteristics of agape. These are a whole-hearted receptivity to God, a sense of gratitude for his love, awareness that this love from on high is a pure gift, and an awakening of reciprocal love. The opening aerial glide over the Alpine mountain peaks and down to the hillsides and valleys below captures the divine movement of agape as a love "that descends, freely and generously, giving of its superabundance" (Nygren 1953: viii–xiii, 212–13). This movement was musically rendered by what one reviewer described as Rodgers and Hammerstein's "great tumbling rivers of sound" (Wilk 2007: 32). Agape is an unearned grace, which Maria thankfully receives and celebrates with a full heart in song. Paradoxically, she is a "problem" that the nuns are not sure how to solve because she personifies the very unpredictability of agape, which cannot be summoned or controlled. Like the clouds and will-o'-the-wisps that drift over the mountain tops, it can only be awaited and humbly accepted when it comes, even if it arrives late—as Maria does for chapel.

Thus, the Mother Abbess's provisional solution to let Maria go is intuitively right and consistent with theological principles still cherished in traditional religious life. Agape is spontaneous and must be allowed to flow freely out to others. Maria has been blessed with "a great capacity to love" and will give it selflessly and abundantly in return to the von Trapp family who is in great need of the grace that she can bestow. Their house is not a home but a mausoleum to Captain von Trapp's dead wife. Maria steps into a cool grey and white interior characterized by shade, silence, absence, and lifelessness. The household is run like a total institution according to rules, regimentation, discipline, and obedience more appropriate to the military or a strict cloister. In contrast, the abbey positively bustles with life and resounds with melodic worship and gentle laughter. Von Trapp is immured in the past by grief for his wife, nostalgia for the imperial era where he was honored as a naval hero, mourning for an Austrian "world that's disappearing," and dread of the coming Nazi order. His children feel neglected, cowed, and unloved.

Maria enters the cheerless von Trapp villa dressed in a dark, coarse peasant dress that even "the poor didn't want." Both it and the dark brown dirndl she wears when she takes the children on their first trip up her beloved mountain have a "Franciscan look." Indeed, she follows St. Francis of Assisi in her spirit of humility and simple poverty, unpretentiousness, and homely love of nature. Critics Anne McLeer and

Rebecca Sullivan have noted her anonymity, the absence of a proper surname or family history, with McLeer concluding that she is not a full person until she acquires the von Trapp married name and becomes part of his family (McLeer 2002: 95; Sullivan 2005: 81). In fact, the recipients of agape often lack social status or prestige (Nygren 1953: 237). When appointed governess to the aristocratic von Trapps, Maria becomes a classic threshold figure who moves between different social roles, classes, and spheres, but she also carries with her an aura of sacred liminality that makes her seem "magical" to viewers (Dyer 1992: 49; Kemp 2002: 4). The opening aerial descent suggests that this glow is not magical but wondrously divine, and that grace can fall on a nobody like Maria—or anybody. Because agape is a pure and selfless form of love, it is associated not only with humility, inferiority, and marginality but sexlessness. For the religious liminar, the universal sentiments of compassion and human kindness may be a greater inner imperative than erotic desire or the reproductive drive (Turner 1969: 94–7, 102–5, 109–11, 143–4).

Film critics have remarked on Julie Andrews's androgynous appearance and antiseptic image as Maria. Pauline Kael regarded her as a Disneyland character, "sexless, inhumanly happy, the sparkling maid" (1970: 177). Richard Dyer saw the physical awkwardness and anxiety Andrews's Maria showed with Captain von Trapp as the exemplification of women's ignorance about their own sexuality and as a negative expression of the "'natural feeling' so positively affirmed in music" (1992: 55). In her queer reading of Mary Martin's star performance in the stage musical, Stacy Wolf shrewdly observed that "Maria seems not so much to love the Captain as to love children, music, playfulness, and nature" (1996: 60). Maria's tomboyish manner, her boisterous behavior, and penchant for getting into scrapes made Wolf conclude that she is "asexual" in the first half of the musical and, as such, a blank page for a lesbian spectator (1996: 52–5). Unsympathetic film critics have drawn another conclusion: that *The Sound of Music* mainly appeals to sentimental women, very young children, and the elderly (Starkman 2000: 65–6; Crist, March 3, 1965).

It can also be inferred from her unruliness and naivety that she is still an adolescent at heart. Indeed, Andrews's Maria seems sister in spirit to another beloved but confused and hoydenish young heroine, Louisa May Alcott's Jo March. Yet it is hardly surprising that a motherless "girl" who becomes a postulant might be a late-bloomer. While sexual experimentation is obviously prohibited in the convent, self-examination is a core requirement of religious life. When Maria takes refuge from her erotic feelings for von Trapp back in the abbey, the Reverend Mother tells her firmly that it's wrong to run away: "These walls were not built to shut out problems. You have to face them. You have to live the life you were born to live." The young, outspoken, lively postulant Maria may be a joyful representation of the "new nuns" of the 1960s who arrived at the convent guitar in hand and wore modified habits (Sullivan 2005: 43, 188, 194, 220–21). Yet while the Mother Abbess is the personification of the traditional nun, she is forward-looking and insists that the cloister was not intended to be a place of safety, shelter, and retreat from the modern world (Novak, *The Saturday Evening Post*, July 30, 1966: 22, 25, 68, 71).

Eros

Maria's vitality and personal charisma make her a cynosure for the nuns, the children, and von Trapp, and indicate that she is far from asexual (Wolf 1996: 58). They are signs of eros, which Lorde called "the lifeforce of women" and source of their creative energy (1984: 55). Eros is apparent in Maria even as a young girl and wells up as a desire for communication and communion through music, which made her long to be one of the sisters (Nelson 1979: 105): "When I was a child, I would come down the mountain and climb a tree and look over into your [abbey] garden. I'd see the sisters at work and I'd hear them sing on their way to Vespers." Climbing a tree is the charming juvenile manifestation of the aspiration and ascent that propel eros and which will be expressed in mature form when Maria sets out to "climb every mountain" at the end of the film (Nygren 1953: 472). Eros will emerge more fully as a passionate capacity for love and for joy, which Lorde insisted must be shared with others. It will be realized through various forms of play that give Maria a sense of belonging and make the children feel they are a family again.

The first stages of the film suggested through breathtaking scenery and stirring song how divine love as agape is generously and abundantly poured out into the human heart (Nygren 1953: 232; Rom. 5:5). As we have seen, the camera moves from the mountain-top to the hillside where Maria stands in joyful surrender, watches her rush down the hill as she is late for Vespers in Salzburg below, and finally arrives before her in the chapel where the religious community assembles for prayer. Her later arrival at the von Trapp villa and battle of wills with the Captain to make play, not drills, a top priority for his children will mark the commencement of eros's counter movement back upward as the film now articulates the desire, the need, the want, the striving, and the struggle for love and happiness (Nygren 1953: 175, 212, 232, 476). *The Sound of*

Music can be read as the articulation of a conservative social and gender ideology in which marriage to the patriarchal Captain makes Maria a whole person (McLeer 2002: 95). However, when eros is no longer seen narrowly as simply a sexual or romantic drive but as the core desires impelling the individual to live life to the full, then the playful activities preceding her marriage to von Trapp assume key importance in determining their relationship.

Play

In his influential essay on "Play and Intrinsic Rewards," Mihaly Csikszentmihalyi argued that "people are most human, whole, free, and creative when they play" (1975: 42). For child psychologist and psychoanalyst Donald Winnicott, the play space is sacred because here the individual can enjoy the intense life experience associated with the imagination, the arts, religion, and scientific discovery (1992: 14, 103). Play is the domain of the liminar who lives "betwixt and between" states (Turner 1969: 95; Turner 1978: 35). Play is the first and the major bone of contention between Maria and von Trapp, a gesture of proto-feminist defiance, and a subversion of his petty patriarchal and fascistic tyranny. Indeed, one of her first acts of disobedience will be to take his children by train back up the mountain where she enjoyed a free and happy childhood. Critics who dislike the film have usually loathed the von Trapp children and regarded Maria's play scenes with them as the most cloying display of the film's kitsch. The world of kitsch has been described as heartless and unfeeling, and the "problem" Maria faces with the children is that they have lost heart. They first present themselves to Maria as little "tin men" trained to callousness by the Captain's military school of a home. Play not only gives them back the heart that they lack but demonstrates Maria's erotic aptitude to give her whole heart to life's small and great adventures and to the relationships they forge.

Maria wins the children over when she neutralizes the *Sturm und Drang* of a thunderstorm by her impromptu song "My Favorite Things." The lyrics of this number communicate the pleasure of simple things, a pleasure expressed in enumerating the familiar objects, activities, and surroundings of everyday life. Maria's list begins with "raindrops on roses and whiskers on kittens, bright copper kettles and warm woolen mittens" but becomes a game of inventory and invention that could go on *ad infinitum*. In the stage musical, "My Favorite Things" was a song that Maria and the Mother Abbess nostalgically remembered from childhood

(Hirsch 1993: 23). In this film scene, the erotic becomes "the nurturer or nursemaid" (Lorde 1984: 56) of a deeper bond with the children in their shared appreciation of the fabric of the world that the bored and the blasé take for granted. Filming "My Favorite Things" so that it appeared as a seamless number required skillful camera work, direction and editing; but the resulting scene succeeded brilliantly in capturing the holistic process of play and its generation of spontaneous intimacy—on Maria's bed and with all in their nightclothes (Dyer 1992: 52–3).

While their father pursues joyless pleasures with Baroness Elsa Schraeder (Eleanor Parker) in Vienna, "gossiping gaily with bores I detest, soaking myself in champagne, stumbling about the waltzes by Strauss," his children enjoy a holiday that dramatizes the intrinsic rewards of play in the succeeding "Do-Re-Mi" number. This sequence required a more complicated and extensive shoot than "My Favorite Things" in scenic locations around Salzburg and featured several dress changes for Maria and the children, yet gave the impression of a continuous voyage of discovery. This is because the extraordinary range of their outdoor activities—sightseeing; trekking; picnicking; ball-throwing; learning to sing, play the guitar, and sight-read music; yodeling; synchronized dancing, playing statues; cavorting; carriage-riding; bicycling; canoeing; and Maria's favorite sport, tree-climbing—suggest not only the human capacity for endless inventiveness and improvisation but the flow experience of play. They move in fluid harmony; they live wholly in the present moment; they find joy, fulfillment, and solidarity through total involvement in their pastimes; they merge with each other through the fusion of action and awareness (Csikszentmihalyi 1975: 43–53).

Julie Andrews

With a background in vaudeville, music hall, and pantomime, Julie Andrews had a flair for comedy and slapstick, which makes her fun to watch on-screen and convincing in her enjoyment of the play state. She had been a child performer herself and appeared to have a natural rapport with the young actors who played the von Trapps. She was happy to lark about with them and raise a laugh, as in the scene where she falls out of the canoe and into the lake in her excitement at the return of Captain von Trapp with Baroness Elsa Schraeder (Hirsch 1993: 119, 130). Kael unkindly called her "the perfect, perky schoolgirl" (1970: 177), but it was the playful heart she showed on-screen, sometimes worn on a clown's sleeve, that made her such a favorite with a popular audience.

Her humor and gusto were enhanced by a legendary singing voice with a rare four-octave, coloratura-soprano range, perfect pitch and diction. As both Richard Dyer and Peter Kemp appreciated, she used this extraordinary vocal instrument to convey her capacity for joy, her delight in music, and the uplifting power of song. This voice conveyed both purity of heart and passion for life, which is another reason why her Maria has captivated viewers. It is a voice that, like play itself, is intermediate between worlds—innocence and experience, childhood and adulthood, the nursery and the nunnery. Her voice will bring grace into von Trapp's life, reminding him that "The Sound of Music" was the song of his own youth, and prompting him to sing aloud the line "like a lark that is learning to pray" from memory.

In her musical *jouissance*, Andrews's Maria had affinities with actual nuns past and present. She resembled the new religious entrants who were animated by Vatican II and inspired by the folk revivalism of the sixties to "come with their guitars . . . full of joy and vivacity" (Novak 68; Sullivan 2005: 166–8). If they remained in the convent after 1965, these new nuns would wear a street-length dress and short veil very similar to Maria's habit as a postulant. Yet with her soaring voice, extremes of register, and rhapsodic joy in the natural world, the figure of Maria also looks back to the twelfth-century visionary and musician, Hildegard of Bingen. Green was an important symbolic color in her vivid theology as it is visually in *The Sound of Music*. She would employ the word "greening," or *viriditas*, to describe how God showered all of creation with his quickening spirit (Dreyer 2005: 77–81). Green is also a color Maria claims, embracing the verdant Alpine hills in the film opening, recycling her green and white bedroom curtains to kit the von Trapp children out in play clothes, choosing green ivy as her bridal wreath, and generally bringing the von Trapp family alive with her own vital spirit.

At the same time the von Trapps quicken new and bewildering feelings in Maria that shake her sense of religious purpose: "I'm not sure I'll make a very good nun." As her attachment to the children grows and her attraction to their father gently unfolds, Maria begins to experience the tension between her desire to give her love without reserve and the need to be loved in return. The von Trapp ball brings the internal conflict between her selfless feelings of agape and the personal longings of eros to a head, and precipitates the turning point of the film with her flight back to the sanctuary, seclusion, and silence of the abbey. Maria's second, reluctant interview with the Mother Abbess is the most revealing scene in *The Sound of Music*, even though it is filmed in semi-darkness with the two principals often looking away from one another. The mise-en-scène with its private altar, sacred shadows, and grilled window turns the superior's office into a confessional and reminds viewers of the historical powers abbesses once exercised as religious leaders, spiritual directors, and wise women.

The Mother Abbess

As Mother Abbess, Peggy Wood takes command of this scene. Although her supporting role is not large, she is Maria's mainstay. Kemp regards her as a fairy godmother (2002: 3), but she is endowed with a religious stature and authority that indicates her symbolic resemblance to *Sophia*, the feminine figuration of Holy Wisdom. She counsels, comforts, and ministers to Maria at crucial film interludes, which mark the initial development, turning point, and denouement of the plot. Her first action in this scene is that of consoler as she places her hand on Maria's bowed head in a gesture of tender blessing: "You've been unhappy. I'm sorry." Wood inflected the simple lines she was given with a gamut of flickering emotions from concern—"Why did they send you back to us?"—to maternal protectiveness and indignation—"Frightened? Were they unkind to you?"—to dawning and pleased intuition that Maria is in love with von Trapp. The dialogue between the two women stands out in this study of cinematic nuns for being not only a demonstration of but an exposition on intimacy. The Mother Abbess shows that although the religious celibate is called to sacrifice sexual activity, this does not mean that she lacks sexual understanding: "Did you let him see how you felt?" Maria's answer is spoken against the backdrop of the abbess's altar crucifix, which commemorates Christ's Sacrifice on the Cross as the most exalted expression of divine love for humanity: "If I did, I didn't know it. That's what's been torturing me. I was there on God's errand. To have asked for his love would have been wrong."

Her halting response articulates a traditional Christian view that there is a dichotomy between agape and eros; that giving love is at odds with receiving it; that self-sacrifice precludes self-fulfillment in love (Nygren 1953: xiii–xiv; Nelson 1979: 110–11). The abbess's reply is one of firm correction and is consistent with Catholic piety, which expressed not only the Augustinian tension of eros and agape but the attempted synthesis and integration of sexuality and spirituality (Nygren 1953: 243, 451–2, 561): "Maria, the love of a man and a woman is holy too." At the time this film was made, Vatican II was redefining the call to holiness and coming to regard marriage "as a true vocation equal in spiritual value to the celibate vocation" (Schneiders 2000: 247). The abbess responds to Maria's plea that she has pledged her life to God and his service by insisting that human and divine love are not opposed to one another: "My daughter, if you love this man, it doesn't mean you love God less. No, you must find out. You must go back." With "Climb Every Mountain," she sends Maria on a new quest for holiness, one in which she does not lose her vocation and bear the stigma of the failed nun, but seeks to find it.[6]

Eros and Agape

If "The Sound of Music" rejoiced in agape as the divine love that descends freely and unreservedly to the world, "Climb Every Mountain" is its musical counterpoint, commemorating the upward longing and struggle of eros. The song expresses the contradictions in the film itself. Its climactic refrain, "follow every rainbow till you find your dream," illustrates the siren call of kitsch to chase fantasized hopes and childish dreams at the end of the rainbow rather than face harder realities (Scruton 2009: 105). However, the middle section of the song resists this kitschification of the religious quest by emphasizing the exertion, perseverance, fortitude, courage, and willingness to forfeit immediate pleasure that eros's constant striving and reaching out demand. Thus, the abbess exhorts Maria to "search high and low, follow every byway, every path you know." As Dyer has suggested, the superior's message is one of tough love, telling Maria that her only course of action is to go on and forward in a spirit of "endurance, self-sacrifice and hope" (1992: 58). Sacrifice is the antidote to the cloying sweetness of kitsch. Sacrifice is the sign of the cross and of agape. The dream that the abbess holds up to Maria is "a dream that will need all the love you can give, every day of your life for as long as you live." In other words, it is a dream that honors love in its totality—the self-giving spirit of agape and the self-seeking spirit of eros.

Maria returns to the von Trapps with the words of the abbess ringing in her ears: "These walls were not built to shut out problems. You have

[6]In her convent memoir, *Particular Friendships*, former nun Kathleen J. Waites remarks that while the film image of Maria fostered her own sense of a religious vocation, "I became so totally absorbed in this image that the demise of her vocation in the end was completely lost on me" (Xlibris, 2005), 15. As I have suggested, the Mother Abbess assures Maria in this scene that she has a calling from God and must discern whether it is to be found in or outside religious life.

to face them." One answer then to "how do you solve a problem like Maria?" is that only Maria can solve this problem. She will do so by facing up to her feelings for the von Trapp family and by recognizing how they impart momentum to self-knowledge and sexual development, and to both altruistic and aspirational impulses (Miles 1988: 124). Maria's now inevitable wedding to von Trapp has been interpreted as an act in which the problem she first posed for the nuns is solved by substituting a bridal veil for a religious veil, making her bride of the Captain rather than Christ, and replacing the walls of the cloister by the strictures of marriage (Sullivan 2005: 82–4). However, the flow of this beautiful wedding spectacle breaks down the binaries that structure both musical theatre and the fairy tale aspects of this film, and dissolves the dualism that presented Maria's problem as an "either–or" choice between agape and eros (Wolf 1996: 56; Csikszentmihalyi 1975: 44–5).

Maria's marriage vow to von Trapp is not depicted as a renunciation of religious life but as a joyful rite of passage. She descends the stairs of the abbey where she was robed in her wedding dress as the Mistress of Postulants fusses with her veil. She kneels for a farewell blessing from the Mother Abbess who symbolically gives her away. She glides across the abbey courtyard accompanied by the religious community that has been her only family to the new family that awaits her on the other side of the cloister gate. A high angle camera watches her proceed down the church

Figure 4-2. This transitional scene depicts the cloistered nun as the "garden enclosed," but shows the Mother Abbess unlock the grille door so that Maria can answer the erotic call of the bridegroom as in *The Song of Songs*: "Open to me, my sister, my love" (5.2).

Figure 4-3. Maria gives new meaning to the nun's gliding walk as she processes down the cathedral nave in a regal wedding dress and train that exemplify the flow state in which there is a joyful merger of action and awareness.

aisle alone in acknowledgment of the virginal independence, autonomy, and singularity that connect her to the convent. Her classical bridal gown with its fitted bodice and graceful cathedral train—woven of the stuff of royal marriages, medieval tapestries, religious clothing ceremonies, and Hollywood princesses—floats like a white cloud behind her as the music of "How Do You Solve a Problem Like Maria?" is triumphantly reprised.[7] She mounts the stairs of the high altar and kneels with von Trapp as the camera pans up to the Baroque reredos above the altar celebrating the coronation of the Virgin Mary in heaven, and then soars to the church tower where the bells joyfully peal following the von Trapp marriage. The answer to Maria's problem is that she does not have to choose between spirituality and sexuality, erotic and sacred love. The answer lies in a God who is "both-and" (O'Murchu 2006: 47).

Finale

What Robert Wise hid from view in this ornate and resplendent altarpiece were the jeweled skeletons of saints that flank the Virgin in her ascent to crowning glory. They are a *memento mori*, or reminder of death,

[7] Any number of fashion commentators have noted the retro touches of Katherine Middleton's royal wedding dress and its resemblance to the iconic gowns that Hollywood star Grace Kelly wore at her wedding to the Prince of Monaco and Julie Andrews wore as Maria in *The Sound of Music*.

and a sense of doom and loss will, in fact, darken the close of the film.[8] The director did not convey this message through the saints' macabre bones, but through the dissolve of the "wildly rejoicing" wedding bells into the somber bell-tolling that mourns Nazi Germany's annexation of Austria with the *Anschluss* and that is a reminder of the wartime close of *The Nun's Story*. Two scene locations in the film denouement allude to the historical fact that early Christianity was founded on suffering and sacrifice. The Salzburg Folk Festival in which the von Trapp family singers perform was staged at the *Felsenreitschule*. Although in actuality a riding school, this cold and forbidding arena of rock had first been developed by the ancient Romans for their games, and its arches and passageways retained the atmosphere of a coliseum where Christians were martyred for their beliefs (Hirsch 1993: 86; von Dassanowsky 2003: 7). Likewise, the abbey graveyard, where the von Trapps conceal themselves after making their escape from the music festival and being hunted down by the Nazis, recalls the ancient catacombs. These early Christian burial sites were popularly, although mistakenly, assumed to have been hiding places from religious persecution.

The von Trapps face persecution for their Austrian patriotism and the Captain's opposition to the Nazis. However, the sisters who give shelter to the family also face a very real threat of persecution for aiding and abetting enemies of the Third Reich. As they rush to hide behind the abbey tombstones, an appalled Maria will apologize to the abbess: "Oh Reverend Mother, we didn't realize we put the abbey in this danger." The Mother Abbess's response gives witness to how selflessly Christians can love one another: "No Maria, it was right for you to come here." The nuns' willingness to endanger their own lives in order to save others becomes one last occasion for kitsch humor and girlish stereotyping. The Mistress of Postulants and Mistress of Novices join forces as co-conspirators in a prank worthy of their naughty postulant Maria, and "confess" to the Mother Abbess that they have removed the car batteries of the Nazis who are hell bent on pursuit of the von Trapps up into the hills. As the family climbs the mountain leading them to the safety of neutral Switzerland, we are left to contemplate the possible fate of the abbey for this early act of resistance to the *Anschluss*. Historically, both Catholic and Protestant leaders submitted to totalitarian authority in the

---

[8] The Baroque reredos and their grisly spectators are in the Church of Mondsee Cathedral, which was used as the site of the Abbey Church wedding. See excellent photos of this altarpiece close up at http://sthugofcluny.org/2009/11/the-reredos-ii-the-german-world.html (accessed July 24, 2011).

Second World War, or strove for the neutrality Sister Luke's community exercises in *The Nun's Story*. Religious who did show civil disobedience ran the risk of violent attacks on their convent, dissolution of their communities, imprisonment, deportation to concentration camps, and death like the Carmelite cloistered nun, Edith Stein, in Auschwitz (Fiand 2001: 168–70; McNamara 1996: 572–3).

In a final tender embrace, the Reverend Mother demonstrates a choir nun's lived knowledge of scripture and love of the psalms when she reminds Maria: "You will not be alone. Remember I will lift up mine eyes unto the hills from whence cometh my help." Mendelssohn turned Psalm 121 into a sonorous hymn of pilgrimage and ascent. The film's opening depiction of the mountainous sublime as the symbol of divine salvation and transcendence is thus reiterated as the family makes its way up the *Obersalzburg* in a flight that is also buoyed by the faith of another psalm: "Here my cry, O God; listen to my prayer . . . when my heart is over-whelmed. Lead me to the rock that is higher than I; for you are my refuge, a strong tower against the enemy" (Ps. 61:1–3).[9] Ironically, this flight will also save Maria from the personal passivity, quiescence, and acquiescence into which she seems to lapse after her marriage to the Captain as though she gave him not simply her virginity but her vital lifeforce on their honeymoon. With flight, she is on the move again, in motion as a character, and in her natural element. She is no longer "frightened" as she was when forced to contemplate her sexual feelings for von Trapp and the prospect of leaving the convent for good. This is not simply because she will be back on the mountain but because she will be free of the trappings of wealth, luxury, estate, and title that define her husband. Maria's background of sacred anonymity, poverty, and simplicity has prepared her to be a stranger and pilgrim on the earth (1 Pet. 2:11). The drama of a family that loses everything—homeland, house, friends, fortune, and social standing, everything except their love for each other and faith that God will provide—had deep appeal not only to an American immigrant audience but to exiles and refugees all over the world who had no place to lay their heads. This trope acquires deeper Christian significance from

---

[9] In fact, as Hirsch notes in *The Sound of Music: The Making of America's Favorite Movie*, 84–6, the film company chose a mountain for the flight into Switzerland that was conveniently reached by road. It did not lead to freedom but deeper into the heart of the Third Reich, straight up to one of Hitler's camps not far from "Eagles Nest." Maria von Trapp complained, "don't they know Geography in Hollywood?," and Robert Wise's response was, "in Hollywood you make your own geography" (Hirsch 1993: 75).

the Son of Man who was homeless and hunted, and who therefore knew the sorrows that people are burdened with as fugitives.

Conclusion

Even though the nuns of Nonnberg Abbey leave the viewer with a final profile of their courage and altruism, they are still dismissed as either sweet and sanctimonious stereotypes or figures of no great significance in *The Sound of Music*. While it is true that their roles are smaller on-screen than in the original stage musical, my reading has contested the critical conclusion that they are superficial characters who provide Catholic window-dressing and bring no religious substance to the film.[10] Indeed, I have argued that the wayward postulant Maria and her wise Mother Abbess exemplify the beauty, the strength, the goodness, and the theological underpinnings of the religious life. Julie Andrews's protagonist Maria embodied the spirit of joy, elation, and energy that continues to attract women to the convent. In a supporting role, the Mother Abbess exemplified the inner core that women religious develop through the tireless pursuit of holiness and that can be a source of comfort, support, conviction, and guidance, especially in times of trouble (Nalevanko 1998: 9, 12; Wolter 1998: 22). Together they project the sacred aura that strikes first-time visitors to the convent.

> There was a curious feeling of reality having been enhanced. I felt as if I was silently being shown how to be alive. It was as if there flowed from the sisters an excitement, an enthusiasm for each moment, a gratitude perhaps. . . . I barely believed in God, yet I felt that I had spent the weekend in God's presence. (Losada 1999: 3)

Julie Andrews's Maria and Peggy Wood's Mother Abbess save *The Sound of Music* from kitsch by communicating this "feeling of reality having been enhanced" through their songs, their full and graced presence to others, their personal faith, and their moments of holy intimacy. In their understandable aversion to the sugar-coated sentimentalism of *The Sound of Music*, early critics paid insufficient attention to the film's

---

[10]For example, David Brown contends that the film version of *The Sound of Music* "lowered the religious content. In effect, Julie Andrews ousted the stage version's larger role for the Abbess and her convent." See *God & Grace of Body: Sacrament in Ordinary* (New York: Oxford University Press, 2007), 371.

visual beauty and sublimity, and to the ways in which its music and play are as uplifting as the prayer sung in Psalm 121. I have joined later revisionists who take the film more seriously and respectfully considered why a world audience came to appreciate it so much (von Dassanowsky 2003: 2–3; Andrew, *Time Out:* September 26 – October 2, 2007). However, my reading has been religiously informed by a sense of the tension, contrast, and eventual convergence of two Christian ideas of love in the film. The film's opening descent and closing ascent capture the sense of agape as a divine movement of love and grace downward to the world, and eros as an upward striving and search for the way to love God and others. Maria's conflict over her religious calling and sexual longings dramatizes a traditional dichotomy between agape and eros. The Mother Abbess insists that agape and eros are not opposed but complementary, and that "if you love this man, it doesn't mean you love God less." The body language of the two women—their gestures of openness, embrace, gratitude, and blessing—demonstrates a continuous and reciprocal movement in which, as David Brown has memorably said, "reaching out . . . is also matched by the divine at the same time coming towards us" (2007: 117). Perhaps one of the many reasons why *The Sound of Music* remains one of the most popular and loved films of all time is that it gave fans the feeling that they, too, had spent time in God's presence.

A Transitional Era for Nuns

The Sound of Music opened in cinemas nine months before the Second Vatican Council ended. While the film falsely claimed it was depicting Austria's last golden days in the thirties, nuns in America would look back on the fifties and first half of the sixties as a genuine "golden age" for religious vocations (Rogers 1996: 103). In 1965, the American Catholic Church could boast a record number of approximately 180,000 nuns. After this historic peak in 1965, however, the numbers began to plummet, and in 1966 alone over 2,000 nuns left the convent. Although there was no shortage of postulants in the sixties, an increasing number did not stay. A Benedictine nun recalls her "feelings of abandonment, as one by one twenty-three of the twenty-six women who entered the postulancy with me left between the years 1961 and 1974" (Hollermann 1998: xvii). A year after *Change of Habit* (1969) appeared, religious communities had lost 19,000 members, with an all-time high of 4,337 leaving in 1970, making the ex-nun a common phenomenon. Some who left grieved for the loss of the "religious family" they had come to love and found the prospect of making a fresh start as "frightening" as Maria does in *The Sound of Music*: "Where would I go? What would I do? Could I get a job? Who would stand by me?" (Nalevanko 1998: 11; Enneking 1998: 44). By 1996, American Catholic sisters had decreased by approximately one half (Ebaugh 1988: 100, 1993b: 2; Fialka 2003: 17, 200; Carey 1997: 7, 29, 33).

Thus, after a long postwar period of growth, stability, and strong corporate identity for American Catholic nuns, they faced changes of considerable magnitude. Although Vatican II was greeted with euphoria and excitement within the Church, the reforms it officially set in motion were not always liberating and empowering but sometimes proved disorientating, threatening, and divisive. *Perfectae Caritatis*, a conciliar document appearing near the end of Vatican II in 1965, called for the general renewal of religious life, and gave nuns the green light to modify cloister restrictions, update religious customs, recover the originating spirit of their founder, and try to design a more practical habit that was "simple and modest, poor and at the same time becoming" (LaFontaine 2008: 78; Carey 1997: 37–8, 58). It was naively assumed that these directives would inspire only minor changes to the externals of religious life.[11] Instead, they triggered intense emotional debate within convents; created political fissures between traditional and more progressive women religious; and led to vocational crisis and the structural unraveling of communities (Wittberg 1994: 213–17; Carey 1997: 176–81).

The habit, in particular, became a visual gauge of a nun's conservative or liberal stance, indicating how she understood her religious identity, responded to higher authority in the Church, and interpreted the renewal and modernization process begun by Vatican II (Kuhns 2003: 151–3; Kaylin 2000: 61; Michelman 1998: 176–86). Feminism made progressive nuns more acutely aware of the patriarchal structure of the institutional Church and the power that its clerical class wielded over them. The wearing of an antiquated habit and veil was associated with pre-modern rules of enclosure and early twentieth-century canonical regulations that not only facilitated their religious control but cut them off from the contemporary world. With the removal of the habit, nuns lost their aura of mysterious otherness; were less prone to stereotyp-

---

[11] As Gene Burns pointed out, however, Pius XII had "originated the idea of the need for the *renewal* and *adaptation* to changed times for all nonessential aspects of religious life" in the 1950s. See Burns, *The Frontiers of Catholicism: The Politics of Ideology in a Liberal World* (Berkeley: University of California Press, 1994), 132–3.

ing as disembodied, asexual, or supernatural beings; and became more conscious of themselves as women. Former nun Mary Jo Leddy vividly remembers being told by her novice mistress in 1965 that she would be buried in the habit that symbolized her burial with Christ, only to be out of the habit for good a year later and realize that Vatican II had changed everything (Rogers 1996: 280–1).[12]

In 1964, the Council document *Lumen Gentium* affirmed that all baptized Christians are called to holiness, and so corrected the common assumption that women religious constituted a privileged, holy elite, and quasi-clerical class in the Church hierarchy, spiritually elevated above the laity but below ordained priests (O'Brien and Schaumber 2009: 178–80; Quinonez and Turner 1992: 3–5, 34–9; Weaver 1995: 71–2). For traditional nuns today, the habit remains a religious sign of the consecrated state that distinguishes them from the laity, a sacred symbol of their total gift of self to God, and a visible badge of their separation from the profane world (Donovan and Wusinich 2009: 34–40).[13] Older nuns may revere the habit as a token of their congregational history and a visual witness to the beauty, nobility, and mission of the religious life (Kuhns 2003: 2–3, 151, 159, 164). Thirty years after Vatican II, a Sister of Mercy in her eighties still recalled the pain she felt when her order put aside the habit: "I love the habit. I felt that it wasn't so much that it distinguished me as the fact that it was a witness. People would see me, they'd know that somebody is trying to serve God to the best of their ability" (Rogers 1996: 5). Yet others only recollect how quickly and comprehensively past habits and traditions were consigned to oblivion. One woman religious likened what nuns went through in the wake of Vatican II to the downfall of communism: "There's no possible going back, even if you didn't know what was ahead. When we changed out of the habit, there

[12]Mother Agnes Mary Donovan, S.V. and Sister Mary Elizabeth Wusinich, S.V. explain the traditional view in "Religious Consecration—A Particular Form of Consecrated Life" that "religious profession is a new 'burial in the death of Christ,'" and caused the professed nun "to 'walk like Christ in the newness of life.'" See Council of Major Superiors of Women Religious, *The Foundations of Religious Life: Revisiting the Vision* (Notre Dame, Ind.: Ave Maria Press, 2009), 22.

[13]See I.H.M. Sister Sandra M. Schneiders's qualification in *Finding the Treasure: Locating Catholic Religious Life in a New Ecclesial and Cultural Context* (New York: Paulist Press, 2000), 127–8, that *Lumen Gentium* and *Perfectae Caritatis* did regard nuns as having a religious life that made them distinct from both priests and laity. She added that "the terminology of states of life in the Church is not only ambiguous but almost hopelessly confused."

was . . . a kind of collective amnesia. . . . None of us can remember what happened to our old habits" (Gordon 2002: 80).

The Second Vatican Council closed with *Gaudium et Spes*, a document that placed the Church squarely in the modern world and called its members to show solidarity with the people of this world in their "joys and hopes, griefs and anxieties" (Schneiders 2000: 103; Quinonez and Turner 1992: 69). In the 1950s, the Sister Formation Movement had already begun to give American nuns the higher education, professional training, and theological briefing that would prepare them to answer this call effectively. Over the course of this decade, active sisters started to move out of the safe enclosures in parochial schools and Catholic hospitals that restricted them in their apostolic ministry to the community of mankind (Carey 1997: 14–15, 133–43). However, the sweeping religious, social, and political changes of the 1960s accelerated the push beyond traditional boundaries and led progressive nuns to become involved in more radical causes such as the civil rights movement and the anti-Vietnam war protest (Chittister 2005: 87; Ebaugh 1993a: 407–8). *Gaudium et Spes*'s affirmation of the dignity of the human person and the nobility of marriage—which the Mother Abbess verified in her own reflections on intimacy with Maria—would lead both nuns and priests to wonder whether they were being called to "fuller intimacy" and humanity through marriage and family life (Rogers 1996: 52; Schneiders 2000: 247). The development of feminist spirituality in the 1970s would make nuns more perceptive about their bodies, feelings, libidinal drive, and core desires, or what Lorde called "the lifeforce of women" (Lorde 1984: 55; Schneiders 2004: 74–5). This erotic lifeforce made them look inward at the connection between their sexuality and spirituality and outward at their connection to others through right relationships, the commitment to peace and social justice, and community-building (Slee 2002: 179–82; Heyward 1989: 3–4, 21–2, 46, 54–5, 101). Their cinematic equivalents gave serious expression to these issues in *Change of Habit*, but in demanding that they be taken seriously on-screen, they also became less sonorous and more strident. The blithe, free, ardent high notes that Maria sang in *The Sound of Music* are not heard from the trio of nuns featured in this 1969 film but from their altogether surprising male lead, Elvis Presley.

Change of Habit (1969)

Even for a film audience liberalized by the counter-cultural values of the 1960s, it must have required a considerable stretch of the imagination to suspend disbelief and buy the premise of a *Change of Habit*—that the screen character Elvis Presley plays, who was invariably a version of himself, would fall in love with a nun or that this bride of Christ would be torn between Christ the King and the King of Rock 'n' Roll. Yet the idea of bringing together two figures who personify sex and the spirit was clever and potentially electric. Directed by TV veteran William Graham, *Change of Habit* was intended as a kind of *aggiornamento* or career update for both Presley and Mary Tyler Moore.

Elvis Presley

Presley had exploded as "a truly revolutionary force" (Guralnick 1999: 119) on the music scene in 1954. He was a poor white Southern boy, born in Mississippi a year before Tyler Moore, in 1935. An early photo of him and his parents huddled together as they face the camera has all the poignancy and vulnerability of a scene from *The Grapes of Wrath*. Presley became a popular artist who embodied a passion that one critic likened to the sacred cinema of Carl Dreyer's 1928 film *The Passion of Joan of Arc* (Brode 2006: 50–3). His original inspiration came from the gospel music he grew up with at the Pentecostal First Assembly of God church and from the black spiritual style of the hymns that encouraged the oppressed soul to sing and soar. His raw and visceral sexual energy as a young pop singer would cause an older generation to condemn his performances as "obscene," and rock 'n' roll as the "devil's music" (Kastin 2002: 180). But as he himself realized, his movements on stage were an extension and artistic expression of the ecstatic body language he had witnessed in the evangelical preachers "who mov(ed) every which way" (Guralnick 1999: 121) to arouse the Holiness congregations of his childhood and to demonstrate their emotional surrender to God (Curran 1989: 138). Indeed, in his performances Elvis used the sensual body to uplift the spirit and so displayed that psychosexuality that Freud had defined as going "lower and also higher than its popular sense . . . all the activities of the tender feelings which have primitive sexual impulses as their source" (1910, *SE* 11: 222).

Elvis made his first Hollywood film, *Love Me Tender*, in 1956. Over the next decade, he made thirty more formulaic "B" movies. *Change of Habit* was pitched to him as the star vehicle that would reverse his fading appeal in the late 1960s and end his boredom with his own talent by showcasing his natural acting ability in a serious social film equivalent to *Midnight Cowboy* (1969) (Moore 1995: 126–7: Guralnick 1999: 134–7). In the role of Dr. John Carpenter, who runs a free medical clinic in a

New York City ghetto, he played a professional maverick with a social conscience. The Hollywood decision to romantically partner him with Mary Tyler Moore's Sister Michelle was a bizarre mismatch based on an interesting premise. The iconic figure of the nun on-screen subliminally reminded an audience that religion had made Elvis a singer and sex symbol. Indeed, the driven stage performer communicated an ardor and intensity that were also notable in the dedicated, real-life sister. Both struck others as being "people who are on fire" (Carey 1997: 30), one consumed by God and the other by profane ambition that nonetheless had sacred origins (Guralnick 1999: 120; Kastin 2002: 176). They also faced parallel challenges. For the heavy-lidded singer, it was how to make his music express the smoldering fires of the hillbillies, African Americans, and migrant whites whose voices had been disenfranchised in the dirt poor South (Kastin 2002: 178; Guralnick 1999: 122). For the chaste nun, it was how to channel erotic energy so as to reach out and touch other lives, and convert it into altruistic service. A School Sister of Notre Dame was frank about the daily challenges of chastity:

> Sometimes when people talk about celibacy, they think of it as abstinence from or lack of or giving up of genital activity. It is all of that. And some days that might be exactly what it feels like. But it's so much more than that. On a better day, it is a vow to love in a less particular way instead of loving *a* single person. (Rogers 1996: 272)

Sister Michelle gives a standard religious reply to Presley's amorous doctor who woos her on-screen, but in her case, it sounds automatic rather than heartfelt: "In marriage you love God through one person. As a nun, I made a commitment to love God through all people." The argument for the non-possessive, non-exclusive, selfless love known as agape will be made again in the 1975 film *In This House of Brede* and the 1995 film *Dead Man Walking*. Falling in love with Carpenter shakes Sister Michelle out of a complacent celibacy and impersonal charity that reflect the rather narrow interpretation of the vow predominant before Vatican II. It makes her realize that chastity was not meant to prohibit human love and friendship, nor can it protect her from the feelings of attraction and affection that run through significant relationships even if they remain non-physical (Rooney 2001: 52–4; Boswell 1986: 36; Schneiders 2001: 62).

The sexual heat and beat of Elvis's rock 'n' roll scandalized the moral guardians of American youth, including the Catholic Church—so much so that the buttoned-up Ed Sullivan ordered his cameramen to shoot the singer from the waist up only when he sang on his national TV show. Music critics, however, extolled the "pure joyousness," "soaring release," and "passion and soul" of his early singing (Guralnick 1999: 120, 139; Kastin 2002: 180). Significantly, while Elvis's familiar voice—at once stirring, suave and provocative—is heard singing the title song during the film's opening credits, the accompanying montage depicts a "chaste strip tease" (Sullivan 2005: 87; Brode 2006: 250) as three good-looking nuns change into mini-dresses, sheer stockings, and heels for social outreach in an inner city ghetto. The camera conveys the virgin sensation of voluptuous liberation as they disrobe by focusing foremost on their tightly coiffed heads. The nun's enclosed face was the semiotic sign of her distance from the world, and the coif becomes a primary metaphor on-screen for her concealed, confined, and sense-muffled body (Campbell-Jones 1978: 175). The sudden release of her cascading hair from the skull cap suggests how the opening of the face will free the psychosexual, social activist, or racial identity that has been tightly bound down by the religious habit and that erupts into unruly life again when the three nun characters leave the convent.

By 1969, the habit had become the most visible sign of the growing split between progressive and traditional nuns over the post-conciliar reforms that should be undertaken in the religious life (Kuhns 2003: 152–60). *Change of Habit*'s clever opening sequence concludes with Sisters Michelle and Irene (Barbara McNair) reprising this political debate.

SISTER IRENE: I suddenly realize how safe I felt in my habit.
SISTER MICHELLE: We argued that out before. . . . We're going to live the way other people live and dress the way they do. For once in our religious lives we're not gonna be different.
SISTER IRENE: There's a lot to be said for being different.
SISTER MICHELLE: We can't be identified with the old order. If we're gonna reach these people, we've got to be accepted first as women, then as nuns.

The decision to remove the habit and "to live the way other people live and dress the way they do" was a cinematic expression of the identification with the wider social community that *Gaudium et Spes* inspired. In "the old order" prior to Vatican II, veiled and habited nuns were regarded as a religious caste, "different," protected, and separate from the modern, secular world. The film opening adroitly suggests the tradeoff. It takes the three nun characters a while to adjust to the fact that they have lost the deference and special treatment that went with a distinctive religious identity. The New York cop who stops traffic so that the sisters in full habit can cross the street yells, "Hey Girls! On this street I stop the traffic" when they automatically begin to cross the same street, against the light, dressed as attractive lay women.

In her final comment on being "accepted first as women, then as nuns," Sister Michelle articulates the controversy that the move to secular dress would cause not only among nuns themselves but within the Church as a whole. It made dismayed Catholic faithful see that the nun had not spiritually transcended her sex but was a real human being with a gendered body, and it made the nun recognize herself more sensuously as a woman (Michelman 1998: 168–9, 185–7). Moreover, as *Change of Habit* dramatizes, and as *Sea Wife* showed earlier, lay clothes complicated nuns' relationships with men, made them more vulnerable to predatory advances and offensive remarks, and added the issue of their desirability to the vexed question of their modern religious identity.

Without the habit and veil, which were the sacred shield of the consecrated virgin, nuns were also more susceptible to sacrilegious representation by popular culture. The film's early attempts at humor are in the worst possible taste, and play on the confusion of women religious on social outreach with streetwalkers. Dr. Carpenter assumes that the three smartly dressed sisters who arrive for work at his clinic are "Park Avenue debutantes" seeking an abortion. When all three follow him into the examining room, he wonders if they worked together as call girls: "Just out of curiosity, was it the same guy?" This flippant and offensive misogyny continues when he tells them that the three previous nurses couldn't take it: "Two got raped, one against her will." Their neighbors in the ghetto will also mistake the sisters for hookers although they are dressed like demure convent graduates (as indeed they are). The local psychopath will conclude that a nun who wears clothes that show off her figure is asking for rape. Their parish priest, Father Gibbons (Regis Toomey), will articulate clerical suspicion that "underground nuns" in "silk stockings" and short skirts are indecent and bring "shame (on) the other fine sisters of the cloth who know their place." He will thus implicitly suggest that the habit neutered nuns and ensured their religious submission. The stockings and mini-skirts to which he objects show that nuns are not dead below the waist; but they also resurrect male celibate fear that attractive women stir the basest passions and lowest instincts of the body (Byrne 1999: 64; Riviere 1991: 325). One man who saw progressive nuns attractively dressed in Paris, said in horror: "It was as if I had encountered for the first time a maiden aunt in hot pants" (Bernstein 1976: 207). In depicting how the nun characters reclaim their identity as women and remove all visible religious insignia, the film's first defensive reaction was to reaffirm the ancient Christian antithesis between the religious and the sexed body.

Elvis made his name as a performer who crossed the boundaries keeping not only religion and sex but blacks and whites apart. The cultural hybridity of his music—part rhythm and blues, gospel, country, and pop—and his marginal position as a Southerner "always living on the edge of town and respectability" (Guralnick 1999: 123; Kastin 2002: 178) made him relate to outsiders, to people who did not fit in and were made to feel uncomfortable in their own skin. Even as he falls for Sister Michelle in *Change of Habit*, Carpenter shows his sympathetic identification with Sister Irene (Barbara McNair), the black sister who joins the trio as a trained nurse. Sister Irene is conflicted by her in-betweenness as an African American nun. Although she grew up in a ghetto where she was "just another nigger in the streets," the local blacks accuse her of being "dipped in maple syrup" and becoming a sugary brown-nose after she "linked up with them ol' beige chicks" in the convent. The very first scene of the film depicts her as the token "other" in a sea of white faces praying in the motherhouse chapel, and so alludes to the tacit racism and segregation that barred black women from admission to many American Catholic orders until the 1960s (Fialka 2003: 115; Thompson 1989: 160). Sister Irene confesses her dilemma to the doctor because he has replaced the callous Irish priest as the good shepherd of the inner city neighborhood. Indeed, he has inherited the popular musical talent, the interest in sports, the border-crossing skills, and the easy-going charm of Father O'Malley in *Going My Way* (1944) and *The Bells of St. Mary's* (1945): "I have used my vocation to get away from all the things I've ever known." Yet Carpenter does not respond by passing judgment on her less than pure, "maple syrup" motives for becoming a nun. Indeed, as actual nuns themselves are now the first to appreciate and as this study underlines, women were motivated by a range of personal, professional, and practical as well as pious desires to embark on religious life (Schneiders 2000: 82–3). What the doctor shows Sister Irene instead is understanding—understanding specifically of the ambition; the flight from racial, economic, and gender oppression; and the desire for higher education, status, and professional purpose that continue to draw women from underprivileged backgrounds to the convent. Carpenter's reply embodies the gospel spirit of that other carpenter from Nazareth: "Poor, hungry, frightened, black—I've been all those things except black." Elvis spoke Carpenter's lines with feeling because they described his own background and drive and not only that of the film character Sister Irene.

When Elvis first burst on the music scene, he was mistaken for a black man by those who heard him on the radio, and he readily acknowledged the influence that a vibrant black musical culture had on his singing. Sam Phillips, who had opened Sun Records studio in Memphis for black recording artists, felt he had at last found "a white man who had the Negro sound and the Negro feel" (Guralnick 1999: 125; Kastin 2002: 178). Like Sister Irene, who was not dark enough for the brotherhood yet "black as the ace of spades" to the bigoted, old Irish biddies who watch her arrive in their neighborhood, so too Elvis's indeterminate identity and cultural doubleness offended both whites and blacks. For Southern redneck disk jockeys, he was "too black" (Guralnick 1999: 129) to play on the radio, and his rock 'n' roll was perceived as reducing "white youth . . . to the level of a nigger" (Kastin 2002: 180). Yet the vicious rumor also circulated that Elvis was a white racist who boasted, "the only thing Negroes can do for me is buy my records and shine my shoes" (Davis 2001: 252–3).

At thirty-four, Elvis had not yet lost the lithe good looks that won him female fans in the 1950s (Davis 2001: 250–1). It was still possible to see why he was hailed, along with his idol James Dean, as the "messianic

Figure 4-4. The on-screen partnership of Elvis Presley's Dr. Carpenter and Mary Tyler Moore's Sister Michelle is a Hollywood take on the "match made in heaven."

figure of a new age" (Curran 1989: 137), to whom a screen nun might understandably transfer her devotion. Elvis also brought his small-town Southern upbringing to the role of the doctor: "I come from a long line of people who believe in getting married, having children, and raising a family." He is warm, relaxed, humorous, attentive, and unflappable—apart from one wonderful moment of disbelief later in the film. Taken aback by the first sight of Michelle back in the habit, he has the same reaction as the producer who later sees Michael Dorsey (Dustin Hoffman) unveiled as a cross-dresser in *Tootsie* (1982): "I'll be damned." He must be the first and only leading man to openly woo a nun inside the convent; to politely inquire if he is "breaking any rules being here;" and to persist in his old-fashioned but environmentally challenged courtship: "Let's try to find a way, Michelle."

Mary Tyler Moore

While Presley comes across as graceful and at ease in his own skin as a performer, Mary Tyler Moore's Sister Michelle hints at the brittle perfectionism and tense discipline that characterized Sister Luke's dedicated nurse in *The Nun's Story*. In a true Hollywood flight of fancy, Michelle emerges from the habit looking like a fashion plate: no ill-fitting or dowdy polyester clothes sully her Fifth Avenue film wardrobe.[14] Her prim little handbags and fastidiously coordinated outfits suggest, however, the exacting and tightly controlled world to which she has grown accustomed as a habited nun. Moore's success in *The Dick Van Dyke Show* from 1961 to 1966 earned her the accolade of "America's TV sweetheart. A vanilla madonna" (Bonderoff 1986: 117). Like Presley, she was looking to break out of the mold and reinvent herself in Hollywood. Unfortunately, *Change of Habit* was panned by the critics as "*The Sound of Music* goes slumming" (Bonderoff 1986: 65). However, in the film she does give a glimpse of the stress behind the all-American girl image that Robert Redford would later probe to elicit a great and dark performance

---

[14]Sister Joan Chittister, O.S.B., described the reality as follows: "Sisters who had been in community for years, who had not combed or styled their hair for decades, who had not chosen so much as socks since they were teenagers found themselves having to find and fit and choose clothes. Those who had families . . . were the lucky ones. Others found themselves adrift, embarrassed, and stripped of their dignity." See Chittister, *The Way We Were: A Story of Conversion and Renewal* (Maryknoll, N.Y.: Orbis Books, 2005), 147.

from her in his 1980 film *Ordinary People*. Even out of the habit, her Sister Michelle is still wearing an invisible veil, one that is a nice foil to Presley's pervasive warmth, and that conveys the cool orderliness of the professional nun and the guarded behavior that acted as a shield of her chastity.

Moore had some insight into the deportment of women religious because she was raised as a Catholic, attended parochial school, and was later taught by the Immaculate Heart of Mary sisters in Los Angeles. In fact, the IHM locked horns with Cardinal James McIntyre at the time *Change of Habit* was made and on the core dilemma that is dramatized in the film—to what extent women religious should have the freedom either individually or collectively to decide whether they will wear the habit, live in community, or explore new apostolates and lifestyles outside convent walls (Carey 1997: 184–91). Indeed, the parish priest in the film could be McIntyre's "mini me." As the three sisters lament, he is not "an apostle of the ecumenical movement" but a throwback to "the inquisition," and has a 'my way or the highway' attitude to the liberal, reforming nuns who challenge his turf. *The Bells of St. Mary's*, *The Nun's Story*, and *Agnes of God* all allude to the institutional gender battles that went on between women religious and their priest overseers. However, *Change of Habit*, *Dead Man Walking*, and *Doubt* show the naked hostility of male clergy to nuns independent of their authority, and dramatize what hard ball they played to remain their gatekeepers (Briggs 2006: 3–7, 174–203; Quinonez and Turner 1992: 98–108). The 2008 film *Doubt* will examine the tussle between a nun superior and parish priest without seniority who nonetheless has the upper hand in the Church hierarchy.

Rather than return to the personal safety of the habit and the security of their uptown Manhattan convent, Sister Barbara (Jane Elliot), the social and feminist activist of the trio, concludes she is "too limited as a nun." This is despite the fact that the three nuns have a string of professional qualifications that testify to the historical success of the Sister Formation Movement in grooming a new generation of highly educated American sisters for expanding apostolates. Sister Barbara is a laboratory technician, while Sister Irene has a degree in public health, and Sister Michelle is a psychiatric social worker with a degree in speech therapy. In other words, the sisters' education, professional training, and range of services are far from "limited." Sister Barbara is referring to the gender political restrictions that would, in fact, contribute to the post-conciliar decline in religious vocations: namely, clerical interference in their work within the parish, lack of decision-making power in a hierarchical Church, and subordination to higher male authority (Burns 1994: 135–6; Ebaugh 1993a: 405–10; Mourao 2002: xxiii–iv, 86). Sister Barbara leaves behind Sister Irene who chooses to remain within a power structure that has given her shelter and advancement as a black woman, and Sister Michelle who is undecided, and for whom the convent has become a half-way house between Christ and Carpenter.

Conclusion

In deciding whether to stay or go, each of the nuns must grapple with one of the three religious vows they took when they entered the convent. For Sister Barbara, the vow of obedience quickly becomes an intolerable infringement of her freedom, openness to the world, and gender equality as a modern liberated woman. For Sister Irene, the vow of obedience returns her to the ghetto poverty from which she escaped and to the moment of truth where she recognizes that the religious vow of poverty has been her passport to a better life. For Sister Michelle, the vow of chastity has left her unprepared not simply for the sexual revolution—represented by Elvis's presence in the film—but for her own sexual awakening. She projects a maturity that is at odds with the youth culture of the times, and yet suggests how women religious might be late bloomers struck by the force of sexual attraction and desire with bewildering suddenness (Schneiders 2001: 133, 206; Bernstein 1976: 329). While the three nuns wrestle with the traditional vows in *Change of Habit*, their real-life counterparts, who led the Sister Formation Movement in the 1950s and 60s, were endeavoring to redefine them more progressively and prophetically as they challenged the profane trinity of modern life—sex, money, and power (Carey 1997: 136–43; Ebaugh 1993b: 19–20).

Interestingly, the film sees the need for a fourth vow that ensures poverty, chastity, and obedience are not a defense against the world but a means of more authentic engagement with it. Sister Michelle tries to make excuses for giving the false impression that she was an unattached woman. When she explains that her religious superiors bound her to silence as a nun—"I took vows"—Carpenter quite rightly retorts: "Didn't you take a vow of honesty?" (Bernstein 1976: 299). The film concludes on the teasing, tantalizing note that characterized its opening, and shows Sister Michelle wavering ambivalently between her love of Carpenter and Christ. However, the semiotics of this final scene, which occurs at an experimental folk mass held in the neighborhood parish church, suggest, like *The Sound of Music*, that she may not be required to make a radical "either-or" choice between them after all. Father Gibbons is now relegated to the sideline, and Carpenter has become the cynosure of the congregation's gaze as he plays his guitar and sings the contemporary Christian hymns sanctioned by Vatican II renewal and later showcased by such musical hits of the early seventies as *Jesus Christ Superstar* and *Godspell* (Brode 2006: 251–2, 257). In the background, the officiating priest expresses his growing distance from the laity by turning to face the altar against the wall and celebrate the Tridentine mass that was a relic of the early modern period. As the altar recedes in visual importance, the Eucharistic focus shifts to a large crucifix with its reminder that Passion and Sacrifice were the genesis of Christian life—and that passionate love for God and humanity led Jesus to offer up his life on the Cross (Haughton 1981: 60–1, 90). In situating Carpenter in front of the cross, the film also alludes to the passion and soul that Elvis brought to his music. When Elvis burst on the musical scene, he was recognized as a revolutionary lifeforce (Guralnick 1999: 119). In *Change of Habit*, he still functions as a revolutionary figure, replacing the priest as the representative of Christ and inviting the congregation to relinquish their Catholic ghetto mentality and adopt the Second Vatican Council's inclusive vision of the Church as the people of God rather than an ecclesiastical hierarchy. With this realignment, the doctor from the Southern Bible belt—who has Jesus's gift for friendship, intimacy, sociability, and communion with others—also asks Michelle to become his partner in the work of the gospel (Chittister 2005: 98, 198–9). This is also an invitation to "find a way" by re-conceiving the vocation as a calling that is not addressed exclusively to women religious or to priests but to all who use the talents God has given them for the greater good (Ebaugh 1993a: 403).

5

SACRED DESIRES

PASSION AND PATHOLOGY IN
IN THIS HOUSE OF BREDE (1975)
AND *AGNES OF GOD* (1985)

Introduction

Reflecting on the effect that the Second Vatican Council had on American Catholic nuns in the 1960s, distinguished Benedictine leader and religious writer Sister Joan Chittister remarked that this decade of unprecedented change and renewal "was wonderful and it was terrible. It started with hope and excitement and ended in a lot of bitterness and difficulty for a long time." Chittister had joined a community with the characteristics that Maria projects so unforgettably in *The Sound of Music*—"high energy, high love" and "a lot of joy" (Rogers 1996: 295–6). She became a postulant in the early fifties at only 16, the same age as Liesl von Trapp, the film's ingénue on the brink of adult life. The Benedictine later speculated that up until the end of the 1930s, both Catholic women in the home and women religious in the convent inhabited a confined world and adhered to similar feminine ideals. As film and cultural critics have observed, this made it possible for Maria to shift her devotion from Christ to Captain von Trapp and his family without feeling ultimately that she had broken faith with the abbey or with God. While Chittister's generation went along with the religious norms from the past because they desired above all else to be nuns, entrants in the 1960s no longer idealized, tolerated, or accepted the older model of devout feminine behavior (Campbell 2003: 86). The habit was described reverently by traditional nuns as a "living cloister," safeguarding and bearing witness to the religious ideals that previous generations of sisters had upheld (Kuhns 2003: 3).[1] Thus, the relinquishment of the habit, dramatically underlined by the film opening and title of *Change of Habit*, was a symbolic break with the old order of the convent (Novak, July 30, 1966: 22). Chittister acknowledged with compassion the "deep resentment from people whose lives were being taken away from them, people who had internalized the system" (Rogers 1996: 296).

In this chapter, I consider two films that seriously investigate why modern women should continue to be drawn to the cloister, even after the radical fall in vocations, decline of religious orders, and alterations to community life in the years following Vatican II. The first film, *In This House of Brede*, was made for TV in the mid-seventies and was based on a Catholic convert's painstaking study of an enclosed Benedictine community in England. It lacked Zinnemann's powers of dispassionate and documentary-like observation in *The Nun's Story* (1959) but had a similar aim—to bring the hidden world of the cloister to life, a world that appeared increasingly obsolete in the cynical decade of the 1970s. In its concern to make contemplative life meaningful, to reconstruct the rhythm and feel of its life cycle of constant prayer, and to explore its counter-cultural spirit, *In This House of Brede* was a film that meshed fiction with cultural and monastic history (Rosenstone 2006: 16, 37, 68). The second film in this chapter, *Agnes of God*, was made ten years later in the mid-eighties and could be classified as a convent mystery or nun noir film that looks back forty years to Powell and Pressburger's 1947 cult classic *Black Narcissus*.

As nun films began to fall out of fashion as a popular genre in the seventies, *In This House of Brede* and *Agnes of God* kept the serious tropes, themes, images, and issues of these earlier postwar films alive. When nuns do appear on-screen in other films of the 1970s, such as *Two Mules for Sister Sara* (1970), *Madron* (1970), *The Devils* (1971), *The Omen* (1976), and *Nasty Habits* (1977), they are masquerade or Halloween dress figures. They provide laughs and semi-pornographic titillation in the Westerns *Two Mules for Sister Sara* and *Madron*, sexually hysterical and sickening spectacle in the historical drama *The Devils*, dark arts in the horror film

---

[1] Until the sixties, young Catholic "ladies" wore girdles, chemises, full slips, gloves, veiled hats, and mantillas to church, which were also a symbolic cloister of their feminine bodies.

The Omen, and political parallels between a power-crazed abbess and American president in the Watergate satire *Nasty Habits*. A decade later, Oliver Stone's *Salvador* (1986) would counter the sexualized or demonized projection of nun figures in these exploitative films by honoring the heroism of the Maryknoll and Ursuline sisters who were murdered by a military death squad because of their social justice work and solidarity with the poor and the victims of El Salvador's civil war. Yet this film also resorts to stereotyping nuns as part-objects when it gives voyeuristic glimpses of their bodies being stripped for gang rape.

The demise of the Legion of Decency as an influential censorship body over the course of the 1960s and 70s made such representations possible (Black 1998: 212–39). However, Catholic lay disapproval of the many actual sisters who adopted secular dress in this period, and angry belief that in abandoning the sacred habit they had forfeited dignity and respect, may have also made the movie industry less wary of debasing their image (Kuhns 2003: 2, 149–58). Furthermore, nuns became iconoclastic targets of desecration because, as Robert Orsi astutely observed, they "had been formidable guardians of the older Catholic way of life and among the most visible representatives of the otherness of Catholic religiosity" (2007: 56–7). Sexual denigration of nuns also recycled American suspicion of the Catholic convent and Protestant horror of Roman devotional and mystical eroticism that dated back to the nineteenth century (Ronan 2009: 14–15, 127; 2008: 325). By the 1980s, negative depictions of religious figures were generally on the rise as society became more secular and more skeptical of church authorities (Miles 2002: 20, 42–3, 49). While *In This House of Brede* and *Agnes of God* are problematic and flawed films in their own representation of nuns, they nonetheless take a serious interest in contemplative life in an enclosed community and show that it can be as radical, hard, and dangerous a calling as that of the sister activist (Byrne 1990: 86–7).[2]

Rumer Godden's 1969 novel, *In This House of Brede*

In 1969, the year *Change of Habit* was released, Rumer Godden published the second of three novels reflecting her long-term fascination

---

[2] As is evident from my argument in Chapters 3 and 4, I do not agree with Lavinia Byrne's view that "the nuns in *Agnes of God* are closer to real people than those of *The Sound of Music* or *The Nun's Story*." See *Women before God* (London: SPCK, 1990), 87.

with nuns, the spirit and mission of their religious life, and the psychology and politics of their community. Her 1939 bestseller, *Black Narcissus*, controversially brought to the screen by Powell and Pressburger, examined the dissolution of an Anglican community dedicated to colonial missionary work in India. Her greater literary achievement with *In This House of Brede* was to bring an English Benedictine monastery alive as a complex microcosm, to dramatize the paradox of how enclosed Catholic nuns remain in touch with the world from behind their cloister grille, and to puncture the secular myth that nothing is achieved by a contemplative life gravitating around prayer (Godden 1989: 247). A number of critical readers have echoed the view of Phyllis Tickle that "*In This House of Brede* is probably the most accessible, accurate, and sympathetic presentation of monastic life in all of English literature" (2005: ix).

Godden was inspired to write *Brede* by the veiled desire of an actual nun, Dame Felicitas Corrigan, a Benedictine cloistered in Stanbrook Abbey, Worcestershire: "I wish that someone would write a book about nuns as they really are, not as the author wants them to be." Godden vividly recalled her involuntary response: "I thought of *Black Narcissus* and blushed" (Godden 1989: 239). Yet *Black Narcissus* held passionate significance for her as a novelist because it had gifted her with the first sweet taste of the "ecstasy, excitement and growth" a writer can experience with literary success (Godden 1987: 138). Moreover, she never forgot that the book was a "wonderful" godsend that rescued her from despair and financial ruin after being saddled with the debts of her feckless husband in Calcutta (Godden 1987: 131, 163). She also realized that when she wrote *Black Narcissus*, she had not altogether exorcised the ghosts of her own childhood hatred for the spiteful Anglican nuns who made her and her beloved sister Jon, with their "chi-chi," British-Indian accents, objects of ridicule and acute misery at English boarding school: "'One day I shall write a book about you,' I thought with darkest intent" (Godden 1987: 20, 25). As an author, she had learned how to mobilize these dark, wild, raw desires, claiming that "when . . . I did write a book about nuns, *Black Narcissus*, I mysteriously could not take that revenge" (Godden 1987: 25). Yet the arrogance, unkindness and "coldness" (Godden 1987: 20) that she saw and suffered at the hands of her Anglican headmistress, Sister Gertrude, are not forgotten but made the chief character flaws of Sister Clodagh, the superior depicted in *Black Narcissus*. Indeed, her candid disclosure of a wish to get even with the women religious who exercised capricious and cruel authority over her as a defenseless child gives insight into films that project grotesque or fairy tale portraits of nun teachers such as *The Dangerous Lives of Altar Boys* (2002) or, to a lesser extent, *Doubt* (2008).

In This House of Brede is regarded as Godden's most ambitious and accomplished work of fiction, one that is "very near a novel of the first rank" (Simpson 1973: 131). If *Black Narcissus* was a form of creative atonement for resentments and transgressive desires lingering from childhood, *Brede* was a novel reflecting her maturity not simply as a writer but as a woman and believer. She wrote this work as she approached her sixties after exploring Hinduism, returning to her Anglican cultural roots, and finally converting to Catholicism.[3] The title of her novel reflected her search as a woman writer not simply for a room but a house of her own, "a house with four rooms, a physical, a mental, an emotional and a spiritual." Each would invite her to develop some core aspect of herself and give her the free space, solid foundation, and passageways to become "a complete person" (Godden 1989: 13; Reichardt 2001: 115–16). Benedictine cloistered nuns uniquely take a vow of stability that binds them for life to the religious house where they make their solemn profession. The permanence that was missing in Godden's migratory colonial life stoked her admiration for the enclosed contemplative nuns she depicted in *Brede* who "abide, keeping their vows" (Godden 1989: 246; Bernstein 1976: 113–14).[4]

Godden's introduction to contemplative nuns was occasioned by grave maternal anxiety. Her daughter Jane had developed life-threatening toxemia during pregnancy but was determined against medical advice to keep the baby. Godden was advised by a friend to "write to Stanbrook Abbey and ask the nuns for their prayers" and quickly the "place . . . bec(a)me a lifeline" (Godden 1989: 244). During this worrying time, she got to know Dame Felicitas who wrote weekly words of encouragement to her daughter, and after her granddaughter was born safely, this contact blossomed into a thirty-year-long friend-

---

[3] Godden became a Catholic in 1957, but because of her divorce and re-marriage, "had to wait years" before she could be formally received and take communion. See her second volume of memoirs, *A House with Four Rooms* (New York: William Morrow, 1989), 249, and Anne Chisholm, *Rumer Godden: A Storyteller's Life*, rev. ed. (Basingstoke & Oxford: Pan Macmillan, 1999), 251.

[4] As Cheryl L. Reed underlined in *Unveiled: The Hidden Lives of Nuns* (New York: Berkley Books, 2004), 295, the specific vows Benedictine nuns take "don't even mention chastity or poverty, although they are implicit with her other vows: stability, conversion of life, and obedience."

ship. The name Godden gave her fictional Benedictine monastery has polyvalent significance and reflects the important place that Stanbrook Abbey came to assume in her own life.[5] She expressed her gratitude as a mother by choosing a name that refers to childbearing (Rosenthal 1996: 85). Perhaps she was also alluding to Paul's stirring vision in *Romans* of "the whole creation . . . groaning in labor pains," and his assurance that when "we do not know how to pray properly, then the Spirit personally makes our petitions for us in groans that cannot be put into words" (8:22–7). She certainly felt that the intercessory prayers of these Benedictine mothers in spirit had been instrumental in saving the lives of her daughter and granddaughter. As a result of her increasing contact with Stanbrook Abbey, Godden also developed a new appreciation not only for the spiritual but artistic and intellectual productivity of cloistered women (McNamara 1996: 574). Dame Felicitas was a renowned organist and award-winning biographer and gave her the encouragement she needed to meet the poet Siegfried Sassoon. She would later marvel that "through knowing nuns who are enclosed, I have met a world of people whom otherwise I would not have encountered" (1989: 257). The abbey was a writer's heaven with its fine library, printing press, and reputation for high-quality publications. The previous abbess, Dame Laurentia McLachlan, had a long and famous friendship with Bernard Shaw, and memorably remarked: "You may be enclosed but you needn't have enclosed minds" (Godden 1989: 247, 255, 258).

Godden discovered other connections between the cloister and the world. The calling to contemplative life did not necessarily come to those who seemed a "perfect" fit or longed to be nuns, but was heard by career women like herself: "doctors, lawyers, artists—one had been a beautician at Elizabeth Arden."[6] Her spiritual mentor, Dame Felicitas, mirrored her own intelligence, strength of mind, sensitivity, and dedication to her craft (Chisholm 1999: 257). Thus, the otherworldly environment of Stanbrook Abbey was paradoxically a place that enhanced her sense of the world—of what Paul called "whole creation"—and enlarged her contacts with the people in it. Behind this paradox lay Godden's growing belief that the enclosed community was "a powerhouse of prayer." The contemplative nuns were the atlases who bore the world on their

[5] Brede was the name of the village next to Godden's home at Little Douce Grove in East Sussex. See *A House with Four Rooms*, 248.

[6] Godden recounted the amusing life story of Dame Felicitas who asked her novice mistress if she really thought she had a vocation. "'Yes dear, I do.' 'Damn!' said Felicitas." See *A House with Four Rooms*, 247.

shoulders and "lift(ed) it up to God in public prayer and praise" through their unceasing commitment to the divine office (Godden 1989: 245, 247, 257).[7] For Godden, this was a hidden labor of love that could have extraordinary results. Yet she realized that *Brede* was a more challenging project than *Black Narcissus*, and that "it would have been far easier to write about an active Order; people can see, understand and admire the good they do" (1989: 246). Indeed, when asked by Ben Huebsch, her literary editor and patron at Viking Press, why she wanted to write a novel about contemplatives—and implicitly risk alienating her wide readership—she replied, "because nuns are dramatic. Theirs is the greatest love story in the world" (Godden 1989: 279).

Godden was aware that this response would be "incomprehensible" to many (1989: 246). Her view is echoed by present-day Franciscan Sister Paula Jean Miller who concedes that "the virgin-spouse paradox (which is implicit in Godden's description of the nun's life as a love story) seems to be particularly incomprehensible to contemporary culture" (2009: 47–8). Dominican contemplative Sister Maria Cabrini recounts a common conviction of being called personally to religious life: "I knelt at the communion railing and, after a few minutes, Our Lord seemed to speak to me. . . . He asked: 'Will you be my bride?'" (2008: 24). Godden's desire to show, as dedicated nuns insist, that religious life offers the prospect of a joyful, liberating, and passionate relationship with God in which "the deepest yearnings of the human heart are awakened" (Donovan and Wusinich 2009: 28; Rogers 1996: 279) inspired a novel that took five years of study and observation of Benedictine ways to complete (Godden 1989: 254). It prompted her to live for a time in the gatehouse outside the Stanbrook Abbey enclosure, and it eventually led her to become a lay oblate and follow the prayer life of the community (Chisholm 1999: 265).[8]

Godden knew that *Brede* would be seen by some as a public declaration of Catholic faith and braced herself for the suspicion and hostility it might provoke. The novel did, in fact, cost her a treasured literary friendship with Noel Coward who "had a phobia about nuns" (Godden 1989: 278–9). But she was unprepared for, and delighted by, the rave

---

[7] After the Second Vatican Council, the divine office became known as the liturgy of the hours.

[8] Godden related in *A House with Four Rooms* that the "Lady Abbess allowed me, for one day only, to follow Stanbrook's day according to the Rule, beginning with Lauds at five minutes to four in the morning, ending with Compline at eight. I was exhausted" (248).

reviews and the "near avalanche" of fan mail that came after her book was published in 1969. Like the popular reception of *The Sound of Music* four years earlier, *In This House of Brede* was a surprise bestseller. Its success proved yet again that Godden's father had been wrong when he warned her during the writing of *Black Narcissus* that no one would read about nuns. It showed that there was great popular interest in a novel that explored why modern women entered a cloistered community and depicted the pivotal importance of prayer not only in their monastic life but in its mysterious power to do good in the world outside (Godden 1989: 245; Chisholm 1999: 267–70).

In This House of Brede was a big, sprawling novel by a consummate storyteller, and its remarkable commercial success, coupled with Godden's track record of film adaptations such as *Black Narcissus* (1947), *The River* (1951), *The Greengage Summer* (1961), and *The Battle of the Villa Fiorita* (1965), helped to ensure that it would be brought to the screen. Godden's long and complex narrative resulted from extensive interviews with the nuns of Stanbrook Abbey. She had found a mother lode as an imaginative writer: "They told me everything I needed to know and more, stories, happenings, far more strange than anything I could have thought of in fiction" (Godden 1989: 254). These stories, told to her in confidence, confirmed her conviction that "nuns are dramatic" and that monastic existence was neither monotonous nor uneventful.[9] Godden conveyed the hidden drama of the "living cloister" and her appreciation of the very different women behind the grille by the use of multiple voices, interior monologue, and viewpoints that move forward and backward in time, in and out of the world, and to life preceding and after entering enclosure (Reichardt 2001: 117; Simpson 1973: 111, 119–21). She not only structurally highlighted the fact that their life histories were not erased, but made this point thematically central to the religious crisis of the central character, Philippa Talbot, who mistakenly thinks she can leave her past self behind and become anonymous when she enters Brede. While Godden's accomplished novel included nearly thirty distinct nun characters in a Benedictine abbey that housed ninety-nine women religious, only eight nuns feature in the TV film that American director George Schaefer made of *In This House of Brede*, and its greatly simplified plot revolves around just four of them.

[9] Godden remarked in *A House with Four Rooms* that her "greatest difficulty was in not betraying to any nun things another nun had told (her)—what is said in the parlour is as secret as in the confessional" (254–5).

In This House of Brede (1975)

Godden had a checkered experience with male film directors. She felt strongly that the film-making partners Powell and Pressburger had made a mockery of her 1939 novel with their 1947 screen version of *Black Narcissus* (Godden 1989: 51–3). Yet she formed a close working relationship with the French film director Jean Renoir when she collaborated with him as a script writer on her 1946 novel *The River*, and indeed regarded his 1951 film as the best and most thoughtful adaptation out of her seven books brought to the screen (Chisholm 1999: 207, 213, 216–17; Godden 1989: 105). Given her great respect and appreciation for the nuns of Stanbrook Abbey and her distaste for what Powell and Pressburger had done to her earlier novel about religious life, she only agreed after some reluctance in 1970 to allow her novel of *Brede* to be made into a film. Unlike Renoir, who insisted that "no-one else (but her) must write this script" (Godden 1989: 97), George Schaefer employed the Hollywood screenwriter James Costigan. Godden was not asked to comment on his draft script until 1974, and when she read it, was dismayed to see how the nuns had been trivialized, the narrative had been truncated, and Brede's place in the story as a religious house of far-reaching social influence had been lost in translation. The word "brede"—like the abbey itself—had a long history suggesting not only how the house had nurtured women but how it had offered them the daily "bread" of communion, "braided" their lives together, and "broadened" the individual nun by making her part of an extended community reaching out to God and each other across time (Simpson 1973: 110–11).

In the novel, the sacred symbolism of Brede and the house's association with breeding and weaving, communion and community are crucial to the resolution of the religious crisis of the mature woman entrant, Philippa Talbot. She conceals the fact that she was once a mother when she enters the cloister, and mistakenly hopes to shut out the memory of her child's accidental death when she passes through the locked doors of the abbey enclosure. Instead, she discovers a complicated society of very human women religious whose behavior is not always edifying and whose attention is not always welcome. Some cry out for her reluctant maternal care. Others require her to draw on her former professional contacts and skills. One young novice forces her to confront the secret tragedy overshadowing her past. Thus, she painfully learns how all their personalities and talents are woven, whether flawed or pristine, into the ongoing tapestry of Benedictine community life. After reading how Costigan's draft script cut her complex and polyphonic narrative, Godden realized that the writer was "obviously out of his depth" (Chisholm 1999: 278) and cunningly arranged what he thought would only be a courtesy call to Stanbrook Abbey. He emerged from the visitors' parlor where he met the Benedictines who acted as a literary review panel, echoing Godden's own appreciation for their skills: "That nun! She's a born dramatist! I learned so much!" (Chisholm 1999: 279).[10] Although the final script was an improvement on the draft, and was at least made acceptable to the nuns, the author herself thought the film never lived up to her literary vision of religious life. Perhaps only a faithful TV mini-series that followed the many strands and characters of her plot could have brought such an intricate and multi-textured novel alive on the screen.

There were also two inherent limitations to Schaefer and Costigan's film version. First, their own vision of religious community in *Brede* was, consciously or otherwise, that of the male in the patriarchal family observing the inter-generational tension of a desirable but needy daughter, withholding or unwilling mother, and jealous, threatened elder matriarch. They thus narrowed the focus of Godden's plot to three principal nun characters: the beautiful virgin-novice Sister Joanna (Judi Bowker) who hates her mother and adores her father; the reluctant surrogate mother Dame Philippa (Diana Rigg) who suppresses her past maternal history and emotions; and the caustic disciplinarian and crone Dame Agnes (Pamela Brown) whose beauty, authority, and lifeforce have faded. I will employ Freud's theories of familial and psychosexual development to read these relations. I will also consider the bond that Dame Philippa develops with a fourth character, Dame Catherine, the Abbess of Brede (Gwen Watford), who assumes a supporting and supportive role like that of the Mother Abbess in *The Sound of Music*. This last relationship, based on the paradox of their difference(s) from one another and their mutual respect and recognition, introduces an alternative dynamic into the film plot. This may not have been what either Schaefer or Costigan intended, but it qualifies their vision of female religious life as a pseudo-primary family disrupted by inter-generational rivalries between matriarchs, mothers, sisters, and daughters. The scriptural discussion of Chris-

---

[10]I am indebted to Anne Chisholm's discussion of the development of the 1975 film in her biography of *Rumer Godden*, 277–9. Godden remarked appreciatively that "one of the nuns, Dame Katharine, ought to have been a detective story writer; I have never met anyone with a stronger sense of plot." See *A House with Four Rooms*, 262.

tian love between these two intelligent women brings the film closer to
Godden's own experience at Stanbrook Abbey of a community called by
Jesus himself to be friends.

Second, Schaefer and Costigan's film of *Brede* lacks historicity, leaving the viewer to conclude that it is set in the 1970s in which it was
made. In fact, the novel begins in 1954 when Philippa Talbot enters the
abbey, takes the reader back in time to the earlier history of Brede and
its inhabitants, and ends after Vatican II closes. Godden had started work
on her novel as Council renewal gathered momentum. As a late convert to Catholicism, she was a traditionalist at heart and felt that real-life
nuns should look like nuns and not "dowdy Edwardian nurses" in their
modified habits. She approved of the fact that the nuns of Stanbrook
Abbey did not materially change their dress,[11] and with her innate sense
of both style and symbolism, she thought "nothing was more becoming
to a woman" than the graceful folds of the Benedictine habit or the veil,
belt, scapular, and cowl that weighted it with sacred meaning (1989: 261;
1969: 375). But she was a truthful writer and, in the closing chapters of
Brede, acknowledged that the winds of change from Vatican II are blowing through the Benedictine monastery and that "the old order was being
shaken out of its ways" (1969: 342). She sketched the developing political
differences between the progressive and traditionalist members of the
community; older generational fear of the young's "muddled thinking
. . . as one cherished tradition after another was felled by popular vote"
(1969: 344); and class tension between the choir nuns who presided over
the abbey chapter and the claustral (or lay) sisters who did much of the
heavy domestic work (Thompson 1989: 151–52; Rogers 1996: 136).
Although the TV film version of *In This House of Brede* was made in 1975,
ten years after the Second Vatican Council ended, it makes no specific
mention of the destabilizing effect that widespread religious reforms had
on actual contemplative nuns.[12] It is as though the women characters in

---

[11] In her novel, *In This House of Brede* (New York: The Viking Press, 1969),
345–6, the Benedictine nuns do alter their habit to make it more practical but continue to wear full-length dress in contrast to the new nuns who adopt street-length
clothes.

[12] Mary Jo Weaver argued that "contemplatives were caught up in the ambi-
guities of the postconciliar era to a greater extent than other sisters," and discussed
how the issue of enclosure politicized progressives within contemplative orders. See
Weaver, *New Catholic Women: A Contemporary Challenge to Traditional Religious Authority* (Bloomington: Indiana University Press, 1995), 102–5. Reed quoted a Carmelite nun who insisted that "if these accidentals—cultural things like the grille and

Schaefer's adaptation of *Brede* are living hermetically sealed off from time in their abbey. However, I will argue that in casting Diana Rigg as the central protagonist Philippa Talbot, and representing her as a new type of aspirant to religious life—one who threatens, challenges, and changes her community—the film nonetheless suggested that contemplative nuns were moving forward not backward in time.

Diana Rigg

Diana Rigg's early life had striking parallels with Rumer Godden's. Like the novelist, she was born in England but moved to India in infancy. Rigg's father was a railway engineer who worked for the Maharajah of Bikaner, while Godden's was a British shipping agent. British India offered these men a career, lifestyle, and status that they could never have enjoyed back home and made them more culturally liberal. Godden's father insisted that his daughter touch the feet in apology of a Brahmin gardener she had sworn at. Rigg's father told an apprentice who humbly beseeched him for a leave of absence that "you must never beg for what is rightfully yours" (Landesman, *The Sunday Times*, July 1, 2007: sec.4.5). Rigg was proud of the fact her father learned Hindi when he arrived in India and that she was taught to speak it as a young child, but she later upbraided her mother for their family's complicity in the British colonial subjugation and exploitation of India. Likewise, Godden complained to her father of her sheltered and blinkered Raj upbringing, and was invited to work with him and gain greater exposure to the country and its people. Both women were sent back to England as young schoolgirls and experienced the culture shock of not belonging. Diana Rigg explained, "I think my upbringing in India made me an outsider. . . . I was moved around a lot until I was about 11. You don't have anything but your parents" (Landesman, sec.4.5). Godden's gypsy existence as a child who never settled down to English schooling and socialization left her with a similar sense of being an outcast and onlooker (Godden 1987: 24–5, 28, 43, 56). Yet India was the making of both Rigg as an actress and Godden as storyteller. Rigg recalled India as larger-than-life and in Technicolor:

---

the habit—are essential to contemplative life, then contemplative life would not be relative to this century. . . . The accidentals are not what make this life. The essentials are prayer, Carmelite spirituality, the solitude, and the silence" (*Unveiled*, 107). In Godden's novel, some Benedictine abbesses review the practices of their houses and rule not to change them, while "others cast away tradition" (1969: 346).

"There's a kind of theatricality to everyday life and I think as a child you absorb that. I remember having a vivid imagination from an early age" (Landesman, sec.4.5). Coincidentally, both left India and returned to postwar Britain for good in the same year—1945 (Reichardt 2001: 114–15; Dukes 1991: 18–22; Lassner 2004: 70–1).

British India made both Rumer Godden and Diana Rigg sister outsiders. One of the reasons why Rigg is so good in the role of Dame Philippa Talbot is that she plays a character who was an alter ego of the actress herself—a strong, independent, private career woman who thinks she must go it alone even after she joins the religious community at Brede Abbey. Trained at the Royal Academy of Dramatic Art (RADA) as a classical stage actress, Rigg distinguished herself with leading roles in *Abelard and Heloise* (1972) and *The Misanthrope* (1975) before making *In This House of Brede*. One of her directors remembers her as "not quite of the mainstream like Dame Judi Dench or Maggie Smith. She remains more aloof with directors and audiences. There is a solitude and privacy about her" (Landesman, sec.4.5). Solitude is also a condition of the cloistered nun and a reminder, as Godden noted, that the word "'monastery' comes from the Latin word *monos*, to be alone, living a community life yet alone with God" (1989: 244; Sipe 1994: 178). Solitude of self also distinguished screen nuns like Sister Clodagh and Sister Luke and reflected both their interior discipline and emotional reserve. Rigg brings these characteristics to the film role of Philippa Talbot, suggests convincingly how they draw her to the monastic life, and then shows how they have become personal defenses erected to cope with a secret tragedy that is both the catalyst and the impediment of her religious vocation. Enclosure exacerbates the temptation to emotionally close herself off from others. As her former lover and only apparent close friend, Sir Richard (Denis Quilley), comments when he comes to Brede to watch Philippa take final vows, "I know that face from time past. It's the one that says 'Help me, help me,' and at the same time says 'You can't. You can't help me. Nobody can.'" Unlike the typical entrant, this nun must learn to curb rather than cultivate the habit of detachment, a detachment so pronounced that on the point of entering the cloister, she admits to Sir Richard, "You're one of the only things I'll miss."

The Politics of Motherhood in the Convent

Philippa is the film prototype of the increasing number of mature women candidates who would be drawn to religious life in the 1970s (Bernstein

1976: 312). At forty-two, she is old enough to be the mother of the other postulants who have joined after finishing secondary school, and indeed conceals the fact that before she became a nun, she was a mother like Mother Miriam Ruth, a principal character in the 1985 film *Agnes of God*.[13] With intimate knowledge as an older woman of marriage, bereavement, and widowhood, and an affair afterwards with the married Sir Richard, it is evident that she cannot aspire to be a consecrated virgin, and challenges by her mere physical presence the traditional incompatibility of sexual experience and holiness (DelRosso 2005: 35). As a high-powered company director who has seen, and it will transpire, traveled the world, she appears to have devoted her prior life to the godless vows of money and power. There is a fear that these worldly values—which are the shadow side of poverty and obedience—will contaminate the cloister. She makes intelligible the real-life tensions that arose between older and more sophisticated candidates and formation directors who felt threatened by their education, professional accomplishments and worldly confidence (Schneiders 2001: 37–9). However, the Benedictines of Stanbrook Abbey had taught Godden a cardinal principle upheld by all nuns, whether traditional or progressive, contemplative or active: namely, that the religious calling is not the result of personal achievement, suitability, or merit (Donovan and Wusinich 2009: 26). It is God's free and mysterious gift of agape (Nygren 1953: ix, 75, 468). As Godden explained further: "no words are more true than Christ's, 'You have not chosen me, I have chosen you.' . . . It can be too the most unlikely person, breaking a settled life, interrupting a career" (Godden 1989: 246). In the film, however, Dame Agnes, the Mistress of Novices, is openly hostile to the very idea that a woman like Philippa should have a contemplative vocation: "I warned Mother. I said she's too old. . . . Think of what she's seen and done at her age, things we know nothing about. I was barely eighteen when I came to Brede and completely innocent."

The hostility between Dame Agnes and Philippa reconstructs a cultural clash that was developing behind actual convent walls by the early 1970s. Even strictly enclosed orders felt challenged not only by the "new ideas, new thoughts, new changes" from Vatican II that Godden depicted "blowing through the monastery" of Brede (1969: 343), but by the gale force winds from the sexual revolution and second wave feminism. Indeed, in the iconic role of the liberated Mrs. Emma Peel—dressed to

---

[13] Reed discusses the new phenomenon of "mother nuns" as older women entered the convent in their forties and fifties (*Unveiled*, 22–3).

kill in svelte leather jumpsuits, and mysteriously unfettered by the ties of marriage—Diana Rigg had dramatized the generation gap between traditional and cool modern England and wittily played it out in the cult TV series *The Avengers* from 1965 to 1968. The actress would cause a sensation a few years later by appearing nude on stage in *Abelard and Heloise*. Rigg's dramatic history and mystique as a ground-breaking sex symbol lent subliminal tension to her charged relationship with Dame Agnes, played by the formidable Pamela Brown, who thirty years before was herself an embodiment of wild and willful sexuality as the exotic Catriona MacLaine in the Powell and Pressburger film *I Know Where I'm Going* (1945).

The dramatic conflict between Philippa and Dame Agnes in the film was given a triangular dimension by the addition of a character who was not present in the novel and who was created to condense, simplify, and romanticize a multi-faceted plot. The ingénue actress Judi Bowker took this new role of Sister Joanna. While her over-wrought relationship with Philippa may reflect male phobia about enclosure as a hothouse of female emotions, it also bears out the psychological observation of experienced vocational directors. Young and immature candidates could treat the convent as an extension of the protective home environment and expect their sister superiors to mother them (Schneiders 2001: 207–11). Yet it is understandable why an older nun like Dame Agnes would still prefer Sister Joanna to Philippa as a candidate. Though needy and girlish, she is eager to please—indeed she is a throwback to the Mistress of Novices' own profile on entry at "barely eighteen" in the early part of the twentieth century.[14] However, after the social changes in the 1960s, formation directors would gradually realize that even young entrants like Sister Joanna were no longer "completely innocent" but were arriving with sexual experience and knowledge that they themselves did not possess (Schneiders 2001: 163).

Schaefer and Costigan seemed oblivious to the fact that feminist consciousness had made both British and American nuns increasingly impatient at being represented as naïve daughters in a patriarchal family (Schneiders 2000: 145–6; Byrne 1990: 89–92). Their decision to place Sister Joanna at the heart of the film plot, to depict her as "a delightful child (who) inspires affection everywhere," and to romanticize the

---

[14]The novel indicates that Philippa Talbot enters Brede in 1954 at 42. Dame Agnes is older, in the film much older than Philippa. Even if we assume that Agnes is in her fifties, she would have entered before 1920. See Rumer Godden, *In This House of Brede*, 34.

clothing ceremony in which she appears before her captivated father as a radiantly beautiful teenage bride of Christ suggests the source of male enchantment with the mystique of the cloister.[15] It is the young virginal nun who repudiates her natural mother and eventually outgrows her dependency on a surrogate spiritual mother but will always remain daddy's girl at heart. However, thanks largely to the choice of Diana Rigg for the leading role, their film does not adulterate the strength of character that Philippa shows in Godden's novel. She becomes the harbinger of a new recruit and change agent who will bring the outlook of a modern, independent, and cosmopolitan career woman to the enclosure of Brede.

The film opens with a thumbnail sketch of the London world Philippa inhabited before entering the cloister. Diana Rigg's character is a handsome, elegant, smartly turned out figure.[16] She is shown briefly taking leave of the staff in her company office—brisk, no-nonsense, stand-offish, and slightly mysterious. Her farewell lunch with Sir Richard establishes a fact that Godden made central to her portrait of contemplative nuns in *Brede* and a correction to *Black Narcissus*: that she is not entering the convent to escape the world or an unhappy love affair.[17] Philippa insists to Richard that she is "running . . . toward not from . . . especially not from you," though she will realize later that she has tried to run away from herself and her tragic past. She collects her suitcase at an apartment that is as tasteful and impersonal as a hotel suite. She leaves her cat with a next-door neighbor to whom she is a polite stranger. The opening scenes of the film thus depict her as a self-sufficient but solitary figure who has no real home before she enters the house of Brede. Her only sign of nerves is the three large whiskies and half-a-pack of cigarettes she consumes in the pub just outside the abbey precinct. But the film does not gloss over the difficulties that an older candidate, used to modern

---

[15] As Marcelle Bernstein pointed out in *Nuns* (London: William Collins, 1976), 123, theologians now insist that Christ's only bride is the Church. See Rebecca Sullivan's related discussion of 1950s vocational books and their bridal motif, which attempted to spiritualize the romantic interest of teenage entrants in *Visual Habits: Nuns, Feminism and American Postwar Popular Culture* (Toronto: University of Toronto Press, 2005), 124–33.

[16] Rigg appears to be dressed in a John Bates signature maxi knit ensemble. Bates was the London designer responsible for the clothes she wore in *The Avengers*.

[17] Godden summarized the reasons most usually expressed: that contemplative nuns enter enclosure "because of a broken heart or are misfits, . . . that they cannot cope with the world and so settle for shelter and security; they want to escape" (*A House with Four Rooms*, 246).

luxuries such as proper plumbing and heating, had in adjusting to the Spartan regime of the cloister.

Lesbian Desire

The film critic Bruce Williams reads close shots such as the one in which Philippa kneels shivering on a burlap mat in her cell, torso bare, attempting to bathe for the first time with only a cold jug of water, as a moment of subliminal eroticism where an unavowed lesbianism begins to "erupt through the fissures in the diegesis" (Williams 2002: 141).[18] Godden herself was emphatic that the nuns she wrote about in *Brede* do not "become lesbians" or sexually seek out each other's company (Godden 1989: 246). Her novel does, however, depict a passionate musical rapport between a senior nun and a novice and makes their artistic bond the occasion to examine the issue of celibate sexuality and sublimation in the religious life, the subject of Chapter 2, or how nuns channel their erotic energy into high cultural, creative, and religious achievements. Costigan transferred this intense bond to Dame Philippa and Sister Joanna, and the Benedictines at Stanbrook Abbey were anxious that this film relationship should continue to be seen as one of "love, but not lesbianism" (Chisholm 1999: 277). The subject of "particular friendships" among women religious had long excited both fascination and fear of the cloister as a transgressive domain where lesbian desire could be freely explored in secret (Mourao 2002: 78–85). It is reasonable to assume from the historical research of John Boswell on homosexuality among male monastics and clergy that religious life in an all-female community was an attractive option for some women with same sex orientation, especially before they could be open about their preference (Boswell 1994: 364–72). However, as Richard Sipe has pointed out, traditional vocational recruitment often occurred at an unfinished and amorphous stage of psychosexual development when adolescent boys and girls like Joanna were inclined toward sentimental friendships and idealistic infatuations for their own sex (1990: 116–18). Convent warnings against particular friendships were thus one way of discouraging passionate fixations that

---

[18]See the only external review of *In This House of Brede* on the IMDB, "A Nunsploitation.Net Review," http://www.nunsploitation.net/movies/inthishouse3 .html (accessed on July 24, 2009), which claims wrongly that Philippa had a lesbian romance with another nun in the novel, and includes the shot of her bathing to illustrate how the "strong sexual elements are all played down in the movie."

were charged with not only tender but more primitive and explosive feelings. Williams argues that lesbian desire is often expressed indirectly through such themes as the mother-daughter-mentor bond, narcissism and neediness, female friendship and sisterhood (2002: 137–41). These themes are indeed present in the parent-child relationship that Philippa and Joanna replay in the cloister, but it eventually develops into a more mature and inclusive friendship.

Looking at this film relationship in the light of Williams's provocative though narrowly focused comments, what stands out is Sister Joanna's narcissism and Philippa's self-loathing, the novice's emotional regression to childhood and the nun's repression of maternal feelings, the neurotic attachment of the young woman and the scrupulous detachment of the older. At the beginning of the film, Joanna symbolically puts herself in the path of Philippa during a chance encounter when she is a schoolgirl and the older woman is walking, suitcase in hand, to enter Brede.

Figure 5-1. Dame Philippa and Sister Joanna reproduce the mother-daughter embrace idealized in *The Bells of St. Mary's* (see Figure 1-1). However, their intimacy is presented as dangerously regressive and exclusive.

Philippa becomes her object of daydreaming and desire in the Catholic family romance: "I thought about you every day after that." This romance is configured very differently from the one in *The Nun's Story*, and features a self-absorbed daughter who heartlessly rejects her natural mother and reinvents herself as an unwanted and neglected child: "Oh she's not my mother. She never has been. She never wanted me in the first place. She's one of those people who simply hate children. . . . I never loved her. I swear it. I love you." For a Victorian patriarch like Freud, the repudiation of the mother as first love object was a necessary step that both boys and girls must take in psychosexual development.[19] It is not followed, however, by Joanna's transfer of attachment to paternal authority or to the authority invested in the abbess by the Church episcopacy, but to Philippa as a phallic mother: "I never once called Lady Abbess 'Mother' like I'm supposed to." The older nun asks, "Why not?" and the neophyte replies, "You know why. You." The fantasy of the phallic mother is a regression to a preoedipal and childish state of narcissistic identification where Philippa becomes Joanna's exclusive love object, and exists as a subject to gratify every need of the novice (Grosz 1992: 314–15; Benjamin 1988: 23–4).[20] This narcissism was by no needs unusual among young entrants who assumed that the community would revolve around them (Schneiders 2001: 61). This is why Joanna has a jealous tantrum when Philippa becomes absorbed in teaching the new Japanese postulants at Brede.

> They all think you're so marvelous. Everyone is talking about how cleverly you've taken over our Japanese sisters and how they do adore you. They haven't learned yet what you're really like under that mask of affection and concern. Tell me, Dame Philippa, how do you say cold, heartless bitch in Japanese?

Freud saw narcissism as the psychological predilection of women, children, and religious believers, and Joanna embodies all three in this

---

[19] Freud outlines his oedipal theory as it applies to girls in his 1931 essay on "Female Sexuality," *SE* 21: 225–8, 235–9. Judith Van Herik analyzes Freud's gender theories in *Freud on Femininity and Faith* (Berkeley: University of California Press, 1985), 129–35.

[20] These female commentators interrogate and extend Freud's speculation on the pre-oedipal phase and its importance for women in "Female Sexuality" (1931), *SE* 21: 230–2, 237–9, 241.

film.[21] Her cloying inability to see either her natural or adopted mother apart from herself illustrates how the narcissist is ruled by the need to be loved. As Freud mused, "it is as though our children had remained for ever unsated, as though they had never sucked long enough at their mother's breast" (1931, SE 21: 234). Yet if the relationship between Joanna and Philippa is not tacitly lesbian as Williams argues, it is certainly homoerotic in so far as narcissism is a love of someone mirroring the self (Benjamin 1988: 162). Freud's interrelated theories of gender, religion, and psychosexual development would help to shape a modern viewpoint that intrudes later in the film—in which religious faith is visualized as not only a childish but a feminized activity, and dispassionate masculinity is implicitly valorized as a model of higher humanity.[22] Rebuffed by Philippa, Joanna asks her former boyfriend David (Nicholas Clay) to visit her at Brede, not for heterosexual but narcissistic reassurance. In the most emotionally powerful scene in the film, she tempts, teases, touches, confuses, and torments him through the cloister grille, only to be told with admirable firmness, integrity, and dignity "not to be childish and unfair, especially to people who love you." As a needy young woman and a naïve religious, Sister Joanna does indeed seem "destined to remain a child for ever" (Freud 1927, SE 21: 24).

If Joanna exhibits Freudian traits of femininity in her proclivity to narcissism, jealousy, neuroticism, and hysteria, Rigg's Dame Philippa presents the psychical strengths Freud equated with masculinity—and the modern woman would claim for herself as a human endowment—such as intellectuality, energy, ambition, independence, and a repudiation of the need for help and consolation.[23] In an earlier religious era, only the holy virgin was privileged to become male in spirit through the renunciation of her female sexuality and reproductive power (Miles 1989: 153). As a nun with a sexual and maternal past, Philippa gives new meaning to the historic accolade *femina virilis*. The nuns of Brede are not sure what to make of Philippa anymore than Freud knew what to do with modern

---

[21] See "On Narcissism: An Introduction" (1914), SE 14: 75–6, 88–91; *The Future of an Illusion* (1927), SE 21: 13–17; and *Civilization and Its Discontents* (1930), SE 21: 72–4.

[22] Sullivan discusses how postwar American Catholic "religion was being devalued through its association with femininity" in *Visual Habits*, 5, 10–17, 25–6, 62, 73. This devaluation can be traced back to Freud's discourse on gender and religion.

[23] See Freud's *Moses and Monotheism*: II (1939), SE 23: 107–15, and Van Herik's discussion in *Freud on Femininity and Faith*, 20–1, 177.

women who did not conform to the feminine mold (Bingaman 2003: 118–19). Philippa's "particular friendship" and traumatic falling out with Sister Joanna will eventually unlock the mystery of her untouchability: "You are never to . . . touch me or call me mother"; of her apparently passionless persona: "I can't deal with your love. I can't cope with it"; and of the "desperate, unhappy self" that she hoped to bury in the convent. When she learns that Joanna plans to leave Brede for another order, Philippa realizes that the strength of the religious community depends on the willingness of its members to risk deeper disclosure, vulnerability, and communion with one another (Slee 2002: 180–1). For Philippa, this means giving her sister in Christ some understanding of the personal tragedy that drew her to the convent after her young daughter Joanna was killed by a car on her way to school:

> Work was my religion in those days. . . . When I came here, it was to find something in place of the nothing my life had become. . . . God would be all. No need of ever saying "I love you" to another human being again. And then you came. You were so like my memory of that other Joanna . . . I thought, "dear God, she's come back to me."

A tragic Job's faith, based on unbearable misfortune, bleak disillusionment with life, and the pathology of work, has brought Philippa to the cloister (Freud 1927, *SE* 21: 15–17; Ricoeur 2004: 141, 450–1). If Joanna must outgrow her childish wish-fulfilling religion, Philippa must move out of the shadow of death—like Sister Luke at the end of *The Nun's Story*—and embrace a faith that makes room for hope and love.

In This House of Brede is not a well-made film, but its distinguished cast of strong actresses performed minor miracles with its indifferent plot and managed to convey "the tragic vulnerability . . . (at) the very core of our humanity" (Sands 1992: 12, 24–5). This vulnerability is inseparable from passionate love because those we care for most can be hurt or die, parted from us or lost. Dame Philippa's daughter Joanna will not return to her anymore than Sister Joanna can return to childhood and be born again to a mother who provides unconditional love. Running through the film is a delicate but complex debate between the principal nuns as to how Christian love can be lived out in religious community and what constitutes right relations with others. For Joanna and Philippa, this will involve a mitigation of their particular form of friendship, a mother-daughter bond that promotes unhealthy regression, narcissism, and immaturity. Costigan's film script pronounces Joanna cured of pathology when she commits herself to agape—the unselfish love and service of her fellow sisters: "We must learn to care less for each other and more for all the rest."

Religious Life as a Community of Friends

However, a Christian love wholly devoid of the intensity and passion of eros and characterized by this bland expression of agape can hardly account for the ardent longing that has compelled women past and present to become nuns. Godden's novel offers a richer, more generous and humane vision of religious community life: "Brede believed in friendship . . . Have as many particular friends as you can . . . but many, not one" (Godden 1969: 71). This is indeed a female world of love and ritual; and like the close female circles of nineteenth-century America, the enclosed community of Brede is made up of a broad spectrum of personalities and emotional temperaments (Smith-Rosenberg 1975: 29). The key question then is not, as Williams suggested, whether the mother-daughter bond suggests a forbidden lesbian relationship. It is rather what the vowed celibate does with her feelings for another—whatever they may be. Can she achieve a balance between the need for self-fulfillment and the necessity of self-sacrifice; between agape, the giver of love, and eros, the seeker of it; and between the duties and desires that constitute religious community life? The love affair that Godden dramatized in her novel and that Schaefer and Costigan tried with only partial success to realize on-screen was not between nuns. It was the love story of a passionate God who calls women to become religious and whom they ultimately desire more than mother, father, children, close friend, or lover (Beattie 2006: 81–2).

Godden's own vision of Brede survives in Philippa's relationship with the fourth principal character in the film, the newly elected abbess, Dame Catherine. While ritual lowliness characterized Sister Luke's encounters with the august Reverend Mother Emmanuel in *The Nun's Story*, there is less formality and more familiarity and frankness between Dame Catherine and Philippa. The shot / reverse shots and reaction shots in their scenes communicate a sense of mutuality in which two remarkable women who are accustomed to giving orders and having people under them—one from the world of the cloister and the other from the city—recognize and respect the authority of the other as did Christ and the centurion. Unknowingly foreshadowing her later dilemma with Joanna, Philippa alludes to Jesus's own gift for intimate connection to others when she cites his gospel message, "This is my commandment that you love one another as I have loved you" (John 15:12). However, as a religious leader, Catherine is cognizant that strong personal attachments, like Joanna's with Philippa, can lead to divisive pairings, while personal animosity, like that of Dame Agnes, can foment divided loyalties that politicize and destroy community life (Loudon 1993: 82–3, Reed 2004: 19–20). The two women show the sympathy, attunement, and trust in one another that distinguished Jesus's community of friends: "I no longer call you servants because a servant does not know what his master is doing. I have called you friends because I have told you everything I have heard from my Father" (John 15:15–16).[24] Jesus also identified those who did the will of his Father as brother, sister, and mother (Mark 3:31–33). However, as we have seen in the case of Joanna and Philippa, religious appellations such as "mother," "daughter," and "child" can replay the unbalanced relationships and co-dependencies in the patriarchal family.

Religious life is dramatized as a hard school in which the nuns aspire to relations that are more authentic than the "virtue-friendships and friendships of charity" some traditional sisters valorize (Allen 2009: 141). No self-respecting person would like to feel she is the undeserving recipient of a charity that makes the other feel virtuous, and the Benedictines in Schaefer's film, like those in Godden's book, are not stereotyped as paragons of either selfless charity or superior virtue. Instead, they must struggle to cultivate Jesus's extraordinary gift for genuine friendship with a motley assortment of people, which includes those who are not particularly likeable or easy to love.[25] In the end, what brings very different women together is a buoyant mystical vision of the community of Brede as "a great, proud ship" that carries "those who were here a hundred years ago and those who will be here a hundred years from now—this long, unbroken line of care and companionship." Such a ship of faith had taken Dame Gertrude More, the direct descendant of St. Thomas More, to France in the seventeenth century to help found an English Benedictine monastery, and it transported this community back to England after the French Revolution where it finally established the enclosed community of Stanbrook Abbey in 1838 (Chisholm 1999: 256). As this history suggests and as Philippa learns when she becomes infirmarian

---

[24] Significantly, Philippa had earlier quoted John 15 but focused on verse 12.

[25] Sister Sandra M. Schneiders, I.H.M., notes among the most positive social attributes of women religious their "generosity, ability to control negative emotions, responsibility for the group, concern for inclusion of the less popular, and capacity to delay gratification." See Schneiders, *Selling All: Commitment, Consecrated Celibacy, and Community in Catholic Religious Life* (New York and Mahwah, N.J.: Paulist Press, 2001), 244.

and swaps the duty of nurturing novices for that of nursing her formidable opponent, Dame Agnes, on her deathbed, the deepest and most enduring foundations of a religious community do not lie in the physical structure of the abbey. The greater the devotion of a nun to her community, the more her life becomes interwoven with its past, present, and future, and the more she comes to embody its common history, spirit, and purpose.[26] As Dame Agnes testifies, "This place is all the world to me, all the world wherever I go. Brede will be there. I am Brede." Her extraordinary declaration could inspire a less tragic reading of *The Nun's Story*. As real-life Benedictine Sister Ephrem Hollermann remarked: "For those who have lived together in the heart of Christ and continue to cling to the desire to seek God, there is no separation, no permanent leave-taking" (1998: xvii).

The Painted Veil (2006)

Schaefer's 1975 film of *In This House of Brede* has disappeared from sight so that when John Curran's screen adaptation of *The Painted Veil* premiered in 2006, more than one critic was amazed to discover that "Diana Rigg, of all people, plays a nun" (Dargis, *The New York Times*, December 20, 2006). Thirty years later, Rigg succeeded to the same position as Pamela Brown in the role of Dame Agnes, playing a religious elder but evoking memories of her beauty, verve, and cult status as a younger actress. As Stephanie Zacharek observed in *Salon.com*, "even though the vibrant Diana Rigg is perhaps the last actress we'd want to see playing an elderly missionary nun, her performance here is so direct and so devastating . . . that even in her wimple and habit, she's not so far removed from the élan of Mrs. Peel" (December 20, 2006). Rigg's weathered face is naked testimony not only to age but to a religious life that has been far from sheltered. Her hunched body and hoarse voice convey the impression that she has habitually braced herself to withstand the harsh vicissitudes of nature. A "miserably poor" and beleaguered French superior working in a Chinese community on the Yangtze River that has been devastated by cholera in the 1920s, she refuses to abandon her mission,

[26]Benedictine Sister Joan Chittister worried that religious communities had lost their common character, mind, and direction, and felt they must reclaim their collective presence and personality before they could expect an upturn in vocations. See *Poverty, Chastity and Change: Lives of Contemporary American Nuns*, ed. Carole Garibaldi Rogers (New York: Twayne, 1996), 300.

Figure 5-2. Film reviewers of *The Painted Veil* did not realize that Diana Rigg had played a nun thirty years earlier in *In This House of Brede*.

although it is "no place for a woman" and although her fellow sisters are falling like flies. Sister in spirit to Dame Philippa, this mother superior shows Job's faith beyond fear of tragedy, need for answers, or desire for divine protection (Ricoeur 2004: 455).

Kitty Fane, played by Naomi Watt, reminds the aged nun of her youthful beauty: "You're very pretty—and very young." But Kitty is also a frivolous and foolish young bride who has had an affair out of sexual boredom and stupidity. Kitty manifests elements of the narcissism that Philippa found in Sister Joanna, but additionally shows the vanity, passivity, and lazy conscience that Freud did not scruple to associate with traditional femininity.[27] It would be wrong to conclude, however, that this woman religious regards herself as "superior" to the younger woman. In a scene that shows great charity and sympathetic identifica-

[27] See Freud's "The Transformations of Puberty," *Three Essays on the Theory of Sexuality* (1905), *SE* 7: 227–30, and Van Herik, *Freud on Femininity and Faith*, 20.

Figure 5-3. Rigg's strong, weathered visage as a French missionary superior is reminiscent of the austere, imposing faces that greet Sister Luke in *The Nun's Story*.

tion, the mother superior sits down next to Kitty, turns to her in close shot, and confides that she too was once a "foolish girl with romantic notions" destined to be shattered. Kitty's illusions were about her marital prospects and the mother superior's about "the life of a religious." What made the idea of writing a novel about the enclosed Benedictines of Brede so attractive to Rumer Godden is what drew Rigg's character into the convent—the belief that nuns did indeed experience "the greatest love story in the world" (Godden 1989: 279). "My love was passionate," she discloses, recognizing in Kitty another passionate and demonstrative woman inevitably disenchanted by the reserved and withholding character of her husband, Walter (Edward Norton). Yet the nun's divine spouse seems no better: "He's disappointed me, ignored me. We've settled into a relationship of peaceful indifference. The old husband and wife who sit side by side on the sofa, but rarely speak. He knows I will never leave Him. This is my duty."

While Freud could offer men no consolation in *Civilization and Its Discontents* (1930, *SE* 21: 145), the mother superior's solace to Kitty is hardly facile or undemanding. Marital fidelity like mature religious faith requires stoicism, perseverance, and forbearance. Walter has thrown himself recklessly as a doctor into the dangerous work of treating cholera in order to dull the pain of his wife's adultery. In so doing, he demonstrates that pathology of duty that bedeviled film nuns such as Sister Clodagh, Sister Luke, and Dame Philippa. Kitty has shown pathology of desire in her reckless affair with Charlie Townsend (Liev Schreiber) and total disregard for the moral and social consequences of her sexual transgression (Bingaman 2003: 57–9). The mother superior concludes her personal homily to Kitty with the profound insight that "when love and duty are one, then grace is within you." As she attests, and as the films in this study have shown, what nuns want from life is no different than that of other women: whether the balance of love and work that eluded Sister Luke, the reconciliation of duty and desire that Sister Clodagh achieved at great cost, the struggle of Dame Philippa and Sister Benedict to integrate both agape and eros into their religious life, or Dame Catherine's efforts to align her "duty" as new abbess to love her whole community with a "natural preference" for some of its members.[28]

Introduction to *Agnes of God* (1985)

By 1985, the optimism that earlier greeted Vatican II calls for renewal of the Church had given way to disillusionment and fear that "things fall apart; the centre cannot hold" (W. B. Yeats, "The Second Coming," 3). Progressive nuns, in particular, were increasingly discontented with the patriarchal family construct, which emphasized their duty as obedient daughters in the Church but did not recognize their desires as mature women religious. With the election of John Paul II to the throne of Peter in 1978, they came up against a pope who was alarmed at the institutional unraveling of religious life, intent on putting the brakes on the Vatican II renewal process, and unresponsive to their pleas for dialogue on further religious reform or consultation on his restorationist policies. When *Agnes of God* premiered, the "I am Brede" *esprit de corps* that buoyed up Godden's English congregation of Benedictine nuns had sharply fallen off in many religious orders. Norman Jewison does not directly address these issues in his 1985 film, which revolves around a French Canadian contemplative community in Montreal—one that loyally displays pictures of John Paul II as supreme pontiff on its walls.

---

[28] In her discussion of "Communion in Community," Sister Mary Prudence Allen, R.S.M. defines "charity-friendships" as those with "persons whom one would not have ordinarily chosen on the basis of natural preference." See *The Foundations of Religious Life: Revisiting the Vision*, Council of Major Superiors of Women Religious (Notre Dame, Ind.: Ave Maria Press, 2009), 151.

However, his sister protagonist, Mother Miriam Ruth (Anne Bancroft), does personify the crisis of faith, spiritual malaise, doubts about the efficacy of her prayer, and loss of the comforting sense of God's presence that became common experiences for many contemporary nuns when their traditional infrastructures were dismantled and community spirit began to collapse (Schneiders 2000: 145–6, 156–8, 165–6, 172–3). This came as a surprise to Joseph D'Angelo of *Films in Review* who seemed to be thinking of Sister Benedict in *The Bells of St. Mary's* (1945) or the Mother Abbess in *The Sound of Music* (1965) when he remarked that Anne Bancroft's Mother Miriam had "a strong but shaken faith, a bit weary without the absolute belief nuns are usually portrayed in films as having" (December 1985: 620). Her antagonist is the single-minded career woman and disbelieving psychiatrist, Dr. Martha Livingston (Jane Fonda), who embodies a vocal, self-righteous feminism that the patriarchal Church blamed for unrest within the ranks of its once most loyal and obedient daughters.[29] Molly Haskell, writing for *Vogue* magazine, bemoaned the fact that Fonda had "lost the generous, engaging quality" (October 1985: 92) she brought to earlier film roles. However, her portrayal of Martha Livingston could also be seen as a projection of the less-than-generous views both the clerical hierarchy and conservative Catholics had of modern feminists.[30]

The first reviewers of *Agnes of God* did not consider that the adversarial relationship between Mother Miriam and Dr. Martha Livingston[31] might be a displacement of the postconciliar encounter between the traditional Church and reforming feminism. Yet the actions of the two women suggest a wider conflict of interests between ruling prelates, sister

[29]Lora Ann Quinonez, C.D.P., and Mary Daniel Turner, S.N.D.deN., captured the masculine mindset of the ecclesiastical Church when they asked an archbishop "what he believed was the major objection of the Congregation for Religious to LCWR (Leadership Conference of Women Religious). Without a pause he answered, 'Feminism.'" See *The Transformation of American Catholic Sisters* (Philadelphia: Temple University Press, 1992), 107.

[30]See, for example, Ann Carey's conservative account of *Sisters in Crisis: The Tragic Unraveling of Women's Religious Communities* (Huntington, Ind.: Our Sunday Visitor, 1997), 31–2. She suggests that in the 1960s nuns began to adopt the militant and zealous feminism portrayed in the inflammatory work of Christina Hoff Sommers, *Who Stole Feminism?* As Weaver despairingly notes in *New Catholic Women*, xiv, the Church found it easy to scapegoat "radical feminists."

[31]There has been some confusion about Martha's last name, which is "Livingstone" in John Pielmeier's stage play but "Livingston" in his screenplay.

loyalists, and outspoken or dissenting nuns. The loyalist Mother Miriam entreats the help of the Montreal diocese when Dr. Livingston insists on pursuing the case of Sister Agnes, a mentally disturbed novice in her convent, while the outspoken Martha fights off mounting opposition to her psychiatric investigation from "the bloody bishop." Martha's political hostility toward the Church derives, in part, from a previous abortion. In 1984, the year before the film release, twenty-four liberal American nuns evoked Vatican ire when they signed an ad in *The New York Times* calling for greater understanding on the social and ethical circumstances that lead to a termination of pregnancy. In 1983 another Sister Agnes—Agnes Mary Mansour—became embroiled in a conflict of Church and State when she was ordered by the pope to resign from her post as Michigan's director of social services administering Medicaid for abortions or else face imposed secularization (Weaver 1995: 97–100; Carey 1997: 214–16; Quinonez and Turner 1992: 85–6). Critics of Jewison's film made no mention of the gender political battles going on at this time within the Church, but focused instead on the dramatic clash between an older and younger woman and between the ideology they each espouse, the venerable religion of Catholicism versus the new science of Freudian psychoanalysis and psychiatry. The source of the woman religious and the woman scientist's profound disagreement is Sister Agnes (Meg Tilly), the novice who triangulates this psychodrama. She has been charged with manslaughter for strangling her newborn baby with the umbilical cord. Dr. Martha Livingston is the forensic psychiatrist assigned by the Montreal court to determine the young nun's mental fitness to stand trial, and Mother Miriam Ruth is the convent superior determined to protect Sister Agnes and her convent secrets.

How to Solve the Problem of Agnes of God

Reviewers could not agree on Agnes's role in the film. *America*'s Richard Blake concluded that Sister Agnes is ultimately "neither a real person, nor a mere symbol," but an enigma who tests both the viewers' and the central characters' willingness to listen and try to understand baffling otherness (October 19, 1985: 242). Kevin Thomas of *The Los Angeles Times* suspected that the novice was a pretext for an ego trip, one dramatized by "the seesawing . . . relationship" between Miriam and Martha in which "each is finally more concerned with herself than with the poor nun" (September 13, 1985: sec.6.1). While virtually all critics regarded *Agnes of God* as primarily a clash of two strong women characters and their opposing cultures, they differed on whether the film succeeded as a convent mystery or failed to rise above the level of histrionic and polarized debate. Tom O'Brien of *Commonweal* dismissed it as "holy hooey" even though appreciative of the visual aesthetics devised by Ingmar Bergman's respected cinematographer, Sven Nykvist (October 4, 1985: 530–1). In contrast, D'Angelo of *Films in Review* deemed *Agnes of God* "one of the more greatly anticipated films of the year . . . that lives up to its advance billing" (619–20). Likewise, *America*'s Blake commended the film for "reworking . . . old material into something fresh and arresting," and for its brave tackling of a story "particularly difficult to develop in today's secularist milieu, which can be hostile to nuns" (242)—as Rumer Godden knew only too well. Yet James Wall of *The Christian Century* shrewdly observed that with its Gothic and theological trappings, this nun noir film "implies a more sophisticated understanding of Roman Catholic tradition than it actually displays" (August 28, 1985: 774).

In her *Vogue* review of Jewison's *Agnes of God* and Jean-Luc Godard's *Hail, Mary*, Haskell was struck by the "sudden interest" that male filmmakers were taking "in childbirth 'from the woman's point of view,'" and the way in which both films appear at first to promote the mother and downplay the role of the father. Yet in an intriguing opener, which she did not develop further in her critique, she speculated that there's "more fear and envy . . . than empathy" for women beneath the film's surface (92). This may be because *Agnes of God* is derived wholly from a 1980 stage play and subsequent screenplay by John Pielmeier, and unlike *Black Narcissus*, *The Nun's Story*, *In This House of Brede*, or *Dead Man Walking*, was not based on a female narrative of religious life and did not have any input from either women artists or nun advisers. Pielmeier was originally inspired by the 1976 newspaper accounts of a Sister of St. Joseph in Rochester, New York who was indicted for first-degree manslaughter after she was found in a pool of blood at her convent and a full-term male infant was discovered suffocated and stuffed into a plastic waste basket. The nun's success in concealing her pregnancy from her fellow nuns and co-workers, her initial denial that she had given birth, and the police search for the father or evidence of rape are the inexplicable elements that Pielmeier wove into a play that was both a murder and a religious mystery. Female commentary probed the issues of celibacy, sexual ignorance or inexperience, bodily awareness, loneliness, and shame that might have led to the Sister of St. Joseph's tragic predicament. However, the playwright was not interested in "a more sophisticated understanding" of Sister Agnes's state of mind, and instead treated her character as a pawn in a metaphysical whodunit (Breslin, *Ms.*, March 1977: 69–71, 99–103; Rosefeldt 1996: 89).

While ostensibly sympathetic to the woman's viewpoint, Jewison's film is distorted by a male perspective, and like Schaefer's *In This House of Brede*, reflects a mindset formed by the oedipal triangular family. Once again, the three principal characters are a projection of the cyclic roles that women have in the patriarchal home as mothers, daughters, and sisters competing for love. Mother Miriam Ruth is the post-menopausal matriarch who gets a second chance at being a good mother and sister in the cloister. Dr. Martha Livingston is the amenorrheic woman nearing the end of her prime, estranged from her mother, and haunted by the death of her own sister in the convent. Sister Agnes is the unstable female in transition from puberty to reproductivity who represents and perverts the mysterious "possibility of motherhood." In contrast to the principals in *Brede*, these three female characters constitute something of an unholy trinity because the tensions between them are more evidently colored by the oedipal psychodynamics of fear, anger, envy, and rivalry. Freud theorized that the girl's consciousness of inherent castration—of femininity as lack—gave rise to the female version of the Oedipus complex, triggered the growth of resentment toward the mother with the discovery that she is not phallic, and led to her shift toward passive attachment to the father, and rivalry with the mother to be paternal love object and bearer of his child. The long-term consequence for the girl was not detachment from either parent, as it ideally was for the boy, or resolution of the Oedipus complex, so much as greater and more conflicted attachment.[32] As Karl Bingaman succinctly expressed it, "the primary ties to parental figures actually become intensified, negatively, toward the mother . . . and positively, toward the father" (2003: 20–3, 121).[33]

[32]See Freud's "The Dissolution of the Oedipus Complex" (1924), *SE* 19: 176–7; "Some Psychical Consequences of the Anatomical Distinction between the Sexes" (1925), *SE* 19:254–8; "Female Sexuality" (1931), *SE* 21: 225–35; and Van Herik, *Freud on Femininity and Faith*, 130–5.

[33]Freud's Oedipus complex focuses on the son in the family with the daughter only a secondary concern and, as a result, insufficiently theorized. In the oedipal triangulation, the boy is conflicted by his desire for his mother and jealousy of his father. The perceived threat of castration is instrumental in his renunciation of the beloved mother. He is released from the psychological bondage of the Oedipus complex through internalization of paternal agency in the super-ego and a consequent shift to permanent psychic identification with the father. Alas, for the girl, there seems to be no real escape in Freud's theory. I am indebted to Kirk A. Bingaman's book *Freud*

Agnes of God dramatizes the psychological intensification of negative ties to the mother and positive ties to the father within the cloister. It does so firstly by representing the enclosed community of *Les Petites Soeurs de Marie Madeleine* as a microcosm of the troubled family, and one that Dr. Livingston finds riddled with "lots of dirty little secrets." While the stage play was inspired by a contemporary Catholic scandal, the film more evidently exploits the popular genre of the convent exposé by setting the religious community in Quebec. This was the nineteenth-century location of Maria Monk's *Awful Disclosures of the Hotel Dieu Nunnery*, which presented a sensational narrative of female victimization, rape, infanticide, and seduction via secret passageways (Franchot 1994: xxv, 154–60). Martha will discover that Mother Miriam is not only Sister Agnes's superior but her aunt and only known relative, and so realize that the pathology within the convent does not derive from its pseudo-primary family structure but from hidden blood ties. As the illegitimate offspring of an alcoholic mother with a history of mental illness, Sister Agnes would have been disqualified for admission to a strict religious order, especially one that is enclosed (Schneiders 2001: 204). It is hard to imagine that even after reform of this longstanding church policy to weed out undesirables, any sensible community would have considered admitting a candidate who was unschooled and simple-minded, and had been "kept home by her mother, never been out, seen a movie or TV show . . . never even read a book." When she showed the inclinations to extreme asceticism, self-harm, and psychosis she exhibits in the film, she would probably have been asked to leave and certainly referred for medical treatment. She was not turned away, however, because Miriam assumed the role of her niece's guardian after the death of her sister and gave her haven in the convent. It is understandable why some of her contemplative sisters believe that Agnes "brought the devil here," for she introduced some of the evils of the modern world, such as family violence and child abuse, into their midst. Yet in the post–Vatican II era, formation directors increasingly had to deal with recruits who had not led sheltered lives and who had been damaged by a dysfunctional family background and by all the sorry experiences of "the broken home" (Ebaugh 1993b: 101; McNamara 1996: 640).

---

and Faith: Living in the Tension (Albany: State University of New York Press, 2003), which I discovered as I began revising this chapter. He confirmed my own long-held view that Christian believers have much to learn from Freud despite his evident disapproval of religion. Yet as his book recognizes, in Western culture we all live in the shadow of Freud whether we accept the fact or not.

Second, Pielmeier employed the trope of the murder / religious mystery to ask the question that is central not only in the detective genre and novels of adultery but Freud's oedipal theory of human development: "Who was the Father, what was the origin, what is the secret?" (Byatt 1991: 238). For Freud, the desire to bear the father's child was the most intense expression of the young girl's oedipal attachment. But whether this desire is perceived as transgressive or transcendent will depend on whether the father of Agnes's child is human or divine. Martha Livingston first suspects that paternal intermediary between God and humanity—the nun's priest—who was often indicted as the rapist in anti-Catholic melodramas of convent life. However, she recognizes the absurdity of this conjecture when she meets the ancient and arthritic Father Martineau (Gratien Gelinas) whose only pleasure is a stiff drink. If the missing natural father holds the key to the desire the daughter lacks in the oedipal family, this is an especially problematic situation for Agnes who could have been fathered by "anyone of a dozen men" and who concludes from her own fatherless childhood that "bad babies cry a lot and make their fathers go away." For a young novice who admits she has "nothing else" but the convent and who lacks intelligence, education, sense of subjectivity, or life experience, identificatory love with a powerful father figure is more liable to take the form of passive submission and masochism.

However, Sister Agnes worships a God who projects not only the phallic power of the unknown father holding the promise of fulfillment but the abusive power of the dead mother who sexually touched her "down there with a cigarette." The masochist's pain and pleasure in surrender to the powerful and punitive parental figures are relived in the nun's "holy" stigmata and rape. Thus the desire for positive identification with the father is coupled by the intensification of negative feelings about the mother, and by an oedipal need to expose, blame, or reject motherhood in which all three women characters participate.[34] Agnes is incapable of consciously admitting that she was a mother, and only under hypnosis will finally confess that she was the worst possible kind who committed infanticide. Her only early role model was a natural mother who was mentally disturbed, alcoholic, promiscuous, and neglectful and who, she

[34]See Rebecca J. Lester's Freudian discussion of "eating daddy's baby and throwing up mommy" in "Like a Natural Woman: Celibacy and the Embodied Self in Anorexia Nervosa," *Celibacy, Culture, and Society: The Anthropology of Sexual Abstinence*, ed. Elisa J. Sobo and Sandra Bell (Madison: The University of Wisconsin Press, 2001), 200–2.

reveals under Martha's abreactive therapy, not only sexually molested her but reviled her as an "ugly" and "stupid" "mistake." Miriam tells Dr. Martha Livingston not to address her by her honorary religious title of "Mother": "I'm afraid the word brings up the most unpleasant connotations in this day and age." It later emerges that Miriam has been alluding to her own troubled familial history. In fact, she exemplifies the growing cultural trend of mother nuns, which would lead widow and mother of ten Arlene Hines to enter a Benedictine monastery in 1980 at the age of sixty-four (Reed 2004: 22). Like Dame Philippa, Mother Miriam was married and had a family, but candidly admits that she was "a failure as a wife and mother," and that her two daughters refuse to see her anymore. Dr. Livingston, too, is ambivalent about motherhood. While she has had an abortion, she still mourns the fact that amenorrhea and age now make it unlikely that she will ever have any children.[35] If Miriam's daughters refuse to see her, Martha's senile mother (Anne Pitoniak)[36] is oblivious to her daughter's presence and curses her existence when Martha visits her in a nursing home.

Why, critics asked in some irritation, do cigarettes acquire such exaggerated importance both as dramatic props and subject of conversation between Martha Livingston and Mother Miriam in this film? The film reviewer for *New York* magazine dryly observed that "*Agnes of God* appears to be an epic about Jane Fonda smoking a cigarette" (September 23, 1985: 95). *Monthly Film Bulletin*'s more charitable Louise Sweet wondered if Martha's obsession with smoking was a sign of her stress as a forensic psychiatrist (March 1986: 74), while *The Christian Century*'s James Wall thought that it revealed her inner battle between religious and scientific faith (774). Peter Schillaci of the *National Catholic Reporter* suggested that chain-smoking was the signature of the liberated woman (October 11, 1985: 16). O'Brien of *Commonweal* concluded his hard-hitting review of *Agnes of God* with an exasperated comment on the scene in which Miriam and Martha steal a smoke together outdoors: "Pielmeier wants a symbol of contemporary spirituality, a common point where mother superior and psychiatrist can meet, but then seizes on—smoking?" (532).

---

[35] See Paul Rosefeldt's detailed discussion of the archetypes of the terrible mother and the absent father as they function in the stage play of *Agnes of God*, "The Search for God, the Father: John Pielmeier's *Agnes of God*, Peter Shaffer's *Equus*," *The Absent Father in Modern Drama* (New York: Peter Lang, 1996), 83–7.

[36] Film critics praised the cameo performance of Anne Pitoniak in *Agnes of God*. In fact, she played Mother Miriam Ruth in the first professional stage production of the play in Louisville, 1980. The play premiered on Broadway in 1982.

Yet in the oedipal dynamics operative in this film, what the nun and psychiatrist have in common is castration, an awareness of their limitation and relative powerlessness in a phallocentric society, whether as women in the Church hierarchy or the State judicial system. This is displaced into the craving to smoke, and resentfully expressed in Martha's habit of furious puffing and angry stubbing out of her unfinished cigarettes (*New York* 95). For Freud, penis envy was a feature of the castration complex and accounted not only for the girl's positive attachment to the father but her compensatory desire for penis substitutes, most notably his baby.[37] While Agnes is emphatic that "I don't want to have a baby . . . I never saw the baby so I can't talk about the baby because I don't believe in the baby," both Martha and Miriam share an obsession with Agnes herself as their surrogate child. The questions of who the father is and who can rightfully claim his child result in a fierce and unresolved competition between Mother Miriam and Martha Livingston who advocate the rival dictates of the father God of ancient Judeo-Christianity and Freud, the father of modern psychoanalysis.

Film critics were also puzzled by the uneven relationship between these two strong, intelligent women, which vacillates between point-scoring animosity and sudden flashes of solidarity, but never leads to the school of friendship noteworthy in *Brede*. However, it is the male and Freudian sense of struggle and strife, not the female striving for *communitas*, that colors their relationship. Indeed, their relationship is destroyed at the film's end by Martha's grossly unfounded suspicion, one she trumpets with almost indecent pleasure, that Miriam is the murderous mother who has smothered Agnes's newborn baby to suppress a convent scandal. Thomas, of *The Los Angeles Times*, suggested that in pruning crucial information from the stage play—such as the disclosure that Dr. Livingston's "sister died of appendicitis because her mother superior wouldn't send her to hospital"—the film made it difficult for an audience to understand why Martha should be so distrustful of Miriam, and why they should be so mortally opposed about the efficacy of faith versus science (sec.6.1). The general critical judgment was that their bitter debate often seems a dramatic end in itself.

[37] See Freud, "The Taboo of Virginity" (1918), *SE* 11: 204–5; "The Dissolution of the Oedipus Complex" (1924), *SE* 19: 177–9; "Some Psychical Consequences of the Anatomical Distinction between the Sexes" (1925), *SE* 19: 256–8; "On Transformations of Instinct as exemplified in Anal Erotism" (1917), *SE* 17: 128–9; "Female Sexuality" (1931), *SE* 21: 240–3; Bingaman, *Freud and Faith*, 20–3; and Van Herik, *Freud on Femininity and Faith*, 132–5.

Meg Tilly's Portrayal of Sister Agnes

The film's disappointing lack of answers and proliferation of questions can also be an occasion for speculative thinking about both God and Freud—a God whom the mystics sought through a cloud of unknowing, and Freud the interrogator who would not be satisfied with the facile answers and consoling words of conventional faith. The key to this alternative reading is Meg Tilly's portrayal of Sister Agnes. This was a difficult role to play convincingly because it is over-determined by religious and psychological symbolism. With a name that evokes the spotless and sacrificial lamb of God, Agnes is a pathological recast of the stereotypic nun who is young, virginal, and pure of heart, and who featured in entertaining films such as *The Sound of Music* (1965) or later, *Sister Act* (1992). Dressed in the all-white habit of a novice, Agnes corroborates Rebecca Sullivan's view that the woman religious often functions as "a blank text on which others can write their own sexual and gender pleasures" (Sullivan 2005: 221; Weaver 1995: 73). Mother Miriam romanticizes Agnes as "an innocent, a slate that hasn't been touched except by God." In a nod to the nuns who sweetly sing divine praise in *The Sound of Music* (1965) and *In This House of Brede* (1975), she professes that Agnes's flawless voice miraculously ended her own crisis of unbelief and restored her world-weary faith. In contrast to Miriam's projection of the novice as a redeemer, Martha's psychiatric project takes a heroic turn. She wishes to save Agnes from a religious life that she believed killed her sister—"My sister died in a convent and it's her voice I hear"—and, implicitly, it's her sister's face that she sees in the Mona Lisa expression of Tilly's novice. Miriam astutely discerns the messianic aspect to Martha's feminist and psychoanalytic inquiry: "Why are you so obsessed with her. You're losing sleep over her. . . . You're bent on saving her. Why?"

Sven Nykvist's camera pictures Meg Tilly's pale face as blending with the wintry Quebec landscape, the pallid but clear northern light of day, the snow, and the white turtle doves that flutter about the convent grounds. Predictably, film critics admired her "radiance"—a favorite accolade for the beatific screen nun but one that does communicate the sense of numinous mystery that Tilly brought to the role of Sister Agnes. The cinematographer highlighted her aura of see-through grace by a shot in which she is portrayed in Vermeer-like repose before an open convent window (O'Brien 531). In close-up, however, his camera is fascinated with the freckles that spot her face and give it an odd beauty. If the visual message is that Agnes is not altogether an *immaculata*, how

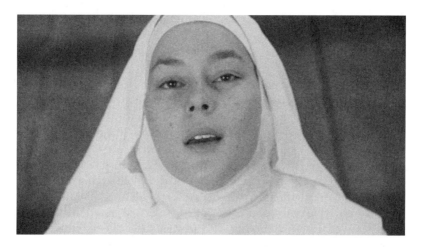

Figure 5–4. Sister Agnes's face reflects the mystery at the heart of *Agnes of God*—whether the novice has experienced erotic or religious ecstasy, sacrilegious rape or sacred rapture.

are we to read her face? Is she an unfaithful bride of Christ, a holy fool, or a simpleton (Miles 2002: 49)? Does she hear the calling of a divine, a schizophrenic, or a daemonic voice? Was this virgin's annunciation a rape or rapture or both? Was she inspired, deluded, or duped into believing that "all of God's angels would want to sleep beside me if they could"? Does conviction of Agnes's holiness or denial of her sexual womanhood lead Mother Miriam to suggest that the infant could have resulted from parthenogenesis and not human intercourse?

Approval of women who remain perpetual children and virgins, suspicion that with puberty they may become tainted sexually, and fear that they will grow "bigger" and acquire the magical omnipotence of the original mother are all imprinted on the placid face, docile body, and malleable mind of Sister Agnes. The novice hears the clashing voices of a bad natural mother and a good "lady" and admits that they "fight over (her) all the time." This "lady" is a mental projection of the Virgin Mary who appeared to the simple peasant girl, Bernadette Soubirous, at Lourdes and who eventually revealed herself as the Immaculate Conception. While this doctrine maintained that Mary was exempt at the moment of her own conception from the stain of original sin and bore the authoritative stamp of papal infallibility, it was commonly misinterpreted as a confirmation of her virginal conception and birth of Jesus. Agnes's inner discord bears out the view that as Immaculate Conception and Virgin Mother, Mary is an impossible role model for a woman and can only be imitated "through self-divisiveness, through splitting her personality into multiple selves" (DelRosso 2005: 47, 68, 86). Yet Mary full of grace, devoid of sin, and untouched by sex was an ideal that remained holy and pleasing to a clerical class that saw the Church—like the fraternity or the secret society—as a sanctuary from female influence (Dinnerstein 1991: 66–7). Just as the ageing student prince Hamlet charges the innocent and bewildered Ophelia to "get thee to a nunnery" lest she become "a breeder of sinners" (Shakespeare, *Hamlet* 3.1.124), so celibate priests also operated within a homosocial culture that facilitated Freudian "defence against femininity" (Freud 1931, *SE* 21: 243). Their unrealistically high expectations of women and their compensatory idealization of the remembered or imagined mother who answered their every need in early childhood, found supreme expression in devotion to the Blessed Virgin Mary (Sipe 1990: 72, 190–3).

The film also uses Sister Agnes to represent the remnants of a Baroque Catholic culture—personified by Bernini's famous sculpture of St. Teresa of Avila in a mystical rapture that fuses eroticism and ecstasy—which Americans now see as "sensual, exotic, sentimental, exaggerated, artificial, and other" (McDannell 1995: 64). However, as *Commonweal*'s hostile reviewer of *Agnes of God* observed, this Catholicism is "creepy" as well (O'Brien 531). Its visual and aural simulacra—a lurid statue of the Blessed Virgin Mary with her sacred heart exposed and elevated in the chest cavity, an elaborate gold-spiked monstrance, the convent's grille padlocked like a large chastity belt, the eerie whisper of words in the confessional, and the talismanic chanting of the rosary in Latin for deliverance from evil—raise the apprehensions of a religious / murder mystery. The discomfort that Martha Livingston shows, as she comes face to face in the convent with the material relics of her Catholic girlhood, illustrates the emotional hold that devotional Catholicism continued to have for those who, like the playwright Pielmeier, lapsed or intellectually abjured their faith in adulthood (Detweiler 1996: 79). Martha will be interrogated by an officious clerical spokesman for the Bishop of Montreal: "Do you still go to church?" and she will be outed by Mother Miriam Ruth who asks, "What have we done to hurt you? . . . I can smell an ex-Catholic a mile away." Even a dedicated skeptic like Livingston is not immune to Tridentine Catholicism's backward pull. As an emancipated modern woman, she derides the "poverty, chastity, and ignorance" of religious life. Yet in the end, the mystery surrounding Sister Agnes still inspires "hope, and love, and desire," and a nostalgic longing for the "belief in miracles" that characterized the Catholic wonder years of her childhood (Gandolfo 1992: 8).

Suzanne Campbell-Jones articulated a pre-modern truth of religious life, one that Jewison forces not only the demystifying psychiatrist but the film viewer to confront in Sister Agnes: "We must accept if we are to understand the nuns, the reality of their belief in the power of the supernatural" (1978: 149). For Martha, this is a dangerous illusion that can lead to psychosis (Freud 1927, SE 21: 31), and the simple novice is quick to realize that the doctor's intended cure will kill: "I know what you want from me. You want to take God away." What distinguishes Meg Tilly's performance as Sister Agnes is the crazy-canny wonderment she brings to a film role where she easily could have remained nothing more than a case study of female delusion, hysteria, and "physiological feeble-mindedness" (Freud 1927, SE 21: 48). Yet as D'Angelo of *Films in Review* perceptively noted, her Agnes is "naïve, mad, sane, simple, complex, and an eerie enigma" (620). Although a promising young actress, the supporting role of Agnes required Tilly to come between the two strong, leading women characters and yet somehow maintain her own intermediate space against the encroachment of both Fonda and Bancroft. However, she was not overshadowed by the two established stars, and indeed, while both she and Bancroft were nominated for a Golden Globe and an Oscar, Tilly alone won a Golden Globe for her performance.

Tilly conveyed Agnes's combination of simplicity and clairvoyance by injecting the character with a dreamy and unnerving liminality.[38] O'Brien complained that "Jewison has no way to film her mind" (530), yet Tilly's rapt expression of face on-screen gives the impression that the novice has a secret interior world where mysterious communication takes place and where the veil between a divine and a human realm might just conceivably have fallen away (Heath 2008: 113; Rizzuto 1980: 134). Martha wants to probe the pathology of this interior and get some straight answers, and Miriam wishes to protect it as a virgin territory closed to her skeptical questions, but Agnes sets them both wondering. While Theresa Sanders concludes that "the film . . . leaves no middle ground between faith and reason . . . the findings of science or the prom-

---

[38]Jane Fonda "came to believe" that while Agnes was "crazy" and "an hysteric," she was also a divine "conduit of sorts." See her interview with Marsha McCreadie in *The Casting Couch and Other Front Row Seats: Women in Films of the 1970s and 1980s* (New York: Praeger, 1990), 125.

ises of religion" (2002: 200), I think *Agnes of God* furnishes the grounds to move beyond futile debate to a more fruitful dialectic between Freud and Catholic faith.[39] Indeed, an ambiguity in both the diegesis and the main characters themselves opens up a space for further discussion.

For Martha, Agnes is living proof of the damning Freudian verdict that religion perpetuates psychical infantilism and neurosis. Freud argued that the primitive helplessness of human infancy and the prolonged dependence on parents in childhood instill a powerful need for protection, love, and security.[40] Agnes's retarded development, her familial history of child abuse, and her little-girl behavior as a novice certainly lend credence to the view that what the convent offers her is the assurance of lifelong safety and refuge. Growing awareness of the precariousness of life impels the child to exalt an almighty God, made in the image of the natural parents but purged of their human fallibility. In Agnes's case, a father God who is both a substitution for the missing father and the imagined progenitor of her child offers protection from the abusive mother of childhood. However, as is evident in *The Nun's Story*, *The Sound of Music*, and *In This House of Brede*, God is never purely or simply the psychic magnification of the oedipal father but can be an exaltation of the mother or other primary caretakers. Furthermore, the image of God cannot be disentangled from the ambivalent feelings of love and hate the vulnerable child has for the more powerful parents who may not only nurture and protect, but punish and abuse her. Thus Agnes's personal God includes fragments of an exalted "Lady" mother as well as the hellish mother of her childhood. Imaginary companions with super powers like guardian angels supplement the aid of the parental imagoes and permit the child to reveal unacceptable aspects of herself to a benevolent third party (Rizzuto 1980: 126–7, 130). In the denouement of the film, Agnes relives what she believes is a visionary encounter with the Archangel Michael in the convent barn. Strikingly, she describes her experience of divine passion there as a "falling into the iris of God's eye," like Carl

[39] Theresa Sanders argues that the film ends by "siding with the claims of science over those of religion." See Sanders, *Celluloid Saints: Images of Sanctity in Film* (Macon, Ga.: Mercer University Press, 2002), 201. However, the *Film Comment* critic, Marcia Pally, felt that the film was weighted much more heavily toward religion than the stage play, which ended with Agnes dying in a psychiatric ward (September–October 1985: 14).

[40] See Freud's *The Future of an Illusion* (1927), SE 21: 24, 43, 49, 53; and *Civilization and Its Discontents* (1930), SE 21: 72, 84–4.

Jung's dream of an ithyphallic god with "a single eye, gazing motionlessly upward" (Jung 1989: 12). The sense of ecstasy, fear, and enormity that pervades her fall suggests the stirring of sexual desire, which she could reveal only to a guardian angel. Her visionary account also pulsates with a longing for symbiotic merger that was a pathological expression in earlier holy anorexics of the visceral need for deep interpersonal communion (Davis 1987: 183–4).

Some critics have concluded from Jewison and Nykvist's attempts to visualize this scene through the interplay of blinding light and brooding shadow that Agnes's God acts like "a demon lover" (O'Brien 531). The film reviewer for *Ms.* complained that her idea of God is not Judeo-Christian but pagan and "more closely resembles an ancient, holistic deity—one that is at once good *and* evil" (December 1985: 29). However, when Agnes declares, "I hate him for what he did to me," and names "God" as her violator, she is revealing to the psychiatrist the immature, fragmentary, and disconnected belief of the child. When asked to free associate by Martha at their initial meeting, the first two words that come to her mind are "God" and "love." This God of Love is an unbalanced and disturbed mix of agape and eros. He seems to call her to both selfless and sexual surrender, self-sacrifice and self-destruction, grace and insemination. Yet her God is also unconsciously pieced together from unacknowledged feelings of anger, fear, suffering, and yearning she has for her natural parents. The radical psychiatric cure that Martha proposes is to rescue her from God and the religious life. "She belongs to God," Mother Miriam insists. "And I intend to take her away from him," is Martha's retort. "She has a right to know that there's a world out there filled with people who don't believe in God."

Martha echoes the view with which Freud drew *The Future of an Illusion* (1927) to a close—that Agnes cannot remain a child forever, must give up the consoling illusions of religion, grow up, and face "hostile life" without the protection of a parental God (*SE* 21: 49). Martha's distaste as a scientist for the Catholic superstition and magical thinking that sustains Agnes's faith is further exacerbated by the nature of Mother Miriam's own belief. Although a clever, shrewd, worldly wise superior, she confides in Martha that the young novice's voice called her back to God. However, this is also a depressing return to the naïve faith of early childhood and regressive search for the guardian angel who was her guide until she reached the age of reason: "All my doubts about myself and God were gone in that one moment. I recognized the voice. Please don't take that away from me again. Those years after six were very bleak."

I suggest that there are some signs that *Agnes of God* attempts to move toward an intermediate position on the psychology of religion that does not require a stark choice between wish-fulfilling faith and demystifying science. In a dramatic monologue omitted from the film, Martha explicitly admits that her own passion for psychiatry is a form of belief: "*My* religion, *my* Christ, is this. The mind" (Pielmeier 1982: 1.3.14). Jewison's screen adaptation visualizes the implications of this statement—that Martha's professional zeal and dedication have parallels with a religious vocation. I will argue in conclusion that the psychiatrist is metaphorically the unrecognized, unacknowledged, and unappreciated sister activist counterpart to the contemplative nuns featured in the film. In so doing, I wish to qualify Margaret Miles's view that in representing religious characters as "sinister, devious or crazy," *Agnes of God* simply reflects the cynicism about "religious conviction or commitment" characteristic of films in the 1980s (2002: 48–9).

Although an avowed agnostic like Freud, Martha too remains absorbed in the phenomenon of religion and cannot eradicate the Catholicism in which she was raised from her psyche (Bingaman 2003: 27). Indeed, the stained glass windows and Gothic arches reflected in the windows of her Montreal apartment indicate that she lives next to a church and is still unconsciously attached to the house of God. This fascination is displaced onto Sister Agnes and is one of the reasons why, as Mother Miriam perceives, she "is thinking about her all the time." The cultural critic Robert Detweiler argues that for all intents and purposes Martha might as well have taken a vow of chastity (1996: 78). As a psychiatrist, she is absorbed in the life of the mind and has little or no time for men or sex. In the film, cloistered nuns have become an endangered minority whom their chaplain describes as "a very special and rare people . . . only a few of them left in this modern world, consecrated to the praise of God." In contrast, Martha is a reminder that the remaining women religious are out in the world. They have not disappeared as persons behind convent walls as her sister Marie did. They may no longer be visually identifiable as nuns or distinguishable from other active professional women. The fact that the psychiatrist is named Martha and her sister the nun was called Marie links her to the harassed and over-worked sister of the contemplative Mary in the gospels. Jane Fonda's prior history of involvement in reform movements and social justice causes where new nuns of the sixties and seventies had become conspicuously active gave her some understanding that a vocation could be a radical call extending from religious to public service (Ebaugh 1993a: 403–8; Byrne 1990: 87–9).

Jane Fonda

Jane Fonda had been a film actress for twenty-five years when she made *Agnes of God* and like American Catholic nuns had undergone a radical transformation of image in that time (Quinonez and Turner 1992: vii–viii). She debuted as an all-American cheerleader in *Tall Story* (1960), but by the end of the decade had become known as the American Brigitte Bardot in *Barbarella* (1968). Like the screen star Ingrid Bergman over thirty years before, Fonda's affair with the French director Roger Vadim led to a sensational shift in her film image from wholesome virgin to willing whore—a binary representation that cinematic nuns did not escape and that is not wholly resolved in *Agnes of God*. Fonda had also embarked on a journey of self-discovery and social activism that had parallels with the decision of progressive American nuns to join the civil rights and anti-war movement, and to leave the security of the convent to start programs for the poor, the marginalized, and the disenfranchised. During the 1970s, Fonda rallied support for the American Indians who occupied Alcatraz, the Black Panther movement, Chavez's boycott of non-union grape pickers, army deserters, and the priests and nuns accused of planning the abduction of Henry Kissinger (Zeidler 1987: 146, 149; Akers 1994: 361–3; Hershberger 2005: 6–23). Tellingly, both her first husband, Vadim, and her father, Henry Fonda, are reputed to have complained that her intense political involvement turned her into a "Joan of Arc" figure—which is how Amanda Plummer played Agnes on the Broadway stage (Perkins 1991: 243; Dyer 1998: 79; Rusinko, *Magill's Cinema Annual* 1986: 59). Her strident anti-war stance made her infamous as "Hanoi Jane" (Perkins 1991: 242) after she visited North Vietnam in 1972 with Tom Hayden, the man who would become her second husband, and spoke out on Radio Hanoi against U.S. saturation bombing (Zeidler 1987: 144–5; DiCanio 1998: 105–6). Sister Joan Chittister recalled that there was a public outcry when the Erie Benedictines active in the peace movement sponsored Jane Fonda's visit to their local community. For years afterward, the townspeople indignantly asked, "Was this treason or was this Christianity? Should sisters be doing such things?" (2005: 87). Like Ingrid Bergman, Fonda would be denounced in the newspapers and on Capitol Hill by congressmen who argued that she should be charged with treason (Zeidler 1987: 145; Akers 1994: 362–3; Holzer and Holzer 1990: 5; Hershberger 2005: 3).

Despite her courage as a political activist, Fonda was regarded with ambivalence by the feminist movement, and would find it difficult to shake off her earlier eroticized image in the 1960s (Perkins 1991: 239–45; Dyer 1998: 79–80; Sullivan 2005: 55–9). Tessa Perkins astutely remarked that her "post-1968 films are characterized by a struggle between a distinctly feminist discourse which inflected much of Fonda's performances and aspects of the narrative and a patriarchal discourse which tends to dominate the overall structure of the film" (1991: 246). While Perkins saw the 1971 film *Klute* as an overt example of these gender politics—with Fonda's controversial portrayal of a prostitute as a pseudo-feminist heroine—the conflict between a feminist and patriarchal discourse is also evident in *Agnes of God*. As I have shown, the film depicts Anne Bancroft's Mother Miriam as a feisty but loyal superior who relies on the protection and political muscle of a clerical power base. The Catholic bishop of Montreal regards Fonda's Livingston as a political troublemaker, aligning her with the social activist sisters whom Church authorities officially opposed and censored in the 1980s (Ebaugh 1993a: 408; Quinonez and Turner 1992: 107–8; Chittister 2005: 224).

Conclusion

While the intense encounter of the three principal women in *Agnes of God* is short-lived, it does not leave the ex-Catholic psychiatrist untouched, and the film ends with a prayer beseeching help for her unbelief: "I hope that she (Sister Agnes) has left something, some little part of herself with *me*. That would be miracle enough." Fonda portrays Dr. Martha Livingston as a solitary figure who must wrestle with the angels and ministers of the psyche. Although obsessed with psychoanalyzing Agnes, she is reluctant to probe her own unconscious motives or childhood complexes. Ironically, although Mother Miriam doesn't approve of "the science of psychiatry," she correctly warns her of the dangers of transference and counter-transference. Over the course of the film, it becomes apparent that Martha's Freudian case against God is also a "j'accuse" against the natural mother who condemns her to hell for having an abortion and the mother superior whose ignorance and indifference led to the death of her sister Marie. Not only is she battling to free Agnes from God but to free herself from the parental hang-ups that this God represents. In a wrenching visit to her mother in a nursing home—one which does show genuine sensitivity to the woman's point of view—Jane Fonda's face in close-up registers the pain and despair, effort and futility of her attempt to be a dutiful daughter. In her senility, Martha's mother mistakes her living daughter for her dead daughter the nun, and Martha must listen as she is damned while her kindness is attributed to Marie. It is understandable from this scene why Martha would not only renounce but also denounce her religious upbringing. Her mother's ramblings are the voice of the harsh, judgmental, accusatory Catholic superego fixated with what has gone wrong in her secular daughter's life—her loss of faith, "son-of-a-bitch" husband, abortion, failed marriage, and divorce—but incapable of seeing her admirable pluck, persistence, and passion as a professional woman. Although her mother's mind is confused, she still rigidly adheres to the black-and-white belief that "Martha's going straight to hell," while Marie, the nun, has naturally gone straight to heaven. Yet what leaves a lasting impression in this scene is not the mother's psychic polarization of her two daughters as either all-good or all-bad. It is Martha's exercise of patience, kindness, generosity, faithfulness, gentleness, and self-control as she tenderly strokes her mother's thinning hair and vacant face. These are the Christian gifts of the spirit, of a God who is Agape and who honors the uphill struggle of eros. They indicate that she, too, is "full of grace" irrespective of whether she regards herself as a failed Catholic or a convert to atheism.

The films in this chapter set in motion an interesting dialectic between the competing claims, on the one hand, of the contemplative and the active life, the cloister and the city, and, on the other hand, of religion and science, Catholic female mysticism and Freudian psychoanalysis / psychiatry. Cinematic nuns move back into enclosed communities in *Agnes of God* and *In This House of Brede*, but I have resisted the conclusion that this should be read symbolically as a reactionary step in which the world is rid of troublesome women religious (Sullivan 2005: 93). *In This House of Brede* tackles the popular perception that contemplative nuns do not engage in work that is important, productive, or influential.[41] Both Godden's novel and Schaefer's film adaptation suggest what they achieve through the power of agapaic prayer for others and through eros's "quest for communion with another, with beauty, with knowledge, with goodness" (Nelson 1979: 112). *Agnes of God* captures some of the beauty of this cloister world through its evocative cinematography but injects a nun noir dimension underlining not only the hardships but also the dangers of enclosed contemplative life for those who are not mature or well-balanced. In *Brede*, Diana Rigg represents a mature women entrant who

---

[41] Godden related the amusing anecdote of Queen Victoria's reaction after the Duke of Clarence visited Stanbrook Abbey: "Someone should give those women something to do." See *A House with Four Rooms*, 247.

brings her experience of the city of man into the contemplative city of God. When she enters Brede Abbey as Dame Philippa, she triggers not only personal and generational tension but also religious and cultural change, culminating in her appointment as abbess of a new Benedictine monastery in Japan. *Agnes of God* continues to show an interest in the phenomenon of the older mother nun with Anne Bancroft in the role of the cloister superior, Mother Miriam. However, it introduces a theme that was touched on earlier in *The Nun's Story*, *The Sound of Music*, and *Change of Habit*: that women religious do not have exclusive claim to a vocation. In a new twist on this theme, the film suggests that nuns may have unacknowledged and even unbelieving sisters like Dr. Martha Livingston who are struggling to carry out their good work in the world. Freud argued that science had superseded religion in performing "great services for human civilization" (1927, *SE* 21: 37–8, 54–6). However, Fonda's Dr. Livingston, like Elvis Presley's Dr. Carpenter in *Change of Habit* or Sister Luke in *The Nun's Story*, shows an intense dedication to healing that blurs the distinction between secular and religious vocational work, and shifts emphasis from the traditional sacrifice of personal passion in religious life to the challenge of how it can be harnessed to serve others (Ebaugh 1993a: 403).

The word "passion" also resonates with the mystery of its original Christian meaning. This is the Passion or redemptive suffering and death of Christ on the Cross, which Agnes somatically relives as a stigmatic in her desire for symbiotic merger with God. However, the cruelty, treachery, and torment memorialized on Good Friday are a reminder of a darker side to eros and the heart's propensity for evil as well as noble desires. These darker desires are the subject of the two films I will consider in my next chapter and book conclusion—*Dead Man Walking* (1995) and *Doubt* (2008). Like *Agnes of God*, they respect the mystery of passionate desire, leaving it deliberately ambiguous whether the human capacity for love has been damaged, perverted, destroyed, or redeemed.

SPIRITUAL DESIRES

SIN, SUFFERING, DEATH, AND SALVATION IN *DEAD MAN WALKING* (1995)

Introduction to *Dead Man Walking*

In the five previous chapters, I have explored the range and complexity of the desires that nuns unveil on-screen and shown how these subvert one view of religious life voiced by Sister Luke, that "a nun is not a person who wishes or desires." While traditional nuns regard the selfless surrender to God in agape as their supreme purpose, they paradoxically allude to the desires associated with eros when they acknowledge that "this letting go" of the self can awaken "the deepest yearnings of the human heart" (Donovan and Wusinich 2009: 28). Indeed, they draw attention to a phenomenon that *Dead Man Walking* will illuminate: which is how eros and agape can become sources of extraordinary energy in religious life when united (Nelson 1979: 17, 28). However while I have interpreted eros as a dynamic lifeforce in the religious life of cinematic nuns, I have also considered how repressed or unavowed desires make their unwelcome presence felt indirectly through involuntary memories, recurrent disobedience, psychosomatic sickness, depression, psychical splitting, and even mental breakdown. Sister Ruth in *Black Narcissus* and Sister Agnes in *Agnes of God* illustrate how eros can take the form of strange, wild, destructive, and ultimately tragic desires. In this chapter, I will first examine the darker face of eros and the venerable question that haunts *Dead Man Walking*: How can a loving Father God allow suffering, harm, and evil to befall his little ones?

Freud's psychoanalytic explanation in *Civilization and Its Discontents* is that while eros is the preserver of life, there is a contrary instinct of death that is alloyed with it and accounts for the aggressive and destructive manifestations of love (1930, *SE* 21: 118–19). From a Freudian point of view, *Dead Man Walking* dramatizes the unceasing contest between eros and thanatos. These are the "Heavenly Powers" that Christianity mythologized into an eternal battle between God and Satan (1930, *SE* 21: 133, 145). The nun protagonist, Sister Helen Prejean (Susan Sarandon), bears witness to a way of life that Freud—like some of the film's characters—viewed as naïve and rose-colored, a life "which makes love the centre of everything" (1930, *SE* 21: 82). Her struggle is to preserve the life and save the soul of a man who appears to have no center and who, as a murderer on death row facing imminent execution, has become a host to darkness and destruction. With his satanic goatee and devil hunter eyes, Sean Penn's Matthew Poncelet awakens the fear that we are descended from a predatory horde, and the film's nightmarish reenactment of the crime as the feral, night-stalking of young human prey in a black wood suggests that we have a lust for killing in our blood.[1] This fear is just barely contained through demonization of Poncelet: by the public as a monster, by the victims' God-fearing families as an abomination, and by the prison chaplain who expounds an old testament God, as the evil that requires retribution and justifies capital punishment. For Sister Helen, however, he personifies the power of thanatos that she must try to withstand through the force of her love and her commitment to living the gospel message of charity, compassion, forgiveness, reconciliation, and redemption. As her mother (Lois Smith) astutely realizes, she is "looking for a love that's so big it takes in all evil." Her desire for a love that engulfs evil in its tender embrace is the core motive that leads her to follow Christ as a woman religious and apprehensively become the spiritual adviser of Poncelet on death row.

Sister Helen's vision of Christian love accords with Freud's view of eros as the power "which holds together everything in the world" (1921,

---

[1] Freud remarked in his 1915 essay on "Thoughts for the Times on War and Death" that "the very emphasis laid on the commandment 'Thou shalt not kill' makes it certain that we spring from an endless series of generations of murderers, who had the lust for killing in their blood, as, perhaps, we ourselves have to-day" (*SE* 14: 296).

SE 18: 92). However, he did not believe the unifying drive of eros was strong enough to prevail over the evil passions of hatred, aggression, and violence that characterized the death instinct (1915, *SE* 14: 280). He saw eros locked in mortal combat with thanatos, and as an atheist, lacked the nun's faith that death was not the end, or that love never dies (1 Cor. 13). Nonetheless, he admired those Christians who achieved sanctity by pursuing the path of universal love for humanity and who moved beyond their immediate family to bind and unite strangers (1923, *SE* 19: 45; 1930, *SE* 21: 101–2). Yet as a master of suspicion, he suspected that what drove them was an underlying fear of the death of those closest. The defense against this was the impersonal charity that nuns like Dame Philippa cultivated in *In This House of Brede* and that became untenable for Sister Luke when her father was barbarously killed in *The Nun's Story*. Indeed, the parents of Poncelet's victims dramatize the acute suffering and helpless misery that the loss of a loved one can cause; and they, too, concluded that only the nun's distance from familial love and intimacy could enable her to show Christian charity to the sadistic murderer of their children.

The contest between eros and thanatos exemplifies the struggle of the natural man for whom the world is, indeed, a dark wood like the crime scene in the film and where, as Thomas Hobbes opined, he lives in "continual fear and danger of violent death" ("The Leviathan," XIII). However, the film nun has another vision of human life that she superimposes like a spiritual transparency on the bleak and savage spectacle of the natural man. This film transparency gives glimpses of a world where eros is not overcome by death, where agape reaches down and comes to human aid, and where natural man can be redeemed by grace (Nygren 1953: 474). The struggle of the woman religious protagonist is to look evil in the face and to resist the fear, dread and horror of death with the pure and unconditional love known as agape. Both the film characters who work in the prison system and the first film critics who reviewed *Dead Man Walking* questioned Sister Helen's motives for becoming spiritual counselor of a hardened criminal on death row.[2] Even the prison chaplain does not appreciate the theology that underpins her religious ministry. She tells him simply that Poncelet "wrote to me and asked me to come," demonstrating by her actions that agape is spontaneous and unmotivated (Nygren 1953: 75), and by her words that God may come

[2] See, for example, Kenneth Turan's review for *The Los Angeles Times* on December 29, 1995.

in answer to prayers we did not know how to express, or been conscious of uttering, and help us in our weakness (Rom. 8:25–27).

The Representation of the Nun in Dead Man Walking (1995)

Dead Man Walking premiered a decade after *Agnes of God* (1985). It was, however, based on real events that took place in the 1980s but were updated to the 1990s after Sister Helen Prejean published her testimonial on Angola death-row prisoners and Louisiana state penitentiary executions in 1993. In the ten-year interlude between these two films, actual women religious began to recover from death themselves—the death of their congregations, the demise of the motherhouses that provided them a surrogate family structure, the decline to the point of extinction in their numbers, and the death of their hopes for significant gender and institutional reform in the Church. Progressive nuns who persevered in religious life, despite the turmoil, divisions, and fragmentation of the post–Vatican II era, branched out from the total, intentional communities of the past and formed the looser associational model that we see in the warm, companionable living arrangement of Sister Helen and Sister Colleen (Margo Martindale). The veteran leaders who emerged from the surviving cohort had the qualities that distinguish Sister Helen on-screen—calmness, quiet, simplicity, humility, steadfastness, and fortitude. Above all, as one sister who weathered these volatile times remarked, there was "a deep trust that God is somewhere, active, in the midst of it all, even the ongoing evil and suffering" (Schneiders 2000: 178). It is no wonder that current-day sisters greatly admire this Hollywood film for its realistic representation of a contemporary woman religious who put Christ's words into action: "I was in prison and you came to see me" (Matt. 25: 36–7; Schneiders 2001: 235, 321; Kuhns 2003: 13).

Yet coupled with the wholly justified praise for *Dead Man Walking* has been a tendency to dismiss earlier films that represented nuns or consign them to the same light entertainment category as *Sister Act*, *The Flying Nun*, and *The Sound of Music*. Indeed the first reviewers of *Dead Man Walking* seemed oblivious to the fact that past film directors such as Powell and Pressburger and Zinnemann had begun the serious study of women religious and their interior life forty or fifty years earlier. *Magill's's* Patricia Kowal exclaimed, "finally, a filmic depiction of a nun that is grounded in human emotion" (*Magill's Cinema Annual*

1996: 126). Critics also admired the luminous intensity of Sarandon's performance, but did not appreciate that the same erotic energy of deep feeling distinguished Ingrid Bergman's vibrant depiction of Sister Benedict in 1945, Deborah Kerr's passionate enactment of Sister Clodagh in 1947, and Audrey Hepburn's ardent portrayal of Sister Luke in 1959 (Ebert, *Chicago Sun-Times*, December 1, 1996; Guthmann, *San Francisco Chronicle*, January 12, 1996; Maslin, *The New York Times*, December 29, 1995). Susan Sarandon's declaration that "I've never seen a nun onscreen who's been a real person" says more about the films she hasn't seen than those she has (Abramowitz, *Premiere*, January 1996: 56). Drawing on her misty memory of *Heaven Knows, Mr. Allison* from Catholic girlhood, she implied that earlier films mainly used the woman religious to fantasize about forbidden and chastely erotic romance. This is a view that I have not disputed as much as opened up for further investigation in this study. Some of these films suggest that the religious state of celibacy is not a denial of sexuality or the need for intimacy but a redirection of these desires into Christian work, service, fellowship, and love (Bell and Sobo 2001: 12–15; Southgate 2001: 249; Abbott 2000: 393, 408). Reviewers of *Dead Man Walking* extolled the fact that Sarandon and Penn could "attain a level of intimacy rarely seen in American films" (Kowal 127; Levy 1999: 297), in their respective roles of dedicated nun and hardened criminal. As I have already shown, this celibate intimacy also complicated and enriched the relationship between the woman religious and an ungodly male in much earlier films like *Black Narcissus* and *Heaven Knows, Mr. Allison*.[3] *The Nun's Story* represented the professional partnership and eroticized bond that arose between a nursing sister and skeptical surgeon as the "sharing of the deepest aspirations of the human soul" (Ewens 1978: 256–7; Gleiberman, *Entertainment Weekly*, January 19, 1996: 37).

Sarandon was right that *Dead Man Walking* is ennobled by its "great love story—a test of absolute unconditional love" (Abramowitz 56). However, the intimacy that develops between this film nun and the death-row convict is not based on personal attraction or affinity, and this is what makes *Dead Man Walking* a significant departure from films

---

[3] Mary Ann Janosik initially explored the nun's call to intimacy in *The Nun's Story* and *Dead Man Walking* in her ground-breaking essay, "Madonnas in our Midst: Representations of Women Religious in Hollywood Film," *U.S. Catholic Historian* 15.3 (1997): 91–7.

of the past, and more theologically profound. Sister Helen must fight to overcome her natural aversion to Poncelet. In this way, the eventual bond that they form becomes emblematic of the love story between God and undeserving humanity, in which agape and eros meet, and the nun's gift of "absolute unconditional love" awakens in the convict a desire for communication, connection, confession, and finally, communion with another. Having confessed, Poncelet is touched with the grace to recognize Sister Helen's presence on death row as an act of love that is pure and generous self-giving, one that, though a prisoner, he has been free all along to reject or accept (Miller 2009: 63, 74). As he says simply, "Thank you for loving me." In his final hour, he testifies to the belief that thanatos does not prevail over eros: "It figures I'd have to die to find love." The nun has also given him an intimation of the divine "gift and mystery" (Donovan and Wusinich 2009: 36–7) that permeates religious life, indeed that makes ordinary life itself sacred. Film director Tim Robbins agreed that *Dead Man Walking* was "not a typical love story. . . . The stakes are much, much higher." He recognized its theological implications by adding, "if they find love out there, they are going to find redemption" (Biskind, *Premiere*, January 1996: 59).

After reading the memoir of her prison ministry, Robbins was struck by how different Sister Helen Prejean was "from some of the religious women and men I was taught by" in her "real hands-on approach to her faith" (Grundmann and Lucia 1996: 7). His film representation of the nun conveys the punishing effort and exhaustion that her hands-on faith required. He shows her willingness to persevere without cause or consolation when faced with a seemingly hopeless case like Poncelet. Indeed, these spiritual qualities distinguish Sister Helen from her clerical antagonist in the film, the morose and defeated Father Farley (Scott Wilson), who regards his prison chaplaincy as a dead-end job.[4] In Prejean's memoir, he is a kind but tired old man who adheres to "an old-school, pre-Vatican" Catholicism (1994: 25), but in the film he is represented as jaded, cynical, and bitter. Although he looks down on the nun, he is not a priest who can be looked up to, a priest like the humble and saintly Father Francis Chisholm in *The Keys of the Kingdom* (1944) or down-to-earth and fallible Father Murphy (Dan Frazer) in *Lilies of the Field* (1963),

---

[4]See Robert A. Orsi's discussion of the equivalent low status given hospital chaplains in *Thank You, St. Jude: Women's Devotion to the Patron Saint of Hopeless Causes* (New Haven: Yale University Press, 1996), 15, 160.

who sweats and drinks a lot. Yet both are represented as faithfully carrying out their pastoral duties and coming to thank God that they were bypassed for advancement and so given the opportunity to imitate Christ more authentically in his lowly status.

The conservative nature of Farley's "pre-Vatican" Catholicism is signaled in the film by his visceral reaction to Sister Helen's appearance at Angola. He interprets her secular dress as an act of religious and gender insubordination. He warns her that "these men don't see many females. For you to wear the habit might help instill respect. If you flout authority, it will only encourage them to do the same." Sympathy with the aims of the women's liberation movement and repeated conflicts with an institutional Church over the postconciliar modernization of religious life made progressive nuns suspicious of this clerical argument that the habit protected them. They were conscious that it often concealed the political desire to put them in their place and maintain the upper hand (Bernstein 1976: 206; Schneiders 2001: 168). The real-life Sister Helen Prejean recalled that in his first draft of the screenplay, Robbins also wanted to put her character back in the habit after this interview with the chaplain: "'No way,' I wrote in the margin. We haven't worn the habit for twenty years, and I surely wouldn't put it on because some chaplain told me to" (Prejean 1997: xii). The outmoded habit is an immediate bone of contention between the nun and the conservative chaplain because it is perceived as a litmus test not only of her unquestioning loyalty to papal authority but of submission to his waning priestly power:

FATHER FARLEY: You are aware of the Papal request regarding nuns' garments aren't you?
SISTER HELEN PREJEAN: The pope said "distinctive clothing" not habits.
FATHER FARLEY: I'm sure you will interpret it your own way. Whatever's convenient.

At the heart of the disagreement between Sister Helen and Father Farley is the issue of formal power over men's souls: "You can save this boy by getting him to receive the sacraments of the church before he dies." In other words, hand him over to me. While administration of the sacraments is still the prerogative of male priests in the Catholic Church, present-day women religious minister to the pressing needs of everyday life that cannot wait the delayed arrival or last-minute intervention of a clergyman.[5] As a spiritual counselor, like Sister Helen Prejean, former Catholic nun Lavinia Byrne found "that some of the tasks which I once understood to be priestly are increasingly coming women's way. In the field of spirituality and retreat direction in particular, . . . you have the care of souls, and you find yourself hearing confessions until you're blue in the face" (Loudon 1993: 179). The year before *Dead Man Walking* debuted, the apostolic letter *Ordinatio Sacerdotalis* defended the argument of the 1976 papal encyclical *Inter Insigniores* and maintained that "the exclusion of women from the priesthood is in accordance with God's plan for his Church," and that Christ only chose men to represent him in his ministry and carry on the mission of the first apostles (Byrne 1999: 128–30). Yet the rich irony of *Dead Man Walking* is that papal pronouncements do not stop either Matt Poncelet or the film viewer from seeing Sister Helen Prejean's incontrovertible resemblance to Christ in her humanity, personal compassion, offer of healing friendship, reconciliation, forgiveness, and "absolute unconditional love" (Abramowitz 56).

A well-meaning Angola prison guard articulates a view of the proverbial "good sister," which is just as conservative as that of Father Farley and indeed which assumes that the role of American women religious has not changed significantly in the fifty years since *The Bells of St. Mary's* was made. "What's a nun doing in a place like this? Shouldn't you be teaching children?" In a way, she still is as I shall indicate later.[6] It is true that earlier cinematic nuns such as Sister Benedict set a conservative benchmark for how women religious should look and deport themselves, what places and occupations they should be identified with, and where they should live and spend their time. However, at the same time, Sister Benedict and Sister Luke also exhibited Sister Helen's "hands–on" gospel faith through their unstinting devotion to teaching and nursing.

[5]Colleen McDannell observed that "when religious objects gain power through their association with the authority of religious institutions, that process is defined and administered by men. When objects are enlivened through the power of relationships, that process is frequently mediated by women." See McDannell, *Material Christianity: Religion and Popular Culture in America* (New Haven: Yale University Press, 1995), 38. This statement is illustrated by the contrasting religious attitudes of Sister Helen Prejean and Father Farley in the film. In her memoir, Sister Helen Prejean elaborates further on the difference between them: "His trust is in the ritual, that it will do its work. . . . For him, the human, personal interaction of trust and love is not part of the sacrament." See *Dead Man Walking: An Eyewitness Account of the Death Penalty in the United States* (New York: Vintage Books, 1994), 81.

[6]As a young nun, Sister Helen Prejean did, in fact, teach.

Although they both had a secure convent base, Sister Benedict, like Sister Helen, lived and worked in a run-down, inner city neighborhood, while Sister Luke did nursing in a mental asylum, the Congo, and a war hospital, which could hardly be called safe postings. Nuns in films of the past—Sister Benedict in *The Bells of St. Mary's*, Sister Luke in *The Nun's Story*, the Mother Abbess in *The Sound of Music*, Dame Philippa and Dame Catherine in *In This House of Brede*, and the missionary superior in *The Painted Veil*—also shared Sister Helen's belief that love could be hard work and that hard work was nothing without love. At the end of *Dead Man Walking*, Earl Delacroix (Raymond J. Barry), the father of one of the murder victims, will tell Sister Helen that he doesn't have her faith, only to receive the response, "It's not faith, I wish it was that easy, it's work." The sanctity of work and the belief in the power of love lie behind her insistence to Poncelet that "redemption isn't some kind of free admission ticket that you get because Jesus paid the price. You gotta participate in your own redemption. You've got some work to do."

While *Dead Man Walking* has been called the first Hollywood film to give a general audience an "honest-to-God" portrayal of the modern woman religious, its realism is the culmination of a postwar body of film work that explored the changing motivation, mentality, and identity of nuns as both women and religious. Yet what sets it apart from earlier films is the depiction of Sister Helen as a woman who reconciles past and present-day conceptions of religious life, who is a progressive nun following the radical call of the gospels but adhering to traditional principles of Catholic theology. Indeed, Robbins suggests how she represents the continuity between progressive and traditional nuns, pre- and post–Vatican II Catholicism, by opening his film with a sequence of shots that are both homage to the traditional figuration of nuns and a re-fashioning of their old image. It cleverly intertwines Sister Helen's former and current sense of identity as a woman religious and so recapitulates the transformational history of American Catholic nuns from the 1950s to the 1990s. At the same time, it alludes to Sister Helen's real-life testimony that she had to grow up out of the childhood faith that first inspired her to become a nun, and leave the convent and habit behind when her religious community changed its mission to ministry among the poor (Prejean 1994: 5).

This opening also establishes the complexity of human perception by suturing together recent and nostalgic personal memories with flashbacks to the crime scene that show how the distinction between the real and the imagined can become blurred. The sequence unfolds like stream of consciousness as Sister Helen drives, lost in thought, to the Louisiana state penitentiary in Angola for her first visit with Matthew Poncelet. Splices from an amateur family home movie, recording her investiture in the full habit of a newly professed nun, are cleverly interwoven with snippets from her contemporary religious life. She is shown dressed casually and living simply with another sister in the poor, black community of the St. Thomas housing project in New Orleans, teaching literacy to high-school dropouts in Hope House, and lending a hand in the nearby Prison Coalition office (Prejean 1994: 3–4). However, her memory narrative begins with a romantic shot of her as a young and happy bride, and so briefly sustains the secular misperception that later puzzles Poncelet. This is that Sister Helen should harbor conventional female desires "to fall in love, get married, have sex."

Subsequent interludes from the home movie correct this first impression and show that Helen was a bride of Christ participating in the traditional clothing ceremony that marked her formal admission to the order of the Sisters of St. Joseph of Medaille.[7] Films like *The Nun's Story* and *In This House of Brede* detailed what went on behind the scenes of her home movie, and give added intertextual meaning to this ceremony by suggesting ironic parallels between the religious formation of Sister Helen Prejean and the incarceration of Matthew Poncelet. As film director Zinnemann showed, there is a superficial resemblance between the rituals of admission to the enclosed convent and to a prison: the stripping of clothes, the removal of all personal effects, the shaving of hair, the loss of identity and privacy, and the assignment to a small cell (Bernstein 1976: 80).[8] The lives that Sister Helen and Poncelet lead are a study in contrastive chastity. For the traditional nun, celibacy is an elected state freeing her to love and serve God whole-heartedly, and a sign of her closeness

---

[7] Customarily, the clothing ceremony took place at the end of postulancy when the religious candidate receives the white veil of the novice as is the case for Sister Luke in *The Nun's Story*. However, Sister Helen is habited in the black veil of the fully professed nun. See Elizabeth Kuhns, *The Habit: A History of the Clothing of Catholic Nuns* (New York: Doubleday, 2003), 15, 22–5; Suzanne Campbell-Jones, *In Habit: A Study of Working Nuns* (New York: Pantheon Books, 1978), 81; and Marcelle Bernstein, *Nuns* (London: Collins, 1976), 99–100.

[8] Bernstein, *Nuns*, 101, notes that "no one is now compelled to crop (their hair) 'like a convict,' as one woman (religious) remembers with a shudder." In Tim Robbins's screenplay, *Dead Man Walking: The Shooting Script* (New York: Newmarket Press, 1997), 6, Poncelet writes to Sister Helen that he occupies a "six-by-eight-foot cell," which is about the size of Sister Luke's cell in *The Nun's Story*.

and gift of her body-self to Christ. For the prisoner, it is a hard punishment and sign of human deprivation, isolation, and alienation from others (Pitts 2009: 93–7; Bell and Sobo 2001: 8). When the real-life Helen Prejean became a nun in 1957, she was embarking on an institutional life that like Angola observed a strict routine and that was largely concealed from the outside world.[9] While contemplative communities observed a liturgical night office, Angola conducted its own gruesome night watch with executions held exactly on the first stroke of midnight. In her book, Sister Helen recalled the outrage of an attorney who defended death-row inmates: "Look how shamefully secret this whole thing is. . . . A few select witnesses brought deep inside this prison in the dead of night to watch a man be killed" (Prejean 1994: 94, 197).

In Kathryn Hulme's narrative close to *The Nun's Story*, Sister Luke spent her last night as a nun in a guest room, alone and apart from her fellow sisters. In *Dead Man Walking* (1995), the condemned man is moved to a separate death house on the eve of his execution. One nun compared religious departures in the pre–Vatican II convent to "a slaughter at a prisoner-of-war camp. The loss was swift and unexpected and no explanation was ever given" (Bernstein 1976: 324). In Zinnemann's film version of *The Nun's Story*, the nun exits the convent in dead silence with no sound, save for the somber tolling of the church bell, heard on the film track. In Robbins's film, Poncelet is not allowed to hear music in the countdown to his execution for fear he will become overly emotional. A traditional religious training in interior silence and celibate aloneness gives Sister Helen an instinctive understanding of his terrible inner loneliness and isolation as a death-row prisoner, though outwardly he is such an unsympathetic and repellant character. She tells Poncelet at their first meeting that they have other things in common: "We both live with the poor." She might have added they both have known life on the inside.

Dead Man Walking privileges the Catholic nun's point of view and introduces us to the characters, especially Poncelet, through the eyes, ears, sensibility, and imagination of Sister Helen (Stadler 2008: 52–5). Some critics assumed that her religious vocation "placed her outside the world" but "gave her the moral courage to face it unflinchingly" (Kamiya, *Salon*). Even traditional nuns hold that sisters in active ministries are most emphatically in the world if, they qualify, not of it (Donovan

---

[9]See George C. Stewart's account of the history and mission of the Sisters of St. Joseph of Medaille in *Marvels of Charity: History of American Sisters and Nuns* (Huntington, Ind.: Our Sunday Visitor Publishing Division, 1994), 151–2, 419–20.

and Wusinich 2009: 40). Sarandon brought this paradox to life in her screen portrayal of Sister Helen. The actress said she "tried to be a vessel through which the truth could be distilled" (Abramowitz 116). She shows a film audience what it is like, and furthermore what it takes, to be fully involved as a contemporary nun in the world. Yet although she is active and progressive, Sister Helen is also the bearer of the film's spiritual transparency and represents the nun as an intermediary who is not entirely of the world and gives witness to the belief that there is life beyond it. Like Hepburn's Sister Luke, Sarandon's Sister Helen acts through the often silent drama of her emotionally expressive face; still, soulful, piercing eyes; and wide, open gaze. Both director Robbins and the first reviewers of his film appreciated the demands of a religious performance that was narrower in dramatic range than Penn's and that required the passive skills of watching, hearing, reading, and reacting to others (Kowal 126; Turan, *The Los Angeles Times*, December 29,1995; Guthmann, January 12, 1996; Grundmann and Lucia 1996: 8). Indeed, just as Sister Helen redefines the vow of poverty by living outside the convent in the St. Thomas housing project and making herself radically available to its community, and will redefine chastity by calling Poncelet to the human vocation of intersubjective intimacy, so her face and eyes reflect the understanding of obedience that emerged in *The Nun's Story*. This is a vow of attentive listening and abiding with others, especially in those dark hours "when men in trouble want to talk about their soul," a vow that she breaks only once on death-row watch with Poncelet when she faints in the prison chaplain's office.

The Collaboration of Tim Robbins, Susan Sarandon, and Sister Helen Prejean, C.S.J.

All the nun films in this study have been shaped by the vision of male directors; but Tim Robbins gave the lead role of a woman religious to his then partner Susan Sarandon, who like him was raised as a Catholic, and collaborated with her on the development and interpretation of his screen script. Indeed, Sarandon was responsible for first bringing Sister Helen Prejean's eye witness account of death row to his attention and persuading him to make a film of her 1993 bestseller (Grundmann and Lucia 1996: 8). The role of an unprepossessing religious was a departure from the sexy, sassy, spirited older women the actress had played in *Bull Durham* (1988), *White Palace* (1990), *Thelma and Louise* (1991), and *The Client* (1994). However, Sarandon's career was intertwined with a commitment to political and feminist activism, sympathy for liberal causes, and concern for social justice that explain her attraction to the part of Sister Helen Prejean (Abramowitz 58, 116). Whereas George Schaefer and James Costigan only cursorily consulted author Godden and the Benedictine nuns of Stanbrook Abbey after drafting the screenplay of *In This House of Brede,* Robbins involved Sister Helen Prejean as a script consultant who "was right in there with him on every line, every scene" (Prejean 1997: xi). The result is a significant alteration in point of view and sympathies.

I suggested in the last chapter how *In This House of Brede* (1975) and *Agnes of God* (1985) are aligned with a Freudian and patriarchal perception of conventional femininity as childish and weak and traditional religiosity as feminized or deluded. In the original memoir and the film adaptation of *Dead Man Walking,* both male officials of the Catholic Church and Louisiana state prison system express the gender view that women are "naïve," "blind" to ugly reality, and "too emotional" (Prejean 1994: 120). Robbins does not gloss over Sister Helen's character flaws, any more than the actual nun did in her eyewitness account, but he certainly does not represent them as weaknesses of faith or femininity. Indeed, the film director followed the book in depicting Sister Helen as an individual who learns on the job, who makes grievous mistakes, who unwittingly causes great anguish to the victims' parents in offering consolation without just cause to the killer of their children, and who often feels out of her depth (Prejean 1994: 26, 32, 64–5, 74, 144). At the same time, Robbins upended gender perceptions by visualizing the blind faith that Sister Helen first needs to see Poncelet through the metal mesh grille of prison security and to hold on to the Christian conviction that "every person is worth more than his worst act." His film gradually illuminates the nun's strength, a strength she does not derive from religious superiority or lack of fear, but from her trust in God, the love of her family, and the practical as well as prayerful support of her sister community.[10]

---

[10]Sister Sandra M. Schneiders, I.H.M., believed that Sister Helen Prejean in *Dead Man Walking* "was affirmed and relieved in her demanding prison ministry by the timely support and even the humor of her local community." See Schneiders, *Selling All: Commitment, Consecrated Celibacy, and Community in Catholic Religious Life* (New York: Paulist Press, 2001), 321. Rebecca Sullivan, however, thought that the "whole community is mere backdrop, rather than an active, motivating force in her life." See Sullivan, *Visual Habits: Nuns, Feminism, and American Postwar Popular Culture* (Toronto: University of Toronto Press, 2005), 225.

Dead Man Walking is also infused with a feminist perspective that human-ized Nygren's austere theological definition of agape by conceptualizing eros as a more positive inner force, particularly for women (Guomunds-dottir 2002: 33–4). The film visualizes how knowledge is colored by emo-tions; moral understanding and judgment require depth in the discernment of personal feelings; and perspicacity depends upon alertness of mind and fully engaged use of the senses (Lauritzen 1998: 213; Stadler 2008: 3, 8, 10; Sarat 1999: 174, 185). Although Robbins amalgamated many of the events in the original book,[11] he put Sister Helen's most heartfelt remarks directly into the mouths of his nun protagonist. As a director, he understood the profound impact that "simple and pure emotions" can make on a film audience (Grundmann and Lucia 1996: 6; Gillett 2008: 1, 7, 20–4). The characters closest to Poncelet in the film are at a loss for words when they are most needed. His mother, Lucille (Roberta Maxwell), breaks down in front of the pardon board and his family sits with him in awkward silence, struggling for something to say, at his last visitor's meeting. After their departure, Sister Helen herself is almost incoherent with grief and dread in the death-house ladies room: "Oh God help me. It's such a terrible place. So cold, so calculated those murders. Help me, Jesus. Help me . . . be strong." Overwhelmed by the sense of death and the cold-blooded actions of both the killer and his executioners, all her efforts to secure a last-min-ute appeal having failed, aware as never before of her human weakness and powerlessness, the nun receives the gift of fortifying and sanctifying grace in answer to her prayer for help. This harrowing scene illustrates in the starkest possible terms that while eros has been reclaimed as a positive lifeforce, sometimes the human effort and striving associated with it are insufficient. Then agape is needed. God does indeed hear her cry and will come to her assistance in the hour of Poncelet's death.

Mother Love

The film also shows how Sister Helen's understanding of God derives from her love for Mrs. Prejean, the mother who first heard her cries, stooped down to take her in her arms, soothed her fears, and consoled

[11] In his screenplay, Robbins created Matthew Poncelet as a composite figure based on the first two condemned men whom Sister Helen befriended and counseled. The first was the Cajun loner Elmo Patrick Sonnier who, with his brother, raped and killed a teenage couple they surprised on "lovers' lane." The other was Robert Lee Willie who went on "an eight-day rampage" of abduction, rape, and stabbing with an accomplice. See Sister Helen Prejean, *Dead Man Walking*, 4, 118–19.

her. Unlike previous film novices like Sister Luke, Maria, Sister Joanna, and Sister Agnes, Sister Helen is fortunate to have the lifelong support of a natural mother, one who is closely identified with her religious vocation from the opening moments of the film. Indeed, Mrs. Prejean stands proudly next to her daughter in the home movie that memorializes her investiture. Sister Helen David Brancato, member of the Servants of the Immaculate Heart of Mary, testified to the influential role that a loving mother could play in the call to religious life.

> Part of that religious experience, part of that call, had to do with the love I received from my mother. My mother and I had this wonderful friendship. I think my relationship with God has an awful lot to do with that mother image, always feeling you could say anything, being very comfortable. (Rogers 1996: 190)

In her memoir, Sister Helen recalled being a daddy's girl (1994: 177). Robbins and Sarandon gave their film version of her book a further feminist accent by eliminating all trace of the daughter's attachment to her father and underlining Mrs. Prejean's position as the wise head of a non-patriarchal household—in effect, a kind of mother superior. Thus it is not the little-girl craving to be liked by the father but the mature desire to actively become like the benevolent mother that is the basis of her religious love and capacity for empathy with others. Mrs. Prejean presciently reminds the nun of what she ought, and initially fails, to do: "What about the parents of those victims. Have you seen them, counseled them?" She watches over her daughter during her troubled sleep the night before Poncelet's execution. In a scene full of Eucharistic significance, the nun acts out a dream in which both Matt and the young murdered couple celebrate his last supper with her family. Poncelet is given her customary seat, the place of honor at the right hand of her mother. Mrs. Prejean is depicted here as a living sign of Eucharistic life, and Matt is presented as the sociable person he might have been—and the person who will be an outcast no longer—if he achieves reconciliation and becomes part of the body of Christ (Rogers 1996: 194). In its surreal depiction of the kingdom of God as a banquet to which all are invited, and the body of Christ as composed of sinners and saints, killers and their victims, devout daughters and prodigal sons, the living and the dead, this scene has the same mystical power of the celebrated communion scene that closes Robert Benton's film *Places in the Heart* (1984).

When Helen wakes from this Eucharistic dream, her mother is there to comfort and support her as she did when her daughter was a feverish little girl: "You screamed, but I held you. I held you tight. A mother's arms are strong when her child's in danger." Her mother's consoling words remind her of the mothering God who can never forget or forsake her children and who guards them from the terrors of the night (Ps. 17:8, 91:5; Isa. 49:15). Helen's mother acts as her spiritual adviser and gives her the strength, in turn, to be a spiritual counselor and confessor to Poncelet and accompany him on his terrifying walk to death. Even her mother's words of concern—"You're in deep water, kid"—which echo Clyde Percy's (R. Lee Ermey) earlier warning—"Sister, you're in waters over your head"—mysteriously resonate with Jesus's gospel message of hope and reassurance to his apostles: "Put out into deep water and let down your nets. . . . Do not be afraid; from now on you will be catching men" (Luke 5:4–11).

As the real-life Sister Helen realized when she spoke to the guard in charge of death row, many of the prisoners were "just little boys inside big men's bodies, little boys who never had much chance to grow up" (Prejean 1994: 180). The spiritual tragedy then of the condemned man is that he is "destined to remain a child for ever" (Freud 1927, *SE* 21: 24). In her interactions with others, Mrs. Prejean's daughter is sensitive to the adult helplessness that lies hidden within evil and crime and is perpetuated by poverty, ignorance and illiteracy. In the opening sequence of the film, Sister Helen listens closely, arm around a mature student's shoulder in encouragement, as the woman softly reads out her composition in a literacy class at Hope House and articulates the nun's own search for "a love so big it takes in all evil": "There's a woman standing there in the dark and she's got big arms to hold you, but you won't feel those arms and that hug until you can see her face." These words also prefigure the loving support and comfort Sister Helen will receive from her mother on the night before Poncelet's execution. The final sentence that the adult student reads aloud becomes the voiceover on the home movie of Helen's investiture: "So you stand there waiting for the light at the end of the road." It is an apt commentary on the symbolic candle she holds as bride of Christ, which calls her to persevere in her religious vocation, "accomplish the desire Thou has given her,"[12] and let her light shine before men (Matt. 5:14–16). The wish to minister to those who are frightened of the dark or walk in darkness—the darkness of thanatos within them-

---

[12]Bernstein quotes the prayer that was said when the lighted candle was given to the bride of Christ at her clothing ceremony: "Grant her grace to persevere, so that with Thy protection and help she may accomplish the desire Thou has given her" (*Nuns* 78).

selves and others—will lead Sister Helen on a spiritual journey in which she brings the light of Christ into the house of death itself. At the time *Dead Man Walking* premiered, nuns still held fast to the belief that despite their dwindling numbers, "the lamps are not going out on religious life" (Rogers 1996: 273). In the dream scene, her mother made the strange, oracular statement: "Annunciations are common. Incarnations are rare. You're not a saint, Helen." The nun is not depicted as a saint in this film, but she is not simply represented as one who proclaims the good news of Christ. In a way, she is an incarnation, someone who embodies his Word, which, in the lofty opening of John's gospel, was "the light shining in the darkness that the darkness could not overcome" (1:5–6).

The more involved she becomes in the ethical complexities of Matt Poncelet's case, the more the nun will be challenged to look at the criminal and the crime through the light of a mother's eyes. The defense attorney, Hilton Barber (Robert Prosky), will advise Poncelet to have his mother at the hearing so that it will be more difficult for the pardon board to see him as a monster. But Sister Helen also considers Mrs. Poncelet's point of view:

> She's your mama, Matt, your mama. . . . What if you die and she hasn't had a chance to speak for you? Don't you think that's going to eat at her? She's always going to wonder if she could have saved you.

Figure 6-1. Sister Helen holds the candle that is symbolic of lumen Christi at her traditional clothing ceremony.

Figure 6-2. The real-life Sister Helen Prejean, dressed in casual clothes, joins the candle vigil before an Angola execution, and is flanked by actresses Susan Sarandon and Margo Martindale, who play Prejean and fellow nun Sister Colleen.

Mrs. Poncelet will bring a photo of her son as a toddler to the panel. She will be prevented from holding Matt one last time before he dies as she once did when he was small: "If I had put my arms around my boy I'd never have let go." Robbins would later recount the story of the shock jock on the radio in the South who changed his mind about the death penalty after seeing this scene: "I don't care what he did. No person, no mother should have to go through that" (Grundmann and Lucia 1996: 5–6). Sister Helen's compassion and heartache as a witness to such scenes will be further compounded by continual reminders of the children who have been lost through Poncelet's crime. Matt will show her a photo of the daughter he has seen only once in his life. Mr. Delacroix will show her a photo of one of Matt's victims, his son Walter (Peter Sarsgaard), as a little boy. Mrs. Mary Beth Percy (Celia Weston) will not allow her to forget that the other victim, her daughter Hope (Missy Yager), was once a child in her womb. She will graphically reconstruct the crime, telling Sister Helen that her daughter was found "nude, legs spread-eagled . . . her vagina all torn up."

Mrs. Percy will assume—as did some film critics of *Dead Man Walking*—that a nun is incapable of understanding her outrage and sorrow as a mother: "You don't know what it's like to carry a child in your womb and give birth, and get up with a sick child in the middle of the night." This essentialization of motherhood and implicit supposition that the celibate nun who forgoes reproduction lacks the emotional feelings "natural" to women were also heard in the angry letters written to the real-life Sister Helen after the execution and Christian burial of the convicted murderer Elmo Patrick Sonnier. These denigrated the women religious who opposed the death sentence as "a bunch of naïve, frustrated women who know nothing of the real world" (Prejean 1994: 109). Film reviewer Damian Cannon echoed these derogatory sentiments in describing her screen character as "a progressive nun who thinks that she understands the world (yet has never experienced something as fundamental as childbirth)" (*Movie Reviews UK*, 1997). In fact, the film makes the case that inspired both Anglican and Catholic nuns earlier in the nineteenth and twentieth century: It is not motherhood but mothering that is a God-given ability, one that both men and women, the sexually active and the celibate, can exercise on behalf of others (Byrne 1999: 38).

It has been said, to the annoyance of many adults, that a son or daughter is always a child to their mother. *Dead Man Walking* takes this minor irritant of family life and turns it into a profound psychological and spiritual truth. Jeffrie Murphy argued that "viewing the wrongdoer in this way—as the child he once was—should make it difficult to hate him with the kind of abandon that would make forgiveness of him utterly impossible" (2003: 266). Yet before Sister Helen can renew Poncelet's baptismal vows and confirm him as a "son of God," she must encourage him to grow up by taking responsibility for the death of Walter Delacroix and the rape of Hope Percy. His final confession to the nun crystallizes the role that the missing father has played in his criminal behavior, identification with the Aryan Brotherhood, and admiration for Hitler. As Freud suggested in *Group Psychology and The Analysis of the Ego*, the attraction to religion, para-military organizations, and fascism can arise out of childish fear and the longing for a paternal leader who will protect the individual from inadequacy, even if the cost is domination and continual threat of punishment (1921, *SE* 18: 93–9, 122–8; Benjamin 1988: 139–46). This identification with an admired but dreaded father figure is often accompanied by emotional detachment from the mother. For this reason, Poncelet must be fully reconciled with his mother by admitting his guilt to her on the phone before he can experience the conversion of heart that agape promises to the person who "surrenders . . . without reserve to God" (Nygren 1953: 213, 223). Then and only then can he make a good confession to Sister Helen.[13] As he tells the nun afterwards, he was intimidated by his partner Carl Vitello (Michael Cullen): "He was older, tough as hell. I was all boozed up trying to be as tough as him. I didn't have the guts to stand up to him. I told my mother I was yellow, goin' along with him." Why, however, does he conclude his confession by saying that "I never had no real love before," when it has been made dramatically evident that his mother loves him unconditionally and he loves her in return? I would argue that Poncelet has known love but he has been unable to show it because of the cult of male toughness that rules his behavior and defines love as weak, belittling, and effeminate (Nelson 1979: 263–4).

The Agape of the Cross

Sister Helen, however, bears witness to a love that is not weak, indeed that is tougher *than* hell, and that derives from her faith in Christ the Redeemer who harrowed hell and brought salvation to souls in captivity. She calls upon this God-man in the cold, clinical, and terrifying confines of the prison death house with its similarity to the Nazi gas chamber. She carries his subversive gospel of transformative love into the very place of execution.

> His love changed things. All those people nobody cared about . . . finally had someone who respected them, loved 'em, made 'em realize their own worth. They had dignity and they were becoming so powerful that the guys at the top . . . had to kill Jesus.

Although Sister Helen is a progressive nun in appearance, living arrangements, and ministry, her spirit of unselfish and whole-hearted service derives from the traditional religious belief that Christ's sacrificial death is the supreme channel of agape. Through the agape of the Cross, divine love pours into the world, offering humankind release from the shackles of sin and redemption to new life (Nygren 1953: 117, 212, 236; Donovan and Wusinich 2009: 23–32). Around her neck, Sister Helen

---

[13] While Tim Robbins told interviewer Peter Biskind that he didn't "think this is a movie about conversion" in "This is the End, My Friend," *Premiere* 9.5 (1996): 59, a view reiterated by Patricia Kowal in her review of *Dead Man Walking* in *Magill's Cinema Annual 1996: A Survey of the Films of 1995*: 127, they are both talking about changing people's minds about the death penalty, whereas I am talking about spiritual *metanoia* or a change of heart.

wears a crucifix, which is the only outward sign she is a nun and icon of her religious dedication to Christ. The crucifix is also the sacred symbol of an older, pre–Vatican II Catholicism valorizing devotional identifica-tion with Christ in his suffering. But Sister Helen never behaves as if her prison ministry to Poncelet is the heavy cross she must bear. Her actions bear witness not only to the Christ who was crucified but who has risen from the dead, and reflect the post–Vatican II accentuation of the resur-rection that prevails over suffering and death (Miller 2009: 74; Pitts 2009: 104; Ronan 2009: 9–11). As if to underline the power of agapaic love and Christ's victory over death, her crucifix sets off the security alarm when she first enters Angola (Reinhartz 2003: 51; Miller 2009: 74).

Prison ministry enabled the actual Sister Helen to see the crucifix with new eyes as the ancient symbol of "the Executed Criminal" (Prejean 1994: 62). This figure on the cross scandalized early Christians in the Roman world because it made the most humiliating and brutal of deaths a symbol of God's unqualified love for both the righteous and the rep-robate. The crucified Christ also bears witness to the Freudian truth that "we are never so defenceless against suffering as when we love" (Freud 1930, *SE* 21: 82), but goes beyond it by insisting that we are never greater or more god-like than when we face suffering and death with love.[14] Traditionally, nuns have seen religious life as a commitment to serve and help transform "the disfigured face of Christ in humanity" (Miller 2009: 75–8). Sister Helen not only imitates Christ but begins to restore his hor-ribly disfigured image in Matthew Poncelet when she tells him, "I want the last thing you see in this world to be the face of love. . . . So you look at me. I will be the face of Christ for you." However, Robbins was care-ful to indicate that Poncelet's suffering did not "make him into a Jesus," and that his upright cruciform position as he says his last words was not designed to be symbolic but rather was a realistic reconstruction of the execution table (Grundmann and Lucia 1996: 7). Indeed, Sister Helen re-coils when Poncelet suggests that in being condemned to death, he bears some likeness to the crucified Christ: "No, Matt. Not at all like you. . . . He changed (the world) with his love. You stood by and watched while two kids were killed." Nonetheless, Matt's cruciform position is a sign of

[14] In an "Angel on Death Row" interview with *Frontline* in 1995, Sister Helen Prejean repudiated the Old Testament image of a vengeful deity who "wants pain for pain, life for life, suffering for suffering, and a death for a death" as "a monster God." See http://www.pbs.org/wgbh/pages/frontline/angel/interviews/hprejean .html (accessed June 10, 2009).

the cross—a reminder that Christ died for incorrigible sinners and with criminals on either side—and symbol of the nun's faith in a God of love who has overcome death and gone before Poncelet to state execution.

Conclusion: The Call to Intimacy

The interviewer Peter Biskind praised Robbins for turning *Dead Man Walking* into "a romance of the soul" (59). As I have indicated, earlier films such as *Black Narcissus, Heaven Knows, Mr. Allison, Sea Wife,* and *The Nun's Story* played with this trope to develop a relationship of chaste eroticism between the nun and an attractive male without religion who articulated a secular, modern, and worldly point of view. The key difference in *Dead Man Walking* is that Poncelet is so repulsive a character as to make any intimacy between him and Sister Helen seem unimaginable. At the same time, the viewer cannot help but admire the nun for not flinching from close contact with him, not recoiling from his insolent stare that combines criminal calculation and sexual appraisal, and for returning it with her steady, sincere, and open gaze. The cynical prison chaplain warns Helen that "there is no romance here, Sister, no Jimmy Cagney, 'I've been wrongly accused if only I had someone who believed in me,' nonsense." There is no danger here of Sister Helen falling in love with Poncelet. A more venerable romance is at work in this film, which is the nun's quest with her searching, bloodhound eyes for some element of humanity—some fragment of the Christ whom she believes still dwells within the soul—to love in Poncelet.

The face-to-face intimacy that Sister Helen warily cultivates with Matt Poncelet does not draw upon the experience of romance that nuns like Sister Benedict and Sister Clodagh brought to religious life. She candidly admits to the condemned man that "I haven't experienced sexual intimacy with anyone. But there are other ways to be close. Sharing your feelings and thoughts . . . your dreams; that's intimacy, too." Helen's template for their developing relationship is the intermediate space that the child occupies with her mother. Indeed, the film acquires added intensity from the fact that the prison visit scenes visually replicate this transitional space where primary bonding first takes place and where the infant is free to play with inner, external, and shared reality. For the object-relations theorist Donald Winnicott, this intermediary realm is the later developmental site of all intense, absorbing, and creative experience (1992: 14); and for the psychoanalyst Ana-Maria Rizzuto, it is the nursery of the very soul where the individual first forms an impression of

God (1981: 177–80). One possible reason why Poncelet seems to have no center, to be so empty and unwilling to connect with others, is that he may not have developed this transitional site and without a psychical space that is alive, the death drive fills the vacuum (Bingaman 2003: 99).

In an illuminating analysis of the shot / reverse shot structure of the prison visits in *Dead Man Walking*, Jane Stadler shows in detail how the film visualizes the gradual reconstitution of this intermediate area of experience and represents it as becoming spiritually transparent (2008: 28–30, 48–61). Here, Sister Helen and Matt Poncelet answer Jesus's call to friendship by finding common ground, establishing rapport, and eventually achieving mutual understanding. This shared, intersubjective space is also the pathway out of the prisoner's inner death chamber: "It figures I'd have to die to find love. . . . Thank you for loving me." The action that produces this transformative statement of love and gratitude is Sister Helen's agapaic gift of herself, her time, and her undivided attention to Poncelet on death row. At first, the Angola security screen acts as a barrier to mutual recognition, which is not helped by Poncelet's inclination to lurk in the shadows like a hooded cobra waiting to strike. The reflections of light on the grille not only make it even more difficult for Helen to see him clearly but turn her into the maternal mirror in which the child need only behold himself and can objectify the woman as a non-person (Benjamin 1988: 23–4). However, as the two tentatively move toward respect, trust, and eventually love, the thick glass partition that separates them in the death house is visualized as more transparent and "thin," as though suddenly porous to the possibility of God.[15]

Matt's act of confession to the rape of Hope Percy and the murder of Walter Delacroix illustrates the potential that this intermediate space contains for reconciling external words and actions with deep, buried psychic needs—or in other words, to become a channel of grace. Robbins staged this turning point in the film as a simulacrum of the sacrament of reconciliation (or *penance* as it was once called) and as a "holy communion" of self-knowledge and acceptance by the other. It begins with Sister Helen sitting sideways and pressing her ear close to hear Poncelet speak through the holes in the thick perspex window of his death-row cell. She has symbolically adopted the position of a priest listening intently to sins con-

[15] In "'What is subordinated, dominates': Mourning, Magic, Masks, and Male Veiling," *The Veil: Women Writers on Its History, Lore and Politics*, ed. Jennifer Heath (Berkeley: University of California Press, 2008), 113, Heath notes that "the ancient Celts spoke of the 'thin,' where the spiritual and material rub against each other."

fided through the screen of the confessional; but she must wait until the last minutes of Poncelet's life for his final, halting admission of guilt and remorse.[16] This zone, intermediate between self and other, separation and connection, interior and exterior reality, becomes the site for a harrowing recollection and reconstruction of Matt's crimes. But it segues into a sacred space where God's forgiving and magnanimous love for humankind is first intimated through a glass darkly and finally is made visible in the face-to-face intimacy between the prisoner and the nun.

Dead Man Walking illustrates the dramatic transformation that cinematic nuns have undergone from early films such as *The Bells of St. Mary's* and *Sea Wife*, where they either silently accepted the fact that few people would take notice of them or wistfully observed that "no one ever looks at the face of a nun." Of course, the charismatic and beautiful actresses who played these nuns belie their characters' words. They not only made an audience look at the religious protagonist but made the nun's veiled and coifed face iconic. However, often it was the nun's face viewers remembered and not the films in which she featured. As a result, they have often seen no need for another backward glance, and so it has escaped their attention that film nuns might give veiled expression to more complex and conflicted desires on-screen, desires that evoke the dilemma of modern women who strive valiantly to follow an ancient religious calling and respond anew to the "Christ (who) plays in ten thousand places" (Gerard Manley Hopkins, "As kingfishers catch fire," l.12). *Dead Man Walking* reverses the movement of these earlier films with a nun protagonist who bids both the film viewer and male protagonist to "look at me" but does so without egotism, vanity, or self-regard. This is not to say that we receive no insight into what personally motivated Sister Helen to don the distinctive black and white habit of a traditional nun in the first place or give it up for unremarkable secular dress when she takes up a more progressive ministry in the late twentieth century. Rather, her limpid gaze, fully turned on Poncelet, directs attention back to the spontaneous, giving, sacrificial, Christocentric desires that make religious life a paradox and a continuing mystery: "I will be the face of Christ for you."

---

[16] Austin Sarat argues that acceptance of responsibility for one's offense, painful recollection of the wrong-doing, genuine sorrow for the harm that one has done, and change of heart affecting behavior and character are the necessary prelude to forgiveness. See Sarat, "Remorse, Responsibility, and Capital Punishment: An Analysis of Popular Culture," in *The Passions of Law*, ed. Susan A. Bandes (New York: New York University Press, 1999), 169–72, 179, 183–4.

CONCLUSION: SUSPECT DESIRES

THE END OF A RELIGIOUS
ILLUSION IN *DOUBT* (2008)?

*W*hen I originally conceived this study, I envisaged *Dead Man Walking* as "the light at the end of the road" for the representational journey that women religious take in postwar popular film. It would have been satisfying to conclude on an uplifting note with a film that means so much to contemporary nuns and that honors their continuing work of making Christ's compassionate presence felt in a troubled world. The intense and life-changing events in *Dead Man Walking* take place at Easter, the supreme Christian celebration, when the God-man who humbled himself on the Cross rose from the dead, and the dark desires alloyed with death were quelled by the power of redemptive love. However, at the end of 2008, more than a decade after *Dead Man Walking*, a darker and more equivocal film portrait of nuns appeared, one that turns back the clock to a conservative American Catholic era in the early 1960s, and is pervaded by a sense of convent atrophy and impending death. This is a dramatic departure from the mood of the film period when religious orders were flourishing; there was still propitious growth in the convent population; and there was a liberal expectation that religious life would be modernized, reformed, and reinvigorated after the Second Vatican Council ended. *Doubt* puts nuns back in their place—in the habit, in the sheltered convent, in the supposedly safe classroom with children, and in subordination to "higher" religious authority. Indeed *Doubt* is a depressing return to the psychodrama of earlier films, which registered the different ways in which the canon law code of 1917 imposed a "great repression" of desire on women religious, and which recorded the struggles of twentieth-century nun protagonists to conform to its antiquated regulation of their lives (Ewens 1979: 272–3; Coburn and Smith 1999: 224–5). Cloistral restrictions hid the lives and aspirations of modern women religious from view, and limited their range of services and scope for achievement. However, as religious historians Carol Coburn and Martha Smith have pointed out, twentieth-century stereotypes continued the work of repression by disregarding the proto-feminist history of American sisterhoods prior to the 1920s and burying the major accomplishments of later nuns "in either negative caricatures of rigid, ruler-wielding drones or in romantic and syrupy discourse describing passive and self-sacrificing martyrs" (1999: 223; McNamara 1996: 615). The harsh principal, Sister Aloysius, and the sweet school teacher, Sister James, bring these repressive stereotypes back to life again in Doubt.

Doubt (2008)

The 2008 film Doubt is set in 1964 when the American Catholic Church was suspended between pessimism and optimism. It was only one year after the sudden and untimely deaths of Pope John XXIII and President John F. Kennedy, and yet the Second Vatican Council (1962–65) was drawing to a close with the promise of renewal and cause for hope. However, Roger Deakins's cold and overcast cinematography underlines the fact that this is a winter of discontent;[1] the opening sermon from which the film takes its name emphasizes the faithful's feelings of unease and uncertainty; and the pressed flowers that the priest keeps in his breviary are the dry memento of a former spring. Doubt brings this study full-circle by mourning the lost innocence of intimacy in The Bells of St. Mary's as the Catholic parish, rectory, convent, and school become places where the young and the weak are threatened by predatory danger, and where priests and sisters may not be so good or happy after all.

Doubt not only punctures the conservative illusion that the preconciliar Church represented a golden age of religious certainty and rectitude, but the progressive illusion that begins to flower in the 1960s—that Vatican II would inaugurate "a glorious liberation from the dark ages of ecclesiastical authoritarianism and rigidity" (Ronan 2008: 326). Doubt is overcast by the postconciliar realization that the rapid and radical transition of religious institutional life from a venerable to a modern frame-

[1] Deakins also worked on Dead Man Walking.

work would precipitate a sharp decline of religious orders and the exodus of many nuns as well as priests from consecrated life (Schneiders 2000: 104). Eclipsing the gloom at the coming loss of the beloved "Father O'Malleys" and "Sister Benedicts" who once stood at the youthful heart of American Catholic life is the film's sense of foreboding as it sketches the religious and gender political roots of the clerical sex scandals that would erode Church moral authority, reputation, attendance, finances, and membership as the twentieth century came to an end.

Director John Patrick Shanley's film was an adaptation of his Pulitzer Prize–winning play, which was staged in 2004 and inspired by the national newspaper reports of clerical and episcopal misconduct that began to rock the Church in 2002. *The Boston Globe* triggered a public outcry with its exposé early that year reporting 250 cases of clerical sex abuse; and 12,000 further accounts were subsequently published by other news organizations. They revealed that over 4,000 American Catholic priests had been accused of molesting more than 10,000 children and youths since 1950. One priest was charged with systematic abuse over three decades.[2] As Anthony Burke Smith has noted, Bing Crosby's Father O'Malley in *Going My Way* became "a common reference point for media discussions" about the most damaging scandal in American Catholic Church history (2008: 124; Ronan 2009: 2). Likewise, O'Malley's woman religious counterpart, Ingrid Bergman's Sister Benedict in *The Bells of St. Mary's*, became a touchstone for Scottish director Peter Mullan in his excoriating depiction of the Irish nuns who ran asylums for fallen women in *The Magdalene Sisters*.

Like *Doubt*, this film was set in 1964, when sexual morality was about to assume increased importance in post–Vatican II church teaching, and sexual repression and self-sacrifice were still identified with Irish-American Catholicism. It premiered in 2002 when the stories of clerical sex abuse began to flood the American media and acquire unstoppable power and momentum (Ronan 2009: 3–4, 11, 71; 2008: 323, 326–7). Indeed, international press reports headlining accusations of "church sex

---

[2] Marian Ronan has written extensively on this topic in "The Clergy Sex Abuse Crisis and the Mourning of American Catholic Innocence," *Pastoral Psychology* 56.3 (2008): 321–39. See the facts and figures she amasses on pages 328–35. In her later book, *Tracing the Sign of the Cross: Sexuality, Mourning, and the Future of American Catholicism* (New York: Columbia University Press, 2009), she eloquently historicizes this crisis. I have found both her works most helpful in crystallizing my own final thoughts.

abuse" first made in 2002 were still circulating in 2012. One gave details of a Philadelphia trial in which "Catholic schoolboys said they had to strip before a priest and endure whippings as they played Christ in a passion play." The report suggests how veneration for the sacred suffering and sacrifice of the crucified Christ could become pathologically twisted by the secret pleasures of sexual sadism and victimization (*The South China Morning Post*, April 19, 2012: A17). Although it scandalized the Catholic Church at the time, *Black Narcissus* (1947) uncannily examined how ascetic severity could lead to the return of the sexual repressed in violent and destructive forms. *The Magdalene Sisters* melodramatizes but does not psychoanalyze this return of the repressed. However, it does represent the Irish Catholic nun in a similar manner to Anglican Sister Ruth in *Black Narcissus*—not as a believable character so much as a cipher who points to a "problem," the problem of sexual desire in the religious life. Thus, the nun again becomes "the unknowable Other, the site and source of Gothic horror" (Stone 2004: 269, 276).

Intertextual Allusion to The Bells of St. Mary's in The Magdalene Sisters (2002)

In Chapter 1, I emphasized the ways in which Bergman's film performance as a woman religious subverts the traditional dichotomy of sexuality and spirituality, passion and religion, eros and agape. She brought the film nun alive as not simply a holy but a whole person, although today "very few even take notice of" her achievement. As *The Bells of St. Mary's* grew old, Sister Benedict began to shrivel into a part object and become the subject of binary splitting. Peter Mullan's 2002 film *The Magdalene Sisters* taps into this binary representation by projecting Sister Benedict's paradigmatic good sister on-screen as an intertextual indictment of the Irish nuns who are malevolent caretakers of a Dublin magdalen asylum for "fallen women" in 1964. By 1964, *The Bells of St. Mary's* was nearly twenty years old. When it debuted back in December 1945, it was recommended as "a nice Christmas present for the whole family" (*Senior Scholastic*, December 10, 1945: 36). Now this "nice Christmas present" is served up as a cheap and—in a touch of devilish black humor—revolting holiday treat for the downtrodden inmates of the Dublin magdalen asylum. The head nun in *The Magdalene Sisters*, the warden Sister Bridget (Geraldine McEwan), is captivated by the film and sentimentally identifies with Sister Benedict as she mothers Patsy and offers up her life at the altar of sacrifice to God's "holy will." However, her captive audience of magdalens grimaces in disgust at the travesty of likeness between the exalted dedication of Sister Benedict and the exultant cruelty of Sister Bridget. While the 1945 film makes the idealized claim that "St. Mary's has grown old doing good," the Irish magdalen asylums have grown into institutions of evil in Mullan's film. Unlike Patsy, the young women in these asylums are treated like depraved children who can never be allowed to grow up. They are kept in protective custody from the romanticized gender desires which Sister Benedict recognized and indeed encouraged—to dress up, attend parties, and go on dates—and subjected to constant surveillance and punishment by harsh authoritarian figures who only see their capacity for sexual transgression (Finnegan 2004: 22–3, 42–3). Sister Benedict's sexual humanity; soulful beauty; and personal, erotic-inflected warmth are the symbolic polar opposite of Sister Bridget's inhumanity, perverted lust for money, and corruption of religious service through sadistic maltreatment of her wards. Her magdalens are not saved but condemned to a "living hell" (Finnegan 2004: 81) where they are indeed tempted to abandon all hope. Their asylum is a place of darkness and despair, notable for its pathological hatred of female sexuality, its demonization of desirable young women, and its cruel rituals for humiliating the sexed body and crushing the youthful spirit.

Bergman's big, beautiful, tear-stained face is a mute reproach to Sister Bridget and her fellow sisters in *The Magdalene Sisters*. They have made the film nun a "mirror, mirror on the wall," flattering their own spiritual vanity, but are blind to how she holds the mirror up to their false piety, religious hypocrisy, and self-deception. Magnified on-screen, Bergman's face reflects a nun who does not think it is a "sin (is) to be beautiful" or have sexuality, and who is spirited and headstrong like the rebellious magdalen Bernadette (Nora-Jane Noone). Indeed, the magdalen asylum is also a ghastly mockery of the cloistered life depicted respectfully in *The Nun's Story* and *In This House of Brede* with its appropriation of mother-daughter address; its involuntary vows of grinding poverty, terrified obedience, and numbing chastity; its rules of silence, strict discipline, and enclosure; its long hours of enforced prayer and hard, unpaid labor in the profitable laundries; its prohibition of friendship inside and communication with family and the world outside; its disfiguring uniform and brutal hair-cropping; and its erasure of the magdalen's sexed body, identity, and past (Finnegan 2004: 23–35).

Mullan's film lambasts the women who ran these asylums and depicts them as a travesty of the proverbial good sister. However, in his damning intertextual allusion to Sister Benedict's iconic role in *The Bells of*

St. Mary's, he implicitly suggests that these ungodly women became nuns because religious life satisfied the most egocentric and prideful aspect of eros, the desire to be socially idealized, revered, and elevated above others. Mullan has been criticized for his gross caricature of women religious. Yet his film was intended as a satire on the conditions that can give rise to religious or clerical malfeasance: namely, the uncritical deference of the faithful to religious figures invested with a high standing in a parochial Irish Catholic community where there is no apparent separation of Church and State; the absolute power that can corrupt those running a total institution not subject to independent inspection and controls; and the extreme repression that forces desire to seek covert, warped, and perverse expression (Harpham 1993: 51–3). Both Frances Finnegan's historical investigation of magdalen asylums in Ireland and Steve Humphries's TV documentary, *Sex in a Cold Climate* (1998), provide firsthand testimony that actual inmates viewed their women religious custodians as cruel bullies and "devils dressed up in nuns' habits."

Bergman's Sister Benedict is full of life on-screen, and embodies Christ's promise of abundant life to those who follow in his footsteps (John 10:10). By comparison, the nuns in *The Magdalene Sisters* are whitened sepulchers, virtuous on the outside but corrupt and dead on the inside (Matt. 23:27). Sister Benedict, however, functions not only as a signifier of reproach but recuperation for the nuns depicted in *Doubt.* Indeed, her personal drama in *The Bells of St. Mary's* has interesting points of comparison and contrast with *Doubt.* Bergman made religious life appear liberating for a woman. She represented Sister Benedict as hard-working and fulfilled professionally, determined and effective as a leader, and charismatic and animated as a teacher. She thus showed how grand it was to be nun. By the end of the film, Sister Benedict's high-spiritedness has been repressed, and her power, authority, convent community, school, teaching job, and the children she loves have all been taken away from her by "Mr. Nice Guy," Father O'Malley. Perhaps this is one reason why *The Bells of St. Mary's* is a film framed in darkness and the threat of death menaces its borders, despite its popular cultural image as a light and innocuous comedy. It is the Christmas film that Michael Corleone (Al Pacino) and his girlfriend Kay Adams (Diana Keaton) see before Michael is sucked into underworld crime and killing in *The Godfather* (1972). Anthony Burke Smith regards *The Godfather,* in turn, as a film that communicates the "longing for the cultural clarity of the old ethnic Catholic world that the postwar era had replaced with suburban, middle-class dreams" (2010: 223). This was a world revolving around urban, immigrant, working-class parishes on the point of decline when Sister Benedict digs her heels in at St. Mary's and Father O'Malley comes to the rescue of St. Dominic's in *Going My Way* (1944).

The religious habit of the nun and the clerical collar and suit of the priest in *The Bells of St. Mary's* also evoke the longing for the black-and-white morality of Catholic childhood that Patsy clung to, where "everything (was) so clean and so good." Sister Benedict personified this morality in her role as the strict school principal who clashed with O'Malley on Patsy's grade requirements for graduation and insisted on upholding St. Mary's high standards, even if it meant failing the student and breaking her heart.[3] Furthermore, the 1945 film light-heartedly dramatized a theme that runs as a continuous but knotty thread through to *Dead Man Walking* and *Doubt*: namely, the gender political skirmishes between nuns and priests, which register male clerical anxiety over the growing authority of confident and professionally competent women religious. The Church could canonically control the religious life but it could not so easily control the minds of the twentieth-century women who brought a modern outlook and aspirations to the convent. *The Bells of St. Mary's* resolved this intractable problem by cutting Sister Benedict down to size, reducing her to a consumptive invalid, and removing her from her dual office as convent superior and school principal. *Doubt's* Father Flynn (Philip Seymour Hoffman) only wishes he could do the same with school principal and superior Sister Aloysius Beauvier (Meryl Streep).

Nun Caricature

In marked contrast to the critical plaudits for Susan Sarandon's realistic representation of the contemporary nun in *Dead Man Walking*, *Doubt's* first film reviewers wondered whether Meryl Streep played Sister Aloysius for laughs. Manohla Dargis of *The New York Times* felt her performance made "no sense in the context of the rest of the film" but was "gratifying nunsense" (December 12, 2008). Critics such as Mick LaSalle from the *San Francisco Chronicle* (December 12, 2008), Stephanie Zacharek from *Salon.com* (December 12, 2008), and Roger Ebert (December 10, 2008) thought she camped it up or was a caricature out of a black comedy on good old Catholic school days. Their implicit question was why such a talented actress did not interpret this nun character more seriously given

---

[3] As I showed at length in Chapter 1, however, Sister Benedict's sexual morality is far less rigid.

the film's grave subject, and my initial concern follows on from this. Why did Streep exaggerate Sister Aloysius rather than interpret her as an imposing figure like Bergman's Sister Benedict in *The Bells of St. Mary's*?

What makes these questions more perplexing is the fact that Shanley, who was both the director and screenwriter of *Doubt*, expressly dedicated his film to "the many orders of Catholic nuns who had devoted their lives to serving others in hospitals, schools, and retirement homes" and who "have been much maligned and ridiculed."[4] Whatever he might say, Ella Taylor of the *Village Voice* observed that his characterization of nuns reflected considerable ambivalence about women, and suggested that this ambivalence could have had autobiographical roots (December 9, 2008). Shanley modeled his two principal women religious characters on his recollections of the Sisters of Charity who taught him when he was six years old. Indeed, he dedicated *Doubt* to his first-grade teacher who was originally called Sister James, and nearly fifty years later as Sister Peggy McEntee, became a technical consultant on the film (Brown, *New York*, January 12, 2009). A possible cause of his filmic ambivalence was visualized at the beginning of *The Bells of St. Mary's* where the community of teacher nuns initially made Father O'Malley feel like an awkward schoolboy again. This film pattern of childhood ambivalence is still at play in *Doubt* when Sister Aloysius sends Father Flynn packing with the order to cut his nails. However, while *The Bells of St. Mary's* was content to reduce Sister Benedict's character through infirmity, Shanley's film relies on the well-worn gender contrivance of splitting the woman religious in two, allocating Benedict's admired qualities of youth, beauty, kindness, compassion, and love to the inoffensive Sister James (Amy Adams), and her dangerous properties of authority, fighting spirit, strength of will, and resolve to the formidable Sister Aloysius.[5] Thus,

---

[4] See "*Doubt*: From Stage to Screen" in the DVD bonus features.

[5] I differ here somewhat from Stephanie Zacharek who concludes her December 12, 2008 film review in *Salon.com* by arguing that "Streep's character is designed to convey the idea that women in the church, circa the 1960s, were powerless yet possibly dangerous, while the men were entitled but confused, and probably mostly harmless." See http://www.salon.com/ent/movies/review/2008/12/12/doubt/index .html (accessed May 26, 2009). In an interview on his original play with Mary Kaye Schilling of *Entertainment Weekly*, Shanley acknowledged that Sister Aloysius was based on the principal of the first school he attended and that "there's a lot of what I believe and think in her." This admiration does not inform Streep's forceful delivery of the character in the film. See http://www.ew.com/ew/article/0,,1041504,00 .html (accessed September 18, 2009).

Sister Aloysius assumes features of the grotesque because the grotesque figure, as Margaret Miles explains, "can be defined only in relation to an ideal, standard, or normative form" (1989: 150)—which is, of course, Sister Benedict. Film reviewers James Berardinelli (*Reelviews.com*, 2009) and Alissa Tallman (*Suite101.com*, May 1, 2009) similarly concluded that Streep brought the monstrous feminine, or mother's shadow side, to life in her performance as a nun.

Shanley called his stage play of *Doubt* a parable. Streep's accentuation of the grotesque elements in Sister Aloysius's personality turns the screenplay into more of a Grimm's fairy tale. The characters in this film do not sleep particularly well at night. Sister James has bad dreams and is later kept awake by guilt over implicating Father Flynn in sexual misconduct with the school's only black student, Donald Miller (Joseph Foster). The school children start up in fear of the dark and of the wind that howls outside their bedroom windows. No mother appears at their side to guard and protect them from the terrors of the night like Mrs. Prejean in *Dead Man Walking*. All are "uniformly terrified" of the school principal, as if Sister Aloysius has stoked their nightmares and assumed a place there alongside the devouring witch and the wicked godmother. Father Flynn jokes with Sister James in the language of fairy tale that "the dragon is hungry" when Sister Aloysius snares her first student of the day for school detention, but betrays his own fear of her magical otherness as an authority figure. Alternating high and low-angle shots convey his further apprehension that she is watching, spying, and lying in wait for him like the all-seeing eye of God that stares down from the stained glass window on the convent landing. This sacred image would mutate into the evil, lidless, unsleeping eye of the Dark Lord in Tolkien's *Lord of the Rings*. This searching orb evokes childish trepidation and awe of the mothers and nuns who seemed to have eyes in the back of their heads. This is a myth perpetuated by the tip the school principal gives rookie teacher Sister James: that hanging a framed photo of Pius XII on the black board, even if he pre-deceased John XXIII, will allow her to see her class reflected in the glass. The irony is that while Pius XII is a ghost from the Catholic past that Sister Aloysius prefers, he was also the pope who anticipated the future work of the Second Vatican Council by perceiving the need for renewal of religious life in the 1950s (Burns 1994: 132–3). Sister Aloysius's lair is delineated by suspiciously bright colors in an otherwise gray landscape—a school entrance as red as Snow White's poison apple and a principal's office in the powerful hue of the green-eyed monster of jealousy. Sister James is played by Amy Adams who starred as the saccharine fairy tale princess in the 2007 Disney film *Enchanted* and who is associated in *Doubt* with a talismanic shade of "Virgin Mary blue" (Saito, *IFC Interviews*, December 12, 2008).

The Patriarchal Bargain

Although Sister Benedict was supported by a sizeable community in *The Bells of St. Mary's*, she dominated the film and effectively gave a solo religious performance like Sister Helen Prejean in *Dead Man Walking*. Sister Aloysius, however, is partnered by Sister James, and the two embody not only the child's fairy tale need to split others into hated or loved, all-good or all-bad objects, but the generational tension of the mother and daughter, the religious elder and young virgin that I explored in Chapter 5. In their contrasting attitudes to religious life, they also personify the conflict between the deeper or darker streak of eros and purer vein of agape that runs as an issue for further scrutiny, contestation, and resolution throughout this study. The relationship between the sister superior and junior nun is dramatized in *Doubt* to allow a complicated exposition of how power routinely worked in the Catholic Church prior to

Figure C-1. While this shot seems to reverse the gender politics of Figure 1-2, in *The Bells of St. Mary's*, with Sisters Aloysius and James looking down at the priests below their classroom window, it also conveys their envy of the power and freedom clergymen have outside where it's still a man's world.

Vatican II reform. Sister Aloysius diagrams the chain of command for Sister James at the outset of the film: "You are answerable to me. I to the monsignor, he to the bishop, and so on, up to the Holy Father." In this hierarchy, Father Flynn may not yet be a monsignor but he nonetheless regards himself as Sister Aloysius's superior, and her influence derives from a "patriarchal bargain," a time-honored strategy whereby women religious obtain secondary power in return for their service, submission, and sacrifice to a male-ruled Church (Ebaugh 1993a: 400–2). This bargain, however, can compromise the pure ideals of agape as selfless and disinterested surrender to God and "obedience to (Him), without any thought of reward" (Nygren 1953: 95). The priest will crudely remind the principal of the gender politics underlying this bargain—putting obedience to man rather than God first—a bargain that Sister Aloysius will come to see as a pact with the devil: "You have no right to act on your own. You have taken vows—obedience being one. You answer to me."

An earlier high-angle shot in which the nun observes Father Flynn conferring with the monsignor of St. Nicholas parish from Sister James's classroom window succinctly captures the gender political cost of the patriarchal bargain. This simple yet nuanced shot conveys the principal's resentful awareness of clerical back-slapping and cliquishness when she

Figure C-2. Father Flynn's self-satisfied face communicates his pleasure at having Sister Aloysius wait on him, and his clerical and sexist assumption that a nun's call to service includes serving him tea.

sees the priests on the sidewalk below, and the fleeting sense that she should not have to answer to men whom she regards as "beneath her" in professional capability. Never were the words of Sister Benedict to Father O'Malley truer than in this classroom scene: "On the outside it's a man's world." Even on the inside, Sister Aloysius's power is demonstrably conditional on priestly approval. In their first hostile interview, Father Flynn reminds her who is boss by sitting down without asking behind her principal's desk and waiting for her and Sister James to serve him tea.

The classic patriarchal bargain allowed older women to compensate for and be complicit in female subordination to male authority by having the upper hand over younger women (Kandiyoti 1988: 279). This is a depressing arrangement in which Sister Aloysius feels entitled to subjugate Sister James—watching her like a child to make sure that she eats up all the unappetizing food on her dinner plate, occupying her classroom desk without permission as Father Flynn later does hers, and going through her drawers for contraband items such as cough drops. Her petty tyranny extends from the classroom to the convent, from the nuns under her as superior to the school children who are at her mercy as principal. As Sister Sandra Schneiders, I.H.M., succinctly remarked, "Patriarchy is the system of domination which legitimizes the oppression of the weak by the powerful" (2004: v). Thus, one of the ironies of the film is that Sister Aloysius does not see the connection between her oppressive behavior to her fellow nuns, her draconian running of the school, and the priest's possible sexual power over a young black loner among the school children. Her authoritarian certainty is buttressed by the dogmatism of the Baltimore Catechism taught in parochial school (Ronan 2009: 6, 53). In one of her few signs of qualms, she acknowledges the truth of Father Flynn's claim that "we are the same, sinners"—a truth that is prefigured in her earlier comment on the accident-prone octogenarian, Sister Veronica: "Nuns fall, you know." Both are participants in a patriarchal food chain that facilitates different forms of predation, and fuels the Hansel and Gretel fears of the school children.

Religious Leadership and the Exercise of Power

American women religious were major beneficiaries of the Church's patriarchal bargain from the 1940s until the 1960s. In the film, we learn that Sister Aloysius became a nun after being widowed in the Second World War. She is therefore representative of the female cohort that entered the American Catholic convent in the immediate postwar era, found scope for the upward-reaching desires of eros, and went on to take the lead in the remarkable expansion of active religious orders (Curran 1989: 155).[6] Her status rewards as a nun include the considerable power she exercises inside St. Nicholas parochial school and the respect and deference she is accorded "on the outside" by the Irish and Italian immigrant parishioners in the Bronx neighborhood. One of the reasons why Sister Aloysius is so resistant to the winds of change that blow through her school and convent, however—despite her resolute closing of mind and shutting of windows—is that they threaten the benefits she has claimed in return for her personal compliance with the patriarchal system (Kandiyoti 1988: 282–5). Indeed, her sexual suspicions of Father Flynn and ruthless determination to "bring him down" are driven in part by the fear that his liberal, Vatican II–inspired views represent the future (Saito, December 12, 2008). This is a future in which she will lose the elite religious standing that compensated her for her position below clergymen by placing her above the laity, and in which she will no longer have more prestige than ordinary women, or be respected as a privileged daughter in the patriarchal family of the Church.

In *Black Narcissus*, Sister Clodagh bemoaned the fact that she "couldn't stop the wind from blowing." Her desire to control what is natural and to micromanage her environment is similar to Sister Aloysius's compulsion for maintaining order and discipline, and grim resolve to withstand the winds of change in *Doubt*. As with Sister Clodagh's censoriousness toward Mr. Dean, Sister Aloysius's hostility to Father Flynn involves a denial of her own sexuality and desire to dominate the feelings that are natural to the people around her (Reed 2004: 108, 307–8). Her unwholesome interest in sniffing out the sexual secrets of others suggests yet again how repression itself can give rise to secret sources of pleasure (Harpham 1993: 52). She represents the dark, unforgiving Irishness that was a feature of American immigrant Catholicism. With a Jansenist enthusiasm for sexual surveillance and prohibition, she is ever on the lookout for mortal sins of

---

[6] As Sister Sandra M. Schneiders, I.H.M., notes, and as I have discussed in Chapter 4, the 1950s and 60s were "the period of the Sister Formation Movement, when (American Catholic) women Religious became not only a spiritual vanguard but some of the best educated and most professionally competent women in the world." See Schneiders, *Finding the Treasure: Locating Catholic Religious Life in a New Ecclesial and Cultural Context* (New York: Paulist Press, 2000), 165. She concluded that "many people have suggested that the 1940s–1960s were the most developed and distinguished period in the history of ministerial Religious Life."

the flesh, even in an eighth grader who is boy-crazy (Ronan 2009: 28–9, 56–7): "Just get her through (grade school) intact," she instructs Sister James. When she arranges a meeting with Donald Miller's mother (Viola Davis), however—an encounter that symbolically takes place outdoors in windswept surroundings she cannot bring under her control—the domineering superior faces desires and needs she cannot subdue by the sheer force of her religious authority.

Film critics have called her dramatic confrontation with Mrs. Miller one of the most emotionally powerful scenes in the film, and rightly so; for Viola Davis plays a cleaning woman who is blessed with the purity of heart the nun lacks. Indeed, she steals this scene from Streep because her character demonstrates her moral superiority to the authoritarian principal. Sister Aloysius goes into this scene with the hierarchical assumption that she can lay down the law and make a poorly educated black woman who works as a lowly cleaner defer to her allegation that Father Flynn has sexually seduced her son. She has a rude shock in discovering that the laywoman does not automatically submit to her religious authority, agree with her moral judgment, or accept her word as gospel. Even the threat of blackmail—"I'll throw your son out of the school"—does not intimidate Mrs. Miller, but is met with the Christian forthrightness and rectitude of a Sister Benedict: "You'll hurt my son to get your way?"

Mrs. Miller also illustrates how the Catholic moral opposition to divorce and homosexuality can intensify the suffering of women and children who are victims of racial and sexual discrimination in society, and poverty and domestic violence in the lower-class black family. Her homophobic husband beats their son and is likely to kill him if given grounds for believing that Donald has had a gay relationship with the priest. In comparison to such violent paternal behavior, Father Flynn's gentle and protective treatment of Donald looks less like sexual abuse and more like surrogate fathering. As Mrs. Miller sums up her morally complex and ambivalent dilemma: "His father don't like him, kids don't like him, one man is good to him—this priest." This priest shows the boy the well-worn road to freedom for the downtrodden, which is the education that Catholic schools, seminaries, and religious congregations could provide. But when Mrs. Miller further defends her son by saying that "I'm talking about the boy's nature now. Not anything he's done. You can't hold a child responsible for what God gave him to be," what else might she be saying indirectly about the priest?

CONCLUSION: SUSPECT DESIRES

Homosexuality and the Homosocial World of the Clergy

The homosocial organization of the institutional Church has offered a haven to priests who felt odd-men-out because they were homosexual in the midst of homophobic Christians, and religious and spiritual in a secular and sexualized gay community. This awareness of being doubly marginalized could make gay priests sensitive to gender stereotyping of masculine behavior and compassionate to those who felt alone and excluded like the black student, Donald, at the all-white St. Nicholas (Boswell 1994: 362–4, 371–2). Where Father O'Malley is socially fluid in *The Bells of St. Mary's* (Burke Smith 2010: 70), Father Flynn exhibits a sexual indeterminacy that the title of the film cleverly alludes to as cause for "doubt." He does not share O'Malley's view that boys need to be toughened up and learn how to fight their corner like real men, lest they become effeminized by the female world of the parochial school and the home. His own interest in personal grooming, manicured nails, and flower-pressing is sexually suspect for Sister Aloysius but indicates a different cultural ideal of masculinity based on refinement and love of beauty. His sermons demonstrate his creative imagination, wit, and power as a narrator, and show his resemblance to Jesus who reached out to the outcast and victimized, and who taught and morally challenged others through the genius of his storytelling. The kindness and tenderness the priest shows the boy are the qualities that many women long to see in men, especially those who are imprisoned in emotionally impoverished definitions of masculinity. However, as Marian Ronan points out, pre-Vatican II American Catholicism was built not only on sexual repression, but on "repression of thought and creativity that dared extend beyond" its narrow definition of the faith (2009: 117). In his heartfelt address to Sister James, Father Flynn defends eros as the hopeful, hazardous love that preserves our humanity and offers resistance to thanatos, the instinct of death and destruction:

> There are people who go after your humanity, Sister. They tell you that the light in your heart is a weakness. Don't believe it. It's an old tactic of cruel people to kill kindness in the name of virtue. There's nothing wrong with love.

In Chapter 5, I explored the pervasive influence of Freud's psychological views on gender and religion. The cultural legacy of these views is that faith is feminized and, as Flynn now warns, love is seen as a weakness.

The Catholic priest who wears long skirted vestments and has become a eunuch for the kingdom of heaven, who articulates the words of a pacifist God of love, and who is also gay, might well feel assailed on all sides by social suspicions of his effeminacy as a man. But there is nothing weak or wrong with being homosexual as there is "nothing wrong with love." Indeed, the exceptional Mrs. Miller declares that gay orientation is God-given; and historian John Boswell and pastoral minister Sister Jeannine Gramick, S.L., have enumerated the gifts gay men brought to the priesthood and to the communities they served. However, films such as *Black Narcissus* and *In This House of Brede* suggested a larger question—not one of sexual orientation but of how the celibate expresses or represses, develops or destroys their capacity for love. As *Black Narcissus*, in particular, has shown, while celibate renunciation of sex is compulsory in religious life, it cannot be practiced successfully without recognition and sublimation of sexuality. The eventual understanding that "what is natural . . . has to flow" (Bourne 1996: 86) ultimately makes both Sister Clodagh and Dame Philippa more appreciative of the celibate gift for non-possessive, non-exclusive, but open-hearted friendships that free them to love more fully (Abbott 2000: 394).

Celibacy, Sexuality, and Abuse

In his extensive interviews with priests on the issue of sexuality, Richard Sipe discovered that those who genuinely felt called to religious celibacy did not feel threatened by women but saw them as equal partners in Christ (Sipe 1990: 281–2). In principle, this means that successful celibacy has the potential to challenge the hierarchical structure of the Church, which promotes male power and domination; the psychical splitting that allows both nuns and priests to divorce their religious life from their gender behavior or sexual (mis)conduct; and the institutional culture of unaccountability, secrecy, and collusion that has shielded both pedophile priests and abusive nuns from exposure (Sipe 1990: 54, 73, 181–6; Cozzens, *Commonweal*, April 22, 2005). The widespread media coverage of Catholic "men of God" who molested minors and reports of predatory behavior that extend back beyond the time of *Doubt* and *The Magdalene Sisters* to the 1950s will make a contemporary film audience wonder whether this culture has facilitated Father Flynn's transfer to three different parishes over a five-year period. The Church's historical adroitness at hushing up sexual scandal will also make them suspicious of the priest's agitated response when he learns that Sister Aloysius has not obtained a character reference by speaking to his previous pastor. Does he fear that she has obtained incriminating information through the informal network of nuns that subverts clerical cover-ups, a network that he indirectly castigates in his sermon on female gossip (Ebaugh 1993a: 401–2, 412)?

Circumstantial evidence—the boy's private visit to the rectory, the smell of altar wine on his breath when he returns to class, a sweaty undershirt the priest stuffed in his school locker—does not resolve the question of what Father Flynn may have "done" with Donald Miller and leaves the motives for his affection and comfort to the boy ambiguous. *Doubt* addresses a subject that has caused great pain and harm to men, women, and children—to the Catholic families whose offspring were prey to seduction or assault because they looked up to the priests in their parish as if they could indeed do no wrong like Father O'Malley; to the women religious whose young charges were abused on their watch; and to the good priests, heterosexual and gay, who have seen both homosexuality and the Catholic priesthood become identified with sexual deviance (Gramick 1989: xii; Dowd, *The New York Times*, March 20, 2002: A29; Ronan 2008: 332). However, *Doubt* is to be credited for not allowing an audience to jump readily to the same conclusion as Sister Aloysius—that the priest is certainly gay and if gay, sexually active or, worse, predatory.[7] Philip Seymour Hoffman's charismatic and complex performance as Father Flynn makes it difficult to demonize him as a "pedophile priest."

In films made fifty or more years ago, such as *Black Narcissus*, *Heaven Knows, Mr. Allison, Sea Wife*, and *The Nun's Story*, sexuality was the elephant in the room threatening to disrupt religious life. *Black Narcissus* suggested that celibacy is not automatic, easy, or necessarily healthy for all women who wish to be religious. *The Nun's Story, In This House of Brede*, and *Agnes of God* depicted the vocational preference for young and impressionable candidates who came directly from school and sheltered homes to the convent. Both *Brede* and *Agnes of God* examined the dangers of admitting novices who were psychosexually immature; had not resolved their primary relationships of love, hate, anger, and rivalry with their mothers or fathers; and whose God was a confused projection of the parents. *The Nun's Story* dramatized the religious drills that inculcated obedience and renunciation, but showed no explicit training

---

[7] In her article on "The Clergy Sex Abuse Crisis" (332–3, 336), Ronan discusses the shameful tendency of the Vatican and ecclesiastical hierarchy "to displace the public humiliation of the sex abuse crisis onto gay Catholic priests and seminarians."

or instruction in chastity. *Brede* tackled the issue of same-sex infatuation that was only hinted at in *The Nun's Story*'s interdict against "particular friendships," but which attested to "the regularity with which adolescent boys and girls form sentimental friendships with others of their own sex" (Freud 1905, *SE* 7: 229).

School leavers like Donald—who wants to become a priest like Father Flynn—would have been able to enter a so-called "minor seminary" after graduating from St. Nicholas at thirteen; and many men entered the seminary proper after high school (Woodward, *Newsweek*, March 4, 2002: 53). The homosocial and adolescent culture of the seminary could leave priests sexually undeveloped or ambiguous and fearful in their attitude to the opposite sex.[8] What is more, Catholic theological misogyny permeated the training for the priesthood, with seminarians instructed to be wary of women and the temptations posed not only by their female sexuality but by their craving for emotional understanding and friendship. Political advancement in the clerical hierarchy was defined by distance from women save the Blessed Virgin Mary and the priest's own blessed mother (Sipe 1990: 72; Orsi 1996: 75–6; Schneiders 2000: 238). The rectory scene in which Flynn gobbles red meat, gulps down wine, and makes crude fun of a female parishioner to his fellow priests gives a thumbnail sketch of a clubby world in which clergymen prefer their own company and derive enjoyment from the sexist devaluation and stereotyping of ordinary women.

Lust, Power, Inequality, and Inequity

In *The Magdalene Sisters*, the priest does not emerge from the seminary as the representative of Christ but as the leader of an Irish male pack that feels entitled to prey sexually on women. Nuns secretly partnered him by emotionally and physically abusing the violated girls placed in their custodial care. The film's protagonist, Sister Bridget, is an extreme caricature of the monstrous feminine, and exhibits Sister Aloysius's prison warden mentality where sexual vigilantism has replaced proper pastoral vigilance of the young. Both women characters suggest that lust for the

---

[8] A. W. Richard Sipe notes that before 1975, many priests entered the seminary in their high school years, thus sealing their sexual development in the adolescent phase. See Sipe, *A Secret World: Sexuality and the Search for Celibacy* (New York: Brunner/Mazel, 1990), 242–3. See his further comments on 54–5, 71–3, 84–5, 116–18, and 189–90.

power they lack in a male-dominated Church—and moreover power that is a displacement of sexual drives—is the occupational temptation of religious superiors with rigid and controlling personalities. The counter side of this lust for power is the priest's abuse of sacerdotal power through sexual lust. Ironically, it is the clear-headed Mrs. Miller who sees that Sister Aloysius can only expect a pyrrhic victory in going after Flynn on the suspicion that he has sexually interfered with her son: "Sister, you ain't going against no man in a robe and win. He's got the position." She is right. A weakness for young adolescent boys, especially one who wants to join the magic circle of clergymen, does not hurt Flynn's career but rather wins him promotion at the film's end as pastor of St. Jerome's parish. While Sister Aloysius's antagonism toward Flynn indicates that the traditional bargain between nuns and priests is breaking down, the clerical men's club closes ranks and keeps the sins and indiscretions of the father secret, leaving patriarchy "intact."

The latest in a long line of nun films that stretches back over sixty years, *Doubt* interrogates the gender and institutional politics that can give rise to abuse and that enabled the Church to conceal its sexual scandals for so long. The 1969 film *Change of Habit* dramatized the fallout from the Second Vatican Council, with active American sisters represented as change agents of reform, and the reactionary Father Gibbons emphatic that they should "know their place" and exercise no independent authority in his parish. *Doubt* is set before the Council has finished its work and depicts a Church in flux as an old school and a more liberal Catholicism jockey for influence. Unlike Sisters Barbara and Michelle in *Change of Habit*, Sister Aloysius fights the change and open-mindedness implicit in John XXIII's call for *aggiornamento*. Yet these two very different films both suggest the second-class status of women religious in a male hierarchal Church that had no real intention of fundamentally changing its own ways. *Doubt* uses the split in personalities between Sister Aloysius and Sister James to outline the complicated reasons why nuns first joined the convent, would soon leave in escalating numbers, lived with religious doubt and decline, or found constructive cause to remain.

If Sister James stays like her actual counterpart Sister Peggy McEntee, it will be because she shares Jesus's love for people, little children, and teaching. If she leaves, like cinematic nuns Sister Luke or Sister Barbara, it will be because her vocational commitment to nurture others is hampered by the institutional politics of religious life and requires an avenue for fuller and freer expression outside the convent (Halbertal 2002: 55). If Sister Aloysius leaves, it will be because her self-interests are increasingly blocked, her hard work is no longer sufficiently rewarded, and her secondary power as school principal and convent superior is diminished. If she stays, as seems likely given her age and inflexibility, she still faces the religious reform that is anathema to her. She will have to take off the close-fitting bonnet of a Sister of Charity that symbolically obstructs a more broad-minded and generous vision.[9] Perhaps, then, she will recognize her own supporting role in a system of domination that leaves weaker women and children vulnerable to the more powerful, and she will deconstruct a religious life that is based on the fiction of an unchanging Church, unambiguous truth, and Catholic faith as the answer to all doubt.

Turning Point

There is a moment of enlightenment in the film where Sister James suddenly realizes that the cost of keeping the patriarchal bargain is too high. This scene is also a symbolic shift from repression toward liberation as she consciously breaks free of the role of docile and obedient junior nun who simply follows the orders of her religious superior. Her class is unruly and she uncharacteristically shouts at them to be quiet. She has just witnessed Father Flynn tenderly comfort and hold Donald in the school corridor after he has been spitefully bullied. She now catches the boy daydreaming in the classroom and loses her temper. The adult viewer knows that this anger is a displacement of her renewed anxiety over the public display of intimacy between him and the priest. The sympathetic classmate sitting next to Donald, Jimmy Hurley (Lloyd Clay Brown), does not understand this, but is sensitive enough to grasp that something else is wrong. In a spontaneous show of Christian solidarity with his neighbor, Jimmy leaps to his feet and answers the question that leaves Donald standing embarrassed and tongue-tied. Sister James punishes him for this act of kindness by sending him to Sister Aloysius's office. When he returns sullen and upset, she shouts at him again in a display of petty territorial power: "This is my classroom, boy, don't you forget that." This threat reduces Jimmy to tears and it is only then that the nun realizes the spiritual temptation implicit in the Church's patriarchal bargain

---

[9] In her cast discussion with Dave Karger of *Entertainment Weekly*, Streep remarked that she used the Sisters of Charity's signature black bonnet as a metaphor for sight and perception, and wore her bonnet close-fitting to show how Sister Aloysius's vision was impeded. See "The Cast of *Doubt*" on the DVD bonus features.

with women religious—of gaining control through the loss of empathy; of being feared rather than loved by her students; of having power over those who are little and uncomprehending without exercising power over her own fearsome emotions; and of compromising or even perverting her religious commitment to agapaic service. Her response—"I'm sorry, Jimmy"—not only preserves her humanity but allows her to reject the bargain that has turned Sister Aloysius into a harsh disciplinarian.

Doubt gives no indication that Sister Aloysius ever had a religious calling but instead focuses on her political contestation of priestly power and higher authority. As a war widow, she shows that women may have had hard-nosed reasons for entering the convent even if they did not receive the gift of a vocation. In the late 1940s and early 50s, religious life gave Catholic women with drive and ambition unparalleled opportunities for an education, a career, managerial responsibility, and job satisfaction they could not obtain in the low-level employment open to them, such as shop and secretarial work, or in marriage and domesticity. In 1964, none of *Doubt*'s characters could foresee that this postwar golden age for American women religious was about to come to an abrupt end. However, like *Change of Habit*, the film sketches one gender political reason why nuns would start leaving religious life in 1966, and that is frustration with a Church that resisted sharing power and privileges more equitably with them, and with the high-handedness of religious authorities who treated them as inferiors or children (Burns 1994: 135, 150; Ebaugh 1993a: 411, 413).

For those who thrived on a Catholic education and have appreciative memories of nuns who stretched their minds and made them strive for excellence, Sister James's moment of lucidity in *Doubt* will be tinged with the nostalgic awareness that both parochial schools and the nuns who staffed them would dramatically decrease in numbers. In 1965, over 104,000 American sisters, out of an all-time peak of around 180,000, were teaching in the classroom. In 1966, they would begin to disappear from the Catholic school system, and by 1975, their numbers would have nearly halved as they either left religious life altogether or pursued new apostolates (Fialka 2003: 200; Carey 1997: 29, 33). Although the Vatican II call for renewal of religious life and revision of the code of canon law heralded the formal end of the "great repression" that had confined and restricted nuns since 1917, American sisters who were progressive would find to their chagrin that they continued to be hampered in their desire for greater liberation as modern women religious. Whether traditional or progressive in thinking, nuns constituted one of the most highly educated female groups in America, and did a great service to women by inspiring their female students to become high achievers. Still, they have yet to achieve decision-making power in a hierarchical Church that remains resolutely patriarchal (Burns 1994: 136–8, 150–6).[10]

While disappointment, disillusionment, and disintegration awaited the nuns who were energized by the liberal promise of Vatican II, *Doubt* dispels religious illusions that have caused needless suffering and bitterness to the cinematic sisters in this study. The first is that nuns can ever hope or should even desire to be perfect. To be sure, the characterization of Sister James and Sister Aloysius borders on stereotype and caricature; but notwithstanding, they know that "nuns fall" because they are fallible human beings. I would argue that this is a liberation of sorts. If we look back at Sister Benedict as a standard of comparison, she may look picture-perfect in *The Bells of St. Mary's*, but she had endearing foibles and forgivable weaknesses that are directly connected to her character strengths. As the film comes to an end, this human frailty is pathologized as "a touch of tuberculosis." Tellingly, it is her doctor who recommends a treatment that will become a story of repression for later cinematic nuns: "When Dr. McKay said you were perfect, he was right for that's what you are." Sister Luke will struggle to no avail to become perfect in *The Nun's Story*. Because "the perfect nun" is also a "living rule" who embodies the cloistral regulations and prescriptions codified by 1917 canon law, she has set herself an unattainable human goal. As she says helplessly, "The more I try, the more imperfect I become." Despite the assurance that she is loved, trusted, admired, and respected as a religious,

---

[10] *New York Times* columnist Maureen Dowd and *Tablet* features writer Phyllis Zagano reported in April 2012 that the Vatican Congregation for the Doctrine of the Faith (CDF) had decided to crack down yet again on the American Leadership Conference of Women Religious (LCWR). It comes as no surprise to hear that that they have rebuked these women religious leaders for their interest in "commentaries on 'patriarchy'" and "radical feminist themes incompatible with the Catholic faith"; for devoting too much attention to social services and causes, and too little to promoting the official Catholic line on female ordination, contraceptives, abortion, and homosexual relationships; and for flouting the authority of bishops as "the church's authentic teachers of faith and morals." Dowd asked why "the church leadership never recoiled in horror from pedophilia, yet it recoils in horror from outspoken nuns." See "Bishops Play Church Queens as Pawns," *The New York Times*, April 28, 2012, http://www.nytimes.com/2012/04/29/opinion/sunday/dowd-bishops-play-church-queen.html (accessed May 2, 2012); and Phyllis Zagano, "A Very Public Rebuke: The CDF and Women Religious," *The Tablet*, April 28, 2012, http://m.thetablet.co.uk/article/162647.html.

she will leave the convent with a heavy sense of failure. Sister Annette Covatta, member of the Sisters of the Holy Names of Jesus and Mary, expressed the relief of letting go of this ideological "baggage with the Second Vatican Council," and described the spirituality of perfectionism, which could intensify guilt and scrupulosity and erode the quality of religious life in the pre-Vatican II era:

> You achieve holiness through being perfect. Being perfect is a hard road, and so the more you suffer, the better chance you have to be perfect. When you have a choice, choose the hardest way, because there's more merit in that and you'll be closer to God. When I had a hard time as a human being and as this person who had so much life in her, I said, "That's what I'm giving up for this way of life." . . . If life was too joyful, I held it suspect. There was a lot of guilt. Life had to be hard. Jesus died on the cross, you know. (Rogers 1996: 131–2)

The second religious illusion that the film subverts is that faith can ever be wholly free of error or doubt. Sister Aloysius's judgmental certainty is a defense not only against the anxiety of unbelief, but against the forces changing the world outside her school window. Her suspicion of the world can be heard in the hostile remarks of some present-day nuns who speak disparagingly of contemporary society as a place of "secularism, hedonism, and utilitarianism" (Donovan and Wusinich 2009: 40); who bemoan "the cynicism and disbelief of this present age;" and who criticize postmodern man's "thwarted search for meaning" in egocentric pleasures and pursuits (Um 2009: 166–8). However, in the films I have studied, often "the world comes thrusting in," as Sister Clodagh exclaims helplessly in *Black Narcissus*; and women religious are thrown into contact with its godless forces of secularism, hedonism, materialism, cynicism, skepticism, and disbelief. Sister Benedict prays at the end of *The Bells of St. Mary's* that God will "remove all bitterness from my heart," when religious disappointment makes her question her faith. Sister Clodagh discovers that the missionary exposure to sacred and sexual alterity at Mopu has stirred her to relive "the struggle and the bitterness" of the dubious motives that led her to become an Anglican nun. Even angelic Sister Angela has momentary doubt about an unquestioned vocation and tells Mr. Allison that "perhaps God doesn't intend me to take my final vows." Sea Wife fears that she is at sea out of the religious habit, that "there's no faith anymore," and that the wellspring of her spiritual life has dried up. Sister Luke is disheartened to find that she has not reached a spiritual plateau "where obedience would be natural and struggle would end," and is told by her sympathetic superior that "there is no resting place ever" in religious life. Maria conveys the joy of hearing God's call in *The Sound of Music*, but when she takes refuge from her feelings for Captain von Trapp back in the convent, the Mother Abbess firmly advises her that the cloister walls "were not built to shut out problems." Sister James's uncertainty is aligned with the spiritual struggles and scruples of these cinematic sisters and reflects a faith that is prepared to give others the benefit of the doubt. In their manifest willingness to work with the forces of modernity and post-modernity and give witness to their counter-cultural values of poverty, chastity, obedience, and compassion, film nuns do project an important message that is consonant with the religious call to greater love—that God did not send his Son into the world to condemn it but to save it (John 3:17).

Doubt closes with a scene that intertextually alludes to the convent garden as a meditative space of tranquil faith in *The Bells of St. Mary's* and an agony of the garden in *The Nun's Story*. In *The Nun's Story*, Sister Luke admits final defeat to Reverend Mother Emmanuel—that she has come to "the end of (her) struggles"—while they sit together on an outdoor bench. As habitually hard on herself as she is scrupulously fair to others, the nun painfully confesses the chronic doubts, questions, imperfections, and infractions of the holy rule, which indicate that she is no longer faithful to the religious life. Repeating the spiritual advice that her superior general gave her when she first entered the convent, Sister Luke concludes, "You can cheat your sisters but you cannot cheat yourself or God." In *Doubt*, by contrast, the superior makes her confession to her subordinate after Sister James finds Sister Aloysius sitting silently outside in the cold, wrestling with a bad conscience, in a snow-covered Christmas garden. When pressed by the young and trusting nun, Sister Aloysius acknowledges that she had no actual proof of Father Flynn's sexual transgressions, but tricked him into resigning from the parish. Sister James exclaims in disbelief, "I can't believe you lied," and receives the morally expedient answer, "In the pursuit of wrongdoing, one steps away from God." There is an almost imperceptible pause as Sister Aloysius becomes conscious of how she has cheated her sisters, herself, and God with the lies that have defended her suspicious, antagonistic, and embattled faith. "Of course there is a price," she admits, instinctively fingering her crucifix, before she breaks down and cries, "Oh Sister James, I have such doubts. I have such doubts." Although *Doubt* is a film clouded by sadness, disillusionment, and bitterness, perhaps there is a wintry glimmer of hope at the end, for the dramatic collapse of Sister Aloysius's obdurate certainty does remove the obstacles to a crisis of faith, which might lead not only to spiritual pain but religious growth and change for the older nun.

Final Remarks

As I was concluding this study of cinematic nuns, the stars who enacted them, and the filmic dramatization of religious life, the Academy of Motion Picture Arts and Sciences announced that *God Is the Bigger Elvis* (2012) had been nominated for an Oscar as best documentary in the short subject category. Showbiz headlines of "The Nun Who Kissed Elvis" reminded the public that Hollywood stars not only played nuns but could, on rare occasions, feel called to become nuns in real life. *The New York Times* reporter Wendy Carlson saw it as "a story straight out of Hollywood" (February 24, 2012). Rebecca Cammisa's documentary profiles the life of Mother Dolores Hart who, in 1963, gave up a promising film career as the beautiful starlet who was poised to become the next Grace Kelly, first kissed Elvis Presley on-screen, and played a medieval nun in the Michael Curtiz film *Francis of Assisi* (1961) in order to enter the cloistered Benedictine Abbey of Regina Laudis in Connecticut. Her life before and after enclosure has both entertaining and arresting points of comparison with the representation of nuns in the movies, and highlights my argument—that feature films about women religious should not simply be dismissed as pure fiction, but have sometimes shown genuine insight into the challenges facing the twentieth-century women who consecrated themselves to a religious life.

The Hollywood Reporter trotted out *The Bells of St. Mary's* stereotype of the nun with the "luminous blue eyes" of a Hollywood beauty who was once romanced by the King of Rock 'n' Roll but whose heart was won by the King of Kings (December 23, 2011). Yet it missed a golden opportunity to note how this love triangle was a variation on the theme of *Change of Habit* (1969) where Elvis Presley's Dr. Carpenter woos a nun and asks her to choose him rather than Christ as her life partner. Mother Dolores remembers Presley for his courtesy and honesty on the set of *Loving You* (1957), qualities that are still apparent on-screen a decade later in *Change of Habit* (Adams, *Yahoo! Movies*, February 21, 2012). When Sister Michelle reappears in a full habit and tells him she is a vowed nun, he famously delights viewers with the retort, "didn't you take a vow of honesty," and so saves a platitudinous film from sinking without trace (Bernstein 1976: 299).

Mother Dolores was engaged before entering the convent. Like Gabrielle Van der Mal's boyfriend Jean in *The Nun's Story*, her fiancé Don Robinson never married. They remained close until his death in 2011, and he admitted, "I never got over Dolores. . . . I have the same thoughts (about her) today as I did 52 years ago" (Leonard, *Mail* Online, February 24, 2012). Struggling to make an interviewer understand how she could love Robinson dearly but long erotically for what he could not give, she said simply, "My search for God was a marital search" (*Elvis Australia*, May 10, 2012). Rumer Godden explained that this was why she felt compelled to write *In This House of Brede*, a novel about enclosed English Benedictines: "Nuns are dramatic. Theirs is the greatest love story in the world" (Godden 1989: 279).

Mother Dolores's own vow of honesty is most evident in her views on sexuality. When interviewer Thelma Adams remarked that one of the most intriguing features of the documentary is that "sexuality doesn't end at the cloister doors—but perhaps our notion of it does," the nun declared what films like *Black Narcissus* have shown—that sexuality features in the religious call to fuller humanity, but "has to go far beyond" sexual relationships to those of emotional and non-physical intimacy. In insisting that sexuality is part of the "total life experience" of all who love, Mother Dolores continues the work of representing nuns as whole persons. Indeed, it is notable that she did not renounce Hollywood with the devil and all his works after her entry into the cloister. She might well have been tempted to do so when the press circulated the ugly rumor that she sought refuge in the convent after having Elvis's love child (Leonard, February 24, 2012). This rumor reflects the anti-Catholic suspicion pervading *Agnes of God* (1985)—that cloistered nuns may have secretly engaged in illicit sexual activities. Instead, Mother Dolores affirmed her love for the movie world and the people she met there: "I adored Hollywood. I didn't leave because it was a place of sin" (Richard, *Huffington Post*, February 19, 2012).

Director Cammisa's mother was a nun for ten years; and her documentary on Mother Dolores Hart was not the first work in which she showed an interest in how and why modern women religious answered the call of a vocation. In 2002, her film subject was "Sister Helen," a Benedictine nun who was active and visible in the world, like Sister Helen Prejean, through her work in a South Bronx half-way house. The director took the title of her documentary on Hart's enclosed Benedictine vocation from the nun's emphasis on the continuity between her former secular and current religious life, the correspondences between human and divine love, and the connection between sacred and worldly experience: "I never felt I was leaving Hollywood. . . . The abbey was like a grace of God that just entered my life in a way that was totally unexpected—and God was the vehicle. He was the bigger Elvis" (Carlson, February 24, 2012). In words that echoed the visual message of *The Sound of Music*, she remarked elsewhere, "I left Hollywood at the urging of a mysterious thing called vocation. It's a call that comes from another place that we call God. . . . Why do you climb a mountain?" (Richard, February 19, 2012).

Yet diffused through her life story is a continual refrain in the films I have studied—that the life of a nun is hard, none more so than life in the cloister. Like Philippa Talbot who also insisted that she was not running from the world but to God when she asks "to try her vocation as a Benedictine in this House of Brede," Hart was not prepared for the austerity of enclosed life. After a life of comfort and luxury as a Hollywood star—she arrived at the abbey in an MGM studio limousine—she found it "very, very difficult" to adjust to the lack of privacy, the physical labor, the unending work of a self-supporting community, the periods of extended silence, and the unceasing dedication to the liturgy of the hours. Indeed, she acknowledged that she had severe doubts about whether she really should remain in the abbey during her first years there. Like Sister Luke, she came to realize that there was never any resting place in the religious life and to accept the fact that she would continue to "struggle" with her vocation. In words that could allow the religious principals in *Doubt* to "go in peace," Mother Dolores remarked, "I can understand why people have doubts. Because who understands God? I don't" (Carlson, February 24, 2012; Leonard, February 24, 2012).

This study has aimed to change the way nuns are seen on-screen by probing the stereotypes in which they have been immured and by considering how these women religious figures came to capture the popular imagination. It lifts the veil on their tumultuous struggle to reconcile conscious convictions and resolutions that have official religious approval with drives and desires that go back into their past and down deep into their unconscious. In looking at the interplay between the divine love of agape and the human passions of eros in the films, it taps into a long history and debate about the nature of love and desire. It challenges the view that Freud and his psychoanalytic disciples have nothing to tell us about faith; and it challenges the Freudian view that religion is largely a privatized and feminized world, and thus women religious should be regarded as mere "nurse-maids try(ing) to appease with their lullaby about

Heaven" (1930, *SE* 21: 122). It asks viewers to reconsider films that made the cinematic nun famous or infamous, beloved or disparaged. It looks closely at films have become frozen in time or preserved as a warm fuzzy memory like *The Bells of St. Mary's* and *Heaven Knows, Mr. Allison*. It offers provocative analyses that will stimulate viewers to reacquaint themselves with serious, disturbing, or problematic film portraits of nuns that still stir controversy such as Powell and Pressburger's *Black Narcissus*, Zinnemann's *The Nun's Story*, Jewison's *Agnes of God*, and even Robert Wise's *The Sound of Music*. It suggests how the film nun was used to explore questions that might once have been viewed as secular, sensational, or unseemly but are now recognized as having spiritual and theological validity. This is how sexuality can be integrated into the religious life without transgressing appropriate boundaries; how celibacy might enhance rather than deprive human intimacy of meaning; how a religious vocation understood only in terms of agape is incomplete without scope for other forms of desire; and how the self-sacrifice and self-giving service at the heart of religious life are a salutary reminder of the generosity, the exertion, the pain, and the cost of Christian love. In their dramatic contention with the lifeforce of eros and the divine force of agape, cinematic nuns occupy a space where the veil momentarily parts between this world and something beyond it, and the darkness of the screen— indeed the darkness of doubt in reaching out for a God eluding human comprehension or verification—is illuminated by their flickering desires.

WORKS CITED

Abbott, Elizabeth. *A History of Celibacy*. New York: Scribner, 2000.

Abramowitz, Rachel. "Mother Superior: Interview with Susan Sarandon." *Premiere* 9.5 (1996): 56–8, 116.

Adams, Thelma. "Love Me Tender: Mother Dolores Hart on Elvis, Her Big Bang Theory of Sexuality, and Her Oscar-Nominated Short 'God Is the Bigger Elvis.'" *Yahoo! Movies* (February 21, 2012). http://movies.yahoo.com/blogs/oscars/love-tender-mother-dolores-hart-elvis.html (accessed May 2, 2012).

Agee, James. Review of *The Bells of St. Mary's*. *The Nation*, January 5, 1946: 24–5.

———. Review of *Black Narcissus*. *The Nation*, August 30, 1947: 209.

Agnes of God (1985). Dir. and Prod. Norman Jewison. Writ. John Pielmeier. Perf. Jane Fonda, Anne Bancroft, and Meg Tilly. DVD. Columbia Pictures, 2002.

Akers, Regina T. "Jane Fonda (1937–)." In *Leaders from the 1960s: A Biographical Sourcebook of American Activism*, edited by David DeLeon, 358–66. Westport, Conn.: Greenwood Press, 1994.

Allen, Mary Prudence, R.S.M. "Communion in Community." In *The Foundations of Religious Life: Revisiting the Vision*, edited by the Council of Major Superiors of Women Religious, 113–54. Notre Dame, Ind.: Ave Maria, 2009.

Alpert, Hollis. "Fortitude." Review of *The Inn of the Sixth Happiness*. *Saturday Review*, December 13, 1958: 26.

———. "The World and the Spirit." Review of *The Nun's Story*. *Saturday Review*, June 27, 1959: 24.

America. "'The Nun's Story'—A Symposium: Author's View, Director's View, Views of Three Nuns, A Critic's View." June 27, 1959: 468–71.

———. "Reactions to *The Nun's Story*." January 26, 1957: 482–3.

Anastasia (1956). Dir. Anatole Litvak. Prod. Buddy Adler. Writ. Arthur Laurents. Perf. Ingrid Bergman, Yul Brynner, and Helen Hayes. DVD. Twentieth Century Fox, 2003.

Andrew, Geoff. Review of *The Sound of Music*. *Time Out*, September 26–October 2, 2007. http://www.timeout.com/film/reviews/75054/the_sound_of_music .html (accessed March 10, 2011).

WORKS CITED

Anonymous Dominican Contemplative Nun. "First Love." In *Vocation in Black and White: Dominican Contemplative Nuns Tell How God Called Them*, edited by the Association of the Monasteries of Nuns of the Order of Preachers of the United States of America, 63–6. New York: iUniverse, 2008.

"A Nunsploitation.Net Review." http://www.nunsploitation.net/movies/inthis house3.html (accessed July 24, 2009).

Armstrong, Karen. *Through the Narrow Gate: A Nun's Story*, rev. ed. London: Flamingo, 1997.

Aronowitz, Alfred G. "The Swinging Nuns." *Saturday Evening Post*, January 4, 1964: 66–7.

Association of the Monasteries of Nuns of the Order of Preachers of the United States of America, *Vocation in Black and White: Dominican Contemplative Nuns Tell How God Called Them*. New York: iUniverse, 2008.

Augustine, Mary, S.M.S.M. "Cross My Heart: Nun's Story JUST THAT!" *Marist Missions*, May–June 1958: 24–8.

Beattie, Tina. *New Catholic Feminism: Theology and Theory*. London: Routledge, 2006.

Bell, Sandra, and Elisa J. Sobo. "Celibacy in Cross-Cultural Perspective: An Overview." In *Celibacy, Culture, and Society: The Anthropology of Sexual Abstinence*, edited by Elisa J. Sobo and Sandra Bell, 3–26. Madison: The University of Wisconsin Press, 2001.

The Bells of St. Mary's (1945). Prod. and Dir. Leo McCarey. Writ. Dudley Nichols. Perf. Bing Crosby, Ingrid Bergman, and Henry Travers. DVD. Republic Pictures, 2003.

Belmont, Claudia. Review of *The Inn of the Sixth Happiness*. *Films in Review*, January 1959: 36–7.

Benjamin, Jessica. *The Bonds of Love: Psychoanalysis, Feminism, and The Problem of Domination*. New York: Pantheon Books, 1988.

Berardinelli, James. *Reelviews.com* 2009. Review of *Doubt*. http://www.reelviews. net/php_review_template.php?identifier=1417 (accessed May 26, 2009).

Bernstein, Marcelle. *Nuns*. London: Collins, 1976.

Bingaman, Kirk A. *Freud and Faith: Living in the Tension*. Albany: State University of New York Press, 2003.

Biskind, Peter. "This is the End, My Friend." *Premiere* 9.5 (1996): 59.

Black, Gregory D. *The Catholic Crusade against the Movies, 1940–1975*. Cambridge: Cambridge University Press, 1998.

Black Narcissus (1947). Prod., Dir., and Writ. Michael Powell and Emeric Pressburger. Perf. Deborah Kerr, David Farrar, Flora Robson, Sabu, Kathleen Bryon, and Jean Simmons. DVD. The Criterion Collection, 2000.

Blake, Richard A. "Women and Madness." Review of *Agnes of God*. *America*, October 19, 1985: 242.

Blye Howe, Mary. "Passionate Love." *Mars Hill Review*, Summer 1998: 53–62.

Bonderoff, Jason. *Mary Tyler Moore*. New York: St. Martin's Press, 1986.

Boswell, John. "Homosexuality and Religious Life: A Historical Approach." In *Sexuality and the Sacred: Sources for Theological Reflection*, edited by James B. Nelson and Sandra P. Longfellow, 361–73. Louisville, Ky.: Westminster / John Knox, 1994.

———. "Old Habits, New Habits." *New Republic*, January 6, 1986: 36–9.

Bourne, Stephen. *Brief Encounters: Lesbians and Gays in British Cinema 1930–1971*. London and New York: Cassell, 1996.

Breslin, Catherine. "Nun on Trial for Her Baby's Death: Will Sister Maureen's Tragedy Shake the Church?" *Ms.* March 1977: 68–71, 99–103.

Briggs, Kenneth A. *Double Crossed: Uncovering the Catholic Church's Betrayal of American Nuns*. New York: Doubleday, 2006.

Brock, Rita Nakashima. *Journeys by Heart: A Christology of Erotic Power*. Eugene, Ore.: Wipf & Stock, 2008.

Brode, Douglas. *Elvis Cinema and Popular Culture*. Jefferson, N.C.: McFarland, 2006.

Brown, David. *God & Grace of Body: Sacrament in Ordinary*. New York: Oxford University Press, 2007.

Brown, Lane. "Director John Patrick Shanley and His First-Grade Teacher on the Difference between *Doubt* and *The Flying Nun*." *New York*, January 12, 2009. http://nymag.com/daily/entertainment/2009/01/doubt_director_john_patrick_sh.html (accessed September 18, 2009).

Buettner, Elizabeth. *Empire Families: Britons and Late Imperial India*. New York: Oxford University Press, 2004.

Burke Smith, Anthony. "America's Favorite Priest: *Going My Way* (1944)." In *Catholics in the Movies*, edited by Colleen McDannell, 107–26. New York: Oxford University Press, 2008.

———. *The Look of Catholics: Portrayals in Popular Culture from the Great Depression to the Cold War*. Lawrence, Kans.: University Press of Kansas, 2010.

Burns, Gene. *The Frontiers of Catholicism: The Politics of Ideology in a Liberal World*. Berkeley: University of California Press, 1994.

Butler, Ivan. *Religion in the Cinema*. New York: A. S. Barnes, 1969.

Byatt, Anita S. *Possession: A Romance*. London: Vintage, 1991.

Byrne, Lavinia. *Woman at the Altar: The Ordination of Women in the Roman Catholic Church*. New York: Continuum, 1999.

———. *Women Before God*. London: SPCK, 1990.

Cabrini, Maria, O.P. "God Called Again." In *Vocation in Black and White: Dominican Contemplative Nuns Tell How God Called Them*, edited by the Association of the Monasteries of Nuns of the Order of Preachers of the United States of America, 23–6. New York: iUniverse, 2008.

Campbell, Debra. *Graceful Exits: Catholic Women and the Art of Departure*. Bloomington: Indiana University Press, 2003.

Campbell-Jones, Suzanne. *In Habit: A Study of Working Nuns*. New York: Pantheon Books, 1978.

Cannon, Damian. Review of *Dead Man Walking*. *Movie Reviews UK* 1997. http://
www.film.u-net.com/Movies/Reviews/Dead_Man_Walking.html (accessed
August 7, 2003).

Carey, Ann. *Sisters in Crisis: The Tragic Unraveling of Women's Religious Communities*.
Huntington, Ind.: Our Sunday Visitor, 1997.

Carlson, Wendy. "A Nun Returns to the Red Carpet: A Preview of 'God Is the
Bigger Elvis,' starring Dolores Hart." *The New York Times*, February 24, 2012.
http://www.nytimes.com/2012/02/26/nyregion/a-preview-of-god-is-the-
bigger-elvis.html (accessed May 2, 2012).

Carr, David. M. *The Erotic Word: Sexuality, Spirituality, and the Bible*. New York:
Oxford University Press, 2003.

Casablanca (1942). Dir. Michael Curtiz. Prod. Hal B. Wallis. Writ. Julius J. Epstein,
Philip G. Epstein, and Howard Koch. Perf. Humphrey Bogart, Ingrid Bergman,
and Paul Henreid. DVD. Turner Entertainment, 2003.

Case, Brian. Review of *Black Narcissus*. *Time Out*, March 8–15, 1995: 153.

Change of Habit (1969). Dir. William Graham. Prod. Joe Connelly. Writ. James Lee,
S. S. Schweitzer, and Eric Bercovici. Perf. Elvis Presley and Mary Tyler Moore.
DVD. Universal, 2002.

Chisholm, Anne. *Rumer Godden: A Storyteller's Life*, rev. ed. London: Pan Books,
1999.

Chittister, Joan, O.S.B. "Sister Says." In *Once a Catholic: Prominent Catholics and
Ex-Catholics Reveal the Influence of the Church on Their Lives and Work*, edited by
Peter Occhiogrosso, 1–23. New York: Ballantine Books, 1987.

———. *The Way We Were: A Story of Conversion and Renewal*. Maryknoll, N.Y.:
Orbis Books, 2005.

Christie, Ian. *Arrows of Desire: The Films of Michael Powell and Emeric Pressburger*.
London: Waterstone, 1985.

Christine, Maria, O.P. "An Extern Sister's Vocation Story." In *Vocation in Black
and White: Dominican Contemplative Nuns Tell How God Called Them*, edited by
the Association of the Monasteries of Nuns of the Order of Preachers of the
United States of America, 50–3. New York: iUniverse, 2008.

Chu, Cindy Yik-yi. *The Maryknoll Sisters in Hong Kong, 1921–1969: In Love with
the Chinese*. New York: Palgrave Macmillan, 2007.

Coakley, Sarah. " 'Batter my heart . . .'? On Sexuality, Spirituality, and the
Christian Doctrine of the Trinity." *Graven Images* 2 (1995): 74–83.

———. "Living into the Mystery of the Holy Trinity: Trinity, Prayer, and
Sexuality." *Anglican Theological Review* 80.2 (1998): 223–32.

Coburn, Carol K., and Martha Smith. *Spirited Lives: How Nuns Shaped Catholic
Culture and American Life, 1836–1920*. Chapel Hill: The University of North
Carolina Press, 1999.

Come to the Stable (1949). Dir. Henry Koster. Prod. Samuel G. Engel. Writ. Oscar
Millard and Sally Benson. Perf. Loretta Young and Celeste Holm. VHS.
Twentieth Century Fox, 1976.

Commonweal. "Come to the Fable." Review of *Heaven Knows, Mr. Allison.* March 29, 1957: 661.

Conn, Joann Wolski. "Dancing in the Dark: Women's Spirituality and Ministry." In *Women's Spirituality: Resources for Christian Development,* edited by Joann Wolski Conn. New York: Paulist Press, 1996.

Council of Major Superiors of Women Religious, ed. *The Foundations of Religious Life: Revisiting the Vision.* Notre Dame, Ind.: Ave Maria Press, 2009.

Cozzens, Donald. "Sex and the seminaries: what really ails them." *Commonweal,* April 22, 2005. http://findarticles.com/p/articles/mi_m1252/is_8_132/ai_n15696628/?tag=rbxcra.2.a.44 (accessed September 18, 2009).

Crist, Judith. "Sugar and Spice, but Not Everything Nice." Review of *The Sound of Music. New York Herald Tribune,* March 3, 1965. n.p.

Crowther, Bosley. "'Bells of St. Mary's' Makes Its Debut at the Music Hall with Bing Crosby, Ingrid Bergman in the Chief Roles." *The New York Times,* December 7, 1945: 26.

———. "'Inn of the Sixth Happiness at Paramount, Plaza.'" *The New York Times,* December 14, 1958: C2.

———. "'The Sound of Music Opens at Rivoli.'" *The New York Times,* March 3, 1965: 34, and online http://movies.nytimes.com/movie/review?res=9804E4 DF153CE733A25750C0A9659C946491D6CF.html (accessed March 10, 2011).

———. "Story of a Marine and a Nun Is at the Roxy." Review of *Heaven Knows, Mr. Allison. The New York Times,* March 24, 1957: sec. 11:22.

Csikszentmihalyi, Mihaly. "Play and Intrinsic Rewards." *Journal of Humanistic Psychology* 15.3 (1975): 41–63.

Curran, Patricia., S.N.D.deN. *Grace Before Meals: Food Culture and Body Discipline in Convent Culture.* Urbana: University of Illinois Press, 1989.

Daly, Mary. *The Church and the Second Sex,* rev. ed. Boston: Beacon Press, 2002.

Damico, James. "Ingrid from Lorraine to Stromboli: Analyzing the Public's Perception of a Film Star." In *Star Texts: Image and Performance in Film and Television,* edited by Jeremy G. Butler, 240–53. Detroit, Mich.: Wayne State University Press, 1991.

D'Angelo, Joseph F. Review of *Agnes of God. Films in Review,* December 1985: 619–20.

Dargis, Manohla. "Between Heaven and Earth, Room for Ambiguity." Review of *Doubt. The New York Times,* December 12, 2008. http://movies.nytimes .com/2008/12/12/movies/12doub.html (accessed May 26, 2009).

———. "A Plague Infects the Land, as Passion Vexes Hearts." Review of *The Painted Veil. The New York Times,* December 20, 2006. http://movies.nytimes .com/2006/12/20/movies/20veil.html (accessed May 26, 2009).

Davis, Francis. *Like Young: Jazz and Pop, Youth and Middle Age.* Cambridge, Mass.: Da Capo Press, 2001.

Davis, William N. "Epilogue." In *Holy Anorexia* by Rudolph M. Bell, 180–90. Chicago: University of Chicago Press, 1987.

Dead Man Walking (1995). Dir., Prod., and Writ. Tim Robbins. Perf. Susan Sarandon and Sean Penn. DVD. MGM Home Entertainment, 2005.

Deedy, John. *The New Nuns: Serving Where The Spirit Leads.* Chicago: Fides/ Claretian, 1982.

Deleyto, Celestino. "The nun's story: femininity and Englishness in the films of Deborah Kerr." In *British Stars and Stardom: From Alma Taylor to Sean Connery,* edited by Bruce Babington, 121–31. Manchester: Manchester University Press, 2001.

DelRosso, Jeana. *Writing Catholic Women: Contemporary International Catholic Girlhood Narratives.* New York: Palgrave Macmillan, 2005.

Denby, David. "Fire and Ice." *Premiere* 7.5 (1994): 43.

Detweiler, Robert. "Sisterhood and Sex: *Agnes of God, Mariette in Ecstasy,* and *The Company of Woman.*" In *Uncivil Rites: American Fiction, Religion, and the Public Sphere,* 75–97. Urbana: University of Illinois, 1996.

Deveau, Vincent. "Honoring the Artistry of Fred Zinnemann" (1994). In *Fred Zinnemann Interviews,* edited by Gabriel Miller, 135–44. Jackson, Miss.: University Press of Mississippi, 2005.

DiCanio, Margaret B. "Jane Fonda (b. 1937)." *Encyclopedia of American Activism: 1960 to the Present.* Santa Barbara, Calif.: ABC-CLIO, 1998, 104–6.

Dinnerstein, Dorothy. *The Mermaid and the Minotaur: Sexual Arrangements and Human Malaise.* New York: Harper Perennial, 1991.

Donovan, Agnes Mary, S.V. and Mary Elizabeth Wusinich, S.V. "Religious Consecration—A Particular Form of Consecrated Life." In *The Foundations of Religious Life: Revisiting the Vision,* edited by the Council of Major Superiors of Women Religious, 15–45. Notre Dame, Ind.: Ave Maria Press, 2009.

Doody, Margaret A. *The True Story of the Novel.* London: Harper Collins, 1997.

Dorsky, Nathaniel. "Devotional Cinema." In *The Religion and Film Reader,* edited by Jolyon Mitchell and S. Brent Plate, 407–15. New York: Routledge, 2007.

Doubt (2008). Dir. and Writ. John Patrick Shanley. Prod. Mark Roybal and Scott Rudin. Perf. Meryl Streep, Philip Seymour Hopkins, and Amy Adams. DVD. Miramax, 2009.

Dowd, Maureen. "Bishops Play Church Queens as Pawns." *The New York Times Sunday Review,* April 28, 2012. http://www.nytimes.com/2012/04/29/ opinion/sunday/dowd-bishops-play-church-queen.html (accessed May 2, 2012).

———. "Father Knows Worst: the lost world of Bing and Barry." *The New York Times,* March 20, 2002: A29.

Dreyer, Elizabeth A. *Passionate Spirituality: Hildegard of Bingen and Hadewijch of Brabant.* New York: Paulist Press, 2005.

Dukes, Thomas. "'Evoking the Significance': The Autobiographies of Rumer Godden." *Women's Studies* 20 (1991): 15–35.

Dyer, Richard. "*The Sound of Music.*" *Only Entertainment.* London: Routledge, 1992. 45–59.

————. *Stars*. London: British Film Institute, 1998.

————. *White*. London: Routledge, 2005.

Ebaugh, Helen R. F. "Leaving Catholic Convents: Toward a Theory of Disengagement." In *Falling from the Faith: Causes and Consequences of Religious Apostasy*, edited by David G. Bromley, 100–21. Newbury Park, Calif.: Sage, 1988.

————. "Patriarchal Bargains and Latent Avenues of Social Mobility: Nuns in the Roman Catholic Church." *Gender & Society* 7.3 (1993a): 400–14.

————. *Women in the Vanishing Cloister: Organizational Decline in Catholic Religious Orders in the United States*. New Brunswick, N.J.: Rutgers University Press, 1993b.

Ebert, Roger. "Audio Commentary." *Casablanca* (1942). DVD. Turner Entertainment, 2003.

————. Review of *Dead Man Walking*. *Chicago Sun-Times*, January 12, 1996. http://www.suntimes.com/ebert/ebert_reviews/1996/01/1015392.html (accessed July 8, 2003).

————. Review of *Doubt*. *Rogerebert.com*, December 10, 2008. http://rogerebert. suntimes.com/apps/pbcs.dll/article?AID=/20081210/REVIEWS/8121 (accessed May 26, 2009).

Eck, Diana L. *Encountering God: A Spiritual Journey from Bozeman to Banares*. Boston: Beacon Press, 1993.

Elvis Australia. "An Interview with Mother Dolores Hart." May 10, 2009. http://www.elvis.com.au/presley/an_interview_with_mother_dolores_hart.html (accessed May 2, 2012).

Enneking, Laura Schneider. "I Will Plunge with My Song." In *Forever Your Sister: Reflections on Leaving Convent Life*, edited by Janice Wedl, O.S.B. and Eileen Maas Nalevanko, 41–8. St. Cloud, Minn.: North Star Press, 1998.

Erikson, Eric H. *Young Man Luther: A Study in Psychoanalysis and History*. New York: Norton, 1993.

Esquire. Review of *The Sound of Music*. August 1966: 20–1.

Everson, William K. "Michael Powell Interviewed by William K. Everson" (1981). In *Michael Powell Interviews*, edited by David Lazar, 79–104. Jackson: University Press of Mississippi, 2003.

————. "Powell and Pressburger Retrospective." *The Museum of Modern Art Department of Film*. November 20, 1980–January 5, 1981. n.p.

Ewens, Mary, O.P. "Removing the Veil: The Liberated American Nun." In *Women of Spirit: Female Leadership in the Jewish and Christian Traditions*, edited by Rosemary Ruether and Eleanor McLaughlin, 256–78. New York: Simon and Schuster, 1979.

Feldman, Gene, and Suzanne Winter, prod. and writ. *Ingrid Bergman: Portrait of a Star. The Definitive Visual Biography*. Dir. Gene Feldman. Narr. John Gielgud. Oak Forest, Ill.: MPI Home Video, c. 1991.

Fialka, John J. *Sisters: Catholic Nuns and the Making of America*. New York: St. Martin's Press, 2003.

Fiand, Barbara. *Refocusing the Vision: Religious Life into the Future*. New York: Crossroad, 2001.

Film Daily. Review of *Heaven Knows, Mr. Allison*. March 15, 1957: 6.

———. Review of *Sea Wife*. August 6, 1957: 8.

Films and Filming. Review of *Sea Wife*. May 1957: 26.

Films in Review. Review of *The Inn of the Sixth Happiness*. January 1959: 36–7.

Finnegan, Frances. *Do Penance or Perish: Magdalen Asylums in Ireland*. New York: Oxford University Press, 2004.

Fitzpatrick, John. "Fred Zinnemann (1907)." In *American Directors, Volume II*, edited by Jean-Pierre Coursodon and Pierre Sauvage, 378–86. New York: McGraw-Hill, 1983.

Franchot, Jenny. *Roads to Rome: The Antebellum Protestant Encounter with Catholicism*. Berkeley: University of California Press, 1994.

Freitas, E. F. "IMDB mini-biography of Ingrid Bergman." n.d. http://www .imbd.com/name/nm0000006/bio.html (accessed December 4, 2007).

French, Brandon. *On the Verge of Revolt: Women in American Films of the Fifties*. New York: Frederick Ungar, 1978.

Freud, Sigmund. "Analysis Terminable and Interminable" (1937). *SE* 23: 216–53.

———. *Civilization and Its Discontents* (1930). *SE* 21: 64–145.

———. "The Dissolution of the Oedipus Complex" (1924). *SE* 19: 173–79.

———. *The Ego and the Id* (1923). *SE* 19: 13–66.

———. "Family Romances" (1909). *SE* 9: 237–41.

———. "Female Sexuality" (1931). *SE* 21: 225–43.

———. *The Future of an Illusion* (1927). *SE* 21: 5–56.

———. *Group Psychology and the Analysis of the Ego* (1921). *SE* 18: 69–143.

———. *Leonardo Da Vinci and a Memory of Childhood* (1910). *SE* 11: 63–137.

———. *Moses and Monotheism: Three Essays* (1939). *SE* 23: 7–137.

———. "On Narcissism: An Introduction" (1914). *SE* 14: 73–102.

———. "On Transformations of Instinct as Exemplified in Anal Eroticism" (1917). *SE* 17: 127–33.

———. *The Question of Lay Analysis: Conversations with an Impartial Person* (1926). *SE* 20: 183–250.

———. "Recommendations to Physicians Practising Psycho-analysis" (1912). *SE* 12: 111–20.

———. "Some Psychical Consequences of the Anatomical Distinction between the Sexes" (1925). *SE* 19: 248–58.

———. "Some Reflections on Schoolboy Psychology" (1914). *SE* 13: 241–4.

———. "The Taboo of Virginity" (1918). *SE* 11: 193–208.

———. "Thoughts for the Times on War and Death" (1915). *SE* 14: 275–300.

———. *Three Essays on the Theory of Sexuality* (1905). *SE* 7: 135–243.

———. "The 'Uncanny'" (1919). *SE* 17: 219–52.

———. "'Wild' Psycho-Analysis" (1910). *SE* 11: 221–7.

Gandolfo, Anita. *Testing the Faith: The New Catholic Fiction in America*. New York: Greenwood Press, 1992.

Gilbert, Helen. "Great Adventures in Nursing: Colonial Discourse and Health Care Delivery in Canada's North." *Jouvert* 7.2 (2003): 1–20. http://social.chass.ncsu.edu/jouvert/v7i2/gilber.html (accessed November 15, 2009).

Gilbert, Sandra M., and Susan Gubar. *The Madwoman in the Attic: The Woman Writer and the Nineteenth-Century Literary Imagination*, New Haven, Conn.: Yale University Press, 1979.

Gill, Brendan. Review of *The Sound of Music*. *The New Yorker*, March 6, 1965: 94–5.

Gillett, Philip. *Movie Greats: A Critical Study of Classic Cinema*. Oxford: Berg, 2008.

Gleiberman, Owen. "A View to Kill." Review of *Dead Man Walking*. *Entertainment Weekly*, January 19, 1996: 36–7.

Gnanadason, Aruna. "Women and Spirituality in Asia." In *Feminist Theology from the Third World*, edited by Ursula King, 351–60. London: SPCK, 1993.

Godden, Rumer. *Black Narcissus*. New York: Dell, 1963. First published 1939 by Peter Davies.

———. *A House with Four Rooms*. New York: William Morrow, 1989.

———. *In This House of Brede*. New York: The Viking Press, 1969.

———. *A Time to Dance, No Time to Weep*. New York: William Morrow, 1987.

Goffman, Erving. *Asylums: Essays on the Social Situation of Mental Patients and Other Inmates*. London: Penguin Books, 1991.

Goldenberg, Naomi R. *Resurrecting the Body: Feminism, Religion, and Psychoanalysis*. New York: Crossroad, 1993.

Good, David, and Ruth Wodak, eds. *World War to Waldheim: Politics and Culture in Austria and the United States*. New York: Berghahn, 1999.

Gordon, Mary. "Father Chuck: A Reading of *Going My Way* and *The Bells of St. Mary's, or* Why Priests Made Us Crazy." *Southern Atlantic Quarterly* 93.3 (1994): 591–601.

———. "Women of God." *Atlantic Monthly* 289.1 (January 2002): 57–91.

Grace, Pamela. *The Religious Film*. Chichester, U.K.: Wiley-Blackwell, 2009.

Gramick, Jeannine, S.L. "Preface." In *Homosexuality in the Priesthood and the Religious Life*, edited by Gramick, ix–xv. New York: Crossroad, 1989.

Grobel, Lawrence. *The Hustons: The Life and Times of a Hollywood Dynasty*. New York: Cooper Square Press, 2000.

Gross, Rita M. "Feminist Theology as Theology of Religions." In *The Cambridge Companion to Feminist Theology*, edited by Susan F. Parsons, 60–78. Cambridge: Cambridge University Press, 2002.

Grosz, Elizabeth. "Julia Kristeva." In *Feminism and Psychoanalysis: A Critical Dictionary*, edited by Elizabeth Wright, 194–200. Oxford: Blackwell, 1992.

———. "Phallic Mother." In *Feminism and Psychoanalysis: A Critical Dictionary*, edited by Elizabeth Wright, 314–15. Oxford: Blackwell, 1992.

Grundmann, Roy, and Cynthia Lucia. "Between Ethics and Politics: An Interview with Tim Robbins." *Cineaste* 22.2 (1996): 4–9.

Guomundsdottir, Arnfriour. "Female Christ-Figures in Films: A Feminist Critical Analysis of *Breaking the Waves* and *Dead Man Walking*." *Studia Theologica* 56 (2002): 27–43.

Guralnick, Peter. "Elvis Presley and the American Dream." In *Lost Highway: Journeys and Arrivals of American Musicians*, 118–40. Boston: Little, Brown, 1999.

Gustafson, Janie. "Celibate Passion." In *Sexuality and the Sacred: Sources for Theological Reflection*, edited by James B. Nelson and Sandra P. Longfellow, 277–81. Louisville, Ky.: Westminster / John Knox, 1994.

Guthmann, Edward. "Sarandon Dead-On in Prison Drama." Review of *Dead Man Walking*. *San Francisco Chronicle*, January 12, 1996. http://www.sfgate.com/cgi-bin/article.cgi?f=/c/a/1996/01/12/DD47500.DTL (accessed August 7, 2003).

Halbertal, Tova H. *Appropriately Subversive: Modern Mothers in Traditional Religions.* Cambridge: Harvard University Press, 2002.

Harpham, Geoffrey Galt. *The Ascetic Imperative in Culture and Criticism.* Chicago: The University of Chicago Press, 1993.

Hart, Henry. "*The Nun's Story.*" *Films in Review*, June–July 1959: 351–4.

Hartung, Philip T. "Drama with a Capital D." Review of *The Bells of St. Mary's. Commonweal*, December 28, 1945: 288–9.

———. "Nuns Fret Not." Review of *The Nun's Story. Commonweal*, July 17, 1959: 374.

———. Review of *Black Narcissus. Commonweal* August 22, 1947: 455.

———. Review of *The Inn of the Sixth Happiness. Commonweal*, December 19, 1958: 317.

Haskell, Molly. "Immaculate Deception." Review of *Agnes of God. Vogue*, October 1985: 92.

Haskins, Susan. *Mary Magdalen: Myth and Metaphor.* London: Harper Collins, 1993.

Haughton, Rosemary. *The Passionate God.* New York: Paulist Press, 1981.

Heath, Jennifer. "'What is subordinated, dominates': Mourning, Magic, Masks, and Male Veiling." In *The Veil: Women Writers on Its History, Lore and Politics*, edited by Jennifer Heath, 99–118. Berkeley: University of California Press, 2008.

Heaven Knows, Mr. Allison (1957). Dir. John Huston. Prod. Buddy Adler and Eugene Frenke. Writ. John Lee Mahin and John Huston. Perf. Deborah Kerr and Robert Mitchum. DVD. Twentieth Century Fox, 2003.

Hershberger, Mary. *Jane Fonda's War: A Political Biography of an Antiwar Icon.* London: The New Press, 2005.

Heyward, Carter. *Touching Our Strength: The Erotic as Power and the Love of God.* New York: Harper Collins, 1989.

Hirsch, Julia Antopol. *The Sound of Music: The Making of America's Favorite Movie.* Chicago: Contemporary Books, 1993.

Hollermann, Ephrem Rita, O.S.B. Introduction to *Forever Your Sister: Reflections on Leaving Convent Life*, edited by Janice Wedl, O.S.B. and Eileen Maas Nalevanko, xv–xviii. St. Cloud, Minn.: North Star Press, 1998.

Hollywood Reporter. "Dolores Hart, the Nun Who Kissed Elvis Presley, Needs Millions to Save Abbey." December 23, 2011. http://www.hollywoodreporter.com/news/dolores-hart-nun-kissed-elvis-presley-276286.html (accessed May 2, 2012).

————. "*'Heaven Knows, Mr. Allison'* Triumph of Artistry." March 15, 1957: 3.

————. "Unusual Theme and Story. Audrey Hepburn in Habit. Needs selling, but worth the effort." Review of *The Nun's Story*. May 6, 1959: 3.

Holzer, Henry M., and Erika Holzer. *"Aid and Comfort": Jane Fonda in North Vietnam*. Jefferson, N.C.: McFarland, 1990.

Hulme, Kathryn C. *The Nun's Story*. New York: Little Brown, 1956.

Hunter, Jane. *The Gospel of Gentility: American Women Missionaries in Turn-of-the-Century China*. New Haven: Yale University Press, 1984.

The Inn of the Sixth Happiness (1958). Dir. Mark Robson. Prod. Buddy Adler. Writ. Isobel Lennart. Perf. Ingrid Bergman, Curt Jurgens, and Robert Donat. Twentieth Century Fox, 2003.

The Internet Movie Data Base (*IMDb*). http://www.imdb.com.html.

In This House of Brede (1975). Dir. and Prod. George Schaefer. Writ. James Costigan. Perf. Diana Rigg, Judi Bowker, Pamela Brown, and Gwen Watford. VCI Entertainment, 2003.

It's a Wonderful Life (1946). Dir. and Prod. Frank Capra. Writ. Frances Goodrich, Albert Hackett, and Frank Capra. Perf. James Stewart, Donna Reed, Thomas Mitchell, and Henry Travers. DVD. Republic Studios, 2001.

Jaikumar, Priya. "'Place' and the Modernist Redemption of Empire in *Black Narcissus* (1947)." *Cinema Journal* 40.2 (2001): 57–77.

Janosik, Mary Ann. "Madonnas in our Midst: Representations of Women Religious in Hollywood Film." *U.S. Catholic Historian* 15.3 (1997): 75–98.

Jantzen, Grace M. *Becoming divine: Towards a Feminist Philosophy of Religion*. Manchester: Manchester University Press, 1998.

Jenkins, Clare. "'A Born Storyteller': Clips from the Interviews." In *Rumer Godden: International and Intermodern Storyteller*, edited by Lucy Le-Guilcher and Phyllis B. Lassner, 173–86. Farnham, U.K.: Ashgate, 2010.

Jones, Sara G. "Sexing the soul: nuns and lesbianism in mainstream film." *Perversions: The International Journal of Gay and Lesbian Studies* 4 (1995): 41–59.

Jung, Carl G. *Memories, Dreams, Reflections*. Edited by Aniela Jaffe. Translated by Richard and Clara Winston. New York: Vintage Books, 1989.

Kael, Pauline. "The Sound of . . . *The Sound of Music* and *The Singing Nun*." In *Kiss Kiss Bang Bang*, 176–8. London: Calder and Boyars, 1970.

Kamiya, Gary. Review of *Dead Man Walking*. "The Meaning of Death." n.d. http://www.salon.com/06/reviews/dead.html (accessed July 8, 2003).

Kandiyoti, Deniz. "Bargaining with Patriarchy." *Gender & Society* 2.3 (1988): 274–90.

Karger, Dave. "Dave Karger Talks to the Cast of *Doubt*." December 18, 2008. http://cinematicpassions.wordpress.com/2008/12/18/dave-karger-talks-to-the-cast-of-doubt.html (accessed September 18, 2009).

Kastin, David. *I Hear America Singing: An Introduction to Popular Music*. Upper Saddle River, N.J.: Prentice Hall, 2002.

Kauffmann, Stanley. "A Use of Beauty." Review of *The Nun's Story*. *The New Republic*, June 29, 1959: 21.

Kaylin, Lucy. *For the Love of God: The Faith and Future of American Nuns.* New York: William Morrow, 2000.

Kehr, Dave. "*The Bells of St. Mary's.*" *Chicago Reader* Online. 2003 http://onfilm .chicagoreader.com/movies/capsules/008.html (accessed July 2, 2006).

———. Introduction to *Black Narcissus* (1947). DVD. The Criterion Collection, 2000.

Kemp, Peter H. "How Do You Solve a 'Problem' like Maria von Poppins?" *Senses of Cinema* 22 (2002) http://www.sensesofcinema.com/2002/22/andrews .html (accessed March 10, 2011).

Kennelly, Karen M. "Women Religious, the Intellectual Life, and Anti-Intellectualism: History and Present Situation." In *Women Religious and the Intellectual Life: The North American Achievement*, edited by Bridget Puzon, 43– 72. San Francisco: International Scholars Publication, 1996.

The Keys of the Kingdom (1944). Dir. John M. Stahl. Prod. and Writ. Joseph L. Mankiewitz. Perf. Gregory Peck, Thomas Mitchell, Vincent Price, and Rosa Stradner. DVD. Twentieth Century Fox, 2006.

Khanna, Madhu. "The Goddess-Woman Equation in Sakta Tantras." In *Gendering the Spirit: Women, Religion & the Post-Colonial Response*, edited by Durre S. Ahmed, 35–59. London: Zed Books, 2002.

Klein, Melanie. *Love, Guilt and Reparation and other works 1921–1945.* London: Virago Press, 1994.

Knight, Arthur. "Two on the Isle." Review of *Heaven Knows, Mr. Allison. Saturday Review*, April 6, 1957: 27.

Kowal, Patricia. Review of *Dead Man Walking. Magill's Cinema Annual 1996: A Survey of the Films of 1995*, edited by Beth A. Fhaner and Christopher B. Scanlon, 125–7. Detroit, Mich.: Gale, 1996.

Kuhns, Elizabeth. *The Habit: A History of the Clothing of Catholic Nuns.* New York: Doubleday, 2003.

Kurth, Peter. Review of *Notorious: A Life of Ingrid Bergman* by Donald Spoto. http:// www.salon.com/july1997/sneaks/sneakb970704.html (accessed December 4, 2007).

Lacourbe, Roland, and Daniele Grivel. "Rediscovering Michael Powell" (1977). In *Michael Powell Interviews*, edited by David Lazar, 44–66. Jackson: University Press of Mississippi, 2003.

LaFontaine, Laurene M. "Out of the Cloister: Unveiling to Better Serve the Gospel." In *The Veil: Women Writers on Its History, Lore and Politics*, edited by Jennifer Heath, 75–89. Berkeley: University of California Press, 2008.

Landesman, Cosmo. "A Passage to India and My Imperial Childhood." *The Sunday Times*, July 1, 2007: sec.4:5.

Landy, Marcia. *British Genres: Cinema and Society, 1930–1960.* Princeton: Princeton University Press, 1991.

Larsen, Deborah. *The Tulip and the Pope: A Nun's Story.* New York: Alfred A. Knopf, 2005.

LaSalle, Mick. Review of *Doubt*. *San Francisco Chronicle*, December 12, 2008. http://www.sfgate.com/cgi-bin/article.cgi?=/c/a/2008/12/12/DDOA14OEC.DTL (accessed May 26, 2009).

Lassner, Phyllis. *Colonial Strangers: Women Writing the End of the British Empire*. New Brunswick, N.J.: Rutgers University Press, 2004.

Lauritzen, Paul. "The Knowing Heart: Moral Argument and the Appeal to Experience." *Soundings* 81 (1998): 213–34.

Lazar, David, ed. *Michael Powell Interviews*. Jackson: University Press of Mississippi, 2003.

Leddy, Mary Jo. *Reweaving Religious Life: Beyond the Liberal Model*. Mystic, Conn.: Twenty-Third Publications, 1990.

Le-Guilcher, Lucy, and Phyllis B. Lassner, eds. *Rumer Godden: International and Intermodern Storyteller*. Farnham, U.K.: Ashgate, 2010.

Leonard, Tom. "The nun who kissed Elvis: Extraordinary story of a starlet who turned her back on Hollywood to live in a convent." *The Daily Mail*, February 24, 2012. http://www.dailymail.co.uk/femail/article-2105662/Dolores-Hart-Elvis-Presleys-flame.html (accessed May 2, 2012).

Lester, Rebecca J. "Like a Natural Woman: Celibacy and the Embodied Self in Anorexia Nervosa." In *Celibacy, Culture, and Society: The Anthropology of Sexual Abstinence*, edited by Elisa J. Sobo and Sandra Bell, 197–213. Madison: The University of Wisconsin Press, 2001.

Levy, Emanuel. *Cinema of Outsiders: The Rise of American Independent Film*. New York: New York University Press, 1999.

Lieblich, Julia. *Sisters: Lives of Devotion and Defiance*. New York: Ballantine Books, 1992.

Life. "Ingrid Portrays a Missionary." Review of *The Inn of the Sixth Happiness*. January 12, 1959: 45.

———. "Movie of the Week: *Black Narcissus*." September 1, 1947: 55–56.

Lightman, Herb A. "'Black Narcissus': Color Masterpiece." *American Cinematographer*, December 1947: 432–57.

Loewald, Hans W. *Sublimation: Inquiries into Theoretical Psychoanalysis*. New Haven: Yale University Press, 1988.

London *Times*. "Britain's Best Bar Nun." Review of *Black Narcissus*. August 4, 2005: sec. T2:17.

———. Review of *The Bells of St. Mary's*. March 22, 1946: 6.

Lorde, Audre. "Uses of the Erotic: The Erotic as Power" (1978). *Sister Outsider: Essays and Speeches*. Freedom, Calif.: The Crossing Press, 1984. 53–9.

Losada, Isabel. *New Habits: Today's Women Who Choose to Become Nuns*. London: Hodder & Stoughton, 1999.

Loudon, Mary. *Unveiled: Nuns Talking*. Springfield, Ill.: Templegate Publishers, 1993.

The Magdalene Sisters (2002). Dir. and Writ. Peter Mullan. Prod. Frances Higson. Perf. Geraldine McEwan, Anne-Marie Duff, Dorothy Duffy, Nora-Jane Noone, and Eileen Walsh. DVD. Momentum Pictures, 2003.

Maio, Kathi. "*Sister Act* and the Habit-Forming Movie Tradition." *Sojourner: The Women's Forum* 17.11 (1992): 19–21.

Marchetti, Gina. *Romance and the "Yellow Peril": Race, Sex and Discursive Strategies in Hollywood Fiction.* Berkeley: University of California Press, 1993.

Marlett, Jeffrey. "Life on the Frontier: *Lilies of the Field* (1963)." In *Catholics in the Movies*, edited by Colleen McDannell, 149–75. New York: Oxford University Press, 2008.

Maslin, Janet. Review of *Dead Man Walking. The New York Times*, December 29, 1995. http://nytimes.com/movie/review.html (accessed July 8, 2003).

McCall, Craig. Documentary: "Painting with Light." *Black Narcissus* (1947). DVD. The Criterion Collection, 2000.

McCreadie, Marsha. *The Casting Couch and Other Front Row Seats: Women in Films of the 1970s and 1980s.* New York: Praeger 1990.

McDannell, Colleen. *Material Christianity: Religion and Popular Culture in America.* New Haven: Yale University Press, 1995.

———. "Why the Movies? Why Religion?" In *Catholics in the Movies*, edited by Colleen McDannell, 3–31. New York: Oxford University Press, 2008.

McLean, Adrienne L. "The Cinderella Princess and the Instrument of Evil: Surveying the Limits of Female Transgression in Two Postwar Hollywood Scandals." *Cinema Journal* 34.3 (1995): 36–56.

McLeer, Anne. "Practical Perfection? The Nanny Negotiates Gender, Class, and Family Contradictions in 1960s Popular Culture." *NWSA Journal* 14.2 (2002): 80–101.

McNamara, Jo Ann K. *Sisters in Arms: Catholic Nuns Through Two Millennia.* Cambridge, Mass.: Harvard University Press, 1996.

Michelman, Susan. "Breaking Habits: Fashion and Identity of Women Religious." *Fashion Theory* 2 (1998): 165–92.

Miles, Margaret R. *Carnal Knowing: Female Nakedness and Religious Meaning in the Christian West.* Boston: Beacon Press, 1989.

———. *Image as Insight: Visual Understanding in Western Christianity and Secular Culture.* Boston: Beacon Press, 1985.

———. *Practicing Christianity: Critical Perspectives for an Embodied Spirituality.* New York: Crossroad, 1988.

———. *Seeing and Believing: Religion and Values in the Movies.* Boston: Beacon Press, 2002.

Milhaven, John G. "Sleeping like Spoons: A Question of Embodiment." In *Sexuality and the Sacred: Sources for Theological Reflection*, edited by James B. Nelson and Sandra P. Longfellow, 85–90. Louisville, Ky.: Westminster / John Knox, 1994.

Miller, Gabriel, ed. *Fred Zinnemann Interviews.* Jackson, Miss.: University Press of Mississippi, 2005.

Miller, Paula Jean, F.S.E. "The Spousal Bond." In *The Foundations of Religious Life: Revisiting the Vision*, edited by the Council of Major Superiors of Women Religious, 47–83. Notre Dame, Ind.: Ave Maria Press, 2009.

Mitchell, Jolyon, and S. Brent Plate. *The Religion and Film Reader*. New York: Routledge, 2007.

Moffitt, Jack. "Adler-Robson Film Remarkable Story of a Modern Saint." Review of *The Inn of the Sixth Happiness*. *The Hollywood Reporter*, November 18, 1958: 3, 8.

Monthly Film Bulletin. Review of *Agnes of God*. March 1986: 73–4.

———. Review of *Heaven Knows, Mr. Allison*. May 1957: 55.

———. Review of *Sea Wife*. May 1957: 56.

———. Review of *The Inn of the Sixth Happiness* January 1959: 3.

Moore, Mary Tyler. *After All*. New York: G. P. Putnam's Sons, 1995.

Moore, Sebastian, O.S.B. "The Crisis of an Ethic without Desire." In *Theology and Sexuality: Classic and Contemporary Readings*, edited by Eugene F. Rogers, Jr., 157–69. Oxford: Blackwell, 2002.

Motion Picture Herald. Review of *Sea Wife*. August 17, 1957, Product Digest sec. 208:489.

Mourao, Manuela. *Altered Habits: Reconsidering the Nun in Fiction*. Gainesville, Fla.: University Press of Florida, 2002.

Ms. Review of *Agnes of God*. December 1985: 29.

Mumm, Susan. *Stolen Daughters, Virgin Mothers: Anglican Sisterhoods in Victorian Britain*. London: Leicester University Press, 1999.

Murphy, Anne F. Review of *Heaven Knows, Mr. Allison*. *Films in Review*, April 1957: 176–7.

Murphy, Jeffrie G. "Christianity and Criminal Punishment." *Punishment and Society* 5.3 (2003): 261–77.

Nalevanko, Eileen Maas. "Wind in the Pine Tree." In *Forever Your Sister: Reflections on Leaving Convent Life*, edited by Janice Wedl, O.S.B. and Eileen Maas Nalevanko, 7–15. St. Cloud, Minn.: North Star Press, 1998.

Nation. Review of *The Nun's Story*. July 4, 1959: 20.

Neal, Marie Augusta, S.N.D.de.N. *From Nuns to Sisters: An Expanding Vocation*. Mystic, Conn.: Twenty-Third Publications, 1990.

Nelson, James B. *Body Theology*. Louisville, Ky.: Westminster / John Knox Press, 1992.

———. *Embodiment: An Approach to Sexuality and Christian Theology*. Minneapolis, Minn.: Augsburg Publishing House, 1978.

Nelson, James B., and Sandra P. Longfellow, eds. *Sexuality and the Sacred: Sources for Theological Reflection*. Louisville, Ky.: Westminster / John Knox, 1994.

Neve, Brian. "A Past Master of his Craft: An Interview with Fred Zinnemann" (1996). In *Fred Zinnemann Interviews*, 145–56. Jackson, Miss.: University Press of Mississippi, 2005.

Newsweek. "Adrift—and a Mystery." Review of *Sea Wife*. August 26, 1957: 96, 98.

———. "Stirring the Melting Pot." Review of *The Inn of the Sixth Happiness*. December 15, 1958: 114.

———. "Storm-Beaten Narcissus." Review of *Black Narcissus*. August 18, 1947: 77–8.

New York. Review of *Agnes of God*. September 23, 1985: 95.

New Yorker. "I'll See You in My Dreams." Review of *Heaven Knows, Mr. Allison*. March 23, 1957: 103.

New York Times. "Thrill is gone from Scott Thriller." Review of *Sea Wife*. December 5, 1957: 45.

Nicholson, Virginia. *Singled Out: How Two Million Women Survived without Men after the First World War*. London: Viking, 2007.

Nolletti, Arthur, Jr. "Conversation with Fred Zinnemann" (1993). In *Fred Zinnemann Interviews*, edited by Gabriel Miller, 109–34. Jackson, Miss.: University Press of Mississippi, 2005.

———. "Spirituality and Style in *The Nun's Story* (1959)." In *The Films of Fred Zinnemann: Critical Perspectives*, edited by Arthur Nolletti, 119–38. Albany: State University of New York Press, 1999.

Novak, Michael. "The New Nuns." *The Saturday Evening Post*, July 30, 1966: 21–5, 66–72.

Nugent, Frank. "Ingrid Bergman of Sweden makes her Hollywood Debut in *Intermezzo* at the Music Hall." *The New York Times*, October 6, 1939: 31.

The Nun's Story (1959). Dir. Fred Zinnemann. Prod. Henry Blanke. Writ. Robert Anderson. Perf. Audrey Hepburn, Peter Finch, Dame Edith Evans, Dame Peggy Ashcroft, and Dean Jagger. DVD. Warner Brothers, 2006.

Nygren, Anders. *Agape and Eros: Pt. I, A Study of the Christian Idea of Love (1932); Pt. II, The History of the Christian Idea of Love (1938–39)*. Translated by Philip S. Watson. Philadelphia, Pa.: The Westminster Press, 1953.

O'Brien, Mary Judith, R.S.M., and Mary Nika Schaumber, R.S.M. Conclusion to *The Foundations of Religious Life: Revisiting the Vision*, edited by the Council of Major Superiors of Women Religious, 177–209. Notre Dame, Ind.: Ave Maria Press, 2009.

O'Brien, Tom. "*Agnes of God*: Rumors of Revelations." *Commonweal*, October 4, 1985: 530–2.

Occhiogrosso, Peter. *Once a Catholic: Prominent Catholics and Ex-Catholics Reveal the Influence of the Church on Their Lives and Work*. New York: Ballantine Books, 1987.

O'Hara, Shirley. Review of *Black Narcissus*. *The New Republic*, September 15, 1947: 37–8.

O'Murchu, Diarmuid, M.S.U. *Consecrated Religious Life: The Changing Paradigms*. Quezon City, Philippines: Claretian Publications, 2006.

Orsi, Robert A. *Between Heaven and Earth: The Religious Worlds People Make and the Scholars Who Study Them*. Princeton: Princeton University Press, 2007.

———. *Thank You, St. Jude: Women's Devotion to the Patron Saint of Hopeless Causes*. New Haven: Yale University Press, 1996.

Ostwalt, Conrad E. Jr. "Conclusion: Religion, Film, and Cultural Analysis." In *Screening the Sacred: Religion, Myth, and Ideology in Popular American Film*, edited by Joel W. Martin and Conrad E. Ostwalt Jr., 152–9. Boulder, Colo.: Westview Press, 1995.

Paietta, Ann C. *Saints, Clergy and Other Religious Figures on Film and Television, 1895–2003.* Jefferson, N.C.: McFarland, 2005.

The Painted Veil (2006). Dir. John Curran. Prod. and Perf. Naomi Watts and Edward Norton. Writ. Ron Nyswaner. DVD. Intercontinental Video, 2007.

Pally, Marcia. Review of *Agnes of God. Film Comment,* September–October 1985: 13–17.

Paris, Barry. *Audrey Hepburn.* London: Weidenfeld & Nicolson, 1997.

Parsons, Susan F., ed. *The Cambridge Companion to Feminist Theology.* Cambridge: Cambridge University Press, 2002.

Perkins, Tessa. "The Politics of 'Jane Fonda.'" In *Stardom: Industry of Desire,* edited by Christine Gledhill, 237–50. London and New York: Routledge, 1991.

Petroff, Elizabeth. *Consolation of the Blessed.* New York: Alta Gaia Society, 1979.

Phillips, Gene. "Fred Zinnemann Talking to Gene Phillips" (1973). In *Fred Zinnemann Interviews,* edited by Gabriel Miller, 37–46. Jackson, Miss.: University Press of Mississippi, 2005.

Pielmeier, John. *Agnes of God: A Drama.* New York: Samuel French, 1982.

Pitts, Mary Dominic, O.P. "The Threefold Response of the Vows." In *The Foundations of Religious Life: Revisiting the Vision,* edited by the Council of Major Superiors of Women Religious, 85–111. Notre Dame, Ind.: Ave Maria Press, 2009.

Powell, Michael. *A Life in Movies: An Autobiography.* London: Faber and Faber, 2000. First published 1986 by William Heinemann.

———. *Michael Powell Special Collection.* Box 4. British Film Institute Library.

———. *Million Dollar Movie.* New York: Random House, 1995.

Powell, Michael, and Martin Scorsese. "Audio Commentary: A Conversation with late director Michael Powell and Martin Scorsese." *Black Narcissus* (1947). DVD. The Criterion Collection, 2000.

Prejean, Helen. "Angel on Death Row" Interview. *Frontline* 1995. http://www.pbs .org/wgbh/pages/frontline/angel/interviews/hprejean.html (accessed June 10, 2009).

———. *Dead Man Walking: An Eyewitness Account of the Death Penalty in the United States.* New York: Vintage Books, 1994.

———. Foreword to *Dead Man Walking: The Shooting Script: Introduction, Screenplay and Notes* by Tim Robbins, xi–xiii. New York: Newmarket Press, 1997.

Prince, Stephen. "Historical Perspective and the Realist Aesthetic in *High Noon* (1952)." In *The Films of Fred Zinnemann: Critical Perspectives,* 79–92, edited by Arthur Nolletti, Jr. Albany: State University of New York Press, 1999.

Quinonez, Lora Ann, C.D.P., and Mary Daniel Turner, S.N.D.deN. *The Transformation of American Catholic Sisters.* Philadelphia: Temple University Press, 1992.

Ragland-Sullivan, Ellie. "The Imaginary." In *Feminism and Psychoanalysis: A Critical Dictionary,* edited by Elizabeth Wright, 173–6. Oxford: Blackwell, 1992.

Rapf, Joanna E. "Mythic Figures: Women and Co-Being in Three Films of Fred Zinnemann." In *The Films of Fred Zinnemann: Critical Perspectives,* edited by Arthur Nolletti, Jr., 235–50. Albany: State University of New York Press, 1999.

Rawlinson, Mark. "'Far More Remote Than It Actually Is': Rumer Godden's *Black Narcissus* and 1930s Mountain Writing." In *Rumer Godden: International and Intermodern Storyteller*, edited by Lucy Le-Guilcher and Phyllis B. Lassner, 39–50. Farnham, U.K.: Ashgate, 2010.

Reed, Cheryl L. *Unveiled: The Hidden Lives of Nuns*. New York: Berkley Books, 2004.

Reichardt, Mary R. "Rumer Godden (1907–1998)." In *Catholic Women Writers: A Bio-Bibliographical Sourcebook*, edited by Reichardt, 114–20. Westport, Conn.: Greenwood Press, 2001.

Reinhartz, Adele. "*Dead Man Walking* and the Riddle of Divine Justice (Leviticus)." *Scripture on the Silver Screen*. Louisville, Ky.: Westminster / John Knox Press, 2003. 39–53.

Richard, Jocelyn. "Oscar 2012: Mother Dolores Hart, Former Elvis Co-Star, to Walk Red Carpet in Religious Garments." *Huffington Post*, February 15, 2012. http://www.huffingtonpost.com/2012/02/15/oscars-2012–mother-dolores-hart-elvis.html (accessed May 2, 2012).

Richards, Jeffrey. "When East Meets West." Review of *Black Narcissus*. *The Daily Telegraph*, October 19, 1987: 13.

Ricoeur, Paul. *The Conflict of Interpretations: Essays in Hermeneutics*. London: Continuum, 2004.

Riviere, Joan. "The unconscious phantasy of an inner world reflected in examples from literature" (1952). In *The Inner World and Joan Riviere: Collected Papers 1920–1958*, edited by Athol Hughes, 302–30. London: Karnac Books, 1991.

Rizzuto, Ana-Maria. *The Birth of the Living God: A Psychoanalytic Study*. Chicago: University of Chicago Press, 1981.

———. "The Psychological Foundations of Belief in God." In *Towards Moral and Religious Maturity*, edited by C. Brusselmans, 115–35. Morristown, N.J.: Silver Burdett, 1980.

Robbins, Tim. *Dead Man Walking: The Shooting Script: Introduction, Screenplay and Notes*. New York: Newmarket Press, 1997.

Rogers, Carol G. *Poverty, Chastity, and Change: Lives of Contemporary American Nuns*. New York: Twayne Publishers, 1996.

Rogers, Eugene F. Jr., ed. *Theology and Sexuality: Classic and Contemporary Readings*. Oxford: Blackwell, 2002.

Ronan, Marian. "The Clergy Sex Abuse Crisis and the Mourning of American Catholic Innocence." *Pastoral Psychology* (2008) 56: 321–39.

———. *Tracing the Sign of the Cross: Sexuality, Mourning, and the Future of American Catholicism*. New York: Columbia University Press, 2009.

Rooney, Kathleen, S.S.J. *Sisters: An Inside Look*. Winona, Minn.: Saint Mary's Press, 2001.

Rosefeldt, Paul. "The Search for God, the Father: John Pielmeier's *Agnes of God*, Peter Shaffer's *Equus*." In *The Absent Father in Modern Drama*. New York: Peter Lang, 1996. 83–96.

Rosen, Ruth. "The Female Generation Gap: Daughters of the Fifties and the Origins of Contemporary American Feminism." In *U.S. History as Women's History: New Feminist Essays*, edited by Linda K. Kerber, Alice Kessler-Harris, and Kathryn Kish Sklar, 313–4. Chapel Hill: University of North Carolina Press, 1995.

Rosenstone, Robert A. *History on Film / Film on History*. Harlow, U.K.: Pearson Education, 2006.

Rosenthal, Lynne M. *Rumer Godden Revisited*. New York: Twayne: 1996.

Rusinko, Susan. Review of *Agnes of God*. *Magill's Cinema Annual 1986: A Survey of the Films of 1985*, edited by Frank N. Magill, 56–9. Pasadena, Calif.: Salem Press, 1986.

Saito, Stephen. "Interview: John Patrick Shanley on 'Doubt.' " *IFC.com*, December 12, 2008. http://www.ifc.com/news/2008/12/john-patrick-shanley-on-doubt.php (accessed September 18, 2009).

Sanders, Theresa. *Celluloid Saints: Images of Sanctity in Film*. Macon, Ga.: Mercer University Press, 2002.

———. "God and Guns: *Seven Cities of Gold* (1955)." In *Catholics in the Movies*, edited by Colleen McDannell, 127–48. New York: Oxford University Press, 2008.

Sands, Kathleen M. "Uses of The Thea(o)logian: Sex and Theodicy in Religious Feminism." *Journal of Feminist Studies in Religion* 8 (1992): 7–33.

Sarat, Austin. "Remorse, Responsibility, and Criminal Punishment: An Analysis of Popular Culture." In *The Passions of Law*, edited by Susan A. Bandes, 168–90. New York: New York University Press, 1999.

Schillaci, Peter F. " 'Agnes of God' a Mystery Story That Probes Hidden Areas of Our Psyche." *National Catholic Reporter*, October 11, 1985: 16.

Schilling, Mary K. "Spotlight on John Patrick Shanley: Un-'Doubt'-edly Good." *Entertainment Weekly*. n.d. http://www.ew.com/ew/article/0,, 1041504,00. html (accessed September 18, 2009).

Schneiders, Sandra M., I.H.M. *Beyond Patching: Faith and Feminism in the Catholic Church*. rev. ed. New York: Paulist Press, 2004.

———. *Finding the Treasure: Locating Catholic Religious Life in a New Ecclesial and Cultural Context*. New York: Paulist Press, 2000.

———. *Selling All: Commitment, Consecrated Celibacy, and Community in Catholic Religious Life*. New York: Paulist Press, 2001.

Scorsese, Martin. Introduction to *Million Dollar Movie* by Michael Powell, ix–xiii. New York: Random House, 1995.

Scruton, Roger. *Beauty*. Oxford: Oxford University Press, 2009.

Sea Wife (1957). Dir. Bob McNaught. Prod. Andre Hakim. Writ. George K. Burke. Perf. Joan Collins, Richard Burton, and Basil Sydney. DVD. Twentieth Century Fox, 2007.

Senior Scholastic. Review of *The Bells of St. Mary's*. December 10, 1945: 36.

Sheehan, Henry. "*Black Narcissus* (1947)." *Film Comment* 26.3 (1990): 37–9.

Simpson, Hassell A. *Rumer Godden.* New York: Twayne, 1973.

Sinyard, Neil. *Fred Zinnemann: Films of Character and Conscience.* Jefferson, N.C.: McFarland, 2003.

Sipe, A. W. Richard. *Celibacy: A Way of Loving, Living, and Serving.* Ligouri, Miss.: Triumph Books, 1996.

———. *A Secret World: Sexuality and the Search for Celibacy.* New York: Brunner/ Mazel, 1990.

Slee, Nicola. "The Holy Spirit and spirituality." In *The Cambridge Companion to Feminist Theology,* edited by Susan F. Parsons, 171–89. Cambridge: Cambridge University Press, 2002.

Smith-Rosenberg, Carroll. "The Female World of Love and Ritual: Relations between Women in Nineteenth-Century America." *Signs* 1.1 (1975): 1–29.

Sobo, Elisa J., and Sandra Bell, eds. *Celibacy, Culture, and Society: The Anthropology of Sexual Abstinence.* Madison: The University of Wisconsin Press, 2001.

The Society of St. Hugh of Cluny. "The Reredos II: The German World." http:// sthughofcluny.org/2009/11/the-reredos-ii-the-german-world.html (accessed July 24, 2011).

The Sound of Music (1965). Dir. and Prod. Robert Wise. Writ. Ernest Lehman. Perf. Julie Andrews, Christopher Plummer, Eleanor Parker, and Peggy Wood. DVD. Twentieth Century Fox, n.d.

South China Morning Post. "Church Sex Abuse: Catholic priest had boys stripped and whipped." April 19, 2012: A17

Southgate, Paul. "A Swallow in Winter: A Catholic Priesthood Viewpoint." In *Celibacy, Culture, and Society: The Anthropology of Sexual Abstinence,* edited by Elisa J. Sobo and Sandra Bell, 246–63. Madison: The University of Wisconsin Press, 2001.

Spoto, Donald. *Enchantment: The Life of Audrey Hepburn.* London: Hutchinson, 2006.

———. *Notorious: The Life of Ingrid Bergman.* Cambridge, Mass.: Da Capo Press, 2001.

Stadler, Jane. *Pulling Focus: Intersubjective Experience, Narrative Film, and Ethics.* London: Continuum, 2008.

Stafford, Roy. "India: The Erotic/Exotic." Review of *Black Narcissus. National Film Theatre Programme Notes.* n.d.

Starkman, Ruth A. "American Imperialism or Local Protectionism? *The Sound of Music (1965)* fails in Germany and Austria." *Historical Journal of Film, Radio and Television.* 20.1 (2000): 63–78.

Steinberg, Leo. *The Sexuality of Christ in Renaissance Art and Modern Oblivion,* rev. ed. Chicago: The University of Chicago Press, 1996.

Stewart, George C., Jr. *Marvels of Charity: History of American Sisters and Nuns.* Huntington, Ind.: Our Sunday Visitor, 1994.

Stokes, Adrian. *Reflections on the Nude.* London: Tavistock Publications, 1967.

Stone, John. "Gothic in the Himalayas: Powell and Pressburger's *Black Narcissus.*" In *The Gothic Other: Racial and Social Constructions in the Literary Imagination,* edited by Ruth Bienstock and Douglas L. Howard, 264–86. Jefferson, N.C.: McFarland, 2004.

Street, Sarah. *Black Narcissus*. British Film Guide. London: I. B. Tauris, 2005.

Suenens, Leon J. *The Nun in the World: Religious and the Apostolate*. Translated by Geoffrey Stevens. Westminster, Md.: The Newman Press, 1963.

Sullivan, Rebecca. "Breaking Habits: Gender, Class and the Sacred in the Dress of Women Religious." In *Consuming Fashion: Adorning the Transnational Body*, edited by Anne Brydon and Sandra Niessen, 109–28. Oxford: Berg, 1998.

———. *Visual Habits: Nuns, Feminism, and American Postwar Popular Culture*. Toronto: University of Toronto Press, 2005.

Sweet, Louise. Review of *Agnes of God*. *Monthly Film Bulletin*, March 1986: 73–4.

Swift, Catherine. *Gladys Aylward*. Minneapolis, Minn.: Bethany House Publishers, 1989.

Tallman, Alissa. "Sister Aloysius in John Patrick Shanley's Doubt." *Suite101.com*, May 1, 2009. http://dvdreviews.suite101.com/article.cfm/sister_aloysius_in_john_patrick_shanleys_doubt (accessed September 18, 2009).

Taylor, Ella. "*Doubt* Wags the Finger of Moral Relativism." *Village Voice*, December 9, 2008. http://www.villagevoice.com/2008-12-10/film/doubt-wags-the-finger-of-moral-relativism (accessed May 26, 2009).

Theatre Arts. Review of *The Bells of St. Mary's*. January 1946: 48–50.

Thomas, Kevin. "Science vs. Faith Issue Resurrected in 'Agnes.' " *The Los Angeles Times*, September 13, 1985: sec. 6:1.

Thompson, Margaret S. "Sisterhood and Power: Class, Culture, and Ethnicity in the American Convent." *Colby Library Quarterly* 25 (1989): 149–75.

Tickle, Phyllis. Introduction to *In This House of Brede* by Rumer Godden, vi–xi. Chicago: Loyola Press, 2005.

Time. "Critic's Goodbye." Review of *The Bells of St. Mary's*. December 10, 1945: 94, 97.

———. Review of *Heaven Knows, Mr. Allison*. March 25, 1957: 106.

Timmerman, Joan H. "The Sexuality of Jesus and the Human Vocation." In *Sexuality and the Sacred: Sources for Theological Reflection*, edited by James B. Nelson and Sandra P. Longfellow, 91–104. Louisville, Ky.: Westminster / John Knox, 1994.

Tromans, Nicholas. "Harem and Home." In *The Lure of the East: British Orientalist Painting*, 128–37. London: Tate, 2008.

———. "Introduction: British Orientalist Painting." In *The Lure of the East: British Orientalist Painting*, 10–21. London: Tate, 2008.

———, ed. *The Lure of the East: British Orientalist Painting*. London: Tate, 2008.

Turan, Kenneth. Review of *Dead Man Walking*. *The Los Angeles Times*, December 29, 1995. http://www.calendarlive.com/movies/reviews/cl-movie960406-2.04564347.html (accessed December 6, 2007).

Turner, Victor W. *The Ritual Process: Structure and Anti-Structure*. London: Routledge & Kegan Paul, 1969.

Turner, Victor W., and Edith Turner. *Image and Pilgrimage in Christian Culture: Anthropological Perspectives*. New York: Columbia University Press, 1978.

Um, M. Maximilia, F.S.G.M. "Evangelical Mission." In *The Foundations of Religious Life: Revisiting the Vision*, edited by the Council of Major Superiors of Women Religious, 157–75. Notre Dame, Ind.: Ave Maria Press, 2009.

Van Herik, Judith. *Freud on Femininity and Faith*. Berkeley: University of California Press, 1985.

Vansant, Jacqueline. "Robert Wise's *The Sound of Music* and the 'Denazification' of Austria in American Cinema." In *World War to Waldheim: Politics and Culture in Austria and the United States*, edited by David Good and Ruth Wodak, 165–86. New York: Berghahn, 1999.

Variety. "Film Preview: *Black Narcissus*." July 8, 1947: 3, 15.

———. "'Narcissus' Banned by Legion, Opens Big in NY." August 14, 1947: 4.

———. Review of *Black Narcissus*. May 7, 1947: 18.

———. Review of *Heaven Knows, Mr. Allison*. March 20, 1957: 6.

———. Review of *The Inn of the Sixth Happiness*. November 19, 1958: 6.

Vineberg, Steve. "Fred Zinnemann's Actors." In *The Films of Fred Zinnemann: Critical Perspectives*, edited by Arthur Nolletti, Jr., 219–33. Albany: State University of New York Press, 1999.

Vizzard, Jack. *See No Evil: Life Inside a Hollywood Censor*. New York: Simon and Schuster, 1971.

Von Dassanowsky, Robert. "An Unclaimed Country: The Austrian Image in American Film and the Sociopolitics of *The Sound of Music*." *Bright Lights Film Journal* 41 (2003). http://www.brightlightsfilm.com/41/soundofmusic.html (accessed March 10, 2011).

Wagnleitner, Reinhold. "The Sound of Forgetting Meets The United States of Amnesia: An Introduction to the Relations between Strange Bedfellows." In *World War to Waldheim: Politics and Culture in Austria and the United State*, edited by David Good and Ruth Wodak, 1–16. New York: Berghahn, 1999.

Waites, Kathleen J. *Particular Friendships: A Convent Memoir*. Xlibris, 2006.

Wakin, Edward, and Fr. Joseph F. Scheuer. "The American Nun: Poor, Chaste, and Restive." *Harper's*, August 1965: 35–40.

Walker, Alexander. *Audrey: Her Real Story*. rev. ed. London: Orion Books, 1997.

Walker, Michael. "*Black Narcissus*." *Framework* 9 (1978–79): 9–13.

Wall, James M. Review of *Agnes of God*. *The Christian Century*, August 28, 1985: 774.

Walsh, Moira. Review of *Heaven Knows, Mr. Allison*. *America*, March 23, 1957: 716.

———. Review of *The Nun's Story*. *Catholic World*, July 1959: 315–16.

———. Review of *The Sound of Music*. *America*, March 13, 1965: 374–5.

Warner, Marina. *Alone of All Her Sex: The Myth and the Cult of the Virgin Mary*. 1976. Reprinted with new afterthoughts. London: Picador, 1990.

Weaver, Mary Jo. *New Catholic Women: A Contemporary Challenge to Traditional Religious Authority*. Bloomington: Indiana University Press, 1995.

Weber, Jeannie M. "Walking among the Saints." In *Forever Your Sister: Reflections on Leaving Convent Life*, edited by Janice Wedl, O.S.B. and Eileen Maas Nalevanko, 83–9. St. Cloud, Minn.: North Star Press, 1998.

Wedl, Janice, O.S.B., and Eileen Maas Nalevanko, eds. *Forever Your Sister: Reflections on Leaving Convent Life*. St. Cloud, Minn.: North Star Press, 1998.

Weisenfeld, Judith. "The Silent Social Problem Film: *Regeneration* (1915)." In *Catholics in the Movies*, edited by Colleen McDannell, 33–58. New York: Oxford University Press, 2008.

Wide Awake (1998). Dir. and Writ. M. Night Shyamalan. Prod. Cathy Conrad and Cary Woods. Perf. Joseph Cross, Dana Delany, Denis Leary, and Rosie O'Donnell. DVD. Buena Vista Home Entertainment, 1999.

Wilk, Max. *The Making of The Sound of Music*. New York: Routledge, 2007.

Williams, Bruce. "A Mirror of Desire: Looking Lesbian in Maria Luisa Bemberg's *I, The Worst of All*." *Quarterly Review of Film & Video* 19 (2002): 133–43.

Williams, Rowan D. "The Body's Grace." In *Theology and Sexuality: Classic and Contemporary Readings*, edited by Eugene F. Rogers, Jr., 309–21. Oxford: Blackwell, 2002.

Winnicott, Donald W. *Playing and Reality*. London: Routledge, 1992. First published 1971 by Tavistock Publications.

Wise, Robert. Foreword to *The Sound of Music: The Making of America's Favorite Movie* by Julia Antopol Hirsch, ix–x. Chicago: Contemporary Books, 1993.

Wittberg, Patricia, S.C. "Feminist Consciousness among American Nuns: Patterns of Ideological Diffusion." *Women's Studies International Forum* 12.5 (1989): 529–37.

———. *The Rise and Fall of Catholic Religious Orders: A Social Movement Perspective*. Albany: State University of New York Press, 1994.

Wolf, Stacy. "The Queer Pleasures of Mary Martin and Broadway: *The Sound of Music* as a Lesbian Musical." *Modern Drama* 39 (1996): 51–63.

Wolter, Rosemary. "The Golden Thread." In *Forever Your Sister: Reflections on Leaving Convent Life*, edited by Janice Wedl, O.S.B. and Eileen Maas Nalevanko, 21–6. St. Cloud, Minn.: North Star Press, 1998.

Woodward, Kenneth. "Bing Crosby Had It Right: Once upon a time, Catholics trusted and respected their parish priests. Are those days gone forever?" *Newsweek*, March 4, 2002: 53.

Wright, Elizabeth, ed. *Feminism and Psychoanalysis: A Critical Dictionary*. Oxford: Blackwell, 1992.

Wright, Wendy M. "Woman-Body, Man-Body: Knowing God." In *Women's Spirituality: Resources for Christian Development*, edited by Joann Wolski Conn, 83–95. New York: Paulist Press, 1996.

Wynn, Judith. "The Sappy and Sublime." *Sojourner* 5.6 (1980): 21, 26.

Young, Colin. "The Old Dependables." *Film Quarterly* 13.1 (1959): 2–17.

Zacharek, Stephanie. "Philip Seymour Hoffman plays a priest who may—or may not!—be a pedophile in this deliberately ambiguous film." Review of

Doubt. *Salon.com*, December 12, 2008. http://www.salon.com/ent/movies/review/2008/12/12/doubt/index.html?CP=IMD&DN (accessed May 26, 2009).

———. "This lush, romantic melodrama, starring Naomi Watts and Edward Norton, is an act of mainstream daring." Review of *The Painted Veil. Salon.com*, December 20, 2006. http://www.salon.com/ent/movies/review/2006/12/20/painted_veil/print.html (accessed May 26, 2009).

Zagano, Phyllis. "A Very Public Rebuke: The CDF and Women Religious." *The Tablet*, April 28, 2012. http://m.thetablet.co.uk/article/162647.html (accessed May 2, 2012).

Zeidler, Jeanne. "Speaking Out, Selling Out, Working Out: The Changing Politics of Jane Fonda." In *Women and American Foreign Policy: Lobbyists, Critics, and Insiders*, edited by Edward P. Crapol, 137–51. Wilmington, Del.: SR Books, 1987.

Zeitlin, David. "A Lovely Audrey in Religious Role." *Life*, June 8, 1959: 141–4.

Zinnemann, Fred. "Dialogue on Film: Fred Zinnemann" (1986). In *Fred Zinnemann Interviews*, edited by Gabriel Miller, 95–102. Jackson, Miss.: University Press of Mississippi, 2005.

INDEX